José del Valle of Central America

Duke Historical Publication

José del Valle
of Central America

Louis E. Bumgartner

DUKE UNIVERSITY PRESS
Durham, N. C.   1963

PRINTED IN THE UNITED STATES OF AMERICA
BY THE SEEMAN PRINTERY, INC., DURHAM, N. C.

For KATHY, JIM, *and* JOHN

This volume has received a subvention from the
Duke University Council on Hispanic Research
under a grant made by the Ford Foundation
for the promotion of international studies.

Preface

As a subject for historical investigation, José del Valle began to attract attention in the 1880's, when Ramón Rosa published the first biography of him. In the early 1900's Rómulo Durón edited a single volume of Valle's papers, and then in 1929, José del Valle and Jorge del Valle Matheu, direct descendants of Valle, published two volumes more of his writings, including a great part of one of his newspapers, *El Amigo de la Patria*. To these outstanding volumes, Rafael Heliodoro Valle (not related to José del Valle) added a volume of Valle's writings, one of letters between Valle and Jeremy Bentham, and a bibliography of works by and about Valle. Professor John Tate Lanning, in his *Academic Culture in the Spanish Colonies* (1940), first saw the significance of the theses of students in the colonial University of San Carlos, and in presenting his findings, he was first to analyze Valle's thesis. Drawing on most of these works, Professor Franklin Dallas Parker published a study of Valle in English (1952 and 1954), and recently Juan Valladares Rodríguez has edited some of Valle's unpublished correspondence.

In the fall of 1952, in search of a thesis topic, I began reading what had been published about Valle. When I finished, two impressions had emerged: (1) Valle was an elusive figure loosely tied to the history of his own time by scanty evidence; (2) unless I could find new information, I could contribute nothing significant. Teased by the perplexing Valle and encouraged by an insistent thesis director, I continued with the subject. In 1954 I received a fellowship that allowed me to work in the Archivo General del Gobierno de Guatemala and to forage for material in Mexico City. After several months I saw plainly, for the first time, what lay behind the encouragement I had had. The manuscripts in the Archivo and Valle's unpublished papers assured me that another work on Valle, far from being repetitious, would make him a different figure and contribute significantly to the history of his time.

In the course of the last ten years I have received more assistance than I can ever hope to repay. My greatest debt is to Dr. John Tate Lanning, James B. Duke Professor of History at Duke University. He suggested the study, taught me how to do the research, and read my manuscript, saving me from my own clumsiness.

Dr. Robert S. Smith, Professor of Economics at Duke University, gave me the advantage of his friendship with Valle's great grandson, the late Jorge del Valle Matheu, who, like his forebear, left a rich scholarly heritage to his children Martha and Mario. To my friends Martha and Mario, to their aunt Luz del Valle, and to other descendants of Valle, including the charming and wide-eyed Beatriz, I owe a debt of gratitude for kindnesses that extend far beyond the ordinary courtesies. Day after day for weeks on end I worked in their home with Valle's papers. Their home almost literally became my home.

Professor J. Joaquín Pardo, Director of the Archivo General del Gobierno de Guatemala, extended me every conceivable courtesy and kindness, putting manuscripts before me that he had catalogued twenty years ago and others that still awaited his sure hand. The staff of the Biblioteca Nacional de Guatemala aided me in every possible way, and Don Héctor Samayoa, Investigador for the Instituto de Antropología e Historia de Guatemala, came to my rescue on many occasions. Don Manuel Rubio Sánchez, an economist of first rank, helped me find a number of necessary books, and Señor José Luis Reyes, former Librarian of the Sociedad de Geografía E Historia de Guatemala, kindly sought out and lent me several rare items.

To Dr. Maury Baker, Professor of History at Kent State University, and to Professors William B. Hamilton, Harold T. Parker, and Richard L. Watson, members of the Department of History at Duke University, I am indebted for their encouragement and many kindnesses. Dr. Frederic B. M. Hollyday, Assistant Professor of History at Duke University, gave the advantage of his judgment on many points, and Professor Cecil Abernethy, Dean of Birmingham-Southern College, read and criticized the first chapter. That my book appears at this time is owing in large part to my late friend and colleague, Professor Henry T. Shanks.

A Buenos Aires Convention fellowship enabled me to do research in Guatemala and Mexico in 1954-1955; a grant and a leave of absence from Birmingham-Southern College allowed me to return to Guatemala in 1958 and to spend the spring quarter of 1960 preparing the manuscript; and additional grants from Birmingham-Southern College and the Southern Fellowships Fund permitted me to complete the manuscript during the following summer. With customary kindness, the Duke University Library put money at my disposal for microfilm and the Birmingham-Southern Library spared no effort or expense in securing much needed materials.

It would be comforting if I could share the shortcomings of my book with those whose generosity made it possible. But, without much courage, I reluctantly claim them all for myself.

Louis E. Bumgartner

Contents

José del Valle of Central America

Family and Education

[1]

On June 5, 1825, George A. Thompson, a British diplomat, called at José del Valle's home in Guatemala City for some information about the affairs of the newly created Federation of Central America. When he arrived, Valle was talking with visitors about the baffling matter of finances. After bidding them God-speed, he showed Thompson into the library. Valle then sat down at a small writing table littered with "manuscripts and printed papers" and began to rummage for the promised data. His guest, a friend of books and scholarly pursuits, had time to observe the surroundings.[1] The library did not fail to impress him. He noted that it was "so completely filled with books, in large masses, not only around the walls but on the floor" that it was difficult to walk. Even more impressive was the slim figure of the "Andean Cicero,"[2] as Thompson called Valle, bent over the writing table sorting through papers. His dark eyes, shaded against the light by still darker, slightly arched eyebrows, leapt from document to document. Thinning black hair groomed forward, perhaps in a deference to a tendency toward baldness, made his naturally high forehead less conspicuous and contrasted pleasantly with the simple elegance so characteristic of his dress: white shirt, high collar, white velvet

1. George A. Thompson, *Narrative of an Official Visit to Guatemala from Mexico* (London, 1829), pp. 208-209. (Hereafter Thompson, *Narrative of an Official Visit.*) Earlier Thompson had written a manuscript entitled "Bosqueo [*sic*] del presente estado de Guatemala." On August 4 he sent a "copy of the preface" to Valle. The manuscript had been sent to England on July 21, 1821. See Thompson to Valle, Mexico City, Aug. 4, 1821, Valle Papers.
2. Thompson, *Narrative of an Official Visit*, pp. 208-209.

tie, and a black suit, expertly tailored.[3] To Thompson, Valle "had all the mania of authorship about him: proofs and revises and lumps of manuscripts, folios and quartos and octavos, opened or interlarded with scraps of memoranda, were scattered" about in profusion. Presently Valle began giving Thompson "paper after paper and document after document" until, as he confessed later, he felt his "appetite satiated at the very sight of them." In contrast, Valle seemed "as though he were inordinate in his requisitions at the feast of the intellect."[4]

The "Andean Cicero" (who will quarrel with an Englishman over a few hundred miles of American geography?) at the time of Thompson's visit was in his forties and midway through the most productive decade of his life. But chances are that Thompson would have been equally impressed fifteen years or so earlier, when Captain General Antonio González Mollinedo y Saravia, head of the royal government in the colony, reported with a hint of disapproval that Valle was "persevering in his studies to the point of ruining his health."[5] His penchant for learning, as Thompson and González suggested, is a major theme running through his entire life. His books were second only to his family in commanding his love and esteem. As he journeyed to Mexico City in 1822 to join Iturbide, one of his small daughters could write: "Everyday, the first job we do is dust your books."[6]

These books in five languages, purchased in Madrid, Paris, London, and New York, early pushed Valle's intellectual "requisitions" far beyond his needs as a lawyer. Thus, he began to view his practice as dull, tiresome, intellectually stifling, and, consequently, irritating. In response to some bitter complaint, his cousin Dionisio de Herrera advised him: "Your ideas, your disposition, and your character are completely contrary to the profession you have chosen to follow. As long as you continue in it, you will not have the independence and the peace and tranquillity that you so zealously desire." Instead of musing on the "greatest natural phenomena," and in place of studying the causes

3. The physical description of Valle does not come from Thompson's work; it is the author's description, based on photographs.
4. Thompson, *Narrative of an Official Visit,* pp. 208-209.
5. Valle Papers. The citation is to a letter of recommendation (undated and unaddressed) written by González in behalf of Valle. (Hereafter González recommends Valle.)
6. Nela del Valle to Valle, June 18, 1822, Valle Papers.

of the "greatness and decline of empires," which might help you in "creating something useful for humanity," you "kill six hours" working on a "tedious brief of sheer trivia." And, finally, you are left "weary and without energy to pursue your desires." "But, my José," his cousin consoled, "you shouldn't have the slightest doubt that your haciendas can provide the means necessary for breaking away from your law practice, even for making you wealthy."[7] Cousin Dionisio knew of what he spoke; he himself lived to become President of Honduras and Nicaragua.

[2]

Haciendas, as cousin Dionisio implied, were an extremely important part of Valle's life. Haciendas, more than books, no doubt, dominated the conversation he heard as a child. Talk of Indian labor, Negro slaves, the price of cattle and hides, the quality of cheese, the difficulty of transportation, and the danger of the *peste* to man and beast were the stuff of conversation to a man such as Valle's father, who had inherited more haciendas than books.[8] These haciendas lay near Choluteca, Honduras, on the Pacific coast, not far from the Bay of Fonseca.

The history of Choluteca, like that of a great many towns and cities of Latin America, stretches back beyond the coming of the conquistadores. When the first Spaniard found his way to the Indian village is vague and uncertain, but there is a strong suggestion that three of Spain's stoutest paused there: Pedrarias Dávila, Pedro de Alvarado, and the eloquent Bernal Díaz del Castillo.[9] Later the Spaniards, probably in response to the suggestion of their dry and dusty throats, changed the name of the village to Jerez de la Frontera, but the Indian name has endured.

7. Dionisio de Herrera to Valle, Tegucigalpa, June 7, 1812, Valle Papers.

8. Archivo General del Gobierno de Guatemala (hereafter AGG), A1.43 (*sección*), 3242 (*expediente*), 348 (*legajo*). Recurso de José Antonio Díaz del Valle, residente en Tegucigalpa, sobre la mortual de su padre, José del Valle. (Hereafter Recurso sobre la mortual de su padre.)

9. Bernal Díaz del Castillo, *The True History of the Conquest of New Spain*, edited and published in Mexico by Genaro García, translated by Alfred Percival Maudslay, printed for the Hakluyt Society (5 vols.; London, 1908-1916), V, 118-119. For information concerning the origin of Choluteca, see Jorge Lardé y Larín, "Orígenes de la villa de Choluteca," *Revista del Archivo y Biblioteca Nacional de Honduras*, XXIV (1946), 103-105; 484-485.

After a half-century Choluteca could claim only "thirty Spanish inhabitants."[10]   Even so, the population declined by ten during the next twenty years.[11]   Early in the seventeenth century, however, the picturesque and charming chronicle of a Carmelite friar injects a note of optimism.   Choluteca counted "some 60 Spanish residents" in 1613, though "not over 30 lived in the town itself," which now had its solid "parish church" as well as "a Mercedarian convent."   Most of the Spaniards earned their living from the "large cattle and mule ranches,"[12] and by the eighteenth century, Choluteca was known throughout the colony for its excellent "breed of mules," but more for the "many breeds of the best cattle."[13]

Choluteca, on November 22, 1776, became the birthplace of José del Valle, or, as he was christened, José Cecilio Díaz del Valle.[14]   He was the "legitimate son of José Antonio Díaz del Valle and Gertrudis Díaz del Valle."[15]   The Valle family had been ranchers in Choluteca at least since 1731, and they were representative of the class of people that made the Spanish empire in America, from the Russian River in California to the Straits of Magellan, a stable society for more three hundred years.

10. Juan López de Velasco, *Geografía y descripción universal de las Indias* (Madrid, 1894), p. 300.

11. Juan de Pineda, "Descripción de la provincia de Guatemala, año 1594," *Relaciones históricas y geográficas de América Central* (Colección de Libros y Documentos Referentes a la Historia de América, VIII; Madrid, 1908), p. 467.

12. Antonio Vázquez de Espinosa, *Compendium and Description of the West Indies,* translated by Charles Upson Clark (Smithsonian Miscellaneous Collection, CII; Washington, 1942), p. 23.

13. AGG, A1.17.1, 13999, 2020.   Autos formados sobre la real cédula para que esta real audiencia, con la brevedad y reserva posible, remita una relación individual de los corregimientos y alcaldías mayores de este reyno (1763).

14. It is a source of satisfaction that my doubt of the date traditionally given as Valle's birthdate has been confirmed by the discovery of his birth certificate. See Juan Valladares Rodríguez, ed., *El pensamiento económico de José Cecilio del Valle* (Tegucigalpa, 1958), p. ii.   (Hereafter Valladares, ed., *Valle.*)   The record of Valle's death (Archivo de la Catedral de Guatemala [hereafter ACG]. Libro de entierros de la Parroquia Sagrario de Guatemala, 1816-1870) shows: "On March 2, 1834, José del Valle died at the age of fifty-eight."   This information was presented in Louis E. Bumgartner, "José Cecilio del Valle: Central American Savant" (unpublished Ph.D. dissertation, Duke University, 1956), p. 22.

15. Archivo y Biblioteca Nacional de Honduras (hereafter ABNH).   Relación de los ejercicios literarios, grados, títulos y méritos patrióticos de Don José del Valle, Auditor Honorario de Guerra del Ejército y provincias de Guatemala (hereafter Títulos y méritos).   The author is grateful to Professor John Bergmann, Department of Geography, University of Alberta, for a photocopy of Ramón Rosa's copy of Valle's record.   A published copy appeared in *Revista del Archivo y Biblioteca Nacional de Honduras,* I (April, 1905), 309-312.   Valle's parents were first cousins.   See ACG, Libro de matrimonios de 1729 a 1821, Parroquia del Sagrario, Oct. 12, 1812 (hereafter Libro de matrimonios).   The parents received permission to marry.   See Valladares, ed., *Valle,* p. iv.

The Valles were creoles, Spaniards born in America who had maintained their purity of race. As such they occupied a station in a class-conscious society subordinate only to Peninsulars, who came from Spain, generally to serve the crown. But creoles were subordinate, and as a rule they were excluded from such positions as that of viceroy, governor, captain general, and from the upper clergy, positions regarded as the exclusive domain of the Spanish-born. The creoles, in the main, occupied the lesser positions in the *audiencia*,[16] the town council,[17] and in the Church. Thus they constituted the majority of royal officials engaged in colonial administration. Equally important, they provided the economic backbone of Spanish society in America. Unlike the Peninsulars, who anticipated retirement at home, in Spain, the creole's home was America. Quite naturally he tried to make his home as comfortable and prosperous as possible and, in so doing, contributed greatly to the prosperity of the Empire. He raised the cattle, cured and shipped the hides, operated the mines, produced the indigo, sold the cacao, and provided a new market for manufactured goods.

José del Valle and his forebears fit exactly into this tradition. Valle's great-grandfather apparently came from Spain about 1700 and in 1731 bid for and finally bought the office of *alférez mayor* of the village of Choluteca.[18] As *alférez mayor,* he was an impor-

16. The *audiencia* was the most important administrative and judicial body in the Spanish colonies. Under certain circumstances it also had legislative authority. In Guatemala, the captain general, the highest royal official in the colony, was president of the *audiencia*.

17. The town council (*ayuntamiento*) also had the function of a court. The offices were salable until the promulgation of the Constitution of 1812.

18. AGG, A1.23, 4609 (*legajo*), fol. 7. Copias de títulos y reales cédulas de los años de 1731 hasta el de 1737. The sale of an office was not complete unless royal confirmation arrived within five years. José Antonio's confirmation, owing to the troubled times in Europe, did not arrive, causing him difficulty in Choluteca. It appears, however, that he had a clear title by 1742. For an account of the trouble, see AGG, A3.10, 1729, 178. Capitán José Díaz del Valle, regidor de la villa de Chuluteca [*sic*], pide que se le otorgue título al oficio de Alférez Real (1736); A3.10, 3561, 193, fol. 26. Títulos y méritos de Joseph Díaz del Valle. Joseph Díaz del Valle, Valle's grandfather, also became *alférez mayor,* and his record contains information about Valle's great-grandfather because proof had to be produced showing that the office was vacant. For information concerning the sale of the office of *alférez mayor,* see J. H. Parry, "The Sale of Public Offices in the Spanish Indies under the Hapsburgs," *Ibero-Americano,* XXXVII (1953), 7. For the necessity of royal confirmation for salable offices, see Antonio de León Pinelo, *Tratado de confirmaciones de encomiendas, oficios, i casos, en que se requieren para las Indias Occidentales* (2 vols., Madrid, 1630), II, capít. 15, fol. 146; *Recopilación de las leyes de los reynos de las Indias* (3 vols., Madrid, 1791), lib. 4, tít. 10, ley 4. Valladares (ed., *Valle,* p. iii) points out that Valle's earliest ancestor in America arrived from Spain about 1700.

tant member of the town council, commanded the militia in time of danger, and carried the municipal standard on ceremonial occasions.[19] Considering the Spanish propensity for pomp and splendor, his was no trivial duty. His son, Valle's grandfather, was also *alférez mayor* and held nearly every office of local government at one time or another. He even found time to serve as the head of the lay brotherhood of his church. And he "carried out the functions of these positions with all exactness, performing the duties of each in the service" of the crown.[20] Valle's father apparently did not hold any offices, but Valle himself was to hold nearly every important one open to a creole. The principal occupation of Valle's forebears was that of raising the cattle[21] that provided much of the meat for the Kingdom of Guatemala,[22] as the colony was often called. Valle broke with the traditional family occupation, but not completely. In the course of his life he owned at least four haciendas, and his ability to manage them reflected the knowledge gained in his youth and contributed substantially to the financial independence necessary for his career as a crown official, public servant, and especially as a man of letters.

Presumably his decision to pursue another career was prompted by his father's desire to provide an education for his son. There were no schools worthy of the name in the province of Comayagua,

19. Parry, "Sale of Public Offices in the Spanish Indies under the Hapsburgs," *Ibero-Americano*, XXXVII (1953), 7.

20. AGG, A3.10, 3561, 193, fol. 26. Títulos y méritos de Joseph Díaz del Valle. Other offices held by Valle's grandfather were: *alcalde* of the Santa Hermandad, two years; *síndico de procurador*, two years; *alcalde ordinario*, four years; and he also was captain of the militia.

21. Valle's great-grandfather owned at least one hacienda, "San Antonio" (33 *caballerías*), which he acquired in 1745 by assuming a mortgage of 630 pesos and the interest on the mortgage held by the Convento de la Merced. It was located in the valley of Guanuale (?) and included "un obraje de labrar tinta añil." Also in the litigation involving "San Antonio," Valle's great-grandfather was credited with the title of Maestre de Campo. See AGG, A1.15, 1818, 181. Francisco Estrada con Don Joseph Antonio Díaz del Valle sobre la propiedad de la hacienda nombrada San Antonio (1780-1782). Joseph Antonio was Valle's father. During the dispute over the hacienda, deeds of ownership were introduced. Valladares (ed., *Valle*, p. iii) writes that Valle's great-grandfather owned five other haciendas. Ownership of two of the five "Pavana" and "Tapatoca," might be confirmed by the fact that Valle's grandfather owned them; they also were the source of a dispute between Valle's father and aunt. See AGG, A1.43, 3242, 348. Recurso sobre la mortual de su padre. Two others, "Ola" and "Santa Bárbara," might be confirmed by the fact that Valle owned them.

22. Valentín Solórzano Fernández, *Historia de la evolución económica de Guatemala* (Mexico, 1947), p. 82. (Hereafter, Solórzano Fernández, *Historia económica de Guatemala.*)

where Choluteca was located, but Guatemala City, the capital of the captaincy general, could boast of a university academically as good as any in America. About 1789 Valle's father, José Antonio Díaz del Valle, moved from Choluteca,[23] and Valle must have entered the University of San Carlos de Guatemala in 1790 or 1791.[24] But the son's education probably was not the only reason why José Antonio pulled up the deep roots of the Valles in Choluteca.

José Antonio, toward the tag end of the 1780's, must have found Choluteca an unpleasant place to live, largely because of a dispute with his sister, Paula, and her husband, Juan Jacinto Herrera, the son of a wealthy and influential family of the same town.[25] The trouble began after the death of the father of Paula and José Antonio. Although Paula was still a minor, she decided to marry Herrera. Ordinarily such a match should have pleased, each being a creole with a background of wealth and influence. But José Antonio, a juridical person and Paula's guardian, refused to sanction the marriage plans. Caught in the web of young love, Paula disregarded her brother's authority. Now a brother's refusal seems a small matter that might have been smoothed over easily, but other problems were involved: the royal "pragmatic of March [23], 1776, and the royal cédula of April [7], 1778" had been violated, charged José Antonio.[26] This was serious.

23. Ramón Rosa, *José Cecilio del Valle* (*Obras de José Cecilio del Valle,* ed. José del Valle and Jorge del Valle Matheu, 2 vols.; Guatemala City, 1929-1930), I, xiii. Rosa's biography of Valle was published in the 1880's and composes the first part of Volume I of the *Obras,* which consist mostly of Valle's writings. Hereafter when the citation is to the biography it will appear as Rosa, *José Cecilio del Valle* (*Obras*); when the citation is to a document, it will appear Valle and Valle Matheu, eds., *Obras.* Rosa's biography also appeared in Rafael Heliodoro Valle, ed., *Oro de Honduras. Antología de Ramón Rosa* (Tegucigalpa, 1948). But to avoid confusion, the author will confine his citations to the edition in Valle and Valle Matheu.

24. A student could secure a bachelor's degree in three years. See John Tate Lanning, *The University in the Kingdom of Guatemala* (Ithaca, New York, 1955), p. 205. (Hereafter Lanning, *University.*)

25. The documents make this relationship plain, but Juan Valladares (*Revista del Archivo y Biblioteca Nacional de Honduras,* XXVIII [1950], 385) confirms it with the record of the birth of Dionisio de Herrera, son of Paula and Juan Jacinto.

26. AGG, A1.15, 1821, 182. Autos de Joseph Díaz del Valle con Don Manuel Batres y Juan Manrique sobre la venta de la hacienda nombrada Santa Cruz, perteniente a los bienes de Juan Félix Briceño (hereafter Santa Cruz). This was a dispute over an hacienda that Valle's father thought he had purchased. Herrera caused him trouble, and Valle's father injected domestic affairs in an attempt to discredit Herrera's case. The specific dates of the royal decrees can be found in José María Ots capdequí, *Instituciones sociales de la América española en el período colonial* (La Plata, Argentina, 1934), pp. 120-122.

These royal decrees dealt with marriage. One section stated that a minor needed permission from his father before a marriage could be solemnized. Should the father be dead, the law empowered the nearest male relative to grant or deny permission. A marriage without permission was, in the eyes of Spanish law and the Catholic Church, not a marriage at all, and a minor violated these decrees at the risk of losing such legal rights as inheritance. It so happened that when Paula married Herrera her father's estate had not been settled. Legally her claim was in doubt, but, determined to have a share, she was ably supported if not prompted by her husband, who used his influence both in Choluteca and in the circle of provincial authority to cause José Antonio no end of trouble.

José Antonio planned to keep the inheritance only until Paula was twenty-five, when he intended to divide it "in a friendly and fraternal manner," but he "immediately began to be on bad terms with his brother-in-law." Soon after the marriage, when the foreman of José Antonio's haciendas "Pavana" and "Tapatoca" was ill, José Antonio had to go to León. In his absence, Paula appeared before the local judge in Choluteca and solicited permission to put her foreman in charge. The judge, who was not "empowered to act in the case," not only permitted her to place her foreman in charge but also granted her "one of the mentioned haciendas." José Antonio complained through clenched teeth that he had been "forcibly stripped of his property," and he successfully had recourse to the office of the *alcalde mayor* of the "district of Nacaome," in whose jurisdiction he claimed the haciendas were located. "But on the night of the same day," Juan Jacinto Herrera, with some "militia and armed persons," seized both haciendas, changed the employees, put his own foreman in charge, and imprisoned the one who worked for José Antonio for no other reason than "that of being my poor employee." Thus Juan Jacinto had become "owner and absolute master of the mentioned haciendas."[27] To counter the high-handed action of his "worst enemy,"[28] José solicited justice from the judge in Choluteca, who previously had favored Paula, but suffered the "misfortune" of "not being heard" because of the prejudice of that

27. AGG, A1.43, 3242, 348. Recurso sobre la mortual de su padre.
28. AGG, A1.15, 1821, 182. Santa Cruz.

official. "Believing that this would not prevail before the *alcalde mayor* of the province," he supplicated before the bar of that royal officer but without success. His only recourse, then, was "to empower" an attorney in Guatemala City to present the case before the *audiencia*. There he asked that the property be restored and that his father's estate be divided according to the judgment of the *alcalde mayor* of Nacaome or any "impartial judge."[29] According to dismal custom, the case, which began in 1780, dragged on and apparently was not concluded until 1804, though the estate was divided in 1788.

While the inheritance case continued, two other litigations pitted José Antonio and Herrera against each other.[30] Each made angry statements that could not be retracted and dredged up and hurled anew scandal that for years had lain dormant. Such matters as these—disputed real estate, a marriage without consent of the guardian, and family squabbles—balloon to gigantic proportions in a small colonial town. People take sides and friends stop speaking. If José Antonio was not sick and tired of the whole matter, he should have been. Moving was a clear solution. Besides, his only son needed an education, and Guatemala City possessed the only respectable facilities in the colony.

[*3*]

Young Valle's thoughts, as he first entered Guatemala City, must have teetered between black despair and high enthusiasm. The capital city in 1790 was anything but pleasing to people much less sensitive than Valle. The devastation delivered by the earthquakes of 1773 had forced Guatemala City from Antigua to its present site. The feeling of security and orderliness evoked by the churches, the monasteries, the university, and the captain general's palace of the ruined capital now gave way to the trauma of moving and rebuilding. The depressed, with features down-

29. AGG, A1.43, 3242, 348. Recurso sobre la mortual de su padre. The petition was acknowledged in September, 1781. In the course of the dispute over the inheritance, it was disclosed that Valle's grandfather died in 1779, and at the time of his death, Valle's father was "twenty-four years and a few months old." Paula, it appears, was born on January 25, 1756.

30. AGG, A1.15, 1821, 182. Santa Cruz; A1.15, 1818, 181. San Antonio.

cast, caught the reflection of their wistful images in mudholes and quagmires.

By the time Valle arrived, the initial shock had passed, but the 20,000 or so inhabitants still bent to the tedious, time-consuming task of putting stone on stone and timber to timber. Streets were still unpaved and, during the rainy season, well nigh impassable. Buildings such as those of the University of San Carlos and the cathedral were not yet finished. But the feelings of urgency and anticipation that half finished buildings demand of the senses must have offset any despair that Valle experienced. And what sensitive undergraduate, especially from a small country town such as Valle came from, does not look forward to first classes with excitement and enthusiasm?

One can reconstruct much of Valle's life at the University of San Carlos through the work of Professor John Tate Lanning. A typical day would find Valle slipping into clothes similar to those of his fellow students. Loud stockings and gold or embroidered passementerie were not permitted. If, before his mirror, he was tempted to fashion a pompadour or try for sideburns, university regulations banished the thought. After arranging his student collar (a necessary part of his attire since he was not studying medicine), he might have decided to wear a long cloak (*manteo*) and cassock (*sotana*). If he did, university statutes demanded that he don his *bonete*, should he be on his way to attend a lecture, defense of a thesis, or Saturday exercises. He was fastidious enough in his dress to wear a pair of starched cuffs—"immemorial custom" and not contrary to academic law until 1798.[31]

In class, the chances are that Valle did not sit next to a Negro, mulatto, or a person born out of wedlock. Negroes and mulattoes were excluded because of race and blood and illegitimates by the "infamy" or dishonor clause of the regulations. Yet he well might have been a class neighbor to an Indian, a person of mixed blood, or an illegitimate son. Indians, legally if not socially or economically, were permitted to matriculate; bastards and persons of mixed blood did attend through devious

31. Lanning, *University*, pp. 191-192.

methods, frequently with the tacit approval of university authorities.[32]

If the professor had decided to meet his class (professors apparently "cut" classes more than the students), Valle doubtless prepared to receive dictation in Latin for thirty minutes,[33] an exercise that would keep down present day enrolment more effectively than high fees. However, he probably experienced little difficulty, since he had studied Latin at the Colegio Tridentino, in Guatemala City, before entering San Carlos.[34] Also the many Latin books in his library attest to his facility with the language. If, by chance, he did have trouble understanding, he could ask for an explanation in Spanish or could question the professor, who, after dismissing the class, lingered a short time at the door to clarify points.[35]

To judge by his later life, Valle spent many hours of his student days in reading, and the university and other "libraries in the Spanish colonies were more numerous and had more books than did those in the English settlements."[36] The library at San Carlos proved no exception to the Spanish tradition. When Valle was a student, the library holdings amounted to at least 5,578 books, which had belonged to the Jesuits, expelled from the Spanish colonies in 1767. If he could not find what he wanted at the University, the libraries of the monasteries were presumably available to serious students.[37] And the supposition that these libraries were devoted largely to Catholic dogma is only as valid as the supposition that the libraries of church-related colleges and universities today are made up largely of nineteenth-century hymnals.

If young Valle's parents were not living in Guatemala City,[38] he retired, after seeking out supplementary reading, to the house of a relative or to one of the seminaries or friaries, where his

32. *Ibid.*, pp. 191-196.
33. *Ibid.*, p. 196.
34. ABNH. Títulos y méritos.
35. Lanning, *University*, p. 196.
36. *Ibid.*, p. 293.
37. *Ibid.*, pp. 294-299.
38. In 1794, Valle's father was described as a "resident of Tegucigalpa" (AGG, A1.43, 3232, 348. Recurso sobre la mortual de su padre). His mother appears to have died in 1795 (Valladares, ed., *Valle*, p. v). But in 1801 Valle's father was living in Choluteca (Josef Antonio Díaz del Valle to Valle, Choluteca, Sept. 2, 1801, Valle Papers).

hours would be regulated by a rigid curfew, specified to reduce the number of student brawls and "town and gown squabbles."[39] But since he held himself aloof and took private lessons in rhetoric, algebra, geometry, literature, English, French, and Italian.[40] in addition to his regular work at the University, it seems certain that he had little time for student pranks. The curfew disturbed him only if it meant that he had to stop working.

Disregarding the physical limitations imposed by the earthquake and subsequent removal to a new city, Valle could not have chosen a more propitious moment to attend the University. Founded by royal decree in 1676,[41] San Carlos offered to her hungry students, for nearly a century, nothing more to gnaw on than the dry bones of scholasticism, which, as Valle lamented later, "made this respectable institution a dark dwelling where no light penetrated save that obscured by fog and mixed with putrid effluvia."[42] The ecclesiastic and philosophic doctrines of scholasticism, which guided Francisco Vitoria to his humanitarian conclusions concerning the right of Spain to colonize America, had degenerated nearly everywhere into sterile controversies among different religious orders, each defending its favorite doctrine.[43] And Valle, without reservations, could declare that Guatemala, before the Enlightenment, was neither "ignorant" nor "enlightened"; it was a country of "error."[44] Fortunately, by the time he matriculated about 1790, the intellectual revolution in Guatemala was reaching its peak.

In the vanguard of this "happy revolution of ideas,"[45] as Valle fondly referred to it, was the good Gray Friar, José Antonio Liendo y Goicoechea. Largely as a result of his efforts, the stale scholasticism scored by Valle gave way to the ideas implicit in the

39. Lanning, *University*, p. 199.
40. ABNH. Títulos y méritos.
41. John Tate Lanning, ed., *Reales cédulas de la Real y Pontificia Universidad de San Carlos de Guatemala* (Guatemala City, 1954), pp. 22-30.   (Hereafter Lanning, ed., *Reales cédulas*.)
42. "Elogio de Goicoechea," *Valle*, edited by Rafael Heliodoro Valle (El Pensamiento de América, X; Mexico, 1943), p. 210. The late Rafael Heliodoro Valle, who with his work called attention to Valle, reproduced in this volume, with few exceptions, selections taken from Valle and Valle Matheu, eds., *Obras*. The author, for the sake of simplicity, will confine the citations, where the material is the same, to Valle and Valle Matheu's work.
43. Lanning, ed., *Reales cédulas*, p. xxii.
44. Valle and Valle Matheu, eds., *Obras*, II, 14.
45. *Ibid.*, II, 21.

Enlightenment as rapidly as the easterly trade winds could blow them from the Continent to the colonies. The transition from Peripateticism to modernity was not made without difficulty, but surmounting obstacles was habit with Goicoechea. Born in 1735, he was orphaned at the age of nine and three years later took the habit of San Francisco.[46] He attended San Carlos when it was still a stronghold of scholasticism, receiving a bachelor's degree in philosophy about 1767. Given his inquiring mind and the rigid discipline of a scholastic education, Goicoechea was admirably suited to receive and absorb the ideas that made a sublime Monday morning seem imminent. Besides teaching for many years at San Carlos, he found time to journey to Europe and, at the end of his sparkling career, to work as a missionary among the Indians of Central America.

Some of his letters written while he served as a missionary reveal a hint of personal traits that must have endeared him to Valle and to everyone connected with the University. Upon occasion he corresponded with his friends in verse, "to amuse myself in my spare time."[47] At the age of seventy-one, after walking "six hours in water up to my knees," he explained that he had experienced little discomfort because of his "habit of going barefoot and getting my feet wet."[48] With compassion, understanding, and a note of Utopian longing, he described the Indians and their life: "They offer one what they have; they never ridicule anyone; and they do not drink except at fiestas, doing so without permitting their children to have any."[49] To an Indian possessing two wives, he explained that the Christian quota allowed only one. The Indian and his wives "broke into tears," and Goicoechea "ruined the whole thing by being on the point of joining them."[50] In a long letter he opposed vigorously an attempt to abolish the method of selling liquor, saying that alcohol, "like all good

46. *Ibid.*, p. 17. In a rough draft (Valle Papers) of his "Elogio de Goicoechea," Valle wrote that Goicoechea's parents were "Dn. Luis Fernando de Liendo y Goicoechea and Da. Baltasara Susa." However, this is not supported by Lázaro Lamadrid, *Una figura centroamericano, Dr. Fr. José Liendo y Goicoechea, O. F. M.* (San Salvador, 1948), p. 5. (Hereafter Lamadrid, *Goicoechea*.) Here the mother's name appears as Baltasara Inza. Another source of information for the life of Goicoechea is Virgilio Rodríguez Beteta, *Evolución de las ideas* (Paris, 1929).

47. Goicoechea to Alejandro Ramírez, Pacura, Aug. 4, 1806, Valle Papers.

48. Goicoechea to (?), Gualaco, Feb. 1, 1806, Valle Papers.

49. *Ibid.*

50. *Ibid.*

things in this life, has its uses and abuses." Take the Church and processions, for example. How many times were they used by "heedless youth" as a "most opportune occasion to see and be seen"? He summed up his argument, in which he presented nearly every point made during our "noble experiment," with a Spanish proverb: Alcohol should be *"ni tan cerca que te abrases, ni tan lejos que te hieles."*[51] Just close enough to warm!

When Goicoechea began teaching at San Carlos, he introduced the subject of experimental physics, using the most modern texts.[52] And it was well known in the University that "in passing" he also taught the principles of geometry, optics, astronomy and geography. In 1782 he submitted to the cloister (*claustro*) or governing body of the University a plan of studies that, for the arts courses, proposed to include "the great works of natural philosophy in vogue in Spain, France, Italy, Germany, and England in the eighteenth century."[53] Valle, who delivered his *Elogio de Goicoechea* shortly after the Gray Friar's death, could not have been in better hands as a student at San Carlos.

As a candidate for the bachelor of arts degree, young Valle spent three years studying logic and philosophy and then passed an examination by defending his thesis successfully in a "public act."[54] He wrote on "general" and "specific" physics. Discussing the general properties of matter, he observed that a "body" was formed of minute atoms.[55] These were not the atoms that scientists tamper with today but resembled more the "magnetic corpuscles" of Pierre Gassendi (1592-1655).[56] Valle then correctly stated the rules for velocity and motion as related to simple and compound moving forces. Implicit in his explanation were the laws formulated by Kepler, Galileo, and Newton. In the field of mechanics he demonstrated the principle of the inclined plane,

51. Goicoechea to Valle, Chinauta, April 13, 1811, Valle Papers.
52. Lamadrid, *Goicoechea*, p. 22; John Tate Lanning, *The Eighteenth-Century Enlightenment in the University of San Carlos de Guatemala* (Ithaca, New York, 1956), pp. 67-69. (Hereafter Lanning, *Enlightenment*.)
53. Lanning, *University*, p. 205.
54. AGG, A1.3-12, 12813, 1927. *Propositiones de rebus naturalibus defendenae a D. Josepho Cecilio del Valle.* Sub disciplina D. Josephi de Leon & Goicoechea Th. Doct. & Ph. Prof. Guatemalae, M.DCC.XCIV. (Hereafter *Propositiones*.) The writer is indebted to Professor John Tate Lanning for the use of his photocopy of Valle's Latin thesis and to Mr. John J. Mahoney for the translation.
55. AGG, A1.3-12, 12813, 1927. Propositiones.
56. See Pierre Duhem, *The Aim and Structure of Physical Theory* (Princeton, 1954), p. 13.

correctly postulated by Stevin (1548-1620),[57] and the parallelo-gram of forces, distinctly and generally formulated by Newton. Valle illustrated three simple levers and then dealt with com-bustion. He explained combustion in terms of the "most subtle substance," phlogiston. The phlogiston theory, first advanced by Joachin Becker (1635-1682), defined the subtle substance as the ingredient necessary in all combustible matter. The theory was generally accepted until Pierre Lavoisier (1743-1794) pre-sented the accepted theory in a note to the French Academy of Science on November 1, 1772. Although Valle, and perforce his instructors, either did not know or did not accept Lavoisier's theory, they, curiously enough, knew the composition of water but inaccurately calculated the proportion of hydrogen to oxy-gen[58]—curious because Joseph Priestley (1733-1804) had isolated oxygen in 1774, only two years after Lavoisier had presented his theory of combustion. But while Valle and his instructors strug-gled in ignorance with the subtle phlogiston, a French judge declared: "The Republic has no need of scientists,"[59] and in 1794, the year Valle received his bachelor's degree, Lavoisier went to the guillotine. Valle concluded his thesis with a discussion of electricity, at that time captivating the imagination of scientists everywhere. He understood the positive and negative nature of electricity and was aware of the thesis of Jean Theophile Desa-gulier (1683-1744) that certain matter would conduct electricity and other matter, such as glass, would not. He mentioned Frank-lin and explained the principle of the lightning rod. Valle's state-ment that electricity aided vegetable growth indicated a knowledge of the Abbé Nollet's experiments. Finally he suggested that "electric fluid" might have some medicinal qualities.[60]

His expression of the medical efficacy of electricity is evidence of the influence of Dr. José Felipe Flores (1751-1824), another progressive faculty member. Flores was known in medical circles throughout Western Europe and America. Last to receive a

57. AGG, A1.3-12, 12813, 1927. *Propositiones.* For a synthesis of the work of Stevin in the science of mechanics, see Abraham Wolf, *A History of Science and Technology, and Philosophy in the Sixteenth and Seventeenth Centuries* (New York, 1935), pp. 219-222; Ernst Mach, *The Science of Mechanics, a Critical and Historical Account of Its Development* (London, 1942), pp. 236-243.
58. AGG, A1.3-12, 12813, 1927. *Propositiones.*
59. Quoted in L. L. Woodruff, ed., *The Development of the Sciences* (New Haven, 1941), p. 129.
60. AGG, A1.3-12, 12813, 1927. *Propositiones.*

degree in medicine before the earthquake destroyed the old capital, he became Guatemala's chief contributor to medicine and medical science.[61]   Immensely interested in electricity, he journeyed to Europe to study more closely the work of Luigi Galvani (1737-1798), whose ideas, Flores learned, were hardly more advanced than those he had been carrying to the classrooms of San Carlos "since the year '90."[62]   The interests of Flores, like those of Goicoechea, were not confined to narrow specialty.   He kept the students of his anatomy classes abreast, if not ahead, of the advances made in Europe.   To make his teaching more graphic and comprehensible, he constructed wax models with removable parts, and although he never claimed to be first with his models, he wrote from France charging his colleagues at San Carlos to take good care of the anatomic figures, which were without parallel "even in Paris."   Only in Florence did he see anything comparable to his own efforts; there he examined the work of the "Great Fontana" (Abbé Fontana, 1720-1805), who "presently is making figures with removable parts like ours."[63]   Flores also was intensely interested in finding a cure for the dread smallpox, and he was apparently in part responsible for the sailing of the Balmis expedition, which carried the vaccine from Spain to her colonies and even to China.[64]

Flores, also like Goicoechea, was a teacher of first rank.   He possessed a contagious enthusiasm for scholarly pursuits and a zest for life not diminished by the failures and foibles of mankind.   A letter, written in Paris (August 13, 1798), provides a candid miniature of the sort of person that helped to mold the impressionable and fertile mind of young Valle.   Almost breathless with excitement, if not from fatigue, Flores wrote to a friend that he had just returned from a trip to "Turin, Pavia, Milan, Parma, Modena, Bolonia, Florence, Siena, Rome, and Naples. I was inside the crater of Vesuvius.   I returned to Rome and went to Loreto, Ancona, Ravena, Terrana, Padua, Venice, and

61. For the date of Flores' death, see José Aznar López, *El Doctor Don José de Flores: una vida al servicio de la ciencia* (Guatemala City, 1960), p. 144.   For the date when Flores received his medical degree, see John Tate Lanning, "Grados académicos en el Reino de Guatemala" (unpublished manuscript), p. 100.   (Hereafter Lanning, "Grados académicos.")
62. Quoted in Lanning, *Enlightenment*, p. 274.
63. José Felipe Flores to (?), Paris, August 13, 1798, Valle Papers.
64. For Flores' contribution, see Lanning, *Enlightenment*, p. 252.

finally to Trieste, with the purpose of continuing to Vienna, but I had passport trouble." He returned to France by a different route, visiting more towns and cities. He sent word to "my friends Carbonel [Dr. Antonio Carbonel, a faculty member] and Goicoechea" that in Paris "not only the stores but also the bridges and streets are full of books, prints, maps, etc., etc." To "the Gutiérrez" (one would be Fray Felipe Gutiérrez, a faculty member), he reported that the French had "turned the balloons into a toy"; even the "women can operate them, . . . I have seen one beautiful young thing do it." But, then, the Parisian "women know more than an entire university." He lost his "small silver watch" to a pickpocket and, traveling with limited funds, he was left asking the time, as he walked around "this Babylonia like a hungry dog, looking at and smelling everything, but that's all." With heartening encouragement to his friends, Flores concluded: "Please tell Córdova [Dr. Matías de Córdova] and the rest of the faculty that I have seen everything and that there is nothing to envy in theory, in practice, or in teaching; that they continue applying themselves and fulfilling their obligations as they always have; and that they suffer with patience the scorn of their countrymen."[65] Flores, unfortunately for Guatemala and San Carlos, never returned. One of his students, a man in the same experimental and inventive tradition, succeeded, however, in making the departure of Flores seem less serious.

Dr. Narciso Esparragosa y Gallardo came to Guatemala from Caracas about 1785. He studied under the direction of Flores, receiving his medical degree in 1788,[66] and he joined the faculty while Valle was still a student. In 1795 the cloister authorized him to give a course in the principles of surgery; later he became chief surgeon of the Royal Hospital and was largely responsible for the decision to build the first medical amphitheater in the Captaincy General of Guatemala. In 1797 and 1798 he earned the praise of his colleagues for removing cataracts by a new surgical method, but he was better known for his invention of a method for delivering in relative safety infants whose position in the uterus made regular procedure impossible. Instead of using iron forceps, which could injure the infant's cranium,

65. Valle Papers.
66. Lanning, "Grados académicos," p. 100.

Esparragosa used elastic bands of whalebristle cloth. He also was active in vaccinating for smallpox after the Balmis expedition arrived, and in 1815 he published a series of instructions for controlling the dread disease. He served as *protomédico,* and when he died, he bequeathed his library to the University.[67]

The progressive ideas of the faculty members of San Carlos, such as Esparragosa, Flores, and Goicoechea, were complemented by enlightened members of the community, who had no formal connection with the University, and together these two groups formed the circle of intellectuals that had such a profound influence on Valle's life. One such person was Jacobo Villa Urrutia, judge *(oidor)* of the *audiencia.* Born in Santo Domingo and schooled in Mexico and the University of Salamanca, he arrived in Guatemala brimming with ideas for raising the standard of living and the level of education.[68] With Flores and others of similar bent, he was the driving force behind the founding of the Economic Society of the Friends of the Country, effected by royal decree in October, 1795. The purpose of the Society, as related in the act of incorporation, was to "promote and encourage agriculture, industry, the arts and crafts, and business of the Kingdom and to improve education."[69]

Directed by Villa Urrutia, the Society made every effort to achieve these goals. In 1796 the members founded a "spinning school," specifying that each student should receive a wage and that a prize should be awarded to the one producing the most thread. Archbishop Félix de Villegas, Dr. Antonio García Redondo, faculty member and ecclesiastic, and Francisco Nájera, all members of the Society, purchased seven spinning wheels with their own money. In the course of the same year the Society

67. For a thorough treatment of Esparragosa, see John Tate Lanning, ed., *Dr. Narciso Esparragosa y Gallardo* (Colección Historia, II; Caracas, 1953), pp. 13-53. When the plans for a College of Surgery were announced, Esparragosa was named vice director, and La Hermandad de Caridad de los Reales Hospitales offered six scholarships, consisting of room, board, and uniforms. In this connection, prospective students were to apply for the scholarships to the secretary of La Hermandad de Caridad, Licenciado José del Valle (Lanning, *Enlightenment,* p. 218; *Gazeta de Guatemala,* March 11, 1805).

68. Carlos Martínez Durán, "La Sociedad Económica de Amigos de Guatemala," *Universidad de San Carlos,* XXVI (1952), 118; Robert Jones Shafer, *The Economic Societies in the Spanish World (1763-1821)* (Syracuse, New York, 1958), pp. 204-205; Antonio Batres Jáuregui, *La América Central ante la historia* (3 vols.; Guatemala City, 1915-1949), II, 464.

69. Quoted in Martínez Durán, "La Sociedad Económica de Amigos de Guatemala," *Universidad de San Carlos,* XXVI (1952), 119.

offered prizes to the Indian or *ladino* (person of mixed blood) who planted and cultivated the most "Chinese cotton." Pamphlets were published to revive interest in cacao and to encourage the cultivation of flax and hemp, nearly unknown in Guatemala.[70] Joseph Longinos Martínez and José Mariano Mociño, naturalists of the royal botanical expedition to Mexico, were invited to found a museum of natural history and a botanical garden at the expense of the Society. In 1796 the captain general of Guatemala lent the dignity of his position to the work when he presided at one of the public functions of the Society and attended the opening of the botanical garden.[71] Two years later the eminent Dr. Matías de Córdova received a gold medal from the Society for his essay on why Indians should dress and wear shoes in the manner of Europeans.[72]

In addition to the Economic Society and the University, the *Gazeta de Guatemala,* "one of the most vigilant defenders of the Enlightenment published in the colonies—English or Spanish,"[73] provided the circle of intellectuals with a third medium for expressing their ideas. Flores submitted articles from Europe telling of the experiments of Galvani and of the wax figures of Fontana. Esparragosa edited the medical information, and Villa Urrutia wrote essays over the pseudonym of Jaime Villa López. Goicoechea, who composed verse in his spare time, apparently strummed his lyre for the *Gazeta* and wrote articles over the pseudonym of El Viejo Licornes.[74]

These men—Goicoechea, Flores, Esparragosa, Carbonel, Gutiérrez, García Redondo, Matías de Córdova, Villa Urrutia, and others—used the University, the *Gazeta,* the Economic Society, and even the Superior Government to put Guatemala abreast of

70. *Junta pública de la Real Sociedad Económica de Amantes de la Patria de Guatemala, celebrada en 12 de diciembre de 1796* (Guatemala City, 1796), pp. 6-18. (Hereafter *Junta de la Sociedad Económica.*)

71. *Ibid.;* Ramón A. Salazar, *Desenvolvimiento intelectual de Guatemala* (Guatemala City, 1897), pp. 262-263; J. Antonio Villacorta, *Historia de la Capitanía General de Guatemala* (Guatemala City, 1942), p. 269.

72. Flavio Guillén, *Un fraile prócer y una fábula poema (estudio acerca de Fray Matías de Córdova)* (Guatemala City, 1932), pp. 205-207.

73. John Tate Lanning, "La recepción, en la América española con especial referencia a Guatemala, de la Ilustración del siglo XVIII," *Anales de la Sociedad de Geografía E Historia de Guatemala* (hereafter *Anales*), XXI (1946), 198.

74. The pseudonyms are shown in Lanning, *Enlightenment,* p. 87. In connection with his poetry, Goicoechea wrote to Alejandro Ramírez (Pacura, June 6, 1806, Valle Papers), remarking: "For Beteta [Ignacio Beteta printed the *Gazeta*], I included some verse, and he has not answered."

the ideas of the eighteenth century and to create an intellectual atmosphere unhampered by tradition and authority. Fresh from a rural setting, Valle entered San Carlos before the departure of Flores, after the arrival of Esparragosa, and while Goicoechea, Carbonel, and Gutiérrez were still teaching. Villa Urrutia became his personal friend, counseling him upon the intricacies in the career of a royal official. García Redondo baptized two of his children, and Esparragosa worked closely with him in the *audiencia*. Valle became Censor of the *Gazeta* and a member of the Economic Society. The deep influence of his student days on the remainder of his life would not have been more obvious if Valle had tattooed the coat of arms of San Carlos on his forehead, "Class of '94."

The range of his interests, including geography, history, the sciences, education, and politics, resembles that of his teachers. His essays on vagabonds and Indians were in the tradition of Matías de Córdova and Goicoechea. His writing on freedom, while lacking the grace of style of Goicoechea, recalls the words of the distinguished teacher: "Freedom is the most useful and precious gift bestowed on mankind by the Creator. . . . Without freedom we live as dumb animals."[75] In the manner of Goicoechea, Valle wanted man to make the best possible use of his freedom. He hectored the merchants: ". . . look to the welfare of the community. Don't be agents of error. Order books. . . . But order the ones that the scholars designate." He appealed to all Guatemalans: "Buy books . . . the ones that, with the reading of each chapter, make us get up out of our chair and jump for joy. . . ."[76] With the enthusiasm displayed by Flores upon seeing the quantity of books in Paris, Valle received word from his cousin in London that "Mr. [Jeremy] Bentham . . . has sent to you by Mr. [John] Bowring, a collection of all his works."[77] Delighted, he wrote to a friend in Mexico that he had just received "the best books on political economy, the encyclopedia that Benjamin Constant and other scholars are publishing; *El viage grande de la Inglaterra* by [François] Dupin; and *La historia de las repúblicas italianas* by [Jean] Sismondi."[78] Two years later, his

75. Goicoechea to Valle, Chinauta, April 13, 1811, Valle Papers.
76. *El Amigo de la Patria*, April 4, 1821. This was Valle's newspaper.
77. Próspero de Herrera to Valle, London, Nov. 27, 1826, Valle Papers.
78. To Miguel González Saravia, July 23, 1827, Valle Papers.

cousin satisfied his request when he sent "4 volumes of *La historia de la India* by [James] Mill."[79] And two years before Valle's death, the future president of El Salvador wrote thanking him for the "2 copies of Bentham's proposed constitution."[80] Such a life, dictated as it often was by research, "lumps of manuscripts," and books that make one "jump for joy," was not likely inspired by two volumes entitled: *Luz de la fe y de la ley (Light of the Faith and of the Law)*, the two volumes that Valle's father inherited.[81]

[4]

Given a glimpse of his future and the quality of his educational environment, it comes as no surprise that his "public act," or defense of his thesis, was "very distinguished" and that the University, in 1794, invested him with the degree of bachelor of arts.[82] In connection with the awarding of the degree, the students made a short address, and likely it was this occasion in Valle's life that prompted a very friendly letter criticizing his oratorical ability. The letter helps to explain how Valle became an accomplished speaker and shows the attention that students could expect at San Carlos. The critic liked the "introduction" of Valle's brief address (*oracioncita*), but the transition leading to the main thought lacked grace of style. The citations of authorities, however, were Valle's chief weakness. It was "necessary to teach oneself, little by little, how to use them," and the cardinal principle to observe was to "digest the doctrine" that was to be used and then deliver it as though it were one's own, never "using the words of the author" unless they should bring to the address "liveliness, energy, and singularity." But even then one had to convince "the listeners that they are coming from the head of the speaker." To bring in lines learned before the address "cools the spirit of the audience," warned the critic. This advice was only part of what was called the "art of the passions," which consisted of "all the skills of eloquence that the pedants ignore." A final criticism concerned Valle's manner of concluding a thought.

79. Próspero de Herrera to Valle, London, Jan. 5, 1828, Valle Papers.
80. Joaquín de San Martín to Valle, July 27, 1832, Valle Papers.
81. AGG, A1.43, 3242, 348. Recurso sobre la mortual de su padre.
82. ABNH. Títulos y méritos.

In order to pound home a point, one had to use "force and movement," which could be done in "a sentence, an exclamation, or a lively flourish." These "flourishes," the critic explained, were the "awakeners" that alerted the audience to the important summation. "St. Jerome used them [awakeners] a great deal, and he called them *acutas argumentorum conclusiones.*"

As a public speaker, Valle must have been superficial, but he was only a youth, and he possessed a desire to learn that moved the critic, who might have been Goicoechea, to urge: "Study without respite; study with intensity." This was the only way to "the star."[83] Valle, probably more than any other student of his generation, kept his eye on that "star" throughout the rest of his life.

83. Valle Papers. The letter is undated. It begins: "Mi Valle," and it is signed "José." And it is the familiarity of the signature that causes the author to doubt that it was written by Goicoechea, though the content has the ring of Goicoechea. At a later date, 1811, when the familiarity might be expected, Goicoechea signed: "Soi de Usted afmo. amigo y siervo Goicoechea."

T W O

A Career at Law: Ambition Unlimited

[*1*]

After receiving his bachelor's degree, Valle began studying law, which he doubtless found irritating in the extreme, for the "happy revolution of ideas" in the arts courses had not yet carried the fortress of Justinian, whose curriculum failed to include a study of the laws of Castile and of the Indies, the current codes of Spain and Spanish America. If the students learned these, they did so by assisting a lawyer licensed to practice before the *audiencia*.[1] With reason, then, according to the editor of the *Gazeta,* the students "complain, lament, in a word, curse the study that uselessly occupies so much time," a study that was "so entangled, so confused, and so contradictory" that they had to spend seven years learning something that could be mastered in two or three. To ease the pain during class, the editor reported approvingly, some students read books that had nothing to do with law.[2] Although editor Simón Bergaño y Villegas doubtless exaggerated, as he did occasionally, he apparently reflected with reasonable accuracy the circumstances in which Valle earned the bachelor's degree in "both laws" (civil and canon, 1799)[3] and about four years later the licentiate.[4] Before he could practice, however, he had to pass an examination, submit documents showing his degrees, age, and racial purity, and pay the required tax (*media anata*). On August 28, 1803, he passed the examination,

1. Lanning, *Enlightenment,* p. 105. The law curriculum was not reformed until 1802.

2. *Gazeta de Guatemala,* Dec. 2, 1805.

3. ABNH. Títulos y méritos; Lanning, "Grados académicos," pp. 82, 93.

4. There is no record showing that Valle received the licentiate, but the conventions of the time would not have permitted the title unless the degree had been properly conferred.

and three days later, he began his career when he swore "to defend the mystery of the Immaculate Conception of Our Virgin Mary" and to use his license "well and faithfully."[5]

Exactly why Valle chose a career at law we do not know. Certainly there were reasons against it. His response to the intellectual environment of San Carlos insured that a "tedious brief of sheer trivia" would be unbearable, and personally he was not so well suited as others for a profession that requires an abiding patience with difference of opinion and plain ignorance. Valle generally thought he was right; and to make relations with others still more difficult, he generally was. The reason that prevailed in the face of these shortcomings was probably the simple necessity of making a living. A law career, besides offering the financial security that comes from a substantial practice, made available positions in colonial government that carried stipends in specie and in status in the community. Money probably took precedence early in his career, for, contrary to popular belief, he did not inherit wealth, but after he achieved a measure of financial security, respect for his position and full recognition of his ability from the society of Guatemala City became increasingly more important to him. But he needed money, as one of his first cases, the defense of his father, shows.

José Antonio, nearly twenty-five years after the dispute began over his father's estate, was still dogged by his brother-in-law and "worst enemy," Juan Jacinto Herrera. While Valle was a student at San Carlos, his father had fallen upon bad days. Deceived by "those he trusted," he lost what money he had, and with mortgages unpaid and bills due, he "signed over to his creditors, in the year 1796 or 1797, all his property," including "even the estate belonging to my wife." Against the wall, because of circumstances not completely revealed, he became the target of Herrera, who instituted proceedings in Comayagua (Honduras) to collect half the profits that José Antonio had earned from his father's estate before it was divided equally with his sister, Herrera's wife.[6] The

5. AGG, A1.47-1, 24915, 2818. Autos del examen de abogado de José del Valle.
6. AGG, A1.15, 7084, 335. José del Valle a nombre de su padre, José Antonio del Valle, pide incitativa para que las justicias de Comayagua remitan los autos con Juan Jacinto Herrera sobre la partición de bienes (hereafter Valle a nombre de su padre).

case dragged on until 1804, when Valle, now a licensed lawyer, intervened to save his father from further embarrassment.

Valle addressed a petition to the *audiencia*, writing with the vigor and incisiveness that were to become the trademark of his legal opinions. He explained that his father had used the profits to support his sister and to maintain the haciendas at a level of profitable production. Angrily, he charged that the "preponderance" of Herrera's influence made a fair trial in Comayagua impossible. Everyone knew that the judge, before whom José Antonio was to appear, was a "friend and debtor of Herrera," as well as an incompetent, "incapable of settling a dispute between children." Equally well known was the fact that José Antonio could not meet the obligations of an unfavorable decision. Herrera's motive, then, as Valle saw it, was purely vindictive, and he implored the court "to extend to my father its royal protection against the outrage that threatens him" and to prohibit "D. Juan Jacinto [Herrera] from interfering in anything that pertains to my father." The *audiencia* acted affirmatively on November 5, 1804.[7]

Valle's defense of his father was only one example of the legal business coming his way from Choluteca, and judging from letters from his father and others, the inhabitants of his home town were happy to have one of their own who could represent them before the *audiencia*.[8] With the years his reputation grew, and he counted as clients the monasteries of Santo Domingo (Guatemala City)[9] and San Francisco (Quetzaltenango)[10] and "nearly all the

7. *Ibid.* If this case did not terminate the enmity, the death of José Antonio, in 1807, did. Valle and Herrera's sons, Dionisio, Próspero, and Justo, were close friends throughout their lives. In connection with his mother's estate, Valle described the sale as most unjust, and in 1799 he might have tried to invalidate the sale. In that year he and his two sisters, all minors, solicited the *audiencia* to invest an attorney, whom they proposed, with their legal rights. They were involved in a litigation with "Presbítero Don Bernardo Orozco concerning the validity of the sale of an hacienda." See AGG, A1.15, 35435, 4361. Don José C. del Valle solicita el nombramiento de curador *ad litem* y propone al Procurador Ballesteros (Feb. 21, 1799); A1.20, 39013, 4561. José C. del Valle transpasa un poder a José Antonio Solís, para que siga cierta mortual (Oct. 5, 1800).

8. For example, see Josef Antonio Díaz del Valle to Valle, Choluteca, April 4, 1804; Diego de Vidaurre to Valle, Comayagua, April 25, 1805; six residents of Tegucigalpa to Valle, May 24, 1809, Valle Papers.

9. ABNH. Títulos y méritos.

10. AGG, A1.47.2, 32250, 4072. El Sor. Licenciado Dn. José del Valle sobre continuar despachando los negocios en que estaba encargado antes de separarse de la carrera de abogado (1813-1814). (Hereafter Valle sobre continuar despachando los negocios.) This document has nothing to do with the Convento de San Fran-

town councils of the Kingdom."[11]   His accounting for the year
1811 reveals still further the extent of his practice; fees for that
year amounted to 2,260 pesos, 4 reales, part of which was compensation for service rendered the government.[12]   The sum was
substantial.   Professors at San Carlos earned about 800 pesos,
judges of the *audiencia*, 3,300 pesos,[13] and Valle paid eight pesos
a month to a foreman of one of his haciendas.[14]   He bought and
sold prime beef cattle (*de buena calidad, de cuerpo y capa, como
dicen los hacendados*) for prices ranging from six pesos to fourteen
pesos each.[15]   Other domestic products were equally reasonable,
but manufactured goods from Europe, such as Valle's English
crystal,[16] and other items, such as his books, were expensive.   If
only half the fees for 1811 came from his practice, he still earned
more than his teachers, a phenomenon that occurs today with
discouraging regularity.   The extent of his private accounts doubtless was owing in part to his reputation for outstanding service to
the government, which began a few days after he was licensed
to practice and continued until 1818, when unusual circumstances
prevailed.

[2]

Valle's first commission, because of the favorable impressions
it created, may have been one of his most important.   In October,
1803, Captain General González appointed him to draw up a set
of instructions on how to combat a plague of locusts that had
befallen Guatemala.   Convinced of the "relationship that must

---

cisco, but in the course of Valle's comments, he mentions that the Convento has
empowered him.

11. González recommends Valle, Valle Papers.   González wrote: ". . . su celo por el
bien común acreditado en los asuntos que ha dirigido como apoderado de casi
todos los ayuntamientos del Reino que distinguiéndolo entre los otros abogados
le han conferido sus poderes. . . ."

12. Quaderno de lo devengado en la abogacía y asesoría, 1811, Valle Papers.

13. Lanning, *Enlightenment*, p. 221; Lanning, *University*, p. 172.

14. Razón de los gastos de la hacienda de La Concepción (no date), Valle Papers.
Valle bought "La Concepción" in 1822.   See AGG, A1.20, 9964, 1484.   Libro de
escribano José Antonio de Solís (April 30).

15. Valle in 1831 contracted to buy cattle at six pesos a head; some time after
1822 he sold cattle of the same quality for 14 pesos, 2 reales each.   See the con-
tracts between José María Lemús and Valle (no date); Juan José Cabrera and Valle,
June 7, 1831, Valle Papers.

16. Razón de lo que dejo en poder del mayordomo de La Concepción en esta
fecha (Feb., 1833), Valle Papers.

exist between the evil and the remedy," Valle's plan of attack took into account the habits of the locust—where it laid its eggs, the stages of growth, and its characteristics when full grown. The attack should begin on the eggs, buried an inch or so in the ground, by plowing them deeper. Failing total destruction, the second assault should be concentrated on the young or unfledged locust, which could be burned, eaten by hogs, or trampled by herds of cattle and by flocks of sheep. Once the insects were full grown, the battle was lost.[17] On October 25, 1803, Valle submitted his manuscript to the crown attorney (*fiscal*) of the *audiencia*, and Captain General González, on January 7, 1804, ordered its publication and circulation throughout Guatemala. The crown attorney praised the work in glowing terms, declaring that the pamphlet was "proof of the talent, exactitude, and thorough knowledge of the young author," who was both "modest and patriotic."[18] Valle's research in the laws of Castile and of the Indies, duly noted at the bottom of the pages, doubtless attracted much of the favorable comment. His mastery of the codes singled him out as one of the "glorious exceptions"[19] and prevented judges from "confusing him with other lawyers of the Kingdom."[20]

Captain General González, unaccustomed to having such talent at his disposal, employed Valle immediately as temporary *asesor* and *relator* for the tribunals of the *audiencia* and as *fiscal específico* for cases that demanded, "because of their gravity," a lawyer of "ability, capable of sustaining the interests of the King."[21] As *asesor* for a given case, Valle submitted a written opinion showing the law that applied and how it had been interpreted in the past. He inserted his opinion into the file of the case, and the judge used it as an aid in reaching a decision. In civil cases the *asesor* could declare on the basis of his research that no grounds for litigation existed. As *relator* he assisted the crown

17. AGG, A1.38,3.4, 655, 23. Instrucción sobre la plaga de langosta; medios de exterminarla, o de disminuir sus efectos; y de precaver la escasez de comestibles (1803). This citation is to the manuscript which was published in 1804. For copies of the publication, see AGG, A1.38.3.4, 22150, 2646; Biblioteca Nacional de Guatemala (hereafter BNG). Colección Valenzuela.
18. AGG, A1.38.3.4, 22150, 2646.
19. Lanning, *Enlightenment,* p. 107. Professor Lanning was not commenting on Valle but was making the point that few lawyers bothered to learn their way through the laws of the Indies.
20. González recommends Valle, Valle Papers. Valle went to the laws of the Indies to find out what had been done in the past.
21. González recommends Valle, Valle Papers.

attorney in preparing briefs. He also stood his turn as court-appointed attorney, accepting any case that came his way.

Occasionally, but inevitably, while serving in these capacities, he experienced the reluctance and captiousness that betray a certain distrust of the ability of a "new man" in any profession. On September 3, 1804, the *audiencia* appointed him to defend one Doña María Ramírez in a case pending in the ecclesiastical court concerning "divorce or annulment of matrimony." Valle asked to be excused, explaining that he already had an enormous amount of work. He was "overburdened with business of *asesoría*" that had to be completed before the next mail, and then there were other legal matters demanding "immediate dispatch."[22] Now for a man accustomed to working from five o'clock in the morning until eleven at night,[23] these excuses appear flimsy. Perhaps the fact that the woman had expressed "little confidence" in his ability had dampened his spirit.[24]

A similar experience occurred a few months later when counsel for a woman blinded by venereal disease initiated proceedings to collect 1000 pesos for "damages" (*daños y perjuicios*) from the man who had communicated it to her. Earlier both plaintiff and defendant had been convicted of "concubinage." Valle decided that the demands, as framed by the woman's lawyer, asked of the court something completely illegal. Plaintiff's counsel replied sharply, charging Valle with "partiality." Valle, reacting as though he had been slapped, suppressed his impulse to declare the petition inadmissible, and calmly reviewed the case in terms calculated to show the ignorance of the lawyer. Concerning the charge of partiality, he "thought of going to the trouble of smashing it." Instead he simply excused it. Still not satisfied and conceding nothing to Valle's interpretation, plaintiff's counsel continued to press his point. Angered beyond objectivity, Valle requested the tribunal to replace him with another *asesor*, who could discuss the case with the "tranquillity of which I am not capable."[25]

22. AGG, A1.15, 26038, 2867. Señora María Josefa Ramírez, sobre que se le nombre de abogado al Sr. Don Josef Tomás de Zelaya, y otros (hereafter Ramírez).
23. Rosa, *José Cecilio del Valle (Obras)*, I, xx.
24. AGG, A1.15, 26038, 2867. Ramírez.
25. AGG, A1.15, 36409, 4415. Manuela García demanda daños y perjuicios de Don Julián González.

In February, 1806, Valle became *asesor* for the Royal Consulado of Guatemala, a position that he held until 1811. Patterned after those in Spain, the Consulado served as a court for commercial cases.[26] In this tribunal he dealt with breaches of contract, disputed sales, and violations of royal laws governing trade. A case in kind, involving the possession of a quantity of indigo, brought against Valle another charge of favoritism. His opinion, according to the plaintiff, was partial to the interests of the defendant, Juan Pedro Lara. Valle, ran the complaint, "has been a student of Lara and until this moment lives in one of his houses without paying any rent."[27]

He might have lived in Lara's house without paying rent; information suitable for gossip quickly becomes public property in a community no larger than Guatemala City was. Conceding Valle's arrangement with Lara, it is entirely conceivable that a disgruntled litigant might cry "foul." But whether Valle acted in an objective manner is impossible to say; however, the charges to the contrary had absolutely no significance, for Captain General González later reported with a sigh of relief that Valle's fairness and objectivity were common knowledge and that he never heard the complaints "against him that were expressed against other lawyers of the country."[28] González, throughout his tenure of office in Guatemala, continued to reward Valle, and in 1805, when the office of censor fell vacant, Valle received the appointment,[29] probably with the thought that it carried more honor than obligation. Special circumstances, however, made the honor onerous.

26. See Robert S. Smith, "Origins of the Consulado of Guatemala," *Hispanic American Historical Review* (hereafter *HAHR*), XXVI (Feb., 1946), 156.

27. AGG, A1.5.7, 2411, 18341. Entre Don Pedro José de Górriz y la testamentaría de Don José Biedna sobre treinta y quatro tercios de tinta (Aug., 1806).

28. González recommends Valle, Valle Papers.

29. ABNH. Títulos y méritos. Valle also was appointed temporary *asesor* (March 12, 1805) for the tribunal of the town council. See AGG, A1.2.2, 15732, 2187. Libro de cabildos de Guatemala, año 1805; Juan Francisco Vilches to Valle, León, April 23, 1805, Valle Papers. And in September, 1805, Captain General González named him Defensor de Obras Pías. See González to Valle, September 10, 1805, Valle Papers; AGG, A1.39, 1758 *(legajo)*, fol. 43. Mercedes y nombramientos, 1805-1807. As Defensor de Obras Pías, Valle provided legal counsel in connection with specified holdings of the Church.

[*3*]

In the histories of Guatemala that have been written since
1821, when independence was achieved, there runs an argument
that sorts out the men who made the history immediately before
and after independence and labels them according to their views
on independence, which is equated with freedom and democracy.
Valle's position as Censor has been one of the strong pieces of
evidence used to counter the charge that he was a sycophant of
the crown. Since Valle had to approve the enlightened and progressive ideas that appeared in the *Gazeta,* the argument runs, he
was equally progressive and enlightened and could not have been
a crown lackey. The purpose here is not to enter the argument
but to show that Censor Valle and editor Bergaño played a part in
and witnessed the end of a singular period in the colony's history.

It is not clear how long Valle acted as Censor, but it is certain
that Bergaño did not edit the paper after September, 1808. Bergaño came to Guatemala from Vera Cruz, where he received his
passport on December 28, 1799, as "an employee named Simón
Carreño" in the service of "Captain Don José Jiménez."[30] Soon
after his arrival, "he fell from a tree in Escuintla, badly fracturing
his pelvis." After long suffering he recovered sufficiently to walk
with crutches, but as a result of the fall he developed a "fistula
that they say is incurable."[31] Except that he was born about
1781,[32] nothing is known of his background. Concerning his
future, however, nothing could have been more certain than
that his ability to criticize, agitate, and ridicule would keep the
staid society of Guatemala City in a tempest. If Valle were the
"Andean Cicero," surely Bergaño was the Guatemalan Socrates,
and if he had lived at an earlier time, his cup of hemlock would
have been a stake and a slow fire.

Bergaño became editor of the *Gazeta* following the retirement

30. AGG, B2.7, 777, 31. Sobre averiguar la conducta de Simón Bergaño y
Villegas. The original passport can be found in this *expediente* and *legajo.*

31. *Ibid.* Captain General González, who received a request from Bergaño in
1810, took the matter up with the tribunal. In the course of the consideration of
the request, González described Bergaño's handicap.

32. AGG, B2.7, 777, 31. Sobre averiguar la conducta de Simón Bergaño y Villegas. Bergaño, at the end of his testimony, October, 1808, said that he was twenty-
seven years old.

of Alejandro Ramírez, close friend of Goicoechea and Villa Urrutia.[33] Under the guidance of Bergaño, the paper continued to be the voice of the cluster of intellectuals. The fact, however, that the paper served as a springboard for their ideas is not meant to imply that Goicoechea, Villa Urrutia, Esparragosa, and the others dictated policy to Bergaño. There was no need to; he agreed with their views. In a letter to Valle, Bergaño explained that he and Villa Urrutia desired "to stir up interest in literature" and to awaken the "talent of Mexico and Guatemala."[34] If Bergaño differed with them, as he did occasionally, the reason was his choleric personality, not his basic views, save perhaps those on religion.

In obvious collaboration with the progressive members of the faculty, Bergaño supported, in a story signed "El Engañado," the assault on "old Aristotle."[35] In the course of the story Engañado (The Deceived), steeped in Peripateticism, made the mistake of allowing a young man with a modern education to examine his library. Appalled with the scholastic "chaff and nonsense," the young man invited Engañado to visit him and see his books. Among those noticed by Engañado were "the works of Massillon, Olavide's *El evangelio en triunfo,* the *Confessions* of St. Augustine, an unbound set of *El viagero universal,* the *Logic* of Condillac, the Marquis of Caracciolo, Fénelon's *El Telémaco,* and the *Memorias políticas* of Larruga."[37] These works and many other titles, ranging from *La Diana enamorada* to the third volume of Tomas Vicente Tosca's *Trigonometría* and including "2 volumes of the *Gazeta de Guatemala;* 9 of the *Diario de México; Genio de Buffon,* in French, one volume; *Espíritu de las leyes,* one volume; and *Cartas marruecas,* one volume," were books found in Bergaño's home[38]—no "chaff and nonsense" here. Save *La Diana enamorada* (Gaspar Gil Polo), spared from the flames in

33. Ramírez died on May 20, 1821. For a summary of his career, see *El Editor Constitucional,* July 30, 1821 (*Escritos de Pedro Molina* [Colección Documentos, X, XI, XII; Guatemala City, 1954]), XII, 707-708. (Hereafter *El Editor Constitucional.*)
34. Valle Papers. The letter was not dated, but it was probably written in February, 1806, in reply to an order that Valle had to convey to him the last of January or the first of February.
35. Lanning, *Enlightenment,* p. 127.
36. *Ibid.,* p. 133.
37. *Ibid.*
38. AGG, B2.7, 777, 31. Sobre averiguar la conducta de Simón Bergaño y Villegas (1808).

the sixteenth century,[39] all were in the best tradition of the eighteenth.

Upon several occasions Bergaño emphasized a second theme of the intellectual circle. In response to a complaint about the "multitude of thieves" in the capital, he quickly pointed out that poverty spawned thieves and that the grinding poverty of Guatemala owed its origin to the fact that there was "no agriculture, industry, or commerce" worthy of the name. Agriculture was chained to decadence by the poor distribution of land, Bergaño asserted. "For every man who has 25 leagues of land (24 uncultivated), there are fifty who do not have enough land to plant an onion." What Guatemala needed, he maintained, was patriotic societies to promote agriculture, industry, and commerce and to encourage the development of the colony's abundant waterways.[40] Another remedy, written in connection with the vagabonds who "scandalize the streets," was to use these people to colonize Guatemala, north and south. In each area there were ranchers who owned "haciendas of eight, fifteen, and even thirty leagues" and whose only interest was the "foolish vanity of having them for their own, with remarkable prejudice to public welfare."[41]

And in explaining what he had found in the records of a certain district, Bergaño pointed up a third theme of the progressive members of the faculty and community. "Of every ten births" in that district "six are native sons" (Indians). These were the children that never would receive an education, and, in many cases, they were fated to watch their mothers die in "destitution." Then, as orphans, they would live in the streets, surrendering themselves to the vices. *¡Cosa increíble!*[42]

Censor Valle had to approve the articles and comments that appeared in the *Gazeta,* and on January 27, 1806, Captain General González had to remind him of the obligations of his position. He explained to Valle that a person of "excellent character" had complained about "certain articles" published in the *Gazeta,* and

39. See Irving A. Leonard, *Books of the Brave, Being an Account of Books and of Men in the Spanish Conquest and Settlement of the Sixteenth-Century New World* (Cambridge, Massachusetts, 1949), p. 230.
40. *Gazeta de Guatemala,* Nov. 21, 1805. Bergaño signed the comment with his initials. The Economic Society suspended operations in 1800.
41. *Ibid.,* Nov. 25, 1805.
42. *Ibid.,* April 9, 1806.

he cautioned Valle "not to approve any writings other than those of general news and discussions, which in no way whatsoever have any connection with religion, legislation, or the customs" of the colony. Further, he directed Valle to check the "contents of the various writings that appear in other publications," making sure that the delicate subjects were treated with circumspection and preventing the circulation of anything containing "sinister concepts."[43] The person of "excellent character," who prompted González' note to Valle, doubtless was Archbishop Luis Peñalver y Cárdenas who, on January 8, 1806, had denounced the *Gazeta* for "its articles contrary to religion, for its satires on certain persons, and for articles 'that excite the carnal passions.' "[44]

With great reluctance—it must have been—Valle communicated to Bergaño the orders from González. Valle and Bergaño enjoyed a limited friendship based on a mutual respect for education. While Valle certainly disapproved of Bergaño's coarseness, he must have admired and applauded, discreetly to be sure, many of Bergaño's forthright statements—statements that propriety and ambition would never allow Valle to make. And Bergaño, who considered Valle one of the two "greatest men in Guatemala," criticized him for those characteristics.[45] The two men, however, saw eye to eye concerning the problems affecting the welfare of Guatemala.

Valle, as early as 1803, was an exponent of a restricted version of free trade. He wrote that the Kingdom of Guatemala covered an extensive area, embracing districts and provinces of very different topography and climate. Each province had an abundance of some product, and in the interest of the colony, it was important for the provinces to exchange their products freely; the "distribution of the abundance," Valle thought, could be accomplished by free trade. This was the "simple principle to which economic science" had been reduced, after it had suffered "the mania of being subjected to all the regulations of an unenlightened policy." If a farmer were "absolutely prohibited from

43. González to Valle, Valle Papers.
44. Lanning, *Enlightenment*, p. 91.
45. The other person was Alejandro Ramírez. Bergaño to Valle, no date (1806), Valle Papers. Bergaño also praised Valle in the *Gazeta* (June 2, 1806) when commenting on men of good taste in Guatemala. He wrote: "Entre ellos el Licenciado D. José Cecilio del Valle . . . es sin disputa uno de los literatos de primer orden aún con respecto a los de Europa."

exchanging his grain," he would cultivate only enough to satisfy the needs of his poor family. However, if he were permitted "to trade with the families of the village," he would produce more, and if the freedom were extended to include "other villages of the district," the crops would "increase in the same proportion." Finally, Valle maintained cautiously, the freedom gradually would include the districts and provinces.[46] His exposition could have included two more steps: free intercolonial trade and free world trade, but these steps went against royal economic policy, and prudent Valle, throughout the colonial period, consistently remained within the bounds of royal authority. Flamboyant Bergaño, however, rarely looked before he leaped. Each recognized this difference in personality, which doubtless strained but never destroyed their mutual respect.

Valle, when he conveyed the order, must have tried to make clear to Bergaño their mutual ground and to persuade him to exercise more prudence. But probably in the manner anticipated by Censor Valle, editor Bergaño replied:

You know much better than I the obligations of a censor, but you don't want to fulfill them. All that does not oppose religion, the government, or the worthy traditions merits approval. Anything that does must be banned. If you, although with regret, wish to respect these; . . . if you are a censor who fears the chatter of the vulgar and some imaginary risks; and if you do not wish to go to the trouble of defending what is right, I shall know that you, as Censor, are not doing your duty. . . . All you want is the gravy [*coger las truchas*], which is to say that you want or do enjoy the honor of being Censor with few obligations and without the fortitude to take a stand in favor of justice. In view of this, it is impossible for me to agree with you, and I shall ask that they name another [censor] for me. Not one person, among the many and well educated, has not accused you of timidity and submission, and I agree and add injustice. I am being perfectly candid and not beating around the bush . . . , and I hope you will be kind enough to forgive me on the basis of my genial, friendly, and philosophic ingenuousness.[47]

Bergaño, probably soon after he addressed the above letter to Valle, decided to reform, "to become a crafty man" with a

46. AGG, A1.38.3.4, 655, 23. Langosta.
47. Valle Papers. If Valle were still Censor in 1807, he received oblique criticism from Bergaño for being too lenient with the press. Bergaño had reprinted an article from a Mexican paper, and in criticizing the article, he wrote: "El papel antecedente se escribió para el Diario de México; pero se hubiera quedado en eterno olvido si reynase en los censores de Guatemala la preocupación que domina el cerebro de revisor mexicano, . . ." See the *Gazeta de Guatemala*, April 6, 1807.

"manner of false prudence and reserve," suppressing his "frank and guileless character." Necessity demanded that he "sacrifice those virtues" so that he might live among the few men that he esteemed, despite the fact that he did not like the rest.[48] If Bergaño had been addicted to the poppy, he would have been better situated to proceed with his reform. His candor apparently continued to attract the attention of authorities,[49] but finally all his indiscretions caught up with him, and he found himself in the toils of the tribunal of the *audiencia:* Sala del Crimen. His prose and poetry that appeared in the *Gazeta,* whose business he managed before the eyes of Captain General González, in his secretariat,[50] had nothing to do with Bergaño's arrest and incarceration. His personal conduct viewed against a new political background was the point of contention.

On October 23, 1808, Francisco Camacho, the senior judge, having received information that Bergaño was engaged in disturbing the peace by creating "dissension between Europeans [Spaniards] and Americans [creoles]," ordered his arrest, the confiscation of his belongings, and a complete investigation.[51] At midnight the order was carried out,[52] and at 1:30 A.M. the following day he was "lodged in jail." On October 27 Captain General González ordered the employees of his secretariat, where Bergaño had been employed since 1805, to testify concerning the conduct of the accused.[53] Miguel Ignacio Talavera, chief of the secretariat and member of an influential family, was first to make

48. Valle Papers. The note, undated and unaddressed, was signed S. B. y Villegas.
49. Ramón A. Salazar, *Historia de veintiún años; la independencia de Guatemala* (Guatemala City, 1928), p. 97. (Hereafter Salazar, *Historia de veintiún años.*) Salazar wrote that Bergaño was denounced to the Holy Tribunal, but Ernesto Chinchilla Aguilar (*La inquisición en Guatemala* [Guatemala City, 1953]) does not support the statement. However, both agree that Valle was denounced for reading prohibited books. See Salazar, *Historia de veintiún años,* p. 98; Chinchilla Aguilar, *La inquisición en Guatemala,* pp. 196, 270. The fact that these denunciations were badges of distinction instead of marks of degradation points up the intellectual freedom of that epoch. Goicoechea and Villa Urrutia were also denounced (Chinchilla Aguilar, *La inquisición en Guatemala,* p. 196).
50. José Toribio Medina, *La imprenta en Guatemala (1660-1821)* (Santiago, Chile, 1910), pp. 340-341.
51. AGG, B2.7, 777, 31. Sobre averiguar la conducta de Simón Bergaño y Villegas.
52. AGG, B2.7, 778, 31. Autos pronunciados por la Real Sala del Crimen denegando la aplicación del indulto a favor de Don Simón Bergaño. In 1812, a general amnesty was granted to political prisoners. Bergaño, languishing in a prison in Havana, applied for his freedom. Thus his case was reviewed, showing among other things that he was apprehended "a las doce de la noche."
53. AGG, B2.7, 777, 31. Sobre averiguar la conducta de Simón Bergaño y Villegas.

his declaration. He denounced Bergaño's "ungovernable and revolutionary character," which was "notorious throughout the city" and which made Talavera view Bergaño with horror.[54] José Ramón Barbarena testified that Bergaño called an employee of the secretariat "*un vil,* a liar, and other similar names," and that he always was exasperating.[55]   Blas Ortiz de Letona could add that several times the employees found it necessary to stop work because Bergaño "offended us with indecent language," and it seemed to follow naturally that Bergaño had "not attended Mass for some time."[56]   Another colleague asserted that Bergaño was "irreligious, sarcastic, and ungrateful,"[57] and Manuel José Fernández held his propriety in abeyance while he quoted the vulgarisms used by Bergaño,[58] vulgarisms that lend validity to Ernest Hemingway's boast that Spanish, at that level, is more flexible than English.   The testimony kindest to Bergaño was that his enthusiasm for literature inspired in him a "monstrous pride that makes him rave."[59]

Bergaño denied nothing, but he did explain that Talavera tried to run the secretariat with "despotism" and that he, Fernández, and Barbarena tried to annoy him at every opportunity. The shabby treatment added to the "implacable hatred" that these men held for him made impossible any respect for Talavera, or anyone like him.   Bergaño hoped that the court would understand and do him the justice that corresponded to a "young man whose crimes have no other origin than the charges of my adversaries or my inclination toward literature."[60]

The investigation took another direction when the "formal scrutiny of his papers" began.   From the "many bundles of newspapers and bundles of poetic works" found in Bergaño's house, only 134 items, some personal correspondence, and unpublished manuscripts were impounded for scrutiny.   One manuscript,

54. AGG, B2.7, 779, 31.   Contra Simón Bergaño y Villegas, oficial escribiente de la secretaría de la capitanía general de Guatemala, por díscolo (Oct. 27, 1808). (Hereafter Contra Simón Bergaño.)
55. *Ibid.*
56. *Ibid.*, Oct. 30, 1808.   Ortiz de Letona confessed that he had done wrong by "not having denounced Bergaño to the Holy Tribunal of the Inquisition."
57. AGG, B2.7, 779, 31.   Contra Simón Bergaño (Oct. 30, 1808).
58. *Ibid.*, Nov. 5, 1808.
59. *Ibid.*
60. *Ibid.*, Oct. 27, 1808.   Bergaño probably did not hear any of the testimony given after October 31, for he apparently was escorted out of the city, on his way to Omoa, before that date.

addressed to "Santísimo Padre," did not improve his chances of going free. Bergaño, in the essay, castigated the Church for allowing young girls to take vows before they realized what they were doing. He knew a nun in the convent of Santa Catalina who was "nearly mad" and whose expressions "were none other than the following: Get me out of here. I don't want to stay here. *I didn't know what I was doing.* . . . If they don't get me out, I'll hang myself." Bergaño recommended that females should not take vows until they were twenty-five, that they should be able to disavow whenever they pleased, that the priests in charge of the convents should be at least fifty years of age, that they should not be friars, and that they must have studied history and other humanities.[61]

In three volumes of the work of Juan Andrés, the notary public (*escribano*) of the Sala del Crimen, Joaquín Calvo, discovered that Bergaño maintained a running argument in the margins with the exiled ex-Jesuit. Calvo dutifully copied passages from the volumes and then the remarks of Bergaño. For example, Andrés "on folio 53, line twenty-two," wrote: "Freedom of thought and of conveying one's thoughts to others is a necessity for literature, and this is enjoyed equally in monarchical states and republics." To which Bergaño replied: "The Abbé Andrés lies. Poppycock. [*Es un tronero.*] No one can deny the freedom of thought, but that of speaking, of writing, of conveying thoughts is what the Spaniards want. The author of this work writes well but thinks poorly; great fluency or eloquence and little substance; plenty of chaff and little grain."[62]

On the basis of less evidence than presented here, Captain General González, in counsel with Judges Camacho and Polo, decided that Bergaño's "seductive genius" could cause "fatal consequences" if he were permitted to remain in "this capital and Kingdom." Not wishing to take any unnecessary risks, he ordered Bergaño transported to Spain under arrest with the charge of "Libertino y Sedicioso" hanging round his neck.[63] Two guards

---

61. AGG, B2.7, 777, 31. Sobre averiguar la conducta de Simón Bergaño y Villegas (Oct. 24, 1808).

62. *Ibid.*, Dec. 5, 1808. The work of Juan Andrés that Bergaño was reading was *Origen, progresos y estado actual de toda la literatura* (10 vols.; Madrid, 1784-1806). Bergaño also criticized the work of Juan Andrés in the *Gazeta* (Oct. 6, 1806).

63. AGG, B2.7, 777, 31. Sobre averiguar la conducta de Simón Bergaño y Villegas (Oct. 24, 1808).

from the department of revenue were to escort him to the Gulf, where he would board a ship bound for Cuba and then Spain, burdened only by "necessary clothing, shaving gear, [and] pillow and mat and bedding," all "inventoried."[64]   Delayed for five months at the port of Omoa (Honduras) waiting for a ship, he arrived in Cuba in March, 1809.[65]   Owing to his "chronic" and "incurable" illness, he went to a hospital after reaching Havana and was never well enough to make the journey to Spain.[66]   On August 29, 1810, still a prisoner, he asked Captain General González to request authorities in Cuba to allow him to "leave the prison (during certain hours) so that he could get some fresh air and take the baths" that would help his illness. González agreed, warning, however, that Bergaño was not to "talk or write anything having to do with government or politics" during those "certain hours."[67]   Apparently González, judging by his acquiescence, had not been greatly affronted by the caricature of him, "with a verse at the bottom reviling his honorable character," found during the investigation in Bergaño's house.[68]

In the spring of 1813 Valle received a letter posted in Havana that contained the following: "Bergaño is alive. Yes, friend, alive."   Alive he was and publishing the *Correo de las Damas, Patriótico Americano,* and the *Diario Cívico.*   And Valle could not have been surprised when he read that Bergaño had a mistress, had experienced some difficulty with a bishop, and had emerged

64. *Ibid.*
65. AGG, B2.7, 778, 31. Autos pronunciados por la Real Sala del Crimen, denegando la aplicación del indulto a favor de Don Simón Bergaño.
66. AGG, A3.1, 380, 18, fol. 3. This document lists the expenses that the government in Cuba sustained as a result of Bergaño's imprisonment there. The government of Guatemala apparently had to pay the bill. Bergaño was confined in the Hospital Real de San Antonio.
67. AGG, B2.7, 777, 31. Sobre averiguar la conducta de Simón Bergaño y Villegas. By this time, Bergaño, who had been charged but not tried, must have recalled a verse he had written earlier for the *Gazeta* (Nov. 14, 1805).
> "Gané un pleyto en que cobraba
> Diez pesos; y el escribano
> Con la planilla en la mano
> Seis de cóstas demandaba.
> Al ver que yo me asustaba
> Dijó, con cariño externo:
> 'y agradézcame Usté a mí
> Que el pleyto no ha sido eterno.'
> Mas yo solo respondí:
> Qué bien hecho está el Infierno."
68. AGG, B2.7, 777, 31. Sobre averiguar la conducta de Simón Bergaño y Villegas.

in triumph.[69] Save for the bill for his care and keep that Cuban authorities sent, the letter to Valle, in 1813, apparently ended his connection with Guatemala.

The Bergaño case, rather than resolve any arguments, serves only to emphasize the intellectual freedom enjoyed in the Captaincy General of Guatemala before Napoleon Bonaparte, in 1808, tried to make Spain a French barracks and Spanish America his commissary. González, with real or imaginary fears, banished Bergaño not for any reason connected with the *Gazeta* but for his alleged activity that pitted creoles against Spaniards. Until 1808 Bergaño cursed and fumed and published the *Gazeta* without consequences more serious than making himself extremely unpopular with Talavera and "anyone like him." At least Talavera, Barbarena, and Fernández were not at all reluctant to record the grossest details of Bergaño's insults, which had rankled in their breasts for three years. And their testimony, completely irrelevant to the main charge against Bergaño, suggests that Captain General González was running scared (which of course he was). Fearing strife between creoles and Peninsulars, González wasted no time in securing testimony that he knew would be damaging. Certainly the complaints against Bergaño could not have come as a surprise, especially since they originated in the secretariat. In addition, González decided, less than twenty-four hours after the arrest, to send Bergaño to Spain, instead of trying him in Guatemala. And two guards escorted the thin, crippled editor, who suffered an "incurable ailment," out of Guatemala before the end of October, 1808. González feared "fatal consequences"; and the singular climate of freedom, in which Valle had been educated, gave way to restrictions imposed in the name of patriotism and security. And an alphabetical list of editors temporarily unemployed because of Napoleon might have begun: Bergaño y Villegas, Simón (Guatemala); Cobbett, William (England). . . .

Apparently Valle's only connection with acts affecting Bergaño was the transmission of an order doubtless inspired by a hyper-

69. Bergaño to Valle, Feb. 1, 1813, Valle Papers. Bergaño, who was refused amnesty by the *audiencia* of Guatemala (1812), wrote: "I got the last amnesty, thus avoiding a voyage that should have cost me my life." But he was not completely free, for he asked Valle to petition the *audiencia* to review its position, because: "I had to leave without a trial, without being convicted of a crime, and it is not possible to vindicate myself of the charges in Spain . . . because of the difficulty of securing evidence. . . ." He wanted nothing less than "absolute freedom."

sensitive archbishop. And Valle did so with regret, knowing that he was caught between the authority of González and the philosophic ingenuousness of Bergaño. In these circumstances, Bergaño's statement that Valle wanted the honor and not the obligation of the office of Censor doubtless struck close to the truth, but what Bergaño and the "many and well educated" took to be timidity and submission was nothing more than the discreetness that attends and favors ambition. And Valle's discretion paid dividends. Less than a month after he received the order concerning the *Gazeta*, González appointed him *asesor* of the Consulado, described above, and in 1807, the commander of the royal artillery and engineering corps successfully proposed Valle's name for the position of crown attorney for the corps.[70]

[4]

These positions were important, but they failed to satisfy Valle, whose ambition kept pace with his talent but, by 1807, ran ahead of his experience. At the age of thirty-one he decided to apply for an appointment to an *audiencia* as a judge. For support of his application, he asked Oidor Jacobo Villa Urrutia, now in Mexico, for a letter of recommendation. Valle did not deceive himself about his chances. He called the selection of judges from the list of candidates a lottery in which many were chosen by chance, more through favor, and only rarely for merit. He thought the odds against him were about 10,000 to 1, but the excitement and enthusiasm emerging from behind the drape of gloom cloaking his prospects betray the thought, fleeting though it might have been, that he would be that one. At least he could not lose anything by making the effort, and "this thought fixed my decision." He expected "very expressive" recommendations but he was sure that Villa Urrutia's would be "more conducive than any other."[71]

But ambition was not the only force driving him in 1807 to ask the crown for an office that might have caused him to move from Guatemala. "How happy I would be," Valle wrote, "with

70. González recommends Valle, Valle Papers.
71. Valle to Villa Urrutia, Dec. 3, 1807, Valle Papers.

a position that would take me a thousand leagues from my enemies." He protested to Villa Urrutia that his signature was "viewed with displeasure" by the judges of every tribunal, and even if they were replaced, "the roots" would remain and would yield "identical fruit." He could escape the unpleasant circumstances by accepting Villa Urrutia's invitation to come to Mexico, but he did not feel that he could leave the country until he definitely had secured a position that would allow him to provide for the family that he already had, despite the fact that he had "remained single."[72] His father had died within the year, and he was caring for his sisters, Manuela and Francisca.[73]

Soon after he wrote to Villa Urrutia, he began preparing his *títulos y méritos* for submission to the Council of the Indies in support of the application he intended to make.[74] In this connection, but at a later date, Captain General González evaluated Valle's work and commented on his character: "I certify that I have known personally Licenciado Dn. José Cecilio Díaz del Valle . . . who has served me in the government of this Kingdom since the time I arrived." Austere in personal life and "pure" in conduct, Valle rarely was seen outside his home unless business demanded; he nearly ruined his health studying, and his education in "several languages, in the humanities, in some fields of mathematics, and in political economy" was generally acknowledged. He had acquired the sound judgment reserved for an *anciano,* and the public and the courts did him the "justice of never confusing him with other lawyers," owing to the "conciseness of his style, the singular gift that he has for perceiving and expressing with clarity the most obscure subjects, . . . and the strength of his principles." Zealously, he had carried out the duties of his many positions to "my satisfaction" and to that of the respective judges, and in view of everything, José del Valle "is very worthy of a toga."[75]

72. *Ibid.*
73. See Pedro Antonio de Zelaya to Valle, Choluteca, Aug. 7, 1807; Miguel López to Valle, Choluteca, Aug. 13, 1807. Each correspondent extended his sympathy to Valle, who "llora por el fallecimiento del Señor su Padre que en paz descansa."
74. Valle Papers. A rough draft (undated) in his handwriting of his *títulos y méritos* was found among his papers. Judging from the positions that he included (and he would not have omitted any), it was written in 1807 or 1808.
75. Valle Papers.

Captain General González' recommendation suggests that Valle, perhaps in a mood of depression, might have exaggerated the displeasure that his presence in the tribunals provoked. Yet the very qualities praised by González well might have been the ones that caused his colleagues to alternate between an envious green and a furious red. Impeccable in his dress, thorough and scholarly in his work, aristocratic in manner, if not in pocket, and cold and aloof, except in his home, Valle offered nothing tangible to his critics. For relaxation, he might have read Alexander Pope's translation of Homer (London, 1794) or *Pensamientos de Pascal sobre la religión* (Madrid, 1805)[76] rather than, say, take a *copita* with the "boys" at the "Lucrecia."[77] Valle had no moral convictions against sipping the wine of the maguey; he kept *aguardiente* and wine within arm's reach,[78] but he used it in the manner suggested by Goicoechea, who declared: "*Aguardiente,* wine, *chicha, pulque,* and the other beverages made by fermentation are susceptible to abuse; however, used with moderation, they are positively good."[79] We are assured by Valle's own hand that he did not frequent the Patio de Gallos (cockpit), where "punctually some men without education, who have abandoned themselves to the vices," gathered.[80]

Thus by his nature and by design, Valle kept his social life severely restricted, a practice regarded as a virtue by Captain General González. He explained in his recommendation that if Valle were appointed he could serve the crown best, owing to his thorough knowledge of the Kingdom, by remaining in Guatemala.

76. These are books that belonged to Valle and that are still a part of his library, which is carefully preserved by his descendants. Valle's sister, Manuela, gave him Pascal's book, as the flyleaf shows.

77. The "Lucrecia" was a tavern in Guatemala City at the time.

78. The statement is based on inventories that Valle periodically made of household goods, kitchen items, and of other things in his hacienda, "La Concepción." See Razón de lo que dejo en poder del mayordomo de La Concepción (after 1822), Valle Papers. On one occasion his sisters wrote to him saying: "Te remitimos el frasco de aguardiente, dos boteyas [*sic*] de vino, . . . y los sigarros [*sic*]." See Francisca and Manuela to Valle, Escuintla, no date, Valle Paper.

79. Goicoechea to Valle, Chinauta, April 13, 1811, Valle Papers. That Valle used alcoholic beverages with moderation is based on the complete lack of evidence to the contrary, which, given the rough and tumble political life of Guatemala after independence, would certainly exist if he had been anything but moderate in any of his habits and appetites. Valle put it another way: "Á una vida laboriosa, acompaño regularmente una conducta irreprensible, porque el trabajo exije recogimento, y el retiro no permite las detracciones del vicio público y privado." Quoted from a rough draft of his títulos y méritos (Valle Papers).

80. Quoted from a letter written by Valle, undated and unaddressed (Valle Papers).

Anticipating the next question, he explained that there was no reason to fear that Valle's "connections would embarrass him in the exercise of his ministry, which would happen with others who are sons of this city and who have ties and connections here."[81]

González, again in praise, touched on another reason that made antipathy for Valle nearly certain. He was from the "province of Tegucigalpa," an outsider without ties and connections in the capital city, a fact of no particular significance when it stands alone. But when the outsider outstripped the "sons of the city," enemies were inevitable, and the obsequious manner that would have salved the wound was totally lacking in Valle's character. And without the energy or the desire to bestir themselves to the pace of the Cholutecan, Valle's enemies seethed within and waited for the indiscretion or weakness that would belie his flawless exterior and allow them to continue in their humdrum lives secure in the knowledge that they were not so inferior as Captain General González thought. Valle finally did make a mistake, not a serious one, but one that they hoped would remove him, in some disgrace, from the scene as a practicing lawyer. The affair, which began in 1814, involved happenings from the previous three years and revealed the anger pent up in the breasts of the sons of the capital, who seemed to possess more talent for petty intrigue than for the law.

[5]

On January 5, 1814, Valle had to appear, in behalf of a client, before the civil court of the *audiencia*. He submitted a routine request, but the notary public refused to admit it, saying that Valle's name had been stricken from the list of lawyers matriculated in the Colegio de Abogados.[82] The purpose of the Ilustre Colegio de Abogados, founded in 1810, was as clearly expressed by the "ruffles of blue muslin or taffeta" that members were permitted to wear on their cuffs as by Article 18 of the statutes: "No one who is not matriculated in the College shall in any manner

81. Valle Papers.
82. AGG, A1.47.2, 32250, 4072. Valle sobre continuar despachando los negocios. Valle explained his experiences of January 5 in his petition dated January 10, 1814.

whatsoever exercise the profession of law in the capital."[83]   Upon hearing the words of the notary, Valle was dumfounded.   When he recovered his poise, he returned to his study, pulled down his copy of the laws of the Indies, and prepared a petition, which, with the response it drew, allowed the story behind the words of the notary public, ". . . he was excluded from matriculation in the Colegio de Abogados," to unfold.

By the spring of 1812, Valle, as suggested by his cousin, was finding the "thousand nothings" of a brief for an "eternal liti-gant" exasperating, and he was thinking of retiring.[84]   He con-tinued, however, for another year.   Then in "June or July," 1813, he decided to quit, and as the senior judge assigned him to crimi-nal cases, he passed them back with a note appended stating that he had resolved to retire in order to recover his health and was not accepting new assignments, though he planned to complete all that he had started.   Throughout the rest of the year he con-tinued to refuse appointments for the same reason.   And on December 9, 1813, Dr. Manuel Talavera, a judge, called on Valle, and in the course of their "friendly conversation," Valle remarked that he had decided to give up his practice.   Talavera offered to make the necessary arrangements and Valle agreed.   Without fur-ther word to Valle, Talavera, on December 11, struck Valle's name from the list of lawyers permitted to practice before the *audiencia* and informed the secretary of the Colegio de Abogados, Dr. Alejandro Díaz Cabeza de Vaca, that Valle had retired.   The Christmas holidays passed, and on January 5, 1814, Valle learned for the first time that he was no longer eligible to practice; conse-quently, he could not complete the processes that had been pend-ing when in June or July he had decided to retire.   These were the facts concerning his retirement, Valle declared, and he defied anyone to find a "memorial, note, or document" of his to the contrary.   Rhetorically, he mused on the spirit that prompted the abrupt termination of his practice, and then he protested that even the most undesirable person of a "fraternity, guild, society, corporation, or company" was informed before he was officially retired.   The "most criminal" man received word of his sentence

83. Quoted in Lanning, *Enlightenment*, p. 111.   Valle became a member of the Colegio on June 6, 1810; at least that was the date when he paid his initiation fee of twenty-five pesos.   See AGG, A1.47, 23784, 2756.   Colegio de Abogados.
84. Dionisio de Herrera to Valle, Tegucigalpa, June 7, 1812, Valle Papers.

before it was executed, and the notary traveled "three or four leagues" outside the city to communicate to the prisoners from Granada (Nicaragua) their sentences. And "I did not even merit the attention of a message of common courtesy." Since he intended to complete the business pending, as the law required, he supplicated the Colegio to rule on the right of the notary to refuse a petition connected with a process that he had begun in May, 1813.[85]

Rather than rule as Valle had asked, secretary Cabeza de Vaca, behind whom stood Talavera, tried to prove that Valle by his own actions had terminated his law career long before January 5, 1814. In 1812 (and Cabeza de Vaca quoted from the records of the Colegio), the Ilustre Colegio de Abogados elected Valle Pro-Secretaría, but since Valle was not present, the secretary sent the news with a doorkeeper (*portero*) to Valle's home. Valle, on the word of the doorkeeper, received the results of the election with great vexation and immediately wrote his "renunciation," dispatching it to the Colegio with the doorkeeper. After brief consultation, the secretary again sent the doorkeeper to Valle's home; his mission now was to collect Valle's dues, which were in arrears. Indeed, Valle had not paid any dues since December, 1812. Parenthetically, Cabeza de Vaca noted that Article 2 of Statute 3 stated explicitly that any member who failed to pay his dues for two consecutive months would be dropped unless he met his obligation within the two-month period of grace. In view of the antipathy toward Valle, the casual observer must have marveled that he had not been disbarred early in 1813. But Valle explained the indulgence of the Colegio when he informed the doorkeeper that it was not "customary that some should pay and others not," and as soon as the dues were collected from the rest his would be forthcoming *prontísimo*. A few days later (allowing the doorkeeper to catch his breath) the secretary again directed that worthy to try once more to persuade Valle to pay up. Irritated beyond civility, Valle flatly refused and told the doorkeeper that "the Colegio cannot count on me for anything." As if bearing news that would lead to a public degradation in which Valle would be stripped of his "ruffles of blue," the door-

85. AGG, A1.47.2, 32250, 4072. Valle sobre continuar despachando los negocios.

keeper reported exactly what Valle said and interpreted it to mean that Valle was breaking with the exclusive Ilustre Colegio de Abogados. Given Valle's attitude, Cabeza de Vaca did not believe that the Colegio had acted abruptly.[86]

To clinch his argument for not allowing Valle to practice, Cabeza de Vaca subjected Valle's explanation for refusing to accept cases to a different interpretation. According to Licenciado Panteleón de Águila, lawyer and son of the capital, Valle refused the assignments not because of his health or of his plans to retire but because the cases would yield little profit. His ill health and anticipated retirement did not deter him from accepting clients whose business was profitable. Was he not at that moment the lawyer for "so and so Cabreras from Tegucigalpa *v.* Florencio Quiñones?" Was it not true that Cabreras had retained him with a fee of seventy pesos? And did Valle not know that his refusal to accept assignments worked a hardship on the other lawyers? Águila, angry because Valle skimmed off the profit, went to the senior judge and complained that Valle's professional conduct was dangerously close to unethical.[87]

These charges threatened to turn what started out as a white-glove controversy into a bare-knuckle brawl. But Valle maintained his composure and used the law, information founded on fact, and stinging innuendo as deftly as though they were a foil in the hands of a fencing master. His discipline and sense of orderliness were offended by the "hodgepodge" (*baturillo*) that the secretary tried to pass off as an answer to a "simple" petition. Valle, however, did not wish to be quarrelsome; he had "sustained no disputes." Nor did he resemble in any manner "the hungry lawyers of some countries who, not having any cases of their own, rave with envy upon seeing on the docket those that belong to someone else and who take measures and make plans for attracting to their poor offices the processes and papers that will allow them to earn some paltry fee." Valle, having decided to give up his practice, cared only to finish "the business piled in abundance on my desk," as the law and professional ethics required. But he

86. *Ibid.,* Jan. 17, 1814. In 1813, Valle was still listed as Pro-Secretaría. See AGG, A1.47, 44926, 5333. Listo de los individuos del Ilustre Colegio de Abogados de este Reyno de Guatemala, y de los que componen tan noble cuerpo, año 1813.

87. AGG, A1.47.2, 32250, 4072. Valle sobre continuar despachando los negocios (January 28, 1814).

larities, which Valle exposed. Their charges were serious and their evidence slight, and this leads to the assumption that what they wanted to charge Valle with and try him for was something that had no place in law or before a tribunal—his resounding success as a lawyer and his refusal to change or to compromise the way he achieved and carried his success. They doubtless regarded him as proud and haughty, words used up to this moment to describe him. And if that forbidding exterior concealed an inarticulate desire to be accepted and recognized in the capital, only his intimate friends could have guessed it. Thus without the necessary evidence, Talavera and Águila had to retreat with an early version of "payola" ringing in their ears.

Actually Valle had less reason to be unhappy than the tone of his personal relations and his letter to Villa Urrutia indicated. Certainly his father's death had saddened him, and the obligation to his sisters contributed to his soberness. But in a few short years he had obtained positions of honor and responsibility and the unstinted support of the highest royal officer in the colony. And, as his cousin Dionisio de Herrera predicted in 1812, the income from Valle's haciendas allowed him to retire from what was probably the most extensive practice in the colony. The Bergaño case did not affect him in any manner; he had nothing to do with it. Impatience for greater success, however, denied him all respite. In December, 1807, he decided to seek a judgeship; in 1808 or 1809, Captain General González recommended him for the position; and, in 1813, Valle's lawyer in Spain, Rafael Antonio Díez y Tovar, wrote that the Council of State was considering Valle for a place in an *audiencia*.[96] Events in Spain between 1808 and 1814, however, delayed all business, domestic and colonial, and while Valle waited in Guatemala, fending off the natural enemies of success, the Spanish struggle against the French forced him to make new decisions concerning his career.

96. To Valle, Cádiz, June 19, 1813, Valle Papers.

THREE

Steadfast Royal Servant,
1808-1815

[1]

On August 13, 1808, Captain General González received a dispatch, by way of Mexico, from the French foreign minister, Jean Champagny, informing Americans that the royal family of Spain had abdicated the throne and had "ceded it with all its rights to the emperor of the French," whose wish it was that Spain should recover "her ancient splendor and luster." To this end, Napoleon had called his brother Joseph to the Spanish throne.[1] After reading the dispatch, González, at 7:00 P.M., called a meeting of his ministers, and together they decided to hold a general meeting on the following day of the principal authorities of the capital.[2] Thus they allowed time to absorb the shock and grasp the details behind the startling news.

Napoleon, through his Continental System, sought to force England to make peace on his terms. If the system were to operate efficiently, intercourse between England and Portugal had to stop. But to get at Portugal, political geography and the battle of Trafalgar dictated that he go through Spain. The pusillanimous Charles IV of Spain, however, posed no serious problems; in 1807 Napoleon reached an agreement that permitted French troops to cross Spanish territory. Once his troops were in Spain, Napoleon, at Bayonne, sprang the snare that trapped both Charles IV and his son, Ferdinand VII, who had succeeded his father, allow-

1. AGG, A1.2.2, 15733, 2187. Libro de cabildos de Guatemala, año 1808. The dispatch was found tucked away in these records of the town council.
2. Laudelino Moreno, "Guatemala y la invasión napoleónica de España," *Anales,* VII (1930), 6.

ing the Emperor to put brother Joseph on the Spanish throne. Spaniards in Madrid, outraged by Napoleon's presumption, revolted on Dos de Mayo, 1808. Quickly the revolt spread throughout Spain, and the Spaniards, in order to organize their efforts against the intruders, established local juntas or governing bodies, which later gave way to the Junta Central, the supreme authority during the first years of Ferdinand VII's unscheduled absence. Napoleon, to his dismay, now had a full scale war on his hands. Except for the Junta Central, these were some of the details that the principal authorities might have pondered on the night of August 13, 1808.

Gathered in the assembly room of the royal palace, on August 14, Captain General González, the ministers of the *audiencia,* the archbishop, members of the town council, the rector of San Carlos, representatives from several monasteries, and the officials of the Royal Consulado heard the reading of the dispatch from Mexico. After González commented briefly, the junta agreed unanimously that the abdications of the royal family "were null and void because they had been obtained by force, in enemy territory, and in the midst of bayonets." The whole Bayonne farce, inspired as it was by the most "perfidious ambitions," merited only contempt. And the members of the junta reaffirmed their loyalty "to our legitimate Sovereign," and to the laws of the Empire.[3]

Thoroughly alarmed by developments in Spain, González began to prepare for trouble in Guatemala. On September 5 he ordered publication of the Spanish declaration of war against the French and announced that property belonging to subjects of the "present French government" would be confiscated. Ports were closed to foreign ships, and Spanish merchantmen, wishing to tie up or embark, should undergo "the most careful examination of their credentials, of their crews, and of whatever else on board." Should the investigation reveal arms or troops or that the ship had "contact with foreigners, especially with the French," it was to be sequestered pending a decision of the government.[4]

3. *Ibid.,* p. 7; *Boletín del Archivo General del Gobierno,* III (1938), 330-331. (Hereafter *Boletín.*) Also see AGG, A1.23, 2317, 273. Declaración y pronunciamiento de las autoridades civiles, eclesiásticas, y militares sobre que no reconozcan ni reconocieren en tiempo alguno la abdicación de Fernando VII (August 14, 1808); B1.1, 00002, 1. Minuta del oficio circulado por el ayuntamiento de la Ciudad de Guatemala con motivo de la prisión de la familia española (Aug. 18, 1808).

4. *Boletín,* III (1938), 347.

A few days after announcing still other precautionary measures, González initiated a public subscription, or a *donativo patriótico y voluntario*.[5] And in December to commemorate a celebration in honor of the Spanish monarch, the Superior Government published a pamphlet entitled *Guatemala por Fernando Séptimo*.[6]

The measures taken by González and the acknowledged leaders, who had gathered in the meeting of August 14, reflect accurately the feeling of the people of Guatemala for Napoleon and his Spanish adventure. A letter written by Simón Bergaño y Villegas, one of the first victims of the tricolor scare, affords a more intimate glimpse of the first reactions to the news. On October 17, 1808, the inhabitants of the capital took advantage of an announcement concerning the subscription to hold a celebration. Two orchestras, with forty musicians each, along with the military band, inspired the crowd in the main plaza, where there was scarcely room for a "grain of wheat," to shout Vivas to Ferdinand and to utter horrible remarks against Napoleon. The illumination provided by 87 big, double flares changed night into day. At 11:00 o'clock, members of the crowd appeared with a portrait of Ferdinand and held it up in the middle of the orchestras. Then, against a background of fife and drum, the crowd paraded forthwith to the royal palace. There the captain general and his wife "revered" and "embraced" the likeness of their sovereign. Later, the enthusiastic crowd paraded through all the streets, and Bergaño, who had joined the throng, lost his hat, handkerchief, and shoes.[7]

But there were also differences of opinion in Guatemala and in all the Spanish colonies in America that sprang from the unusual turn of events in Spain. The absence of the king and the

5. Moreno, "Guatemala y la invasión napoleónica de España," *Anales*, VII (1930), 12; *Gazeta de Guatemala*, Sept. 26, 1808. After about a year of silence the *Gazeta* resumed publication on September 19, 1808. In the issue for October 6, 1808, the editor informed subscribers: "El 19 de Septiembre último se restableció en esta capital la gaceta, que se había suspendido ínterin se arreglaba la nueva imprenta."

6. Medina, *La imprenta en Guatemala*, p. 490.

7. AGG, B2.7, 777, 31. Sobre averiguar la conducta de Simón Bergaño y Villegas. On the authority of the records of the investigation, these are faithful copies of Bergaño's letters, which were found in his home. This letter, according to the records, was written on October 18, 1808 and addressed to Ramón, who apparently lived in Mexico. During the happier period of Spanish-French relations, Bergaño glorified Napoleon in a sonnet, "A Napoleon" (*Gazeta de Guatemala*, July 28, 1806). But when Napoleon invaded Spain, he wrote a vilification of France, in verse (*Proclama* [Guatemala City, no date]).

interregnum rule, first by the Junta Central and then by the Regency and the Constitution of 1812, created special problems concerning the procedure of government in the colonies. Some groups insisted on recognizing the supreme authority of the Junta Central; others argued that juntas should be formed in the colonies to govern in the name of the crown. Generally, the creoles were in sympathy with the idea of local government under the guise of fidelity to Ferdinand, not simply because they were enthralled with the idea of more democratic government but also because of their own interests. Local juntas, locally elected, promised the opportunity of sharing authority with Spaniards or of controlling it completely. Mexico, in 1808 and 1809, manifested most clearly this difference of opinion, which has been interpreted as the first step toward independence.

Differences between creoles and Peninsulars, though not nearly so great as in Mexico, also existed in Guatemala, as other letters of Bergaño show. About two weeks after the news arrived from Mexico, he complained that "the people are without a king, and they don't care." He blamed the apathy on the fact that there were only about a hundred or hundred and fifty Spaniards in the capital. Nothing whatsoever could be expected of the creoles, who were "egoists, sluggards, poltroons, and disloyal." They wished only "to change the system without taking into consideration the benefits that they derive from it." They had a king who did not take one red cent (*un medio real*) from Guatemala. On the contrary, he made a thousand concessions in agriculture and commerce and provided a supplement to offset the difference between the expense of government and the inadequate revenue from the colony. "I assure you," Bergaño continued, "their attitude makes me uneasy." In the province of Quetzaltenango, the creoles informed the Indians of the events in Spain, and now they have refused to pay their taxes. Other provinces, he feared, would follow their example, and sooner or later someone would assault an official, which could be sufficient provocation for a revolution that would have "fatal results."[8]

Two weeks later, Bergaño wrote that the government was

8. AGG, B2.7, 777, 31. Sobre averiguar la conducta de Simón Bergaño y Villegas. Dated September 3, 1808, the letter was addressed to Agustín Fernández, who apparently lived in Mexico.

hearing the "confessions" of a "subversive (Spanish American)." Denounced secretly, the authorities took him by surprise and found copies of some "pasquinades," which he already had circulated, and a "proclamation or exhortation" admonishing Guatemalans "literally to drink the blood of the Spaniards just as they have been sucking up the money that belongs to us." The prisoner, Bergaño noted wryly, had divulged everything (*vomitado lindamente*), and the government "has just realized that the friars with the most influence are the ones that they ought to hang first." Bergaño estimated that there were only about "30 or 40 prodigals," but they were capable of inflicting on Guatemala an equal number of embarrassments.[9] And he worried because the government had not given orders to the military, which was "composed of 200 infantrymen of the militia and 40 dragoons." But since the troops were "all of mixed blood and despicable for their habits and vices," they in any event could not be relied on.[10]

In the testimony that Bergaño gave during his own investigation, he presented other evidence of the rivalry between creoles and Spaniards. On October 17, when he had lost his shoes, Bergaño had gone to the home of José María Peinada, alderman (*regidor*) of the municipal council of the capital, just as the crowd was filling the plaza. On the corner, near Peinada's home, Bergaño heard shouts of "Death to the Chapetones" (Peninsulars). He started out the door to punish the guilty persons when Peinada stopped him and shouted out: *"Boys, now is not the time."* Struck by the remark, Bergaño asked Peinada when he thought the time would be. His only reply was: "Now is not the time to create dissensions." A few days later Peinada confided in Bergaño that Guatemala should have elected a junta as the Spaniards had done in Spain, and on October 21, when it was known that the Spaniards had arrested Viceroy Iturrigaray of Mexico for favoring just such a junta, Peinada called from his front door to Bergaño, who was on horseback, saying that he disapproved of the arrest of the viceroy.[11]

In the afternoon of the same day, Antonio Rivas, an account-

9. AGG, B2.7, 777, 31. Sobre averiguar la conducta de Simón Bergaño y Villegas. This letter, dated September 18, 1808, was addressed to Ramón.
10. *Ibid.*, Oct. 3, 1808.
11. *Ibid.* Bergaño testified on October 23, 1808.

ant, chatted with Bergaño about politics, remarking that there were rumors of replacing Captain General González. To learn more about the rumors, Bergaño that evening asked an official what he thought about "our situation." The official replied that he was "persuaded that the creoles still wanted to drink the blood of the Spaniards." Expressions of such force convinced Bergaño that there existed in Guatemala the two factions that everyone knew "divided South America."[12]

On January 22, 1809, the Junta Central of Seville, aware of the dissension between creoles and Peninsulars, declared that the "vast and valuable dominions" in America were no longer "colonies nor commercial establishments but an integral part of the Spanish monarchy."[13] Consequently, Spanish Americans should begin immediately to elect representatives to the Junta Central. The declaration and instructions for electing deputies to the Junta arrived in Guatemala City a month or so later, and Captain General González, on April 30, 1809, published the news and ordered preparations for the elections. The method of choosing representatives was a curious combination of election and lottery. The town councils of each district seat of government were "to name three individuals of known honesty, talent, and education," who were free from "all that might detract from them." After the election of the three men, the town councils should then select by lot one of the three, and the name of the one chosen should be sent to Guatemala City. From the names submitted to the capital, the members of the *audiencia* together with the captain general (*real acuerdo*) were to elect three whom they considered best qualified to represent the Kingdom. Then, by drawing lots, the members of the *audiencia,* supervised by the captain general, should choose Guatemala's representative to the Junta Central.[14]

As soon as district authorities learned the procedure, elections began, and the town councils of León, Tegucigalpa, San Vicente, and Sonsonate elected Valle. In the lottery, three chose his

12. *Ibid.* Moreno ("Guatemala y la invasión napoleónica de España," *Anales,* VII [1930], 13-15) quotes a long and vigorous complaint registered by the municipal council of the capital that also emphasizes the dissension, but in view of the events during the subsequent twelve years, both the council and Bergaño exaggerated.
13. *Boletín,* III (1938), 380-381.
14. *Ibid.*

name.[15] Captain General González observed that, of all the lawyers, Valle was the only one thus distinguished, and González
ascribed the success to Valle's ability and to the reputation he
enjoyed throughout the colony.[16] But Valle refused to accept the
voter's mandate and the fortune of "blind luck" that had put him
in a position to become a deputy to the Junta. On October 9,
1809, he wrote that he "was not insensitive to an honor so great,"
but the office, which "perhaps would flatter the vanity of others,"
caused him no illusion. He had always thought of himself with
modesty, and he had "no reason for varying this opinion." These
were critical times for the Spanish government, and he confessed
that he was "incapable of filling even the smallest part of a position so important." This "sole consideration" was reason enough
for his withdrawal, but he added that the weakness of his constitution, and the responsibility of caring for his two sisters helped
to fix his decision.[17]

Eleven months were required to complete the elections in
Guatemala,[18] and by the time the representatives to the Junta
were chosen, political changes in Spain obviated the necessity of
their attendance. The Junta had fled before French troops from
Seville to Cádiz, where it appointed a regency of five men who
were to make preparations for calling a constituent congress, the
Cortes. Thereupon the Junta dissolved itself.[19] On February 4,
1810, the Council of Regency decreed that elections for representatives to the Cortes should be held in Spain and Spanish
America. The election procedure was nearly the same as that
for the Junta Central. The decree was published in Guatemala
in the spring of 1810.[20] At first glance it appeared that Americans
were to be represented in proportion to their numbers, but this
was not true. Political leaders in Spain had quickly recognized

15. AGG, A1.1, 4347, 37. This *legajo* contains the replies from the various town
councils informing the *real acuerdo* of the persons elected. Also see the *Gazeta
de Guatemala*, March 7, 1810; Crisanto Sacasa to Valle, Granada, June 22, 1809;
Juan Francisco Vilches to Valle, León, June 23, 1809, Valle Papers. Sacasa (and
the *Gazeta*) pointed out that the *ayuntamiento* of Sonsonate was the only one of
the four that did not choose Valle's name in the lottery, and he explained further
that Valle's name had been introduced in the initial election in Granada.
16. González recommends Valle, Valle Papers.
17. AGG, A1.1, 4347, 37.
18. *Boletín*, III (1938), 381. See the note by Professor J. Joaquín Pardo.
19. Charles E. Chapman, *A History of Spain* (New York, 1918), pp. 492-493.
(Hereafter Chapman, *Spain*.)
20. Medina, *La imprenta en Guatemala*, p. 504; *Boletín*, III (1938), 470.

that proportional representation would have permitted Americans to control the Cortes. For this reason representation was rigged to favor the Spaniards.[21]

Guatemala, nevertheless, took advantage of its first opportunity to assist in a supreme governing body of the Empire. Elections began immediately, and on July 24, 1810, the province of Guatemala elected Dr. Antonio Larrazábal, a faculty member of San Carlos and the most distinguished of the representatives from the captaincy general. The town council of the capital gave Larrazábal a set of instructions, and he set out for Jalapa (Mexico), where, in February, 1811, he was still awaiting transportation to Spain. Finally he arrived in Cádiz on August 17, and about a week later he took the oath of office.[22] The Cortes, however, had been in session since September 24, 1810. Thus Larrazábal, as was the case with other American representatives, contributed little to the constitution promulgated in March, 1812.

[2]

The Spanish struggle for freedom, which enlisted heartfelt sympathy throughout the colonies, also plucked at Valle's patriotic heartstrings. He must have shared the feeling of outrage for Napoleon and deplored the dissension between creole and Peninsular, else Captain General González, in 1809, would not have written that Valle, "in the present circumstances," had shown "sentiments distinguished by fidelity," which he had publicized in a pamphlet entitled *Public Demonstrations of Loyalty and Patriotism by the Merchants of Guatemala City in the Present Circumstances.*[23] Valle, however, was not convinced that the Junta Central promised much of a future, for his excuses were polite ways of saying that he was not interested. The office of deputy to the Junta, simply put, lacked the prestige to compete

21. Chapman, *Spain*, p. 493.

22. *Boletín*, III (1938), 479, 482, 489, 499-500. For a copy of the controversial instructions given to Larrazábal by the town council, see *Instrucciones para la constitución fundamental de la monarquía española y su gobierno de que ha de tratarse en las próximas cortes generales de la nación dadas por El M. I. Ayuntamiento de la M.N.Y. L. Ciudad de Guatemala* (Guatemala City, 1953).

23. González recommends Valle, Valle Papers.

successfully for Valle's favor against the old and highly esteemed office of *oidor*.

After the initial shock and excitement, Valle settled back into the routine of day-to-day living. His sisters, who never married, still looked to him for guidance and care. He attended the business of his practice and minded the affairs of his haciendas, finding pleasure, as always, in his books. He still kept a record of the weather, which he had begun in 1801,[24] and a complaint registered against exorbitant taxes by "six citizens of Tegucigalpa" took more of his time.[25]   Doubtless he was also busy gathering the personal data necessary for admission to the Colegio de Abogados.[26]

The year 1810, however, brought news that must have distressed Valle and disturbed his routine: Captain General González received orders to new duty. His replacement, who assumed command on March 14, 1811, was to be José de Bustamante y Guerra.[27]   In the Spanish colonies the period of transition involved in the transfer of authority, tedious even today in a society based on tenure, was a period of helpless uncertainty for men like Valle who did not enjoy a royal appointment. Frequently, almost inevitably, men of capacity who had gained favor with one superior were viewed with disfavor by another. González, however, made the transition for Valle a little less uncertain. Upon terminating a tour of duty, the law required superior officers (viceroys, captain generals, and governors) to report in writing on the political, economic, and social conditions of the colony, pointing out peculiarities, problems, advantages, and the personnel available to the incumbent. In this connection Bustamante asked González for the names of the best educated lawyers whose "integrity and

24. Diario del Thermometer [*sic*] de Fahrenheit en Guatemala, 1801-1825, Valle Papers.
25. March 24, 1809, Valle Papers.
26. For the details of the credentials that a lawyer had to present, see Lanning, *Enlightenment*, p. 111.
27. *Boletín*, III (1938), 490; Pedro Torres Lanzas, ed., *Independencia de América, fuentes para su estudio. Catálogo de documentos conservados en el Archivo General de Indias de Sevilla* (6 vols.; Madrid, 1912), II, 483. (Hereafter Torres Lanzas, ed., *Independencia de América*.) Bustamante wrote from Jalapa informing authorities in Guatemala that the Council of Regency had appointed him to relieve González (AGG, B1.4, 582, 20. Correspondencia general). González went to Mexico and participated in the fighting against the insurgents led by José María Morelos, whose forces captured and executed González. See AGG, A3.1, 2852, 1790. Minuta del informe sobre que a fines de noviembre de 1814 fué ejecutado el ex-presidente Antonio González por Morelos (May 12, 1815); Lucas Alamán, *Historia de Méjico* (5 vols.; Mexico, 1849-1852), III, 324-325. Medina (*La imprenta en Guatemala*, p. 555) notes that González was killed at an earlier date.

adherence to the just cause of the king, Nuestro Señor," was beyond question.[28] González recommended only two that he thought could meet the requirements. On the basis of the recommendation, Bustamante selected "D. José del Valle."[29] Valle still had to prove himself, but his characteristics and those of Bustamante made harmonious relations a foregone conclusion.

Less than a month after Vice Admiral Bustamante arrived in the capital, he published a pamphlet that ended once and for all the speculation about the new commander. The first page of the publication made the remaining eighteen superfluous. Indeed, two sentences established his position beyond the slightest doubt. Bustamante announced that he had learned the "art of commanding" by the only true method—"that of obeying." A series of voyages one of which was a "scientific expedition that circumnavigated the world,"[30] had been sufficient to make him value highly that wise doctrine. After an apprenticeship, he received orders to assume the position of "political and military commander of Montevideo and commandant of the naval station." This tour of duty (1790's) had provided him with occurrences that allowed him to display the "qualifications that ought to adorn a commander." Two of these "I will joyfully boast about all my life": that of being a "pure Spaniard, inflexible in protecting the dignity of this name"; and that of possessing "steadfastness in defense of justice."[31]

Sailor Bustamante hardly had stowed his gear when occurrences in Guatemala tested his vaunted qualifications. Word of Father Hidalgo's Cry of Dolores (September 16, 1810) had

28. Bustamante to José de Alós, Secretario Interino de Estado y del Despacho Universal, Madrid, Nov. 13, 1819, Valle Papers. Bustamante, when he made this observation, was recommending Valle for the position of *auditor de guerra*.
29. *Ibid.*
30. AGG, A1.1, 56930, 6921. *El Presidente, Gobernador y Capitán General de Guatemala, Teniente General de la Real Armada D. José de Bustamante a todas las autoridades y habitantes del Reyno de su mando* (Guatemala City, April 13, 1811). He was referring to the Malaspina expedition.
31. *Ibid.* Bustamante went to Montevideo in 1796, and the occurrence that he mentioned was an engagement with an English fleet. For further information on the life of Bustamante, see AGG, B1.14, 582, 20. Correspondencia general; José Mariano Beristain de Souza, *Biblioteca hispano americana septentrional; o, catálogo y noticia de los literatos, que o nacidos, o educados, o florecientes en la América septentrional española, han dado a luz algún escrito, o lo han dexado preparado para la prensa* (3 vols.; Mexico, 1816), I, 199 (hereafter Beristain, *Biblioteca hispano americana);* Domingo Juarros, *Compendio de la historia de la Ciudad de Guatemala* (2 vols.; Guatemala City, 1937), II, 10; Ricardo Levene, *Historia de la nación argentina (desde los orígenes hasta la organización definitiva en 1862)* (10 vols.; Buenos Aires, 1936-1941), IV, 314, V, 392-394; Medina, *La imprenta en Guatemala,* p. 515.

reached Guatemala before the arrival of Bustamante, and the news of open rebellion in Mexico found sympathetic readers in Guatemala. As though following the example set by Hidalgo, a faction in the city of San Salvador under the leadership of Dr. Matías Delgado, Juan Manuel Rodríguez, Pablo Castillo, and others revolted on November 5, 1811. They seized arms and ammunition from the local arsenal and soon controlled the city, receiving some support from neighboring towns. Most of the province, however, denounced the revolt and two town councils were commended for their opposition to the insurgents. The revolt was soon isolated, and Bustamante, trying to understand and to deal fairly, granted a general amnesty.

Before Bustamante had pacified San Salvador, another insurrection, without organization and leadership, broke out in León. On December 13, 1811, during a celebration, shouts of "Down with the Spaniards," and "Death to José Salvador," the local governor, started the uprising, and the city soon passed into the hands of the insurgents, whose main interest, apparently, was to rid themselves of José Salvador. When Bustamante, observing admirable patience, replaced the governor and offered a general amnesty, the revolt collapsed.

Nine days after the outbreak in León, a similar occurrence began in the city of Granada. Colonial officials fled to neighboring villages, and the rebels, in possession of the city, prepared to stand off any force coming against them. Bustamante, his patience growing thinner, sent about a thousand troops and again offered a general amnesty, allowing the Granadinos to take their choice. When they refused, the troops moved into position (April, 1812), but before firing, Bustamante once more authorized an amnesty. After a second refusal, the troops engaged the insurgents, who very quickly decided that the defense of their cause was not worth the trouble. Representatives from the hostile forces parleyed, and the commander of the loyal troops guaranteed an amnesty if the insurgents would surrender. On this basis the hostile forces reached an agreement, and the loyal troops invested the city. Bustamante, who had extended an amnesty before the fighting began, repudiated the agreement made after the rebels had chosen to fight. He ordered the arrest and prosecution of all involved. Several got death sentences (though they were never executed); nine heard themselves committed for life; and shorter sentences went to 133 others. All who were still alive in 1817 received a general pardon.[32]

One of Valle's first reactions to these uprisings, described as the first steps toward independence, was one of irritation. Recently he had contracted to buy some cattle, which were to be driven from the province of San Salvador to his haciendas near Choluteca. But on November 19, 1811, he had to warn that "the incidents in San Salvador" made the prescribed route of delivery dangerous. He suggested other roads.[33] He also shared the irritation of one of his friends who complained that the uprisings were responsible for the demands of the Indians for higher wages.[34]

Letters from other friends, however, suggested that the revolts were more than trifling affairs to Valle. Colonel José Rafael Molina described the action in San Salvador as a "diabolical insurrection,"[35] and on January 25, 1812, he expressed happiness that it had been smothered, noting obliquely that he and Valle, owing to the "unanimity of their sentiments," had a new bond uniting their friendship.[36]

When the prisoners from Granada arrived in Guatemala City in September, 1813, having walked the entire distance from Granada,[37] Valle made his sentiments still clearer. He observed with disapproval that "individuals of the so-called first families"

32. In connection with the uprising in León and Granada, the intendant of the province took advantage of an earthquake of small proportion to write that the "Omnipotent" had spoken a warning to the conspirators. "And it would be an opportune moment," the intendant thought, to remind the people what happened on "Holy Thursday of last year" in Venezuela, where a "great earthquake struck down" those who were "disloyal to our Sovereign," causing "no harm" to those who were loyal. See AGG, B2.2, 701, 24. El Gobernador de Nicaragua al ayuntamiento de la ciudad de Granada y León, 7 de julio, 1813. For accounts of these uprisings, see Hubert Howe Bancroft, *History of Central America* (3 vols.; New York, 1883-1887), III, 12-16; Francisco Gavidia, *Historia moderna de El Salvador* (San Salvador, 1918), pp. 74-75; Francis Merriman Stanger, "The Struggle for Nationality in Central America" (unpublished Ph.D. dissertation, University of California, 1930), pp. 36-45; Laudelino Moreno, "Independencia de la Capitanía General de Guatemala" (Asociación Española para el Progreso de la Ciencia de Cádiz, sección 6; Madrid, 1927), pp. 26-28; Pedro Zamora Castellanos, *El grito de independencia* (Guatemala City, 1935) pp. 55-61.
33. Valle to Mariano José Gálvez, Valle Papers.
34. Juan Francisco Vilches to Valle, León, July 30, 1812, Valle Papers.
35. To Valle, San Vicente, Nov. 25, 1811, Valle Papers.
36. Valle Papers.
37. Salazar, *Historia de veintiún años*, pp. 171-172.

of the capital had gone to visit and to present gifts to the Granadinos.   Yet these same individuals never troubled themselves to
visit the other unhappy criminals who had no funds, no family,
and no friends to succor them.   Nor did these individuals visit
the hospital where the "unfortunate sick" were in need of compassion and sympathy.[38]

[*3*]

Following the revolutions of 1811-1812, Valle had to cope
with another innovation.   The Constitution of 1812, promulgated in Spain on March 19, appeared on September 24 in Guatemala.   Although it did not extend equal representation to the
colonies, it provided measures for improving local government.
The Constitution specified that offices of the town council would
be elective rather than salable and hereditary and created a new
governing body, the provincial deputation *(diputación provincial)*, to consist of seven members and to share specified authority
with the captain general, who under the Constitution became
Jefe Político.   Bustamante, against his better judgment as a "pure
Spaniard," swore to defend the new system.[39]

Valle, who in public referred kindly to the Constitution,[40]
helped to prepare for the first elections.   Bustamante had appointed him secretary of the Junta Preparatoria,[41] and the Junta
asked him to draw up instructions explaining the electoral procedure.   In his explanation he pointed out that the Constitution
stipulated that only citizens could vote, and Negroes were not
considered citizens.   He apologized for their exclusion, but noted,
with citations from Greek and Roman history, that citizenship was
an honor bestowed only on the deserving.[42]

38. Valle Papers.   This information comes from a rough draft of an incomplete
essay entitled "Espíritu del oficio."
39. *Boletín*, III (1938), 517-518.   For a description of the promulgation of the
Constitution, see *Gaceta del Gobierno de Guatemala*, Sept. 28, 1812.   March 19, the
day the document saw light in Spain, was declared a national holiday, which
should be celebrated "con gala besa-manos e iluminación general, un solemne *Te
Deum* en todas las iglesias y salvas de artillería."   See AGG, A1.2.2, 15739, 2190.
Libro de cabildos de Guatemala, año 1813.
40. *El Amigo de la Patria*, Oct. 26, 1820.   Valle read an essay entitled "El
economista" in September, 1812, and published it in his newspaper.   In a long
adverbial clause, he spoke kindly of the Constitution.
41. Torres Lanzas, ed., *Independencia de América*, III, 238.
42. AGG, A1.2.2, 15738, 2190.   Libro de cabildos de Guatemala, año 1812.   A

As soon as the members of the town council of the capital were elected, they, together with the members of the provincial deputation, began to be on bad terms with Bustamante. The members of the deputation, after waiting and beseeching, were finally installed in September, 1813, only to be ignored.[43] The town council, duly elected and installed, immediately protested Bustamante's reluctance to implement and to obey the Constitution. He restricted the freedom of press, delayed the election of deputies to the Cortes, refused to dignify the conclusion of the elections with a *Te Deum,* and deprived the town council of its constitutional authority. In short, Bustamante, from the time the town councils were made elective until they reverted to their traditional form, did everything possible to keep authority in his own hands.[44] It is entirely possible, however, that the squabble between him and the town council of the capital was not a simple case of "tyrant" versus freedom. The members, with few exceptions, could easily have been as interested in embarrassing Bustamante as they were in securing the freedom provided by the Constitution.

The exchanges between Bustamante and the town council, however, did provide a further clue to Valle's position during the constitutional period. In what likely was the beginning of a false rumor, the members of the town council, in the session of August 27, 1813, claimed that they had received information that several other municipal councils had "asked the Supreme Government [in Spain] that Bustamante remain in his command in perpetuity." The instigator, whose motive was "personal advantage," was "Lic. Dn. José Cecilio del Valle." To undermine the

copy of the instructions was found filed in the pages of the record of the town council for this year.

43. Manuel Josef Pavón, José María Delgado, Bruno Medina, Eulogia Correo, José Simeón Cañas, Mariano García to Bustamante, August 17, 1813, Valle Papers. These six members of the deputation (the seventh member was Dr. Matías Delgado) requested Bustamante to install the deputation, which he finally did. But in a rough draft written by Valle, Bustamante passed judgment on each of the members and decided that Canon Bruno Medina was the only one of reliable loyalty. Thus Bustamante requested the extinction of that body. See Report on the members of the diputación provincial (no date, no signature), Valle Papers.

44. Information relative to the differences between Bustamante and the town council and the deputation can be found in Torres Lanzas, ed., *Independencia de América,* III, 357, 362, 390, 402, *passim; Boletín,* III (1938), 521-524; AGG, A1.2.5, 25296, 2835. Cuaderno de correspondencia del ayuntamiento (letter of September 1, 1813); A1.2.2, 15739, 2190. Libro de cabildos de Guatemala, año 1813 (Aug. 31, Sept. 3).

so-called "intrigue," the members of the town council ordered a dispatch to other cities asking them not to make such an ill-advised request.[45]   The members of the town council of the capital were in a vengeful mood; the Cortes had rebuked them for their opposition to Bustamante, as this letter to Valle shows: "The news that the Cortes has approved what His Excellency the Captain General has done toward implementing the Constitution and has condemned the town council's opposition to him has made me very happy.   I don't think that you [Valle] have sent me any news that has pleased me more."[46]   Distraught by the message from the Cortes and reminded of Bustamante's stern discipline by the recent arrival of the prisoners from Granada, the members of the town council struck out at him with a rumor calculated to arouse hostility sufficient to convince the Cortes that he was as arbitrary as they claimed.   By linking Valle with the "intrigue," the members of the council manifested the hostility toward the successful man from Choluteca who had captured Bustamante's favor.   At the very moment that the municipal council aimed the accusation, Valle, owing to his procrastination about his retirement, was distressing Manuel Talavera and Alejandro Díaz Cabeza de Vaca.   That Cabeza de Vaca was a member of the town council is significant.   The rumor, however, was no more preposterous than another that spoke of Valle and Bustamante departing together for Spain.[47]   A comment by Valle (which might or might not have been made in connection with the rumor) seems appropriate.   In October, 1813, he wrote that the "spirit of inventing news, of exaggerating the adversities, and of belying or making doubtful the plausible continues."[48]

In the same month Valle, with accuracy not available to prophets, noted that malcontents, who publicly affected the greatest loyalty, were working secretly to excite those lacking sufficient

45. AGG, A1.2.2, 15739, 2190.   Libro de cabildos de Guatemala, año 1813.   For another interpretation, see Salazar, *Historia de veintiún años,* pp. 172-174.

46. José Rafael de Molina to Valle, San Vicente, Sept. 25, 1813, Valle Papers. José Rafael and his brother, Father Manuel Antonio, contributed 1,000 pesos to the *donativo* (*Gazeta de Guatemala,* Oct. 17, 1808).

47. Joaquín Arechavala to Valle, León, Nov. 19, 1814, Valle Papers.   Colonel Arechavala wrote: "Aquí ha corrido la voz de que V. se va a España acompañando al Señor Bustamante; es muy buena proporción y una compañía inmejorable, pues ese Señor Capitán General tiene en España nombre, brazos y excelente concepto, muy merecido."   Arechavala was in charge of collecting for the *donativo* in León. See *Gazeta de Guatemala,* Sept. 26, 1808.

48. "Espíritu del oficio" (Oct., 1813), Valle Papers.

perspicacity to perceive the objective of the plan.[49] Two months later Bustamante exposed a plot to overthrow the government. The monastery of Belén, in Guatemala City, was the center of the conspiracy. The persons involved had planned to seize and incarcerate Bustamante, to release the Granadinos, to seduce the military, and to proclaim independence. An informer whispered the plans to Bustamante, and he ordered the arrest of all who appeared to be implicated in any way. And before the Belén conspiracy was settled another abortive uprising occurred, in January, 1814, in San Salvador. The revolt, however, was put down quickly and those captured were imprisoned.[50]

Following these ill-planned affairs, Valle's position during the critical epoch became unmistakably clear. Bustamante had appointed Valle, in 1812 and 1813, to two relatively unimportant positions, but Valle was much closer than these perfunctory appointments indicate. He apparently worked in Bustamante's secretariat and then became his closest and most trusted secretary. A hint of the favor that Valle enjoyed appeared in a letter from a friend, written on July 17, 1812: "Tell me if it is true, as they say, that you are in the secretariat of His Excellency, the President."[51] Three years later, in a complaint to the crown, an accurate observation was made that in Bustamante's writing were seen "the style and character" of José del Valle.[52] When Valle began writing reports and dispatches for Bustamante is uncertain, but the number that he did write establishes that Bustamante put complete trust in Valle.

After the first revolt in San Salvador, the Regency appointed José María Peinada intendant of that province. After the second revolt, Valle prepared for Peinada the instructions that should guide him in maintaining "peace and general tranquillity." San Salvador, Valle began, was the first "to manifest publicly" the

49. *Ibid.*
50. Alejandro Marure, *Bosquejo histórico de las revoluciones de Centro América desde 1811 hasta 1834* (2 vols.; Guatemala City, 1877), I, 19 (hereafter Marure, *Bosquejo histórico*); Torres Lanzas, ed., *Independencia de América*, III, 329-330.
51. Miguel José Castro to Valle, San Marcos, Valle Papers.
52. Valle Papers. The document referred to is a rough draft of a dispatch in which José del Barrio, José Ingenieros Palomo, and Miguel Larreinaga were protesting against Bustamante's attempt to invalidate their title of *oidor*, which each received, on March 29, 1814, by grace of the Regency. (Hereafter Barrio, Palomo, and Larreinaga protest against Bustamante, Valle Papers.)

"regrettable spirit of restlessness," and according "to your [Peinada's] correspondence, which I have before me," the province "has never been completely pacified since the first disturbance." Valle praised Peinada for the zeals that cut short the second disorder and urged him to prevent the third by extending his "vigilance to the most obscure hideout [*última manida*] that cloaks the conspiracy" and by making "profound and penetrating investigations concerning the causes of the evil."

Political systems, Valle explained, operated on the basis of reward and punishment, the only concepts that man understood. Reward inspired man to work hard, and punishment not only castigated the wrongdoer but made plain to everyone the consequence of crime. The province of San Salvador, like the other provinces where revolts had occurred, had three classes of people: *Los malos y perversos,* who abused the amnesty extended to them after the first disorder when they started the second; the law-abiding people who had displayed their loyalty to the "just cause of the nation"; and those who had not declared themselves but who "manifested a peaceful indifference."[53]

Valle emphasized the importance of dealing quickly with the first class. Experience with the insurgents from Granada had taught the Superior Government that even though the Granadinos were "separated from their province and confined in prison, they continued their malignant influence." But in each case, special care had to be taken with the "interrogations" in an attempt to learn any results of the correspondence that the rebels were supposed to have initiated with José María Morelos.[54]

"Inform the second class," Valle stressed, "that the Superior Government will reward each one in proportion to his merit." Any employment controlled by that government would be made available only to those who had shown "incontrovertible proof of their fidelity and sincere patriotism." To impress this class with the intentions of the government, Valle commissioned Peinada to inform the town council of San Vicente that the

53. Instrucción reservada de este Superior Gobierno al Sr. Intendente Jefe Político de San Salvador, Dn. José María Peinada (no date), Valle Papers. The document bears no signature, but the handwriting and the style unmistakably belong to Valle.

54. *Ibid.* After the execution of Miguel Hidalgo, Father Morelos led the Mexican revolutionaries until his execution on Dec. 22, 1815.

Supreme Government acknowledged the "distinguished service" made during the second revolt. Also he was to convey to Father Manuel Antonio Molina and his brother, Colonel José Rafael Molina (Valle's friends), that their service would be rewarded with appropriate recommendations. And Valle instructed Peinada to work with zeal in rewarding the worthy mulattoes and Indians with some land, unless they already were property owners. Peinada was also to inform them that the Superior Government would extend credit not exceeding 100 pesos to those who could put up sufficient security. The money would come from the public funds of Indian towns (*fondo de comunidades*) and was to be used for buying tools. Equally important, Peinada learned, the Superior Government had begun to lay plans for improving the standard of living, for as the viceroy of Mexico noted in his plan of pacification of February 10, 1812, people living at the subsistence level have a tendency to join subversive movements.[65]

The section of the instructions dealing with the government's intention to employ or to recommend for employment only those whose fidelity and patriotism were unimpeachable was zealously carried out. In a report that Valle wrote for Bustamante, recommendations were made for the deanship of the cathedral chapter, vacant because of the death of Dr. Antonio Carbonel. Exercising the privilege extended by the Royal Patronage, Bustamante sorted through the candidates indicating his approval or disapproval. The archdeacon, Dr. Antonio García Redondo, received the recommendation and Bustamante's fulsome praise. For the position of archdeacon, which would be vacant if García Redondo moved up, Dr. Bernardo Pavón, the canon highest in the hierarchy of the cathedral chapter, had a legitimate claim. Pavón, however, had close ties with those who had "signed the revolutionary instructions published by this town council in the year '11," and his friendship with Deputy Larrazábal was so close that he had hung Larrazábal's portrait in the salon of the University with an inscription immediately below it.[56] Pavón's rela-

55. *Ibid.* In connection with the plan to raise the standard of living, Valle noted that the Superior Government would invest money but not to the "prejudice of the treasury."

56. Valle Papers. The report (undated and unsigned) is an incomplete rough draft, and the handwriting belongs to Valle. (Hereafter Report on the personnel of the cathedral chapter.) The University also presented Larrazábal with a set of instructions, which Dr. Bernardo Pavón helped to prepare. See Lanning, *Enlighten-*

tions extended even into the "nocturnal society" of his brother, Manuel, and linked Bernardo with the "suspected" Dr. Matías Delgado and his brother, Miguel. Matías, according to reliable sources was the "author of the first disorders in San Salvador," and Miguel was in prison for his complicity in the uprising and for his correspondence with Morelos. In view of this, Bustamante could not recommend Dr. Bernardo Pavón.[57]

In another report, Valle, writing for Bustamante, interpreted an amnesty for political prisoners to apply only to those "simple people" who had been "seduced and deceived" by the "iniquity" of the leaders of the uprisings. Certainly the amnesty was not meant for the Aguilares, Delgados, and Rodríguez, who had abused the pardon granted to them after the first revolt in San Salvador.[58]

On March 3, 1814, Valle stole enough time from his work to write to his friend, Gregorio de Castriciones, a wealthy Spanish merchant, about the elections and uprisings in San Salvador. Valle complained that the men with the "worst name" were elected to the municipal council of that city. "It is sufficient to say . . . that Dn. Juan Manuel Rodríguez, alias Malilapa, and . . . Pablo Castillo were elected." These men had been involved in the first disorder. Following the elections of December, 1813, "there were secret juntas," and on the night of January 24, at the sound of a bell, more than 1,000 men rushed into the streets. They threatened "the life of Intendant Peinada, that of Commandant Rosi, of Peninsulars, and of those fond of Spain." Happily the "patrols of volunteers and some troops from the regular garrison" were sufficient to crush this, the second uprising, killing only two or three and wounding several. "Malilapa, Dn. Miguel Delgado . . . [here the letter is torn away] and various others have been imprisoned, but Pablo Castillo escaped and has not been captured." To guard against further disturbance, "Bus-

---

ment, p. 329. Bustamante also requested that the members of the town council who had signed the instructions, except José de Isasi, Sebastián Melón, Miguel González, and Juan Antonio Aqueche, should not be permitted any employment controlled by the government. See AGG, A1.2.2, 15741, 2191. Libro de cabildos de Guatemala, año 1815 (Aug. 22); Salazar, *Historia de veintiún años,* p. 182.

57. Report on the personnel of the cathedral chapter, Valle Papers. For additional information about the Pavón family, see *Noticia Biográfica del Señor D. Manuel Francisco Pavón, Consejero de Estado y Ministro de lo Interior del Gobierno de la República de Guatemala* (Guatemala City, 1855), pp. 1-21.

58. Valle Papers. The document cited is a rough draft, dated Aug. 18, 1814. (Hereafter Report concerning amnesty.) The Aguilares were the brothers Nicolás, Manuel, and Vicente.

tamante has ordered artillery Colonel Dn. José Méndez with some troops from the regular garrison" of Guatemala City to San Salvador and "has taken other measures worthy of the wisdom with which he governs." The province was now peaceful, but Valle thought that it was very possible that the fire was still smoldering. Emphatically he declared to his friend that "popular elections are dangerous in such grave circumstances." "Wouldn't you think," given the "spirit of disorder in America," that the people would elect those "most loyal to the just cause?" Instead, they invested their future with the "most suspected" and the "conspirators." And Deputy "Larrazábal, whom they call *fide* [*digno*] . . . [here the letter is torn away], unaware of the state of things in the Kingdom . . ., has asked that they declare that even . . . [one word and part of the following are torn away] *cestuosos* and sacreligious are citizens, that confirmation of the elections are not necessary, and that the people should engage freely in elections."[59]

Two months later, Ferdinand VII, who had been restored to his throne, tried to preclude such spectacles as popular elections under any circumstances. On May 4, 1814, after suspending all decrees passed during his absence and dismissing the Cortes, he declared that "respectable persons" from various parts of the Empire had "expressed unanimously their repugnance and disgust" for the Constitution. Ferdinand the Desired, as it happened, agreed with these persons, and with one sentence he restored royal absolutism to the Spanish Empire.[60] Guatemala received the news some time during the summer, and Bustamante dedicated himself to destroying every vestige of the Constitution of 1812. With one whiff of decretory grapeshot, he dispatched the provincial deputation and the elective town council to the limbo for progressive ideas from the Spanish Empire.[61] And in the course of the first year of royal absolutism, the last shred of

59. Valle Papers. Castriciones contributed 4,000 pesos during the first collection for the *donativo patriótico voluntario*. See *Gazeta de Guatemala*, Oct. 17, 1808.

60. A text of this pronouncement by Ferdinand can be found in AGG, A1.2.2, 15740, 2191. Libro de cabildos de Guatemala, año 1814. Also see *Boletín*, IV (1938), 13-18.

61. AGG, A1.2.2, 15740, 2191. Libro de cabildos de Guatemala, año 1814 (Sept. 20). For orders restricting freedom of press, for gathering and burning "pernicious books," and for recalling the Jesuits, see Medina, *La imprenta en Guatemala*, pp. 568-569, 595; Torres Lanzas, ed., *Independencia de América*, IV, 121; AGG, A1.2.2, 15742, 2192. Libro de cabildos de Guatemala, año 1816 (Feb. 6).

the veil that has obscured Valle's position for nearly a century and a half was torn away.

[4]

Bustamante, with the help of the reliable Valle, now bombarded the crown with confessions of faith and complaints against the "humiliating constitution" that had spread the "principles of subversion" throughout America.[62] In one of his early memorials, which Valle wrote, Bustamante was quick to point out to Ferdinand that some people had changed "their language" since his return, but that Bustamante always had "spoken the same," and if his "Spanish obedience" made him accept the Constitution of 1812, he desired to make clear that he had "never ceased to protest" against it and had "never ceased talking like a pure Spaniard who is delighted to be your subject." Owing to his loyalty, he had been "calumniated by the town council and the provincial deputation, offended publicly in the Cortes, and censured in some newspapers." Adamant before the opposition, he reported in a dispatch, dated October 27, 1813, that the instructions the town council of the capital had given to Deputy Larrazábal were one of the primary causes for the revolts. Clearly, they were a "literal copy of the Declaration of the Rights of Man drawn up by the National Assembly of France during the epoch of her horrible revolution." Brazenly, the instructions allotted "Your Majesty" only the executive power and gave the legislative power to a congress of deputies, elected by the people, with a "salary of 1,200 pesos, and the title of Excellency." The person largely responsible for writing the instructions was José María Peinada, who according to general opinion was a "son of a Frenchman."[63]

Another document prepared by Valle for Bustamante illuminates more clearly the characteristics that the two had in common

62. Valle Papers. The document is a rough draft (undated, unsigned, and written by Valle) reviewing events that occurred in Guatemala during Ferdinand's absence from the throne (hereafter Report of events during the absence of Ferdinand).

63. *Ibid.* These dispatches were reaching Spain, according to Canon Juan Francisco Vilches (to Valle, León, July 19, 1814, Valle Papers), who wrote that Bustamante had informed Archbishop Ramón Casaus y Torres that he had received an acknowledgment from Spain of his "memorial concerning the revolutions in these parts."

and shows that there were few men that Bustamante felt he could rely on. In compliance with the laws of the Indies (Valle of course cited the laws), Valle drew up a report on the personnel of the *audiencia*. The senior *oidor* at the time (late 1814 or early 1815) was Joaquín Bernardo de Campuzano, who had been forced to leave the *audiencia* in Buenos Aires because he had "married a daughter of that country without previous license" from the Council of the Indies. Campuzano, however, had not profited from his experience. Soon after he arrived in Guatemala, he established close relations with the families of the capital. After 11:00 A.M., when the *audiencia* concluded its business, in the afternoons, and at nights, for days on end, he had been seen visiting with the people of the city. Most of his friends were creoles or "creolized Europeans" (*europeos acriollados*), and he had little to do with Spaniards. He was a frequent guest in the home of the Marquis de Aycinena, a wealthy merchant, and in the home of the Pavóns, who were also merchants.[64]   A more serious breach of the conduct demanded of an *oidor*, however, was that Campuzano visited the Marquis "even now when he is involved in a litigation with the Real Hacienda over 35,000 pesos which he owes for taxes."[65] Neither did Campuzano observe the proper decorum "during the epoch when the gloomy news from Spain made diversion repugnant." He gave parties attended by many people. Finally, it was known that he corresponded with some of the intendants of the provinces, and, in view of this, subjects in these provinces were reluctant to initiate proceedings against the intendants.[66]

Oidor Juan Gualberto González, "an intimate friend of Oidor Campuzano," had ties equally close with the community. "Dominated by his passion for music, he spends a great deal of his time copying music [*papeles de solfa*], teaching Italian arias to several children, and playing the violin in Campuzano's orchestra, which is integrated [*confundida*] with the musicians of the city, some of

64. The Pavón family and the Aycinena family, two of the wealthiest in Guatemala, were tied together by marriage. See Report on the personnel of the cathedral chapter, Valle Papers.

65. The House of Aycinena apparently was having financial difficulty at this time, as Valle indicated (to Julián Valladares, March 18, 1814) when he wrote that there was "a scarcity of money in the House of the Marquis."

66. Valle Papers. The report bears neither date nor signature but was written by Valle (hereafter Report on the personnel of the *audiencia*).

whom are barefoot, barelegged little mulattoes [*mulatillos descalsos de pie y pierna*]." González was also negligent about matters of protocol. When the news arrived telling of the "return of our Sovereign" from exile, the employees came "to congratulate the government, as was proper," but González had not taken advantage of any of the occasions to extend his good wishes. His indifference, however, probably was owing to the fact that when the Cortes ordered the government to sell the king's houses, they were sold, including that of González.[67]

Honorary Oidor Manuel de Talavera was a "subject whose personal relations, lack of professional dignity, lethargy, and slight scrupulousness in the business of the Real Hacienda" made him of little value to the government. (Imagine Valle's zeal at this point.) Also, he had favored free trade during the critical period and had been seen in the company of men who had "little or no dignity." He had been "admonished privately," but he had not changed. A separate report would be sent concerning him.[68]

Oidor Antonio Serrano Polo, "elderly and ailing," manifested by his "retiring manner" the "dignity becoming a toga." But when the Belén conspiracy was discovered, he went to Antigua, in the province of Guatemala, and did not extend his sympathy to the government. Polo had no connection with the conspiracy—Bustamante also had sold his house.[69]

Not long after these reports were prepared, a royal order arrived (May 9, 1815) informing Bustamante that Ferdinand wished him to select one or more subjects whose "education, wisdom, maturity, and judgment" would enable them to write, "in a simple and correct style," a memorial describing "with truth and objectivity" the revolutions that had occurred in the Kingdom of Guatemala.[70] Bustamante, with the privilege of selecting anyone in the capital or from anywhere in the provinces, put his

67. *Ibid.*
68. *Ibid.*
69. *Ibid.*
70. Archivo General de Indias (hereafter AGI). Audiencia de Guatemala, 629. El presidente y capitán general de Guatemala acusa el recibo de la real orden de 31 de julio del año próximo pasado, acompañando quatro documentos en comprobación de inconvenientes que se pulsaron para escribir por ahora las memorias que previene dicha real orden y hasta que S.M. en su vista se digne resolver lo que sea de su soberano agrado. The order was received on May 9, 1815, and the replies were dated July 18, 1815. The author is grateful to Professor John J. TePaske, Department of History, Ohio State University, for the copy of this document.

trust in three: Archbishop Ramón Casaus y Torres; Rafael Trullé, treasurer of the Consulado and editor of the government newspaper; and José del Valle. Archbishop Casaus begged to be excused, noting that news of such documents generally became known to the "insurgents and conspirators." Earlier, he had written a memorial similar to the one desired, and he knew that the repercussions could violate his dignity and threaten his life.[71] Trullé also knew that a copy of the memorial, if it were written, would remain in the secretariat of the government, and he supplicated His Majesty to be excused for the same reasons suggested by Casaus.[72]

Valle's reply, a model of how to refuse a king without actually saying no, points up his loyalty and his ambition. In three centuries, he wrote, the Spanish colonies had not experienced anything comparable to the events that had "occurred in the brief absence of our beloved Sovereign." The first news of the struggle in Spain inspired a restless spirit in the American colonies. Passions were inflamed and subversive ideas soon deprived Americans of the joys of peace and pushed them into the horrors of a civil war. A memorial pointing out and describing the "causes, the instigators, the methods, and the results" of the revolutions would be of great value to Ferdinand, whose decisions had "rescued us from such a delicate crisis" and would serve as a warning to "perfidious conspirators."

If Valle should write the memorial, he knew generally the outline that he would follow. The origins of the conflict lay deep in the history of the colonies. He would begin, then, by discussing the spirit of conquered countries, in general, and that of America, in particular, and attempt to show how that spirit had been affected by "works published by foreigners," whose purpose had been "to obscure the glory of Spain" and to make the conquistadores odious in the eyes of the world. The influence of the "doctrines of some philosophers," the "example of the Anglo-Americans in their war for independence" and that "subsequently provided by the French," along with their "seditious

---

71. Casaus had written a pamphlet against Hidalgo. See Lanning, *Enlightenment*, p. 83. For additional information on the life of Casaus, see Beristain, *Biblioteca hispano americana*, I, 263-264; *Boletín*, III (1938), 492; Medina, *La imprenta en Guatemala*, p. 518.

72. AGI, Audiencia de Guatemala, 629.

constitutions and writings," also would have to be considered. More specifically, if he wrote the memorial, he would have to try to determine the influence of these ideas and actions on the thinking of the people who lived in the capitals of America, where the inhabitants were better educated than those in the provinces. Against this background, the revolutions in Guatemala would be comprehensible.   But to trace the course of the revolutions, pointing out "the names and character of those who clandestinely inspired the riots and insurrections—to unravel the whole plan of their machinations—this, Señor, cannot be done with accuracy in the same country where the families and friends of the conspirators live."   The person that learns the details of the revolutions will be the "victim of diverse sufferings."   The Conde de Revillagigedo, viceroy of Mexico during the last of the eighteenth century, stated once that Mexico should never forget that she was a colony of Spain.   "Until this moment, they hate the memory of his name."   Feeling in Guatemala, much more intense than in Mexico during the days of Revillagigedo, would expose the author of the proposed memorial to many dangers, and Valle, fearing for his personal safety, also asked to be excused, unless he received an appointment that would take him to Spain.   In a "memorial of November 3, of last year [1814]," Valle had supplicated an appointment to an *audiencia* in Spain so that he might live in a "country more analogous" to his character, where he would be "less exposed to embarrassments."   Now, "if His Majesty condescends to hear my solicitations, I shall present immediately the memorial, which I shall begin to write confidentially."[73]

From these reports and reasons for not writing reports emerges a profile of Bustamante and Valle.   Bustamante, pure Spaniard with Spanish obedience ingrained in his character, had spent all his mature life in the military.   He had learned to command by

73. *Ibid.* The fiscal of the Council of the Indies noted: ". . . que siendo de bastante peso las razones que exponen los indicados M. R. Arzobispo, Valle, y Trullé para que se les tenga por escusados, y más para una cosa que ha de ser enteramente voluntaria, le parece que este asunto no demanda providencia."   Fragments of this document have been published in Rómulo E. Durón, ed., *Obras de Don José Cecilio del Valle* (Tegucigalpa, 1906), pp. viii-x; R. Fernández Guardia, "La independencia: una gran sorpresa," *Revista de los Archivos Nacionales de Costa Rica,* IV (March-April, 1940), 152.   Also see Rómulo E. Durón, "José Cecilio del Valle," *Bulletin of the Pan American Union,* LXIX (Jan.-Dec., 1935), 39-45.   But for the document in its entirety, see Louis E. Bumgartner, ed., "Documentos de la independencia de Guatemala," *Antropología e Historia de Guatemala,* XIII (July, 1961), 56-61.

learning first to obey, and as a subject of Ferdinand, he exempli-
fied the obedience that he demanded from royal subjects under
his command. The laws of the Indies were explicit about the
conduct of *oidores*. Bustamante's mentality did not allow him
to question the reasoning behind the laws or to interpret them
according to time and circumstance. He lived by the royal codes,
by the book, and he was extremely proud of the attainments that
he had achieved by a spartan life. Under no circumstances could
he countenance apathy, frivolity, and Italian arias from a royal
minister dignified by a toga. Given his demeanor, Bustamante's
response to the burst of revolutionary activity in Guatemala was
predictable. He had not been sent to the Indies to destroy the
bond between crown and colony but rather to keep it taut and
toned to the wishes of the king. When the royal subjects in
Guatemala set their sights on independence, his duty was clear
and he did it. He tried amnesty first, but when the Granadinos
"twice scorned the amnesty, it was necessary to make them respect
force, to prosecute them, and to send them to the Peninsula."[74]
No Spanish officer could have done more. And if he confused
"the authority of his distinguished position with his personal
authority,"[75] he did so in the interest of the crown and because he
viewed himself as a military commander and the subjects in
Guatemala as enlisted men. No less repugnant but more difficult
to cope with was the Constitution of 1812, promulgated in the
absence of the king. Bustamante could not conceive of government under a document that insulted "our ancestors."[76] That
mere town councils should be accorded the title of "most serene
highness" and that the Spanish codes should be set aside escaped
his wildest imagination.[77] Thus faced with the choice of "tyrant"
or traitor, Bustamante remained loyal, and as the Spanish Empire
staggered and lurched under the blows that were to bring it to a
close, his loyalty to the crown stood out as a tribute to the spirit
and courage with which the Empire had been built.

By July, 1815, when these reports had been written, the ease
with which Valle had bridged the period of uncertainty after the
departure of Captain General González was limpidly clear. By

---

74. Report concerning amnesty, Valle Papers.
75. Barrio, Palomo, and Larreinaga protest against Bustamante, Valle Papers.
76. Report of events during the absence of Ferdinand, Valle Papers.
77. *Ibid.*

the time Ferdinand VII had returned, Valle was as close to Bustamante as he ever had been to González—if not closer. Valle's
rigid discipline, aristocratic dignity, and incontrovertible loyalty
to the crown could not have escaped the notice of Bustamante,
surrounded as he was by two musicians, a waster, and the crotchety
Polo. And Bustamante, in the manner of González, appointed
Valle to new offices and recommended him for the office of Honorary Judge Advocate of the Army, which Valle received in June,
1813.[78] Later he became outright Judge Advocate (1821). Bustamante's recommendation in this connection, then, should remove any remaining doubt about Valle's loyalty during the
critical epoch. Writing in 1819, Bustamante noted that he had
"employed D. José del Valle throughout my command, entrusting
him with serious matters," which he discharged faithfully. And
his "well known loyalty" (*lealtad notoria*) to the crown caused
him to suffer "harassment and displeasure at the hands of some
corporations."[79] Valle's talent and "adherence to the just cause"
were as impressive to Bustamante as they had been to González.

Valle, however, was as dissatisfied in 1815 as he had been in
1807. In chasing the elusive toga and fending off his enemies,
he rapidly approached the point of not caring what happened in
Guatemala. At any rate, his ambition to sally forth to Spain
draped in a toga had been sufficiently great to allow him to bargain with Ferdinand VII.

As quickly as Valle received new appointments, however small,
he sent the information to Rafael Díez y Tovar, who, in Spain,
guided and pushed Valle's candidacy for a toga. In October and
November, 1812, Valle had served as secretary of the Junta Preparatoria and had explained, in a pamphlet, the electoral procedure. On January 3, 1813, he sent news of his "new services"
and a copy of the instructions, which had been circulated
throughout Guatemala.[80] On June 3, 1814, he informed Díez y
Tovar that Bustamante had written to his brother, Francisco, a

78. Bustamante to Valle, May 10, 1813, Valle Papers. Bustamante passed to
Valle a copy of a note, "for your knowledge and satisfaction," telling him of the
appointment.
79. Bustamante to José de Alós, Secretario Interino de Estado y del Despacho
Universal, Madrid, Nov. 13, 1819, Valle Papers.
80. Rafael Antonio Díez y Tovar to Valle, Cádiz, June 19, 1813, Valle Papers.
Díez y Tovar remarked that he had received Valle's letter, of January 3, 1813,
containing the information.

merchant in Cádiz, asking him to apply himself in Valle's behalf. Bubbling with enthusiasm, Valle emphasized that "the recommendation of Sr. Dn. Francisco will be very effective owing to his close friendship with Sr. García Herrera, Ministro de Gracias y Justicia." To make his application for a toga still more attractive, Valle asked Archbishop Casaus y Torres for a recommendation. Casaus, happy to oblige, wrote to the Secretario del Consejo de Estado and to Santiago Martínez del Rincón, "secretary of the Conde de Altamira,"[81] whose *señorío*, at an earlier date, included the entire city of Elche, in Valencia.[82]

For a moment, Díez y Tovar made these recommendations seem unnecessary when he raced to his home in Madrid, "with inexpressible anxiety," to inform Valle that the "Longed for Ferdinand" would arrive soon and that it was anticipated that he would make appointments to the *audiencia* of Guadalajara (Spain), for which Valle, "the best situated," would be considered.[83] A few months after Valle received this news from Díez y Tovar, a friend wrote saying that word from Madrid stated that the "Council of the Indies has proposed Señor D. Cecilio del Valle for Honorary Oidor" and further that there was "no doubt that His Majesty will confirm the proposal."[84] Valle, sure that the time had come, began informing his friends of his imminent departure. And Joaquín Arechavala wrote that he would be sorry to see Valle leaving for Spain.[85] On November 1, 1814, Díez y Tovar, however, caused Valle's enthusiasm to subside when he explained that no decision had been made "concerning the

81. Valle to Díez y Tovar, Valle Papers. The letter cited is a rough draft, but Díez y Tovar received the information, as his letter of November 1, 1814 (Valle Papers) shows. Casaus also wrote to "Sr. Colomarde, oficial del Ministerio de Indias, diciéndole que se interese en proporcionarme colocación. Sirvase V. hablarle ofreciéndole mis afectos. Creo que será atendida una recomendación tan expresiva." (Valle to Díez y Tovar, July 3, 1815, Valle Papers.) It was probably at this time that Casaus wrote the expressive paragraph in behalf of Valle that appears in Valle's títulos y méritos (ABNH). In the same connection, Oidor Campuzano, who was transferred to Cuba before 1819, wrote a recommendation for Valle. See ABNH. Títulos y méritos.

82. Richard Herr, *The Eighteenth-Century Revolution in Spain* (Princeton, New Jersey, 1958), p. 95.

83. Rafael Antonio Díez y Tovar to Valle, Madrid, April 6, 1814.

84. Florencio Castillo to Juan José Zelaya, Madrid, Oct. 4, 1814, Valle Papers. Juan José Zelaya was likely the son or close relative of Pedro Antonio de Zelaya who lived in Choluteca and who described himself as a cousin of Valle's father. See Pedro Antonio de Zelaya to Valle, Choluteca, Aug. 7, 1807, Valle Papers. Valladares (ed., *Valle*, p. iv) also suggests a relationship between the two families.

85. To Valle, León, Nov. 9, 1814, Valle Papers. He noted, however, that Valle's "wisdom" would be an honor to Guatemala.

togas for Guadalajara."[86]   Then on December 1, he sent Valle's optimism scurrying before the grim news that the king, disregarding the list of recommendations, had appointed an ex-deputy.[87]

After reading Díez y Tovar's letter, Valle, for the moment, had to be satisfied with the office of Honorary Judge Advocate, but even this satisfaction was blunted and he became embittered when his enemies tried to deprive him of the dignity due that position. A series of royal orders, beginning in 1745 and extending to March 3, 1803, invested judge advocates with the title of lordship (*señoría*) and with the other privileges enjoyed by *oidores*.[88]   The *oidores* of the *audiencia,* knowing how to offend others of the tongue of Spain, refused to accord Valle the title and slighted his position in other small ways.   Valle took steps to correct the erring *oidores,* and on October 17, 1814, Gregorio de Castriciones, now in Spain, wrote that he had learned from Díez y Tovar that an order would force the *oidores* to extend to Valle his title and privileges.[89]   But the order, issued on October 4, 1814,[90] and expedited on May 7, 1815,[91] failed to end the controversy.   In high temper, Valle informed Díez y Tovar that the order had arrived but that the "spirit of rivalry has inspired new caviling." The ministers now asserted that the royal order requiring them to accord him the title and privileges did not impose on the *audiencia* the same obligation.   Further, Valle accused, they denied that they ever had refused him the title of lordship while they continued to do so.   Consequently Valle had entered an appeal with the fiscal of the *audiencia,* but fearing his prejudice, Valle urged Díez y Tovar to explain the difficulty at court.   "I will send you plenty of proof that attests that they have denied me the title.   No one could think that I am so stupid as to appeal for something that has not been denied me, or that the

86. To Valle, Madrid, Valle Papers.
87. *Ibid.*
88. AGG, A1.40-58, 14218, 2045.   Juramento de José del Valle, auditor de guerra de ejército (June 10, 1813).   Escribano Antonio Arroyave witnessed and recorded the oath of office, noting explicitly the dates of the royal orders granting the privileges: January 10, 1745; April 7, 1745; April 15, 1760; June 26, 1788.   And Valle pointed out the subsequent order of March 3, 1803 (Valle to Díez y Tovar, July 3, 1815, Valle Papers).
89. To Valle, Cádiz, Valle Papers.
90. Valle to Díez y Tovar, July 3, 1815, Valle Papers.
91. AGG, A1.2.2, 15741, 2191.   Libro de cabildos de Guatemala año 1815.   On May 7 the town council acknowledged receipt of a copy of the order of October 4, 1814, confirming Valle's claim to the title of señoría.   Bustamante sent the copy to the town council.

captain general would have supported the appeal if he had not witnessed the obstinacy with which the *oidores* have refused to grant that which is due me."⁹² For at least two more years the *audiencia* and Valle tilted at each other, and by 1815, if not earlier, the town council had closed ranks with the *audiencia,*⁹³ indicating that the years following the return of Ferdinand would bring Valle more unhappiness and drive him to the point of wishing to leave Guatemala without a toga.

[5]

Thus Valle emerged from the critical period of insurrection and constitutional rule with powerful friends and dedicated enemies and an outstanding record of loyalty. He had viewed the dissension between creoles and Spaniards with the same repugnance that Juan de Dios Mayorga, future deputy to Mexico, expressed in a letter: ". . . the opinion against the Peninsulars is heard from even the most rustic. . . . I have told them that the persecution of the Spaniards was a sign of the worst barbarity."⁹⁴ Though Valle was not as vehement concerning the revolutions as Mariano Murillo, a Spaniard threatened during the uprising in León, Valle shared the sentiments underlying Murillo's denunciations of the "despicable and monomaniacal spirit" that prompted them.⁹⁵ Valle did not esteem the Junta Central suffi-

92. Valle to Díez y Tovar, July 13, 1815, Valle Papers. Valle explained that, as far as he knew, the fiscal had done nothing, but: "Temo que su objeto sea dar cuenta sin noticia mía para sorprender a S. M. Espero por lo mismo que vea V. si han dado cuenta y en el caso de haber dado, haga las gestiones correspondientes entendido de que yo sigo agitando. . . ." José del Barrio, Miguel Larreinaga, and José Ingenieros Palomo denied that they had refused to accord Valle the title of lordship and that they would discuss "his false assumption" in another letter. See Larreinaga, Barrio, and Palomo protest against Bustamante, March 18, 1815, Valle Papers.

93. AGG, A1.2.2, 15741, 2191. Libro de cabildos de Guatemala, año 1815 (May 7).

94. To Valle, Dec. 24, 1811, Valle Papers. In addition Dios Mayorga explained that the feeling against the Spaniards seemed to be subsiding.

95. To Valle, León, Jan. 14, 1813, Valle Papers. Murillo did not confine his remarks to the revolutions in Guatemala but also included those in Mexico. Morelos, at that time, was operating in the south of Mexico, and there was some apprehension in Guatemala, which was indicated in a letter from Isidoro de Valle Castriciones (San Salvador, April 24, 1814, Valle Papers) when he wrote: "Certainly the news from Oaxaca is very pleasing, for we no longer need to fear the insurgents of that Kingdom, according to the newspapers that I have seen from that capital. And pray God that they have been destroyed." That Murillo was a Spaniard was shown when he wrote (to Valle, León, June 19, 1820, Valle Papers)

ciently to run the risk of being elected, and he wrote, for Bustamante, that the instructions that the town council gave to Deputy
Larrazábal were designed to destroy the laws of the Indies and
"to set forth a plan of independence."[96]   And Valle nodded
approvingly when he read Dionisio de Herrera's comment: "Yes, I
saw the instructions. What plans! What designs! God couldn't
have made better ones."[97]   Valle was contemptuous of Larrazábal's
blissful ignorance, and Valle and Bustamante accepted the Constitution with reluctance.

Herrera's letter, however, suggests a difference between Bustamante and Valle. Bustamante opposed the Constitution because
his character and training made a departure from the tradition
of royal authority unthinkable. Valle, owing to his education
and intimate knowledge of Guatemala, opposed the Constitution
because it was completely out of touch with reality. To Valle,
constitutional government and independence were ideas that
might be discussed over a cup of chocolate by scholars whose place
and privilege were secured by tradition and royal authority. Certainly they were not suitable topics for times of crisis. But even
to mention these ideas in connection with Valle, between 1808
and 1815, except in a negative way, is to exaggerate their importance in his thinking. And in his plans for the future, he gave
them no consideration whatsoever. His overwhelming desire was
to go to Spain as an *oidor*. In view of this, if a difference of
opinion did exist between Bustamante and Valle, Bustamante's
unstinted support assures us that Valle never revealed the nature
of the difference, if at that time he were aware of it himself. Together, then, they received the restoration of royal authority with
the feeling that they had just driven the last nail re-securing the
lid on Pandora's box.

that his wife had died, noting that "we came together to this Kingdom from the
Peninsula."

96. Report on the members of the diputación provincial, Valle Papers.

97. To Valle, May 1, 1814, Valle Papers. Valle certainly agreed with his friend
Colonel Arechavala, who wrote (León, Dec. 24, 1812, Valle Papers): "I am convinced
that Guatemalans want everything for themselves and desire to be deputies for the
whole world."

Years of Frustration,
1815-1820

[*1*]

Moments of happiness for Valle, between 1808 and 1815, seem to have been few and fleeting and confined to his anticipation of a better life in Spain. One exception was his marriage, on October 12, 1812, to María Josefa Valero y Morales, not from Guatemala City but from Comayagua (Honduras). Valle's friend, Archbishop Ramón Casaus y Torres solemnized the marriage, and the parents of the bride were in attendance.[1] María Josefa was an intelligent and loving wife who bore Valle three children, of whom we have definite record, two daughters and a son, Bernardo. The eminent Dr. Antonio García Redondo baptized two of the children, and Valle's faithful sister, María Francisca, was the godmother to all three. But the troubled times and Valle's work and ambition robbed him even of some of the happiness of his marriage and family. He took his marriage vows less than three weeks after the publication of the Constitution. His first child, María Dolores, was born on March 29, 1814,[2] immediately after the controversy over his practice and shortly before Ferdinand abolished the Constitution. His second child, María Josefa, was born on March 28, 1817,[3] shortly after Valle's benefactor,

1. ACG, Libro de matrimonios de 1729 a 1821, Parroquia del Sagrario.
2. ACG, Volumen sexto de bautismos de españoles, desde 6 de febrero de 1772 hasta el año de 1822 (hereafter Volumen sexto de bautismos). García Redondo baptized María Dolores on March 30, 1814. In the Libro de Inhumaciones en Mausoleos, at the general cemetery in Guatemala City, it appears that María Dolores died on November 5, 1893.
3. ACG, Volumen sexto de bautismos. María Josefa was baptized on March 29, 1817.

Bustamante, received orders back to Spain. And Bernardo Maca-
beo arrived on August 1, 1820,[4] less than a month after the Constitution of 1812 was re-established. However, as long as Bustamante remained, Valle's future, despite his unhappiness, was relatively secure in Guatemala. His detractors confined themselves
to whining and sniping.

[2]

In January, 1817, Bustamante skipped over Honorary Oidor
Manuel Talavera (as Captain General González also had done)
and appointed Valle interim crown attorney (*fiscal interino*).[5]
The fiscal, as was the case with other officers in colonial institutions, had specified privileges and prerogatives. One was that he
should occupy a certain chair of "preference" in meetings of the
captain general and his councilors.[6] Valle hardly had an opportunity to try any of the chairs for comfort before the members of
the town council began to whimper that he had no right to the
preferred seat. The *real acuerdo,* which had entertained the
"protest," replied in a note signed by Bustamante that decisions
of January 30 and February 20, 1817 had assured Valle the rights
that he had been exercising.[7] Simply because Bustamante said
so was not sufficient. Could the *real acuerdo* please send the
documents showing the agreements of "January 30 and February
20, last?" No, as a matter of fact, the *real acuerdo* could not. So

4. ACG, Volumen sexto de bautismos. Bernardo was baptized on the day of
his birth by Dean García Redondo. The Valles appear to have had two other
children. See Rosa, *José Cecilio del Valle (Obras),* I, xxvii.
5. AGG, A1.40-29, 22383, 2657. Juramento del fiscal interino José del Valle
(Jan. 30, 1817). Oidor Antonio Norberto Serrano Polo wrote a recommendation
for Valle, and Polo noted that Captain General González failed to appoint Talavera,
who, "in addition to other deficiencies that decorum renders inexpressible, is also
married to a daughter of this country." Polo noted further that Bustamante,
whenever possible, refused to employ Talavera. See Dn. Antonio Norberto Serrano
Polo, del Consejo de S. M., Oidor Decano de la Real Audiencia y Chancillería de
este Reyno, Ministro Consultor Togado del Tribunal de Santo Oficio de la Inquisición de México, Superintendente de esta Real Casa de Moneda [a favor de José
del Valle], Sept. 12, 1819, Valle Papers. (Hereafter Polo recommends Valle.)
Talavera died on April 15, 1821. See *El Editor Constitucional,* May 14, 1821.
6. The reference is to the meeting of the captain general with the ministers of
the *audiencia* (*real acuerdo*) and to the meeting of the *real acuerdo* with members
of the exchequer (*junta superior*).
7. AGG, A1.29, 25427, 2841. El ayuntamiento de Guatemala protesta por el
asiento asignado al auditor de guerra, Lic. José C. del Valle. The note signed by
Bustamante was dated March 28, 1817.

the squabble continued.[8] What Valle's reactions were can be inferred from a letter written by Dionisio de Herrera, but in another
connection: "Your [Valle's] reflections concerning the intermi-
nable trouble that lawsuits produce are certainly true."[9] The
puerile bickering of the town council, however, did serve to
emphasize Bustamante's statement that Valle suffered persecutions because "of having been distinguished by the Government."[10]

While the argument continued, Valle performed the duties of
the fiscal with characteristic thoroughness until November, 1817,
when he made way for the permanent appointment.[11] As fiscal, he
defended the interests of the crown in both civil and criminal
cases, most of which will be dealt with below (Chapter VI), but
one illumines his continuing interest in economics.

[*3*]

The rainy season of 1816 (June through October) had brought
downpours that ruined crops and caused, in 1817, a frightening
shortage of corn in the province of Comayagua. The Superior
Government, in an attempt to arrest the emergency, permitted
the governor of the province to borrow 3,500 pesos from the
public funds of Indian towns, and Juan Antonio Tornos, the
governor, bought corn "at a great distance." The cost of trans-
poration, however, raised the price higher than that of grain in
the immediate vicinity of Comayagua. Governor Tornos, em-
barrassed by corn he could not sell, chose "to violate the public"
when he posted an order that "no one should sell corn until he
had sold the bushels that he had bought," promising at the same
time to prosecute all transgressors. He then asked the Superior
Government to stand behind him.[12]

Valle had to decide whether to invalidate the order, causing

8. AGG, A1.2.2, 15743, 2192. Libro de cabildos de Guatemala, año 1817. See
the records for April 10, June 10, and September 2.
9. To Valle, Oct. 8, 1816, Valle Papers. However, Valle well might have been
writing about his appeal to force the *oidores* to extend him the title of lordship.
10. Bustamante to José de Alós, Secretario Interino de Estado y del Despacho
Universal, Madrid, Nov. 13, 1819, Valle Papers.
11. Polo recommends Valle, Valle Papers.
12. AGG, A1.22.22, 5772, 262. Autos acerca de la falta de maíz en Comayagua.
Valle wrote his opinion on May 28, 1817.

a loss of part of the borrowed principal, or to support Tornos. In a display of insight that came from first-hand experience with colonial trade and a knowledge of the theories of the economists, he wrote that Tornos' order violated the right of property— that right of each to buy and sell crops as he pleases. Only the "Sovereign and the authorities" to whom he had delegated such great power had the prerogative "to modify, to limit, and to suspend" that right. And the fiscal had not seen any law that concedes such power to the intendants. Valle shrank from the thought of the damage caused by an order that choked off trade, violating thereby the laws of the Kingdom and the views of the scholars. "When the flow of domestic trade possesses all its natural energy, and when the hand of authority does not impose obstacles twisting its course, the businessmen are continually seeking out abundance and scarcity." Valle referred to his essay on the locust plague (1804), in which he had stated essentially the same opinion, and he called Tornos' attention to the wisdom of the Economic Society of Madrid when its members informed the Council of Castile: "It is in vain, Señor, to expect a decline of prices for any reason other than that of abundance, and it is useless to hope for abundance without the free exchange of goods." Tornos, accordingly, had some expensive corn to sell, and at a price that would not return the borrowed principal.[13]

Valle had first shown an interest in economics in 1803, and he may well have contributed articles on economics to the *Gazeta*, though none of the contributions have been identified as his.[14] Periodically, beginning during the time of González, Valle served as legal adviser for the exchequer,[15] and, on January 29, 1811, after the Sociedad Económica had been re-established,[16] he be-

13 *Ibid.* Valle wrote: "El primer derecho que se ha hollado en ellos es el de propiedad, protegido en todas las legislaciones cultas: el de vender cada uno sus frutos como le parezca; el de comprarlos como le convenga. Solo el Soberano y las autoridades a quienes haya delegado tamaño poder lo tienen para modificar, limitar, o suspender aquel derecho; y no ha visto el Fiscal ley alguna que lo conceda a los intendentes." The author read this document in 1958. Recently it has been published in its entirety. See Pedro Tobar Cruz, *Valle, el hombre, el político, el sabio* (Guatemala City, 1961), pp. 289-297.

14. The reader, however, is invited to compare the essays on political economy that appeared in the *Gazeta* (April 30, May 7, and June 11, 1804) signed "El Imparcial y Buen Patriota" with Valle's articles on economics that appeared in *El Amigo de la Patria*.

15. González recommends Valle, Valle Papers.

16. AGG, A1.6, 31117, 4035. Oficio del Capitán General Antonio González,

came a member.[17] About a year later he began to draw up plans for a class in economics, which the Sociedad intended to sponsor. Teaching would not be a new experience, for at the time he published his outline for the course in economics (March, 1812), he was giving classes in philosophy at the University of San Carlos.[18] But his outline lent validity to Captain General González' statement that political economy was Valle's favorite subject.[19]

Since the subject was relatively new, Valle noted that few economists had given thought to a "complete course in the science." His reading had taught him that "Count Galeani,"[20] Linguet,[21] and Necker[22] had fixed their attention on agriculture. Campomanes[23] concentrated on industry, and Baudeau[24] dedicated himself to resolving the problem of free trade, "which has divided opinion." Jovellanos,[25] "educated and zealous protector of the peasants," limited his observations to Spanish agriculture. Condillac,[26] "worthy successor of Locke in the art of precise discussion," confined himself to trade as it related to government. And even Hume,[27] "thorough as are all the English economists," had not presented a complete course in economics. Adam Smith, though "his style was not very good," approached what Valle

---

transcribiendo la orden por cual es restablecida la Sociedad Económica (Dec. 12, 1810); A1.6, 31118, 4035. Autos relativos al restablecimiento de la Sociedad Económica. For additional information concerning the re-established Society, see Shafer, *The Economic Societies in the Spanish World*, pp. 223-224; Lanning, *Enlightenment*, pp. 102-104.

17. Antonio de Juarros to Valle, Jan. 29, 1811, Valle Papers. Dues were eight pesos each year. Among Valle's papers are receipts for this amount for the years 1813, 1814, 1818, and 1820. The treasurer for 1818 was Mateo Ibarra and for 1820, José Santa Cruz.

18. AGG, A1.3-4, 12340, 1892. Libro de claustros de la Universidad de San Carlos, 1808-1831 (Nov. 9, 1811). Appointments were made in November, and Valle apparently was substituting until the permanent "election" was made the following year, on Nov. 10, 1812.

19. González recommends Valle, Valle Papers.

20. Valle apparently was referring to Fernando Galiani, *Diálogos sobre el comercio de trigo* (Madrid, 1775). For an excellent treatment on the departure of Spanish thought from the mercantile theory, see Robert S. Smith, "The *Wealth of Nations* in Spain and Hispanic America, 1780-1830," *Journal of Political Economy*, LXV (April, 1957), 104-125.

21. Simon Linguet (1736-1794).

22. Jacques Necker (1732-1803).

23. Pedro Rodríguez Campomanes (1723-1803).

24. Nicholas Baudeau (1730-1792).

25. Gaspar Melchor de Jovellanos (1744-1811).

26. Étienne Bonnot de Condillac (1715-1780).

27. David Hume (1711-1776).

wanted, but Smith's work was advanced for an "elementary course" and "obscure in many places."[28]

Throughout the summer of 1812 Valle continued to read and reflect on political economy, and in September he presented a paper before the Sociedad Económica, in which he developed his ideas more fully than at any time since 1804.[29] The main question that a political economist had to grapple with was: Why was wealth not distributed with more equity?[30] Before proceeding to answer this question, the economist should avail himself of the tools necessary for his profession. A knowledge of mathematics was not only a practical tool but one that increased man's capacity to reason, and by steeping himself in the history of the country of his interest, the economist could perceive trends of industry, trade, and agriculture that he otherwise would fail to see.[31]

Tools in hand, the economist could proceed to investigate the problems connected with the distribution of wealth. To begin with, he should form the hypothesis that seemed valid to Valle: "Labor is the origin of all wealth . . . and is the beginning of the immense scale of values." The society that had the least unemployment should be the wealthiest—"This is the true scales of politics." And the "nations that wish to tip them in their favor ought to augment employment, the only weight that favors one side over the other."[32] If, however, in his investigation, the economist found that from the capital cities down to the provincial villages there was a "decreasing amount of wealth" and an "increasing amount of work," it would be fallacious to conclude that the hypothesis was wrong. Such a phenomenon meant only that someone who exerted influence on the life of the villages was following an erroneous theory. The economist, then, would need to ferret out the error that had resulted in poverty for the

28. Valle and Valle Matheu, eds., *Obras*, II, 25-29; *El Amigo de la Patria*, April 12, 1821. When, in 1821, he learned that Heinruch von Storch (1766-1835) had published a *Curso completo de economía política*, Valle remarked that it filled a need for the study of economics (*El Amigo de la Patria*, June 27, 1821).

29. Valle and Valle Matheu, eds., *Obras*, II, 32-41. The editors of the work cited reprinted much of Valle's writing that appeared in *El Amigo de la Patria*, then as now, not easily available. Quite naturally they did not reprint everything, and thus the author will alternate between volume II of the *Obras* and *El Amigo*.

30. Valle and Valle Matheu, eds., *Obras*, II, 33-34.

31. *Ibid.*, II, 34-35.

32. *Ibid.*, II, 35.

countryside, where the people planted and harvested, and in wealth for the cities, "which produce nothing."[33]

The investigation would extend to the most minute details and include an analysis of the language that had influenced the distribution of wealth. A glossary of terms peculiar to economics would be useful, and in this connection the economist was bound to root out and destroy the baseness that had been attached to the crafts and the injustice that had labeled those institutions profane that served the general public and that stigmatized the "worker who lives in the center of his property, cultivating the land where he was born."[34]

Valle's economist had many more obligations to society. It was his duty to peruse the laws, one by one, singling out those that were contradictory, that violated "one's right to choose freely his occupation," that restricted "one's free use of the holdings created by his work," and that did not "extend equal protection to all."[35] He had to be familiar with farm and factory, mine and bank, and understand the function of the agents of trade, from the greatest speculator to the meanest market woman. Equally important was the interest the economist should take in the education of youth, not filling them with information fit only for mouthing in halls of learning but with knowledge that should make them men, which was to say "laborers, artisans, merchants, and employees capable of fulfilling what they set out to do."[36] In short, the economist that Valle had in mind was a man like himself, one with a broad education, rigid discipline, boundless energy, and more time than Valle had in 1812.

In 1814 Valle presented his "Elogio to Goicoechea," denouncing scholastic authority and praising the modernity ushered in by the distinguished teacher, and in the following year he helped to edit and write articles for a new newspaper. The first number of the *Periódico de la Sociedad Económica de Guatemala* appeared on May 1, 1815; the director of the fortnightly was Archbishop Casaus, who contributed 400 pesos to the enterprise and a monthly stipend of twenty pesos for operations. Dr. Antonio García Redondo was the assistant director, and the editors, in addition to

33. *Ibid.*, II, 35-36.
34. *Ibid.*, II, 36.
35. *Ibid.*, II, 37.
36. *Ibid.*, II, 38.

Valle, were Dr. Mariano López Rayón, eminent member of the faculty of San Carlos; Dr. José María Castilla, a Spaniard and future editor of *El Editor Constitucional;* and Antonio Gutiérrez y Ulloa.[37]   At first glance, these men appeared to be trying to recapture the spirit of the defunct *Gazeta,* but the *Periódico de la Sociedad* never got off the ground.   The penultimate copy (April 1, 1816) warned the readers that the next number would be the last, since there were only "40 subscribers in the capital and 70 outside."   The archbishop's stipend for the year (240 pesos) was gone, and the paper had lost an additional 200 pesos, which Casaus "generously suffered."[38]

In signed articles Valle approached the problem of a nation's wealth from another angle.   The personality of a state, he maintained, was nothing more than a compound of the perfections and imperfections of the people who composed the state.   And a state, in order to reap the full measure of prosperity promised by its natural resources, had to possess the qualities considered virtuous in individuals.   "Idleness . . . intemperance . . . and egoism" would push a state into the poorhouse, while the "impiety" of "attacking the Religion" was a thrust at the vitals threatening the very existence of the state.   "In order to be a good vassal," it was necessary "to have a good son, a good brother, a good father, and a good friend."   A "nation not composed of virtuous families" would be "poor and helpless," a mere "plaything for adventurers."   The "good vassals" necessary for sustaining the empire could be produced by "education of the youth" and by "property for the man."   Education and property, however, would not solve all the problems, and Valle, in words recalling his advice to Intendant Peinada, pointed out the advantages of "penal law for those who do not conduct themselves well" and of "remunerative laws for those who conduct themselves with honor."   There was "no other theory for forming the habits that decided whether man's fate" was to be one of misery or happiness.[39]

Valle's comments in connection with the scarcity of corn in

37. BNG.
38. April 15, 1816.
39. BNG, *Periódico de la Sociedad Económica de Guatemala,* July 15, 1815. The article cited was entitled "Ciencias morales" and was part of a series of articles on *ciencias.* Fragments of the rough drafts of these articles can be found in Valle Papers.

Comayagua, his reflections on a course in economics, and the
paper that he read before the Sociedad Económica attest that he
was keeping abreast of the writings coming out of Spain, the
Italian peninsula, France, and England. He accepted the cliché
concerning work and wealth, and the almost total lack of industry
in Guatemala, along with his intimate knowledge of rural life,
made the writings of the physiocrats, or of those holding similar
views, more meaningful. More important, however, Valle was
applying his knowledge to specific circumstances, and in the future, after he had decided to remain in Guatemala, he would
begin the investigation that he suggested in 1812.

His essay "Ciencias morales," however, appeared to be in line
with the policy of the Superior Government to attach and hold
the devotion of subjects whose standard of living tended to make
their loyalty to the crown doubtful. The policy, which Valle had
explained to Peinada in 1814, also complemented the royal plan
of 1817, to elicit devotion by granting scholarships to "American
Spaniards" for study in the "Colegios Mayores" of San Bartolomé,
Cuenca, and Oviedo.[40] And in view of his past life and the fact
that he was interim crown attorney, his respect for royal authority,
expressed in connection with the corn shortage, could have been
anticipated.

[4]

The office of temporary fiscal, which had provided Valle with
several opportunities to use his knowledge of economics, was the
last appointment that he received from Bustamante, who learned
from a letter posted in Madrid (March 18, 1817) that he was to be
replaced by the captain general of Santo Domingo, Sub-Inspector

40. Lanning, *Enlightenment*, p. 334. While more evidence is necessary to establish clearly that Valle was following the plan that he expressed to Peinada, if the
plan were in effect at all, there is information that permits the assumption. Casaus
offered 500 pesos toward the expense of bringing the noted mineralogist, Andrés
del Río, of Mexico, to Guatemala to teach mineralogy (*El Periódico de la Sociedad
Económica*, May 15, 1815). Bustamante also was interested in mining. In a note
to the *ayuntamiento* (Aug. 19, 1813), he wrote that such a revival would increase
the "prosperity" and "happiness," but at the moment, the mining industry was
in *total decadencia*. See AGG, A1.2.5, 25296, 2835. Correspondencia del ayuntamiento de Guatemala. In addition both Bustamante and Casaus tried to encourage
the cultivation of cereals. See *El Amigo de la Patria*, Jan. 20, 1821.

Carlos Urrutia.[41]   With the arrival of the news began the period
of transition from one superior to another, accompanied of course
by the usual rumors about the new captain general.   Colonel
Arechavala learned from a friend in Trujillo that Urrutia embarked for Guatemala, on February 22, 1818, aboard the *Hermosa
Catalina,* and "they say that he is a worthy gentleman, very kind
and very well situated."[42]   Fray Manuel de la Madre de Dios,
Bustamante's nephew, wrote from Mexico, saying that there were
many people from Vera Cruz in Campeche and that they all
"spoke of the ineptitude of Sor. Urrutia for commanding" and
related some of the celebrated passages he had written when
he was "governor intendant" of the province of Vera Cruz.[43]
Valle doubtless had traversed several times the distance between
these extremes.   In the end he nearly talked himself into believing
that Bustamante was not leaving at all.   "Time has been disabus-
ing us; and all have seen that the order to turn over the command
to the Sub-Inspector has not come, that Bustamante continues on,
and that everything has not been so certain as claimed."[44]

Time also disabused Valle of his wishful thinking.   On March
28, 1818, Bustamante, who had received Guatemala "in a state
of perfect tranquillity,"[45] turned over the Kingdom, whose tranquillity he had preserved, to Carlos Urrutia, sixty-five and in
failing health.   Bustamante took leave of the capital on April
4,[46] bound for Mexico,[47] Havana, and ultimately for Spain, and
he was as happy to depart from Guatemala as many Guatemalans
were to see him go.   Writing from Cuba, in good spirits, he
expressed satisfaction that his delayed journey and three-month
stay outside of Havana had restored his "health and strength"
in a manner that caused all to marvel, but especially those who
viewed his existence "sorrowfully."[48]   In February, 1819, he

41. AGG, A1.2.5, 25305, 2835. Correspondencia del ayuntamiento de Guatemala,
año 1817. A copy of the letter, over the signature of Bustamante and dated
August 13, 1817, was sent to the town council.
42. Joaquín Arechavala to Valle, March 18, 1818, León, Valle Papers.
43. To Valle, Campeche, July 12, 1818, Valle Papers.
44. To José Simón de Castroviejo, Jan. 18, 1818, Valle Papers.
45. Torres Lanzas, ed., *Independencia de América,* II, 483.
46. Valle to Gregorio de Castriciones, June 18, 1818, Valle Papers.
47. Manuel de la Madre de Dios to Valle, Campeche, July 12, 1818, Valle Papers.
48. To Gregorio Urruela, Havana, Feb. 12, 1819, Valle Papers. Bustamante
wrote: "La demora de mi viaje, y la benéfica residencia de tres meses fuera de esta
ciudad han restablecido mi salud y fuerzos en términos que se admiran todos, y
mucho más los que creyeron tristemente de mi existencia."   Urruela gave 4,000
pesos to the *donativo.* See *Gazeta de Guatemala,* Oct. 6, 1808.

boarded a ship bound for Spain, where he awaited the outcome of his *residencia*. (A *residencia* was a thorough but routine investigation that every superior officer had to stand upon leaving a post. It was conducted by a royal official, specially appointed, who reported his findings directly to the crown. If irregularities were disclosed, the crown prosecuted; if the record were clean, the superior officer was protected against future charges and innuendos based on a previous tour of duty.) Bustamante emerged from this review of his term with flying colors. Soon he was flying the flag of the Minister of the Navy, a resounding reward for a loyal subject.[49]

Bustamante's ship probably had not dropped Cuba below the horizon, however, before his "evil-wishers" began to spread the rumor that ship, crew, passengers, and Bustamante had gone to a watery grave.[50] And following the departure of the "true Spaniard,"[51] Valle's home became the wailing wall for those who mourned the departure of that "great chief"[52] and the clearing house for complaints against the mistreatment of Bustamante's friends and against the new government. Chief of operations was "Friend Valle, who is the one who is working in connection with what happens to us." He "will have communicated to you [Bustamante] that most worthy of your attention."[53] Letters of condolence to Valle, praise for Bustamante, and charges against

49. José Simón de Castroviejo, León, Jan. 19, 1819, Valle Papers. Castroviejo was reporting that he had heard a rumor that Bustamante had received the appointment. Later, Valle sent information to his friends concerning Bustamante's fortune. Mariano Murillo wrote (to Valle, León, March 19, 1820. Valle Papers); "Aprecio las noticias que me comunica celebrando la distinción y aprecio, que se ha hecho del Sor. Bustamante quien la merece justamente." Also see Salazar, *Historia de veintiún años,* p. 200.

50. Mariano Murillo to Valle, León, Oct. 4, 1819; Joaquín Arechavala to Valle, Oct. 18, 1819, Valle Papers.

51. Valle Papers. The following comes from a rough draft of a note that Valle probably submitted or intended to submit in behalf of Bustamante during his *residencia*: ". . . fué verdadero español, amante de su Rey y de la Península donde nació; y a excepción de los malquerientes que es preciso tengan los que manden . . . en época de tanto calor y fermentación, de tanto extravío y error, podría probar, que su conducta privada y pública fué intachable y digno de elogio."

52. Ramón Lagos to Valle, Choluteca, Oct. 1, 1818, Valle Papers.

53. Valle to Bustamante, May 18, 1819. Valle was writing for someone who had lived in Guatemala for "forty years" and who had been *alcalde* and *regidor* "several times," serving in the *ayuntamiento* during the *tiempo más crítico*. This information leads to the assumption that he was writing for Sebastián Melón, who refused to sign the instructions, who had been singled out by Bustamante for not signing, and who was *alcalde* of the *ayuntamiento*. In writing the letter, Valle first stated that Melón had lived in Guatemala fifty years but then changed it to forty.

Urrutia began to arrive before Bustamante was out of the Kingdom and continued into March, 1820. "Each day, Amigo, we
miss the presence of Bustamante more and more";[54] "Here [León]
it is thought that Sor. Bustamante is Minister of the Navy";[55] "I
have seen the news which must be of great satisfaction for Bustamante and of *contusión* for his many enemies";[56] "I always believed false the news of the re-baptism of the passengers of the
frigate *Sabina,* on which Señor Bustamante had passage";[57] "I
have learned with pleasure that he has been decorated with the
Gran Cruz de San Hermenegildo."[58]   And Valle's friend, Colonel
Joaquín Arechavala, was convinced that a "statue should be
erected in this Kingdom" of Bustamante.[59]   A note from Valle's
hand will serve as an inscription for the statue (which will be
completed about the same time as the one of Theodore Roosevelt
in Colombia):

> El Excmo. Sr. D. José Bustamante y Guerra was president of this
> Kingdom from March, 1811, until the same month of 1818.   During
> such a critical period, he knew how to rule . . . to meet such extraor-
> dinary circumstances.   Vigilantly, he tried to maintain it [the King-
> dom] in peace and tranquillity, and he worked to achieve this objec-
> tive, the one uppermost in his preoccupations, to the point of breaking
> his health, which was vigorous when he came to the Kingdom and
> debilitated when he left.   He made authority respected . . . supported
> with firmness the cause of our King, which was so opposed in that
> time . . . , and upheld religion, prohibiting anything that could
> upset the throne or the altar.[60]

A lampoon that made the rounds in the capital hinted at one
of the main reasons why Valle and the other friends of Bustamante longed for the "pure Spaniard."   Valle addressed to
Bustamante a "Diario de diversas incidencias ocurridas en los

54. José Simón de Castroviejo to Valle, León, Jan. 4, 1819, Valle Papers.
55. *Ibid.,* Jan. 19, 1819.
56. Ramón Lagos to Valle, Choluteca, Oct. 1, 1818, Valle Papers.
57. Mariano Murillo to Valle, León, Oct. 4, 1819, Valle Papers.   Murillo wrote:
"Siempre creí que era falsa la noticia del rebautimiento de la tripulación de la
fragata *Sabina* en que iba el Señor Bustamante.   Ya V. conoce que todos los
hombres, según la situación en que nos hallamos, tenemos otros enemigos.   Yo
sabía que había llegado felizmente el expresado Señor antes de recibir su anterior,
y ahora lo he visto en la gaceta de 20 de abril que me cita."
58. Joaquín Arechavala to Valle, Oct. 18, 1819, Valle Papers.
59. *Ibid.,* March 18, 1818.   Writing of the imminent arrival of Urrutia, Arechavala
remarked: ". . . juzgándole un digno sucesor de nuestro amado el benemérito
Exmo. Sor. Dn. José de Bustamante (a quien debía erigírsele una estatua en este
Reyno)."
60. Valle Papers.   The quotation comes from another rough draft of a report
that Valle probably submitted or intended to submit in behalf of Bustamante.

meses corridos de Septiembre de '18 a Febrero" in which the following appeared:

On October 7, the following pasquinade was found on the house of Perales: "to . . . those disturbers of the peace, Valle and the ex-inquisitor Martínez [Bernardo]. The people ask D. J. del V., isolated in his home without mixing in anything, not to commit any crime other than that of communicating with the Commissary of the Holy Office, B. M." The offensiveness of this is that it has been assumed that he [Valle] has instituted proceedings in connection with the incidents of the Monja Aycinena. Though it is not true, it is supposed that he is favorably disposed toward the Commissary. This is only a manifestation of the hatred for him and the aversion for the Holy Office.[61]

The key to Valle's misery, which was greater after the departure of Bustamante than at any previous time, was the phrase that began: "isolated in his home." Grammatically unrestrictive though it is, the phrase was of utmost significance for Valle, and his correspondence illumines the full meaning. Writing to Gregorio de Castriciones, Valle laconically reported that "the new president took possession last March" and that "D. Manuel Pavón received him and continues in close relations with him. D. Ignacio Palomo, a relative of nearly all these families, is the *director secreto*."[62] A year later, on May 18, 1819, Friend Valle, this time writing to Bustamante but for someone else, noted that Francisco de Paula Vilches, charged with conducting Bustamante's *residencia*, had arrived (April 11, 1819) and had come from Havana "with the ex-deputy of the Cortes, D. Antonio Larrazábal and D. Antonio Batres y Nájera." And Valle must have been ill to the point of retching when he learned that "Manuel Talavera" also enjoyed the confidence of Vilches.[63] A month later Valle, writing to Bustamante for the same person, acidly noted that Talavera, the Palomos (Domingo, Antonio, and Ignacio), Larrazábal, and

61. Valle Papers. For information concerning Teresa Aycinena, see Chinchilla Aguilar, *La inquisición en Guatemala*, pp. 175-176.
62. June 18, 1818, Valle Papers. Manuel Pavón, brother of Bernardo, whom Bustamante refused to recommend for archdeacon, had been elected to the Junta Central.
63. Valle Papers. Valle, probably writing for Melón, stated: "El 11 del próximo anterior llegó a ésta el Sr. Regente Francisco de Paula Vilches, comisionado en primer lugar para la residencia de V.E. Vino desde Havana con el ex-diputado de cortes D. Antonio Larrazábal, y D. Antonio Batres y Nájera y le recibió en el público el Oidor Moreno. No asiste todavía a la audiencia, ni ha abierto aún la residencia. Ignoramos lo que será; pero vemos con sentimientos que el sugeto de sus confianzas es hasta ahora el agente fiscal D. Manuel Talavera y que éste y otros enemigos de V. E. son los que rodean."

other "individuals of these families absolutely surrounded" Vilches.[64] Writing for himself, Valle brought into sharper focus the picture of colonial politics: "The influence in the palace of said Pavón is without doubt. There is evidence from several negotiations that prove it. The new president has made cadets of the sons of the same Pavóns and of some of the Aycinenas." And Urrutia, according to Valle, had awarded the commissions extralegally.[65]

Valle, who had basked in the favor of González and Busta-mante, was agonizingly aware that he had failed to make the transition to Urrutia, who was hemmed in and hermetically sealed off by a Talavera, the Pavón family, the Aycinena family, Larrazá-bal, and the Palomos. These were some of the people who had failed to gain favor with González and Bustamante, and when Urrutia was appointed, they made a successful bid for favor by surrounding him as soon as he arrived. And when the evidence is all in, we most likely will find that a stream of letters were flowing from the Pavóns, Aycinenas, and others of "these families" to Urrutia before he ever boarded the *Hermosa Catalina*.

The important point of the struggle, however, was not that Valle lost and that his enemies won but rather that it laid the basis for the first political parties in Central America. And owing to the fact that these parties soon became involved with inde-pendence, the notion that the issue of independence was the main source of enmity separating "these families" from Bustamante and Valle has clouded a political quarrel as undignified as any in this country for the spoils of office. But to mention inde-pendence as a serious issue, in 1818, is to distort the objective of Valle's enemies. And the argument that would make patriots of some of the men who surrounded Urrutia or who had opposed Bustamante because they were to become leaders after independ-ence carries no more validity than a claim that Valle worked for independence because he figured so prominently afterward.

The idea of independence, however, did cross Valle's mind in 1818. He reported to Gregorio de Castriciones that Urrutia had "manifested desires for free trade" and that some members

64. Valle Papers.
65. Diario de diversas incidencias ocurridas en los meses corridos de Septiembre de '18 a Febrero, Valle Papers. Valle claimed that Urrutia had invested the com-missions "sin practicar su recepción las diligencias que previene la ordenanza."

of the town council and the Consulado had encouraged him. Valle warned that if Urrutia did not enforce "the laws that prohibited it, the commerce with the Peninsula will cease, its relations with America will be cut off, and the independence of this Kingdom will be prepared."[66]

In 1818, however, the most important result for Valle of the political race for Urrutia's favor was that all of those who had been Bustamante's friends (*adictos*) "lived retired and [were] reduced to talking with each other."[67] Unhappy, miserable, and the target of lampoons, which sprang from the "phlegmatic temperament of these countries,"[68] Valle doubled his efforts to leave, and he prevailed upon Castriciones to supplicate Bustamante, when he arrived in Cádiz, "to get me out of this country and bring me to that one with any job." Tell him, Valle implored, "that you will handle all the expenses at my cost and that this horizon is more doleful each day."[69] These were the words of a man who desperately wanted to leave Guatemala, but what he sincerely wanted was to leave with the ever-elusive toga of an *oidor*.

[5]

Since he had received the frustrating setback that Díez y Tovar explained in his letter of December 1, 1814, a royal order to the Council of Castile had put Valle in contention for any vacancy that might occur in an *audiencia* in Spain.[70] Díez y Tovar

66. June 18, 1818, Valle Papers. Whether owing to Urrutia's alleged desire for free trade or for other reasons, Guatemala's coasts, if we can believe Valle's notes, were not so well guarded after the departure of Bustamante. Writing, probably for Melón, Valle stated: "Un año ha que V. E. [Bustamante] salió de este Reino; y en tan corto tiempo son tantas las mutaciones que no es posible referirlas en una breve carta. El contrabando se ha aumentado extraordinariamente: el comercio de la metrópoli se ha destruido casi enteramente: los corsarios que en el Gobierno de V. E. jamás insultaron nuestras costas, ahora han tenido el atrevimiento de entrar en la boca del San Juan, primero, luego Sonsonate, después Realejo y últimamente en Omoa, apresando dos barcos en San Juan, uno en Sonsonate y cuatro en el Realejo." See Valle (for Melón ?) to Bustamante, no date (April, 1819), Valle Papers.
67. Valle to Gregorio de Castriciones, June 18, 1818, Valle Papers.
68. Valle to (?), June 18, 1818, Valle Papers. The document is a rough draft of a letter, but there is no indication concerning the destination. It was not intended for Castriciones, for the letter included many things that Castriciones already knew.
69. Valle Papers.
70. Antonio Díez y Tovar to Valle, Madrid, July 25, 1815, Valle Papers. Díez

assured that he would guard Valle's interests "until the day."
"Would to God that it's in Granada" where the "land is beautiful,"[71] he teased Valle, who upon reading the letter must have
paused a moment to imagine himself in historic Granada, walking
the roads of the Romans, admiring the architecture of the Moors,
corresponding, even chatting, with the scholars of the Old World,
and "reading, writing, and enjoying the life I long for."[72] But
the months ahead were not encouraging, and then came the
dismal letter from Díez y Tovar: "They still have not announced
the vacancy that they told me would occur in Granada, but—"[73]
And Valle once more was left dangling on promises to push his
candidacy, and his reaction must have been forceful and to the
point, for Diéz y Tovar stressed that Valle had insisted, against
all advice, to seek a place in Spain; consequently, he would have
to suffer the frustration pointed out in advance.[74]

Doggedly, Valle persisted in his efforts, and he even choked
down some of his pride when he wrote to Juan Gualberto González, who had played violin in Campuzano's orchestra before
departing for Spain, asking him to make his influence available.[75]
González was somewhat surprised that Valle wanted to leave
"that Ethiopia, as you call it," and he told Valle very frankly that
he would have a better chance of securing an appointment if he
came to Spain and acted as his own agent. The respect for
recommendations coming from America, "for and against," had
"fallen a great deal." Besides, there were an "infinite number
with the same recommendations" that Valle possessed, and the
Council of Castile always preferred to appoint one of the in-
numerable persons known personally. Since many of these same
people were "without a job and with a salary," they were high
on the list. "I would like to see you here, but if you expect
to be appointed in the Peninsula as a result of my influence, I

y Tovar wrote: "Tengo la satisfacción de que se ha comunicado orden a la Cámara
de Castilla para que sea Vm. colocado en plaza togada de la Península." The order
was given on June 15, 1815. See Polo recommends Valle, Sept. 12, 1819, Valle
Papers; ABNH, Títulos y méritos.

71. Madrid, July 25, 1815, Valle Papers.

72. Valle to (?), June 18, 1818, Valle Papers. Valle was writing about his plans
to go to Spain, and he fancied that it would be pleasant "leer, escribir, y gozar la
vida que apetezco."

73. Madrid, Sept. 24, 1816, Valle Papers.

74. Madrid, Jan. 24, 1817, Valle Papers.

75. González acknowledged (Madrid, April 24, 1817, Valle Papers) Valle's letter
of Aug. 18, 1816.

tell you that I have no connections to offer you."[76]   The ratio, "10,000 to 1," must have flashed through Valle's mind, but driven by frustration and bitterness, he felt that the odds were unimportant and again wrote to González,[77] whose second reply revealed that Valle was so determined to go to Spain that he was thinking of selling his haciendas.[78]

On November 24, 1817, Díez y Tovar disclosed the extent of the predicament causing Valle's frustration.   The order had gone out putting Valle in contention for an appointment in an *audiencia* in the Peninsula, but Díez y Tovar was in the difficult position of "desiring vacancies and looking for the means of securing the title of *oidor*."   Valle, consoled Díez y Tovar, was "experiencing the miserable life of the suppliant."[79]   Undismayed by the difficulty and goaded on by Bustamante's departure, Valle wrote, in June, 1818, that his first wish was to go to Spain, but while he was awaiting an appointment, he would accept with pleasure the post of "*oidor, alcalde de crimen,* or fiscal in the *audiencia* in Mexico."   But if he did not receive a position in the Peninsula "in the coming year [1819]," he would go to Spain without one. "My patience is nearly exhausted."[80]

In 1819 he asked for and received an excellent recommendation from Serrano Polo, who commended Valle for his loyalty, talent, and capacity for work.   But he received a disheartening letter in February, 1820: "If you solicit or wish anything from the court [Spain], it is necessary to find another agent, because a certain Tovar isn't worth anything, except for asking for reales; he works for the government."[81]   After nearly thirteen years, this brash note apparently ended Valle's attempt to secure a position in an *audiencia* in Spain.

76. González to Valle, Madrid, April 24, 1817, Valle Papers.
77. On July 3, 1817.
78. González to Valle, Madrid, Dec. 29, 1817, Valle Papers.   González wrote: "Me parece atrevido el pensamiento de vender sus fincas para trasladarse acá o a otras partes."
79. To Valle, Madrid, Valle Papers.
80. Valle to (?), June 18, 1818, Valle Papers.   Valle wrote: "La copa de la paciencia se va llenando."
81. (?) to Valle, Cádiz, Feb. 3, 1820, Valle Papers.

[6]

While Valle mourned the transfer of Bustamante and failed in his efforts to get out of Guatemala, he also was having trouble with his haciendas, "Santa Bárbara," "Ola," and "San José."[82] These were the acres that were making Valle wealthy. In December, 1813, and January, 1814, he sold 604 head of cattle,[83] and two years later he had 300 head at "San José" and 180 at "Ola."[84] However, in 1816, the cheese making was behind schedule, because all the hands had come down with the *peste:* "Some of them died." In the same letter, the foreman, Juan José Pinel, reported that the Negro slaves, though they were well behaved, were of little value in the field, because they did not understand such work. But they had taught him an "easy way to kill coyotes," and as soon as he tried it, he would tell Valle the results.[85] In June, 1819, Juan José had worse news. "This year has been bad for all the haciendas on this coast [Pacific]." The "pest of murrain, the barrenness of the fields, [and] the lack of rain" had resulted in the death of 186 head of cattle.[86] Six months later Valle learned in addition that the 150 head of cattle that he had bought in October, 1819, were not the ones that were delivered.[87]

This gloomy picture must have changed during the next three years, for in April, 1822, Valle bought a large hacienda near Chiquimula, in the province of Guatemala. "La Concepción" covered more than 3,000 acres, and with equipment and livestock, cost Valle 10,000 pesos.[88] And his reminder to himself that he could increase the income from "La Concepción" by reducing expenses and stepping up production was sufficiently simple to suggest a note of apprehension concerning the obligation that he

82. Arechavala to Valle, León, June 2, 1815, Valle Papers. Colonel Arechavala, commenting on his own haciendas (he had six in Guatemala, some of which he had not seen for fifteen years, and four in Spain) mentioned the three that Valle owned.

83. Razón de las partidas de novillas que vienen de haciendas en diciembre de 1813 y enero de 1814, Valle Papers.

84. Juan José Pinel to Valle, Choluteca, May 31, 1816, Valle Papers.

85. *Ibid.*

86. *Ibid.*, June 1, 1819.

87. AGG, A1.20, 39054, 4562. Obligación escrita entre José del Valle y José Antonio García Zelaya, sobre la venta de una partida de novillas.

88. AGG, A1.20, 9964, 1484, fol. 5. Libro de escribano José Antonio de Solís. The sale was registered on April 30, 1822.

had contracted.[89]   Under normal circumstances a transaction of this magnitude would be concluded only after serious reflection and then with some misgivings, but the year 1822 was a troubled year, and Valle well might have contemplated even more the wisdom of his action.   Between 1818 and April, 1822, Guatemala, from the Isthmus of Tehuantepec to Panama, became independent from Spain, passed through four chaotic months of freedom, and then surrendered to rumors and became a part of Mexico.

[7]

As the colonial period drew to a close, Valle agreed with Canon Bruno Medina that "this Kingdom is a place of banishment" *(un destierro)*, and Valle's plans were to go to Spain, where he, at the suggestion of Medina, could "enjoy the good climate of Europe," free from all the "capricious people"[90]—people such as those who had denied him the title of lordship and who had contested his "place of preference."   And when he read an invitation from some of these same people to assist the town council in "solemnizing" the "annual passing of the royal standard," we can only guess at his thoughts.[91]   His overwhelming desire to leave Guatemala, however, was certain, and in 1818 he had reached the point of thinking of selling his haciendas and going to Spain without employment.   But he preferred to go as an *oidor,* and he watched the "sons of Guatemala—beardless children"[92]—receiving royal appointments while his own hopes were shattered and his buoyant confidence changed to resentful bitterness.

His only happiness and moments of contentment during the last years of the colony came when he escaped into the bosom of his family, but even then the paralytic bitterness crept in, and he could write that "Larreinaga and the oldest son of Barrio have left for that place [Spain].   I envy his fortune, but I do not de-

89. Valle Papers.

90. Bruno Medina to Valle, Danlí, Oct. 16, 1819, Valle Papers.   Canon Medina was the one member of the *diputación* that received Bustamante's approval (Report on the members of the diputación provincial, Valle Papers).

91. AGG, A1.2.2, 15745, 2194.   Libro de cabildos de Guatemala, año 1819.

92. Valle to (?), June 18, 1818, Valle Papers.   Valle wrote: "Los hijos de Guatemala, niños imberbes, están casi todos colocados; y yo no lo estoy después de trabajo, y sacrificios."

spair to follow his path. I wish to learn, and if I aspire to a position it is to facilitate the trip [to Spain] and to leave honor and *mont[epio?]* to the two little ones that I have."[93]   He also tried to escape by burying himself in his study.   In February, 1818, he received five boxes of books from Gregorio de Castriciones.   "They are good ones, and I have had moments of pleasure."[94]   And Dionisio de Herrera replied, in June, 1819, to a letter: "I received your profound reflections concerning a universal language.   They are worthy of the most serious thought."[95] Valle also had read widely, and with pleasure, in the field of economics, but whenever the tenets of that discipline carried the reader into the labyrinth beyond the bounds of royal authority or threatened the bond between crown and colony, he proceeded with circumspection and warned against the consequences for Spain of free trade.   Thus in every respect, he had earned Bustamante's compliment: "well-deserving subject."[96]   But there was no escape from the fact that Bustamante was gone, that Valle had not received the desired royal appointment, that the sons of Guatemala—the families of the capital—surrounded Urrutia, and that the horizon of "that Ethiopia" became more doleful each day.

93. Valle to (?), June 18, 1818, Valle Papers. Doubtless Valle referred to José del Barrio. Larreinaga apparently did not return until August, 1821. See Salazar, *Historia de veintiún años,* p. 230.
94. Valle to Gregorio de Castriciones, June 18, 1818. The books were mailed from Spain on February 23, 1818.
95. To Valle, June 16, 1819, Valle Papers. It is possible that Valle's interest in a universal language came from Villa Urrutia. See Lanning, *Enlightenment,* p. 31.
96. "Vasallo benemérito," wrote Bustamante. See Bustamante to José de Alós, Secretario Interino de Estado y del Despacho Universal, Madrid, Nov. 13, 1819, Valle Papers.

F I V E

The Year of Decision,
1820

[*1*]

Throughout 1819 and into the following year, anticipation of a life in Spain still teased Valle's fancy, and if in his reveries he saw himself supervising the last trunk of belongings aboard a frigate bound for Spain, he at least gained some relief from the "days of mortification" visited upon him by the biting squibs circulating throughout the colony.[1] He of course agreed that he would be worth "one hundred per cent more"[2] in Spain, where he would be appreciated and "rewarded for his continuous services in behalf of king and country."[3]

Still, on the periphery of his anticipation—which had come to be the answer to all his problems—he began to feel the pinch of parting from friends that the journey promised. He was close to Mariano Murillo, who wrote: "You already know that your trip will be grievous to me, because I had counted on your kindness for the education and instruction of my little Mariano."[4] Separation from cousin Dionisio de Herrera, who probably was closer than anyone outside Valle's immediate family, would be even more grievous for Valle. Their friendship extended into intimate family affairs, including a candid and friendly discussion of the trouble that had separated their fathers.[5] And of Valle's correspondents, outside his immediate family, Dionisio was the only

1. Valle to (?), June 18, 1818, Valle Papers.
2. Juan Gualberto González to Valle, Madrid, Dec. 29, 1817, Valle Papers.
3. Mariano Murillo to Valle, León, Sept. 19, 1819, Valle Papers.
4. *Idem* to *idem*, Oct. 19, 1819.
5. Dionisio de Herrera to Valle, Aug. 17, 1812, Valle Papers.

one to write to Valle using the familiar forms of the language. Thus Valle's invitation to Dionisio to share the joy of a journey to Spain was both sincere and natural.[6] The about-face of Peninsular politics, however, cooled Valle's ardor; he must needs consider adjustments that might make life in America more pleasant.

[2]

In March, 1820, Ferdinand VII, forced by a revolution aimed at royal absolutism, re-established the Constitution of 1812. Later that spring, when the news arrived in America, the colonists in the Kingdom of Guatemala stood at the same threshold through which they had passed in 1812. Everything was as it had been—constitutional guarantees, elected town councils and provincial deputations, elected representatives to the Cortes in Spain, and executive authority vested in a monarch. There was, however, one great difference in Guatemala; ailing Urrutia had replaced the stern hand of the "great chief" at the helm. There would be no authoritative opposition to the basic law.

Guatemala responded quickly to the new freedom, and vague lines of two political groups commenced to form. Each group, in the beginning, had a newspaper for a rallying point. *El Editor Constitucional,* the first of the two papers founded in 1820, was conceived in periodic meetings (*una tertulia*) of "liberal Spaniards and creoles" in the home of the Señor Canon Doctor José María Castilla. Those who attended were Juan and Manuel Montúfar, Marcial Zebadúa, José Barrundia, José Beteta, Vicente García Granados, two artillery captains, and the Doctor Médico Pedro Molina. Manuel Montúfar, employed in the secretariat of Urrutia, was the logical person to report the news. Dr. Pedro Molina agreed to write the section devoted to "physical and moral education," and the columns under the title "Variedades" were charged to José Barrundia, Canon Castilla, and the other members.[7]

6. *Idem* to *idem,* Oct. 8, 1816.

7. Pedro Molina, "Memorias acerca de la revolución de Centro-América, desde el año de 1820, hasta el de 1840" (hereafter "Memorias"), *Centro-Americano,* XIII (April, Sept., 1921), 278. The writer is indebted to Señor José Luis Reyes, former Librarian of the Sociedad de Geografía E Historia de Guatemala for permission to use this fragment of Molina's "Memorias," which were first published some time

The newspaper of the second group was *El Amigo de la Patria,* whose origin appears to have been prompted by the need to balance the views expressed in *El Editor* and to serve as an organ of expression for those opposing the group that included Barrundia and Molina. A report submitted to the crown by the treasurer, who later refused to accept independence, sheds some light on the conception of *El Amigo.* "The good Spaniards, realizing the danger and aware that the Constitution aided in many ways the disloyal ones, tried to establish another newspaper with the name *El Amigo de la Patria* that should oppose the first one." But its principal author, with as much talent as dissimulation, finally became the owner of the paper, and he followed the impulses of his disposition, also sowing with skill "the seeds of independence."[8] The principal author was José del Valle, and he well might have combined with others to found a paper opposed to *El Editor,* and in view of the abrupt cessation of outspoken opposition to *El Editor,* Valle probably did assume complete control. But it seems highly implausible that independence was the main issue, or even an important one, in the elections of 1820. The difference between the two groups appears rather to have been nothing more than a continuation of the rivalry for positions of influence and prestige that had begun for Valle during the time of Captain General González. The only change that occurred was that the two groups assumed the dignity of political parties. The Gazistas or Bacos (Drunks) rallied round *El Amigo,* and those who clustered about *El Editor* became known as Cacos (Thieves). The positions sought by each group, whose influence extended beyond the province of the capital, were the seven seats of the provincial deputation, those of the town council of Guatemala City, and the seats in the Cortes in Spain.[9]

---

between 1840 and Molina's death in 1854. For further information concerning the life of Molina, see J. Joaquín Pardo, *Bibliografía del Doctor Pedro Molina* (Colección Documentos, XVI; Guatemala City, 1954).

8. "Guatemala, hace ciento catorce años. Informe (inédito hasta ahora) del Ministro Tesorero de las Reales Cajas de Guatemala, acerca del estado deficiente del erario antes y después del 15 de septiembre de 1821" (hereafter "Informe"), *Anales,* XII (Sept., 1935), 10-11. The report was dated March 11, 1824.

9. Each province was to have a provincial deputation of nine members, two appointed and seven elected. Membership was to be renewed by one-half every two years. See *Constitución Política de la Monarquía Española,* Tít. VI, Capít. II, Art. 325-335. In connection with the seats in the Cortes, the Cacos seemed content to elect one of several Guatemalans who happened, at that moment, to be in Spain. See *El Editor Constitucional,* July 31, 1820.

Valle, it is possible, became the leading candidate of the Bacos as a result of a letter from José Venancio López and José Ignacio Foronda, both residents of the capital but neither a member of the "family." Each was an elector, and along with four others, they would elect the deputies to the Cortes and to the provincial deputation. Valle was at loose ends after the arrival of the news of the revolution in Spain. No longer could he count on the peace and tranquillity that the Peninsula had promised. Nor had he gained the favor of Urrutia that would have given him positions of responsibility and prestige. Thus, when electors López and Foronda explained that they wished to elect a provincial deputy, who possessed all the qualities that the Constitution demanded, and that they had decided on Valle, he accepted. But there was one small item that needed clarification. "We do not doubt your adherence to the Constitution, for if we did we would not have chosen you." However, "three or four persons" had protested. If Valle could give them "some documents" that would prove his "patriotism" and "adherence to the great charter," they quickly could squelch the opposition.[10]   Valle, who became a candidate for the deputation and the town council of the capital, had to supply the proper credentials.

On the same day that López and Foronda wrote, Canon Juan Miguel Fiallos of Comayagua also addressed a letter to Valle that probably caught him about midway in his transition from wishing to leave "that Ethiopia" to becoming a candidate for important local offices. At any rate, Fiallos' letter emphasized the decision that Valle had to make. The cleric had been canvassing Comayagua and the environs in behalf of Valle for the office of deputy to the Cortes, and he wrote to Valle, saying that the people were kindly disposed toward his candidacy. "If it is true, as I have learned, that you are thinking of going to Spain, this commission will not burden you, and our province would rapidly advance if you would take charge of its political interests."[11]   Valle replied in words recalling his withdrawal, in 1809, from the elections for the Junta Central. In 1820, however, his motives were different. The bright, chatty anticipation of going to Spain as an *oidor* had faded and gone glum. He was no longer a bachelor; only a month

10. Sept. 6, 1820, Valle Papers.
11. Comayagua, Sept. 6, 1820, Valle Papers.

before Fiallos wrote, Valle's third child was born, and despite all his unhappiness, he was becoming wealthy. For the moment, then, he would bide his time in Guatemala, and he wrote that the journey was too much for his family and that the short time before the Cortes should meet was not sufficient for arranging his affairs.[12]

Valle's decision to remain in Guatemala might be construed in a manner that suggests that he would be, at best, a perfunctory candidate. But one of the main reasons for his wish to leave was the enmity that existed between him and the families of the capital. They had beaten him after the arrival of Urrutia, but now the elections offered Valle a way to succeed that did not lead him, hat in hand, past grinning Aycinenas, Palomos, and Pavóns to Urrutia. The Constitution, regardless of what he thought of it, reduced the odds to a point where he could compete, and competition with the "sons of Guatemala" had nurtured Valle since the time of Captain General González. In 1820, however, the lines of the opposition included the illegitimate Molina[13] and the one-time fugitive from the garrote, José Francisco Barrundia. They were to give the Cacos excellent support, but who knows what their motives were and whether they led or were led?

[3]

The Cacos, who began publishing their paper on July 24, 1820, drew first blood when Liberato Cauto[14] came out swinging against the Bacos, reviling the egoism and self-interest that inspired their attempt to destroy the freedom of the Constitution. Why were these "filthy harpies" allowed to nest in Guatemala? Why had they come to tear into shreds "with their talons" the "feast of the liberals," spoiling the rest with their "foul droppings?" "Citizens! Do you want to know? Look back at the times;

12. *El Amigo de la Patria*, Nov. 3, 1820. Valle, who undoubtedly wrote part of a reply to charges made against him in *El Editor*, noted that he had been invited to be a candidate, quoting a sentence from Fiallos' letter, and then gave his reason for declining. If Valle did not write the reply, Foronda and López, who signed it, had read Fiallos' letter.

13. Carlos Gándara Durán, *Pedro Molina* (Guatemala City, 1936), p. 16.

14. This in all probability was a pseudonym for Pedro Molina. See Molina, "Memorias," *Centro-Americano*, XIII (April-Sept., 1921), 278.

remember the despotism that a short time ago dominated us. Who were its ministers? Who mourned the day of triumph of Spanish liberty?" These were the people to guard against. *¡Alerta guatemaltecos!* Watch the "serviles" who intend to destroy "beneficent liberalism" by "means of division."[15]

Soon after this assault, Liberato Cauto fired point blank at electors López and Foronda,[16] who were known to be supporting Valle, denuding the reference to "despotism" so that all could see. The Bacos plainly were the party of "Sr. Bustamante, predecessor of our present humane Chief." From this party, composed of "Europeans and creoles," came the "spies and informers" who had been responsible for the "sepulchral silence" that suited only a "despotic and inquisitorial government." This is the party that "nearly exterminated Granada," that "defamed the instructions of Señor Peinada," and that opposed the fulfilment of those "repeated amnesties that the piety of His Majesty inspired in favor of the so-called insurgents of Guatemala [the Belén conspiracy]." In light of this, Liberato Cauto groped to understand how López, who had been imprisoned for complicity in the Belén conspiracy, could support the Bacos. Neither could Liberato Cauto understand Foronda, who also had "suffered arrest, insults, and persecutions" at the hands of Bustamante.[17] But Liberato Cauto's primary target was not López and Foronda; he was only trying to turn them from supporting Valle, whom he derided, not by name, for being Bustamante's minister. And in a footnote, Caco Cauto pointed out the "loud murmurs of disapprobation" heard in the hall when electors López and Foronda put Valle's name in nomination, charging by innuendo that Valle did not adhere to the Constitution.[18]

15. *El Editor Constitucional*, Sept. 18, 1820. Later, however, Molina identified Valle by name as Bustamante's "intimate advisor" in that "despotic government." See Pedro Molina, José Francisco Barrundia, and José Francisco Córdova to Agustín de Iturbide, Nov. 3, 1821, Hernández Dávalos Collection, HD, 14-3, 1450, University of Texas Library. The date of the letter should be November 30, or a date immediately thereafter, for the terminal event mentioned in the letter, occurred on that date.

16. On October 3, 1820, López and Foronda published a reply to Liberato Cauto's essay of September 18, 1820. See *El Editor Constitucional*, Oct. 16, 1820.

17. *El Editor Constitucional*, Oct. 16, 1820.

18. *Ibid.* In the same issue, Liberato Cauto charged that Valle had written the reply that López and Foronda published on October 3, and Cauto addressed Valle: "Oíd esta verdad, hombre obscuro, que hablas por boca de otros y te ocultas." To this and all the other charges, *El Amigo* (Dec. 2, 1820) replied:

These charges threw Valle, López, Foronda, and the Bacos on the defensive, and smarting from such names as ignoramuses, slaves, and harpies, they tried to answer twenty-one separate charges that the angry Cauto had drawn from an arsenal stocked during Bustamante's days. In an attempt to destroy the veil of doubt that Cauto had thrown over their faith in the basic law, they declared their most decided adherence to the Constitution, shaming at the same time the spirit that drove Cauto to calumniate and to promote the spirit of the family. That the Bacos were the party of Bustamante, of course, was ridiculous. "Does a man who ceased commanding, on March 28, 1818, have a party— a man who is no longer chief of these provinces, a man who is absent and who some supposed expatriated in Portugal?"[19]

Foronda, though Liberato Cauto had tried to flatter him, was angered by the charge that he had been arrested, insulted, and persecuted, and he related exactly what Caco Cauto had reference to, blaming Ignacio Larrazábal, brother of the former deputy, for all the trouble.

In 1814 there was a bullfight. I was outside the ring in which they were fighting, behind the retaining wall with Colonel Lagrava. The youths who were on the roof over the seats began throwing fruit rinds and peelings. Francisco Argüello, second secretary of the government, reported this to the owner of the seats, Francisco Rodríguez. He climbed onto the roof, which was made of leather, to scold those who were causing the disturbance. The boys were scared and began running and making the noise one would expect. The people in the seats [below], unaware of the cause, became excited, thinking, some of them, that it was an earthquake and, others, that it was an uprising. Larrazábal (Learn it wise men)[,] Larrazábal believing the latter and supposing that I was the author went to tell Sr. Bustamante.[20]

Bustamante called Foronda in, and he explained everything to the captain general's satisfaction. There had been no arrests, no insults, and no persecutions, only the brother of Antonio Larrazábal running to Bustamante.

In connection with the innuendos aimed at Valle, López and Foronda declared that they were as proud to back him as the

---

"Que cuatro veces al mes un Zoilo insolente
Levante rabiosa una voz impotente.
Yo no oigo sus gritos por el odio formados:
Yo no veo sus pasos en el fango estampados."
19. *El Amigo de la Patria,* Nov. 3, 1820. Though Valle did not sign the answer, he doubtless wrote the sections that applied to him.
20. *Ibid.*

"four provinces, León, Sonsonate, San Vicente, and Tegucigalpa" had been in 1809. That Comayagua now wished to support him for the office of deputy of the Cortes made them equally proud. Caco Cauto, they agreed, however, was correct in reporting that there had been murmurs of disapproval when Valle's name had been put in nomination, but Liberato Cauto, quite understandably, failed to mention that the "loud murmuring" came from a member of the family who was pushing the candidacy of two nephews.[21]

And it was in connection with the family, who supported the Cacos, that Bacos Valle, López, and Foronda struck their most effective blows. In nearly all their arguments, they had referred to the family, implying that the members held a strangle hold on the economic and political life of Guatemala. The term "family," however, was somewhat intangible and did not convey the full meaning that the Bacos desired. To correct this, they published, in a special edition of *El Amigo,* the names of the members of the family, showing their relationship to each other, their occupations, and their salaries. Fifty-nine members with sixty-four positions in government and church and a combined salary of 89,025 pesos were figures that readers could readily grasp. At the head of the family stood José Aycinena, employed in the Council of State in Madrid, at a salary of 6,000 pesos. He was the son of Juan Fermín de Aycinena who, by three marriages, had tied the Aycinena family to the Nájera, Muñoz, and Piñol families, and the children of the marriages had extended the ties to the families Aguado, Aguirre, Asturias, Arrivillaga, Barrio, Barrutia, Batres, Beltranena, Céspedes, Coronado, Croquer, Echeverría, Lara, Larrazábal, Letona, Manrique, Matute, Montúfar, Olaverri, Pacheco, Palomo, Pavón, and Vallecillo. The list included three judges, five mayors, and many other important and well paid officials.[22] These were the families that composed "the family."

21. *Ibid.* Valle probably wrote this section in which he quotes almost word for word a sentence from the letter he received from Fiallos. Fiallos wrote: ". . . nuestra provincia adelantaría mucho si V. tomara a su cargo sus intereses políticos." The following appeared in *El Amigo:* ". . . la provincia adelantaría mucho si V. tomara a su cargo sus intereses políticos." Fiallos could use the possessive form because he and Valle were from that province. Valle simply substituted the definite article.

22. *El Amigo de la Patria,* Oct. 29, 1820. Also see Thompson, *Narrative of an Official Visit,* pp. 521-522; Troy S. Floyd, "The Guatemalan Merchants, the Government, and the *Provincianos,* 1750-1800," *HAHR,* XLI (Feb., 1961), 98.

They were Cacos during the elections of 1820, as the in-fighting shows.

[4]

Baco Mateo Ibarra, official of the Consulado, was accused of and then charged with exercising persuasion beyond the point of prudence in his zeal to elect Valle and other Bacos. His testimony and the reaction it drew show more clearly the political alignment and reveal what likely was the main issue between the Cacos and Bacos.

On November 16, 1820, Ibarra went to Antigua (about twenty-five miles from the capital) to take the baths that his health demanded. The day after he arrived, two weavers asked him whether an answer had been given to the petition asking prohibition of foreign trade, which the weavers of Antigua had submitted to the provincial deputation in the capital. "The question in the street where I met them was a casual one," declared Ibarra, who explained to the weavers that he would "talk about this at Tomás Arroyave's house." That night the two weavers, accompanied by about twenty others, went to Arroyave's house to hear what Ibarra had to say. And Ibarra hastened to add that he had not invited the twenty others.

Soon after the weavers arrived, they asked Ibarra to tell them in whom they could place their confidence in the elections. "The best people," Ibarra replied. All those at Arroyave's house were "men of honor." The weavers were "good men" too. And they should guard against the "spirit of the family"—the family that "always has tried to dominate the elections." This spirit, according to Ibarra, was the "origin of nearly all the obstreperous differences that occur in Guatemala." Now, it was alarming to learn that the family had been taking such measures to win the coming elections that the weavers felt compelled to seek his advice. The juntas in the capital had been public and scandalous. The objective of some had "not been innocent," but the family had not started legal proceedings. "There also have been juntas in Antigua . . . and no case has been made in connection with them." Several members of the family had gone to Antigua in the days preceding the elections for provincial deputy. Isidoro Montúfar and Máximo Coronado, both members of the family, were the ones that worked hardest passing out lists. Still they feared defeat; thus Mayor Máximo Coronado of Antigua began proceedings against Ibarra. This was gross injustice, Ibarra charged, especially in light of the fact that Rafael Montúfar y Coronado had gone to Antigua with Antonio Arrivillaga y Coronado and Manuel Pavón y Muñoz to sway opinion for the Cacos. And "according to general opinion," Ignacio Larrazábal, "exceeding his authority" as sergeant major of the plaza of Guatemala City (salary: 1,000 pesos) dispatched to Antigua "seven dragoons with knives and carbines, doubtless to consummate the scandalous violence that Mayor Coronado lawlessly visited upon me that night." And injured Ibarra added that Pedro Arrivillaga y Coronado was "Colonel of the battalion of dragoons and Manuel Montúfar y Coronado the Adjutant."[23]

Mayor Coronado, of course, challenged Ibarra's testimony, claiming that the meeting at Arroyave's house was something other than a casual visit and discussion: it was part of a deliberate and premeditated scheme to attract the votes of the weavers by promising them that the Bacos would work to cut off textiles coming into Guatemala from Walis (British Honduras).[24] When the weavers arrived at Arroyave's house, they were met by Ibarra, Pablo Figueroa, Manuel Rivera, and Mariano Vides. All present, Ibarra addressed them in effect: "It is necessary that each should reflect on the person that is to be named elector so that he elects those who love their country, who will benefit the poor, and who are God-fearing men." And he asked the weavers to focus their attention on the Bacos *and not the Cacos."* Further Caco Coronado accused Ibarra of inspiring the petition signed by 210 weavers and submitted to the deputation[25] "asking the total ex-

23. AGG, B1.13, 8337, 494. Testimonio de los autos tramitados en la Antigua Guatemala contra los asistentes a la junta celebrada el 17 de noviembre, en casa de Don Tomás Arroyave, convocada por Don Mateo Ibarra, para tratar de la elección de miembros del ayuntamiento de dicha ciudad (hereafter Junta convocada por Mateo Ibarra), Nov. 28, 1820.

24. *Ibid.,* Dec. 13, 1820.

25. In *El Amigo de la Patria* (Nov. 11, 1820), Valle published the weavers' petition, in which they maintained that the textile industry had been nearly destroyed by the imports from British Honduras. The deputation received the weavers' request on November 13, 1820. See AGG, B1.13, 478, 16. Actas de la diputación provincial de Guatemala.

tinction of commerce with Walis." What infuriated the Cacos was not the ridiculous request but that Ibarra had tried to pass off as signatures of weavers those of "tailors, cobblers, barbers, firecracker makers, and of other artisans who have never exercised the function of weavers." "We are assured," Coronado testified, that the only reason that Ibarra favored the extinction of trade with British Honduras was that he had "twenty thousand pesos worth of cotton goods" that he wished to sell at the higher price promised by the prohibition.[26]

In conclusion, Coronado moved in for the kill. With confidence, he explained that in Antigua, where lived men of "true piety," Ibarra's activities were "not so fearful." But in the "villages where the ignorance is so crass and where they believe a charlatan as though he were an infallible oracle," Ibarra's influence was "truly frightening." Coronado, who had been investigating Ibarra's past, was convinced that he was a charlatan. "When he was denounced to me," Coronado continued, "I decided to find out what kind of a man he was—his origin and circumstances. I learned . . . that he was a native American [Indian] from Mixteca, Mexico, and that his last name is Pérez and not Ibarra. But in no document . . . has he presented proof of his Christianity."[27]

Christian or no, Ibarra and the Bacos had won the support of the weavers, as they called themselves when they testified. "Several members of the family," they swore, "made trips to Antigua during the last days before the elections"; everyone knew that the Marquis de Aycinena and his relatives came. But the weavers, wanting nothing to do with the family, had elected electors who were of the same opinion. Concerning the charge made by Coronado that some weaver voted illegally because they were involved in processes that could send them to prison, the weavers supplicated that they be permitted to say, with all due respect, "that our conduct is better than that of Alcalde Máximo Coronado and his confidant, Isidoro Montúfar y Coronado." "We can prove," the weavers continued, "and we would if it were necessary (when we have an impartial judge) that . . . they are in debt to public

26. AGG, B1.13, 8337, 494. Junta convocada por Mateo Ibarra (Dec. 13, 1820). *El Editor* had taken a firm stand in favor of free trade. For example, see the issue for September 18, 1820.

27. AGG, B1.13, 8337, 494. Junta convocada por Mateo Ibarra (Dec. 13, 1820).

funds and that the former has been prosecuted for bootlegging *aguardiente.*"[28]

The rivalry between Bacos and Cacos extended even into the halls where the electors cast their votes for the provincial deputy of the province of the capital. A note to Valle described briefly what happened. The six electors were trying to elect one of the three candidates, but time and again the balloting resulted in three votes for Mariano Beltranena, two for Valle, and one for someone else. A majority was necessary for election, and in an attempt to break the deadlock, a decision was made to confine the voting to Beltranena and Valle. The first ballot resulted in another deadlock: three votes for Beltranena; three for Valle. At this juncture, tempers on short fuse, it was decided to draw lots for the seat, but before the electors could proceed, Mariano Aycinena demanded that they "suspend the act" or exclude "from the drawing Señor Valle," who had not presented "proof of his adherence to the Constitution." Over the protest, the electors continued, drawing the name of Mariano Beltranena,[29] which must have calmed ruffled relative Aycinena. Thus the Cacos won a seat in the provincial deputation, but the Bacos were not left empty handed.

Valle, with the aid of another elector and friend, Dr. Mariano Larrave, won the office of mayor of the town council. According to Molina, Barrundia, and Córdova, Larrave passed around a "handwritten proclamation" among the "ignorant people." The manuscript, Molina and company continued, was aimed at the "family" and attracted the "low class" to the Bacos. Thus Valle became mayor, and in addition, in March, 1821, Mateo Ibarra was elected to the Cortes and Valle to the provincial deputation.[30]

28. *Ibid.,* no date [Dec., 1820]. Pedro Molina ("Memorias," *Centro-Americano,* XIII [April-Sept., 1921], 278-279), verified that the weavers supported Valle. Also see Manuel Montúfar y Coronado, *Memorias para la historia de la revolución de Centro-América* (Guatemala City, 1934), p. 45. Montúfar wrote his memoirs while in exile in Mexico, and they were first published anonymously in Jalapa in 1832. They were popularly known as *Memorias de Jalapa;* hereafter they will be cited in that manner. Montúfar implied that Valle and the Bacos bought the votes.

29. Nov. 18, Valle Papers. The note bears no signature.

30. Molina, Barrundia, Córdova to Iturbide, Nov. 3, 1821, Hernández Dávalos Collection, HD, 14-3, 1450, University of Texas Library. The election for the town council occurred on December 31, 1820, and the winners were announced in *El Editor Constitucional,* January 1, 1821. The election of Ibarra to the Cortes and Valle to the deputation was announced in *El Amigo de la Patria,* March 17, 1821. Also see the congratulatory letters to Valle from Juan Antonio López (Quetzalte-nango, April 7, 1821) and Joseph Tinoco (Comayagua, April 25, 1821), Valle Papers.

[5]

For Valle, the elections of 1820 had provided the means of escaping from a set of circumstances that, in 1818 and 1819, he had found unbearable. Surrounded by enemies and without the favor of Urrutia, he found Spain more attractive than ever before; but then, in 1820, the Peninsula became revolutionary; his retreat in that direction was cut off and he was left at the mercy of his enemies. Juan Joseph Zelaya likely touched on Valle's thoughts. Writing in connection with the possibility that Valle might go to Spain as a deputy, Zelaya suggested that it might be wise, "while the turbulence of the Peninsula is calming, to serve as a substitute [deputy] for those [Guatemalans] who are in Spain, and when the sea is calm, then, if you like, you can go."[31] Valle doubtless agreed with "the old one." On the basis of economics alone, Valle certainly saw the impracticality of selling the haciendas that, by 1813, had made him sufficiently wealthy to retire from his law practice, "not needing the fees for the gracious living of his family."[32] He had not carried out his threat to go to Spain, in 1819, without employment, and the Peninsula in that year was much more attractive to him than in the following. Thus he refused the candidacy for the Cortes. But Valle, who always was miserable when he did not have a hand in government, colonial or republican, was still on the "retired" list and "isolated in his home" as a result of Bustamante's departure. Thus when Valle received an invitation from electors López and Foronda, he accepted with pleasure the chance to become again actively involved in political life, and his enthusiasm spilled over into the columns of *El Amigo*. By September, 1820, then, he had accepted constitutions as a fact of life; there were few other alternatives, and he never considered living in the Germanies, Russia, China, or Ethiopia.

For the Cacos, the elections also offered an opportunity to satisfy personal interests, which probably were as varied as the persons composing that group. It is difficult to imagine that Molina and Barrundia along with Mariano Bedoya[33] and José

31. To Valle, Sept. 4, 1820, Valle Papers.
32. Polo recommends Valle, Sept. 12, 1819, Valle Papers.
33. Bedoya was Molina's brother-in-law.

Francisco Córdova, both stout campaigners for the Cacos,[34] had anything in common with Aycinenas, Beltranenas, and the rest of the family, save a mutual dislike for Bustamante. In view of their past and future, Molina, Barrundia, Bedoya, and Córdova well might have been thinking about independence. But if they were, they were working at cross-purposes with the family, whose main interest seems to have been to protect its traditional positions of influence, while fending off Valle, the traditional and most effective challenger from the provinces. The dislike for Bustamante had little to do with political philosophy but was owing almost entirely to the fact that the family circle did not enjoy his favor. When Bustamante proposed to deny the title of *oidor* to José del Barrio, José Ingenieros Palomo, and Miguel Larreinaga, because of their ties and connections, they wrote that it was a mistake "to suppose that we have opposed the re-establishment of the system of administration of justice of 1808." And when, in point three of their petition, they blamed Valle for Bustamante's actions,[35] they were not engaging in a polemic concerning political ideology. Barrio and Palomo were members of the family, and Larreinaga, though from León, was tied so closely that he took Barrio's eldest son on the grand tour. The family, however, apparently had reason to be angry with Bustamante, who had brought suit for a tax debt of 35,000 pesos[36] against the Aycinenas and who appears to have prosecuted the Beltranenas for smuggling.[37]

Yet certain members of the family never allowed their anger

34. In a complaint from a parish priest and others appears the following: "The foreman of the hacienda . . . that belongs to Julián Batres [a member of the family] called a meeting of all the tenants, and afterward several of these unfortunates have come to me, the parish priest, complaining that they were threatened with the loss of their milpas, with beatings, and with fines if they did not vote for the list that was given to them." The men most responsible were José María Santa Cruz and Mariano Bedoya. The priest also called attention to José Francisco Córdova, "who comes at night." See AGG, B1.13, 8338, 494.

35. Barrio, Palomo, and Larreinaga protest against Bustamante, Valle Papers. For the order establishing the system of 1808, see AGG, B1.9, 00426, 12. Oficio de Exmo. Sor. Capitán General sobre que la Real Audiencia se restablezca el estado del año 1808 (Jan. 16, 1815). A royal decree of June 25, 1814, was the authority for Bustamante's order.

36. Report on the personnel of the *audiencia*, Valle Papers.

37. Salazar, *Historia de veintiún años*, pp. 242-243; José Simón Castroviejo to Valle, Jan. 19, 1819, Valle Papers. Castroviejo, writing about Bustamante, reported a rumor that the "Beltranenas have won their case in every respect," indicating that the case had been initiated before Bustamante departed and suggesting that the favorable settlement was owing to his departure. This might have been the case that Salazar referred to.

to jeopardize their positions by complaining too vigorously against Bustamante. When the members of the town council of 1810, who had signed the instructions given to Deputy Larrazábal, petitioned Ferdinand VII to lift the penalty that barred them from government employment, the Marquis de Aycinena signed the petition, which also was a complaint against Bustamante. But a few days later, he wrote apologizing and withdrawing his name.[38] And the fact that the other signers of the instructions (who almost to a man were members of the family) petitioned to have the penalty removed raises a question. Did they petition Ferdinand to set aside his decision in order that they might participate in a government as absolute as any west of the Oder River? Some members of course did participate without any feeling of revulsion. An Aycinena, José, served in the Council of State in Madrid, while relative Antonio Larrazábal languished in a Spanish prison in behalf of freedom. A Larrazábal ran to tell Bustamante on Foronda, and Máximo Coronado, who doubted Ibarra's Christianity, denounced the same Ibarra as a "revolutionary," claiming that he had been involved in the uprisings in León and San Salvador.[39] And Aycinenas, Palomos, and Pavóns surrounded Urrutia, whom Ferdinand the Desired, had appointed. That Urrutia winked at smuggling, or (to put it politely) free trade, made his relationship with the family congenial. But then a revolution restored the Constitution, and Urrutia, as Jefe Político, had to share important decisions with the provincial deputation. Thus the family not only had to maintain close relations with Urrutia but also needed to put a member in the deputation to protect its interests. And when Beltranena succeeded in capturing a seat, by a lucky draw, the family could relax a bit. With the possible exception of a few members, then, the interest of the Cacos was to serve their own interests, which included keeping Valle "retired" and "isolated in his home."

But the Cacos failed to keep Valle out, and the elections of 1820 demonstrated a second time that aversion for him was confined largely to the family and to those whose political philosophy caused them to view with repugnance the royal absolutism of

38. AGG, A1.30-4, 22002, 2639. Peticiones del ayuntamiento en la residencia contra el Capitán General Bustamante, no date [1818-1819].
39. AGG, B1.13, 8337, 494. Junta convocada por Mateo Ibarra (Dec. 13, 1820).

Ferdinand, as it was expressed in Guatemala by Bustamante. Each time, in 1809 and 1820, that a test of strength occurred, in which all but Negroes could participate, Valle fared well, a fact, however, that can be interpreted either as a sign of protest against the grip of the family on the capital and the capital on the provinces or as a display of genuine confidence in Valle. Doubtless a good deal of both was present in each election.

But the elections were over, and Mayor Valle prepared to present a positive program for the capital that, together with his essays in *El Amigo* and his legal opinions, provide a glimpse of Guatemala immediately before the bonds with Spain were cut.

Mayor of Guatemala City

A Glimpse of Guatemala on the Eve of Independence

[*1*]

With the tedious and frustrating idleness at an end, Valle assumed the office of mayor on January 2, 1821,[1] and for five months the many and varied functions of the town council occupied his time in a manner unknown to him since the arrival of Urrutia. The Constitution of 1812 charged that body with supervision of public health, preservation of public order and maintenance of prisons, administration and investment of municipal funds, care of primary schools, hospitals, and beneficent organizations, upkeep of roads and bridges, and with the promotion of agriculture, industry, and trade.[2] Fresh in spirit and brimming with ideas, Valle sought answers for each of the many problems, and his views on public order and crime and punishment made the reference to the Marquis di Beccaria (1735?-1794) in *El Amigo* more significant.[3]

On January 10, 1821, Valle included in *El Amigo* a brief account of the public execution of a man convicted of murder. He found the spectacle appalling, not only for the grisly details of the execution but also for the fact that he thought that homicide and crimes of violence occurred more frequently in Guate-

1. AGG, A1.2.2, 15747, 2194. Libro de cabildos de Guatemala, año 1821. The first meeting was given to organization of committees, and Valle became chairman of the one on education.
2. *Constitución Política de la Monarquía Española,* Tít. VI, Capít. I, Art. 321.
3. Dec. 2, 1820.

mala City than in other places of equal population. As fiscal, in 1817, he listened to a plea for mercy by the attorney for a woman guilty of murder. Unmoved by the sentiment, Valle explained that her crime was as inhuman as any committed by the most criminal men, and then he lectured the attorney, declaring that "the scandalous butchery" in the capital demanded "exemplary punishment." With each year the violence increased. "When Sor. D. Miguel Batalla was fiscal, only five hundred wounded entered the hospital in a year. Now there are no longer five hundred but eight or nine hundred." Why only during the last week of Lent, Valle continued, forty or so had entered the hospital, and one had gone to the morgue.[4] In connection with the sentence of a man convicted of murder while intoxicated, Valle, with wrathful disgust, wrote that the Ley de Partida, promulgated in thirteenth-century Spain by Alfonso X, condemned intoxicated murderers to only five years banishment on an island, but if "King Dn. Alfonso had known Guatemala and had seen the bloody character of the people," he surely "would have imposed a more severe penalty."[5] But in a "country where the laziness and immorality of the people multiply the excesses," Valle did not find the violence incredible.[6] Neither did he accept it philo-

4. AGG, A1.15, 37774, 4474. Contra María Arriola por homicidio en Gregorio Mendoza. Valle wrote his opinion on March 22, 1817, and concerning the fact that the murderer was a female, he stated: "Se dice que la debilidad del sexo merece equidad; pero es contradicción vergonzosa alegar debilidades en el acto mismo en que se cometen delitos tan inhumanos, de que sólo parecían capaces los hombres más criminosos." The fact that one man went to the morgue came from another case. See AGG, A1.15, 37856, 4479. Contra Rito Orantes por homicidio en José María Fuentes. Valle wrote: "Este ministro ha visto un estado formado por el contador del hospital; y del aparece que en siete corridos desde 16 hasta 23 de febrero último entraron 25 hombres y 16 mugeres y a más de esto un cadáver."

5. AGG, A1.15, 37856, 4479. Contra Manuel Eugenio Lito por homicidio en Miguel Lemús. Lito's attorney tried to secure an easier decision for his client on the basis that he was intoxicated when he committed the murder. On May 30, 1817, Valle wrote: La Ley de Partida que condena a cinco años de destierro en una isla a los homicidios ebrios fué expedida para España en siglo muy diverso del nuestro. Si el Rey Dn. Alfonso hubiera conocido a Guatemala y visto el carácter sanguinario de este pueblo . . . seguramente habría impuesto pena más severa." Valle was not the only person to express such an opinion. A report in *El Editor Constitucional* (February 21, 1821) began: "Guatemala, que por desgracia abriga en el seno de 40,000 almas una plebe libertina y sanguinaria, ve con horror, que sus archivos en lo criminal puedan exceder a los de la Europa entera." After this exaggeration came a more accurate statement: "Por los estados del hospital que obran en el expediente se verá: que en el año '19 hubo 476 hombres heridos, 158 mugeres, 70 soldados, y entre todos 19 muertos. . . . En el de '20 pasaron de 900."

6. AGG, A1.15, 37812, 4477. Sobre la formación de estados y modo de dar cuenta en las causas criminales para que se arreglen a lo dispuesto en la real cédula de 1800. Valle wrote on March 12, 1817.

sophically; he sought to learn the reasons and then tried to remove them.

Idleness and poverty, he thought, were two chief reasons, and he implored the Superior Government to root out the obstacles besetting agriculture, industry, and trade, making available, thereby, the employment necessary for happiness and prosperity. The town council, he wrote, could contribute by facilitating the diversions and recreation that the youth of the capital lacked. Government, however, could not provide all the solutions. Most of the burden should weigh on the backs of the citizens, who could form a society or club dedicated to preventing young people from going astray. If the members of the proposed organization, Valle explained, would take charge of the conduct of a boy when he first showed signs of "giving himself up to vice," the capital would be most honorable and the number of criminals would be less astonishing.[7]

Adult misconduct and crime were vulnerable to the same approach but demanded more stringent measures. In the absence of a police force, Mayor Valle proposed a plan to prevent crime by closer supervision of conduct in the capital. His intention was to subdivide each of the four districts of Guatemala City into sections of three or four blocks. From each section the town council, Valle proposed, should select a citizen of known virtue and integrity to help preserve "order and morality" by reporting to the municipal council all "gambling, drunkenness, and concubinage." These "vigilantes" (*celadores*), however, were to have no police authority.[8]

Valle realized, of course, that even in ideal circumstances there would be wayward ones who would eventually find themselves accused, convicted, and imprisoned for criminal offenses. But society, he insisted, still had obligations to these unfortunates, and the first duty was to insure the accused a speedy trial. Justice, according to Valle, came exceedingly slow in Guatemala. When, for example, he reported the execution in *El Amigo,* he singled out and criticized the delay that had kept justice patiently waiting

7. *El Amigo de la Patria,* Jan. 20, 1821.
8. Valle to the provincial deputation, April 6, 1821, AGG, B1.13, 345, 18. If the deputation answered Valle's request to put his plan in effect, the author was unable to find the reply.

four years.⁹   But he could recall cases from his own career.   In
the Crown *v.* Rito Orantes for the murder of José María Fuentes,
appealed from the muncipal court to the *audiencia,* Fiscal Valle,
with unconcealed disgust, wrote that he should "focus his attention" not on the charge against Orantes but on the tribunal of
the town council, which had proceeded slowly and haphazardly.
That the case was a simple one made Valle more contemptuous.
On September 15, 1814, in the course of a fight, Orantes hit
Fuentes on the head with a machete.   Fuentes died in the hospital on October 7, and finally on March 7, 1815, the tribunal
solicited the surgeon's report concerning the "seriousness of the
wound."¹⁰   The report came in on May 12, 1815, but then "without any reason" the case was suspended.   "The prisoner has not
escaped," Valle noted.   On the contrary Orantes readily admitted
that he had dealt Fuentes the death blow but contended that he
had done so in self defense.   Thus in view of the transcript, a
paltry seventeen pages,¹¹ Valle found the only point beyond
proof was who had started the fight.   The obscurity of the point
in addition to the fact that Orantes already had "suffered two
and one-half years of prison because of the delay in his case"
moved Valle to recommend that the *oidor* of the *sala del crimen*
sustain the sentence of "six years in the Petén prison" pronounced
by the municipal court.¹²   But Valle also recommended that the
oidor reprimand the court for the remarkable delay which it
had evidenced "in the dispatch of criminal cases, especially those
involving violence and murder, which occur so frequently."¹³

9. Jan. 20, 1821. *El Editor Constitucional* (Jan. 22, 1821) also commented on
the execution.
10. In case the wound were made with a knife or machete (and if the weapon
were found), the examining surgeon frequently drew a picture of the weapon, and
if the knife or machete were too long for the page, the picture continued on a
foldout or on the next page. Dr. Esparragosa served as examining surgeon for a
time.
11. AGG, A1.15, 37856, 4479. Valle wrote his opinion on April 14, 1817, and in
connection with the shoddy procedure, he noted: "Desde el auto cabeza de proceso
hasta la sentencia definitiva no se componen la causa más que 17 fojas. . . . Los
testigos examinados no han sido más que tres. Para recibir las declaraciones no ha
sido necesario librar exhortos porque todos son de esta ciudad. El reo no ha
hecho fugo; y no aparece causa alguna de aquéllas que suspenden el curso de
un proceso. Sin embargo, comenzado el presente en 15 de septiembre de 1814, no
se pronuncía la sentencia hasta 27 de marzo próximo anterior [1817]; y se han
empleado dos años seis meses para escribir diez y siete fojas."
12. Valle considered requesting the death sentence.
13. AGG, A1.15, 37856, 4479. Valle wrote: ". . . que se extrañe al Juzgado 2
la notable morosidad con que se ha procedido en la sustanciación en el despacho
de las criminales, especialmente sobre heridas y homicidios que tanto abundan en

After assuring the accused a speedy trial, the judges, Valle thought, had the obligation to impose a penalty that corresponded to the crime. "It is a constant observation of criminologists," he observed, "that excessive severity of punishment produces effects contrary to the objective for which it was employed."[14] In connection with a case in which a young man from the rural area (*un rústico de menor edad*) was convicted of sodomy, Valle wrote that the Ley de Partida demanded the death penalty and that the laws of Castile went further and added by fire. But "capital punishment," Valle wrote, was a "violent remedy," useful only when exercised with "greatest economy."[15] He opposed flogging as an unfair penalty that not only punished the guilty party physically but also degraded him publicly. And confined as it was to the "so-called plebeians," flogging was discriminatory, and everyone, Valle asserted, should be equal before the law.[16]

If the criminal were sentenced to confinement, society and government, Valle thought, were obliged to assure that the prison was fit for habitation and that the food was substantial. Soon after becoming mayor, he discovered that more than forty prisoners depended for their daily sustenance on the meat that could

---

el lugar: que se prevenga al asesor del mismo juzgado la brevedad en que debe despachar dichos asuntos. . . ." In addition he criticized the same court for not imposing sentences that suited the crimes. See AGG, A1.15, 37781, 4474. Contra Mariano Garóz. Garóz was convicted of seven charges, including the wounding of four men, and the tribunal of the *ayuntamiento* sentenced him to two years imprisonment. Valle recommended an additional year. For further criticism of the court, see AGG, A1.15, 37829, 4477. Contra Gaspar Lucho por homicidio en Vicente Pacheco (April 15, 1817).

14. AGG, A1.15, 37619, 4466. Contra José María Flores por arma corta. Flores had been caught carrying a weapon that he had not used, and the court of the *ayuntamiento* sentenced him to two hundred lashes in the public plaza and six years in prison in Havana. In addition, he had been confined eight months while waiting for his trial. Valle thought the penalty was much too severe, and he wrote (June 26, 1813): "Muchos podría discurrirse sobre la sentencia del juzgado; pero basta presentar sencillamente el hecho. Flores es acusado de haber portado una sola vez arma corta. Es dudosa si la portación fué casual o maliciosa; y cierta que no abusó de ella. Por este solo cargo se le imponen tres penas: ocho meses de prisión, 200 azotes en la plaza pública, y 6 años de presidio en los arsenales de la Havana. . . . Es observación constante de todos los criminalistas de juicio que la severidad excesiva de las penas produce efectos contrarios al objeto de su establecimiento."

15. Valle Papers. The citation is to a rough draft of an opinion that Valle doubtless wrote in 1817, though the author was unable to find the case in the Archivo General del Gobierno. Valle wrote: "Capital punishment is a violent remedy, useful only when used with greatest economy, as the criminologists have written . . . after seeing it abused."

be purchased with "four reales."[17]   Moved by their hunger and misery, he declared before the town council that such treatment was inhuman and failed to conform to the laws that stated explicitly that prisons were not for "tormenting prisoners but for keeping them in custody."   Since municipal funds were notoriously limited, he proposed to supplement the diet of the poor prisoners with broth from the head bones of cattle, which yielded substantial nourishment and was very cheap.[18]

Mayor Valle also recognized the danger of confining convicted criminals with those "detained for correction and only for minor offenses," and he proposed to the town council a plan for separating the prisoners.   Limited funds, however, restricted his project to a partition or to the acquisition of an old school building that also had served as the Convento de Santa Clara.   Alderman Pedro Sorogastúa was appointed to inspect the building, and on the following day, he reported that it was unfit for habitation. The town council, however, did set aside 206 pesos for making a more accommodating arrangement for the prisoners.[19]

[2]

In an effort to fulfil every obligation imposed by the Constitution on the town council, Valle made recommendations for industry and agriculture.   In the modern sense of the term, Guatemala had no industry.   The textiles of Antigua, the center of attention during the elections, were a handcraft product.   Mining, once a profitable industry, especially in the province of Comayagua, had long ceased to attract investments.[20]   Valle's purpose, then, was to call attention to the lack of any industry worthy of the name and to suggest what possibilities, in view of the depleted treasury, lay open to Guatemala.   When in March, 1821, the province of the capital elected Baco Mateo Ibarra to the Cortes, Mayor Valle proposed that the instructions from the town council

17. A *real* was the smallest coin in circulation.
18. AGG, A1.2.2, 15747, 2194. Libro de cabildos de Guatemala, año 1821 (February 1 and April 25). Apparently Valle was responding to an act of the Cortes concerning prisons. See *El Editor Constitucional*, April 16, 1821.
19. AGG, A1.2.2, 15747, 2194. Libro de cabildos de Guatemala, año 1821 (January 16, 1821).
20. See Bustamante to the town council, Aug. 19, 1813, AGG, A1.2.5, 25296, 2835; *El Amigo de la Patria*, March 17, 1821.

to Ibarra should include a statement about the ease with which paper mills and glass and dye factories could be established.[21]

Agriculture, however, was and always had been the main source of wealth, but in the eighteenth century agriculture had begun to decline. The Consulado had been warning of the decline and, in 1817, reviewed the dismal developments that pointed toward disaster. About 1750 Guatemala lost the "source of her ancient wealth" when she lost her cacao trade. Cargoes of cacao had gone from the ports of Omoa and Trujillo, on the Gulf, to Mexico, Spain, and then to all Europe and from the ports on the Pacific to Peru and the rest of South America. Peru and Mexico, however, began cultivating cacao, and their competition netted them Guatemala's trade. Fortunately the demand for indigo offset, at least in large part, the loss from cacao, but by 1817, the indigo trade, the only source of wealth, was in extreme decline, and the Consulado, to save the trade from absolute ruin, felt impelled to inform the Superior Government of the causes and to suggest a remedy. The causes for the decline were many. The distance from the ports, the poor roads, the periodic locust plagues, and Spain's continuous wars had contributed immeasurably. But as long as Guatemala had remained one of the primary sources of indigo, the simple expedient of raising prices had offset the additional costs imposed by these obstacles. There were years in which Guatemalan indigo had "sold for forty reales a pound" in Spain,[22] and a harvest of 1,100,000 pounds had not been unusual. Recently, however, the sale of indigo at almost any price was well-nigh impossible. The warehouses in Cádiz and Guatemala were full to overflowing, and at prices of "six and seven reales" per pound few cared to buy. The English, with their indigo from the east, had captured the market. In order to stave off complete ruin by competing successfully with the English, the Consulado recommended a reduction of the taxes on indigo, which amounted to nearly 30 per cent.[23]

21. AGG, A1.2.2, 15747, 2194. Libro de cabildos de Guatemala, año 1821 (March 20, 1821). Also see *El Amigo de la Patria*, August 22, 1821.

22. AGG, A1.5, 1273, 51. El Real Tribunal del Consulado, sobre fomentar la agricultura, industria y comercio (hereafter El Consulado sobre fomentar la agricultura), April 15, 1817. This price seems extremely high. See Robert S. Smith, "Indigo Production and Trade in Colonial Guatemala," *HAHR*, XXXIX (May, 1959), 200-201.

23. AGG, A1.5, 1273, 51. El Consulado sobre fomentar la agricultura. The Consulado calculated that from the time that a *tercio* of indigo left the "hand of

Valle, who, as fiscal, had read this report from the Consulado,[24] was keenly alive to the depressed state of agriculture, as his actions in the town council and his essays in *El Amigo* show. When he learned that the Cortes was considering the removal of taxes on indigo, he introduced a motion in the town council to supplicate the Cortes also to remove taxes on grain, which Valle considered the most likely substitute for the ruined indigo.[25] Further, with the support of the municipal council, he proposed to request ten thousand pesos from the public funds of Indian towns for subsidizing the cultivation of cereals.[26]

In *El Amigo,* in essays on the value of statistics, he presented information that explained more clearly the reason for the penury of agriculture and industry. "We are in almost absolute ignorance concerning our provinces," he wrote, not knowing the "extent of their areas nor the true positions of the principal places." Even the "plants that grace their surface" and the "minerals hidden in their mountains" were unknown. The "most barbarous countries" had been mapped—"the country of the Hottentots has a map." But "Guatemala after three centuries of what is called civilization still does not have one." "A government," Valle insisted, "that does not know the lands that it rules, the fruits of the land, nor the people who inhabit it, is as a blind person who does not see the house in which he lives."[27] The economic state of a nation was closely related to the success or failure of government, and a statistical profile showing the natural resources would signal the direction leading to prosperity.

---

the laborer" until it arrived at a port of departure on the Gulf the sale price had been raised "twenty-seven and one-fourth per cent," which was to say "more than two reales per pound." The chief complaint, however, was against the four-peso levy on each *zurrón* (214 pounds) of indigo that went to the Indigo Growers' Society. For details of the Society and the basis for the complaint, see Robert S. Smith, "Indigo Production and Trade in Colonial Guatemala," *HAHR*, XXXIX (May, 1959), 194-197.

24. Valle, as fiscal, commented briefly on the report, on May 16, 1817 (AGG, A1.5, 1273, 51).

25. AGG, A1.2.2, 15747, 2194. Libro de cabildos de Guatemala, año 1821 (Jan. 30 and Feb. 1). Valle also saw possibilities for coffee, tobacco, maguey, and cotton. See *El Amigo de la Patria*, June 9 and Aug. 22, 1821.

26. AGG, A1.2.2, 15747, 2194. Libro de cabildos de Guatemala, año 1821. He made the proposal on the basis that an act of the Cortes permitted such a loan and that Ciudad Real had borrowed a like amount for a similar project.

27. *El Amigo de la Patria*, Jan. 20, 1821. Valle was exaggerating. Periodic reports on nearly every aspect of colonial life were forwarded to the *audiencia* and the Council of the Indies by nearly every colonial official, civil and ecclesiastic. Lack of money and royal preoccupation with other matters seems to have been the difficulty rather than a dearth of information.

A statistical survey, for example, of the district of Suchite-péquez showed that "three fourths of the population owned only one third of the land," and closer inspection disclosed that the three fourths were Indians, who were, as Valle put it, "uncultured, ignorant, poor, miserable, nearly savage men." He inferred from these statistics that the Indians lacked the strength and fortitude to struggle longer against the odds favoring the "one fourth," and he proposed to subsidize their strength with education and small parcels of land.[28]

In response to an act of the Cortes aimed at the financial power of the Church, Valle elaborated his remarks, criticizing the ecclesiastic grip on the land of Guatemala. Hardly a "measure of land" he noted with alarm, was free of financial obligation to the Church. To buy an hacienda by simply assuming mortgages held by the Church was not unusual.[29] When Valle bought "La Concepción," he had to pay 2,000 pesos to the Convento de la Merced and 3,000 to the Convento de la Concepción. These mortgages amounted to one-half the sale price.[30] Thus his fears that all the land in Guatemala soon would be in the hands of the "seculars and regulars" were not entirely groundless. He of course recognized the services performed by the Church. "But would it be right for one class to become proprietors of all the land, rural and urban? . . . Would it be right that the persons of the other classes remain reduced to tenants or renters . . . ? Would it be just if the land were not cultivated by the hands of its owner . . .?"[31] Agriculture was the "mother of prosperity,"[32] and in the interest of agriculture, Valle continued, the owners should be the ones who worked the land, the fruit of the land should not be burdened by excessive taxes, land should be parceled out to the Indians, and the Indians should be educated.

28. *El Amigo de la Patria*, May 15, 1821.
29. *Ibid.*, March 23, 1821.
30. AGG, A1.20, 9964, 1484. Libro de escribano José Antonio de Solís (April 30, 1822).
31. *El Amigo de la Patria*, March 23, 1821. Valle of course did not mention that he was an absentee landlord, and he apparently saw no danger in the fact that relatively few families might gain control of most of the land. The Aycinenas, in 1819, had seven estates (Robert S. Smith, "Indigo Production and Trade in Colonial Guatemala," *HAHR*, XXXIX [May, 1959], 186); Valle's friend Colonel Arechavala had six and Valle had three and soon would acquire a fourth.
32. *El Amigo de la Patria*, Oct. 26, 1820.

[*3*]

How to educate the "two-thirds" concerned Valle in the town council and in *El Amigo*.[33] The ever-recurring obstacle, of course, was lack of money, which he well knew, but with characteristic imagination he made the depleted treasury seem less stifling. On February 27, 1821, he introduced in the town council a plan of taxation for the support and expansion of education in the capital. His plan was to levy a direct tax on the head of each family; the amount, however, would vary according to the individual's ability to pay. While some families would pay only one real others would pay ten or more. The advantages of the tax, he emphasized, lay in its simplicity and in the fact that the "income would be fixed or the same each year," allowing the town council to plan more efficiently for the needs of education. Equally important, the new tax would free that part of the regular monies reserved in the past for education for other projects such as the urgent need of more water for the capital.[34]

Education of the Indians presented an obstacle in addition to restricted funds that Valle summed up in the title of a short editorial: "Let's Merit the Confidence of the Indian."[35] He noted the laws forbidding Spaniards and *ladinos* from living in Indian villages, averring, though the laws had been decreed to protect the Indian, that they had failed in their purpose and served only as a "wall of separation," preventing the transfer of culture from the Spaniards to the Indians. Much could be accomplished toward breaking down that wall and inculcating the Indians with Spanish culture by increasing the number of primary schools; demanding that the different societies, organizations, and town councils "always be composed of Indians, Spaniards, and *ladinos*"; and by encouraging "marriage of Indians with other classes."[36]

33. Valle maintained that two-thirds of the population could not read and that one-half of those who could read could not extract square or cube roots (*El Amigo de la Patria*, Jan. 27, 1821).

34. AGG, A1.2.2, 15747, 2194. Libro de cabildos de Guatemala, año 1821 (Feb. 27). Valle also tried to eliminate the expense of hiring tax collectors by prevailing on men of known integrity who would collect the taxes without fee because of their "love of public service." See AGG, A1.2.2, 15747, 2194. Libro de cabildos de Guatemala, año 1821 (Jan. 16, 17, 19, 30; Feb. 6, 9; March 6).

35. *El Amigo de la Patria*, Oct. 26, 1821.

36. *Ibid.*, August 7, 1821.

While Valle was searching for means to expand education, the provincial deputation offended his sense of economy with the proposal to establish the new tribunal (*jueces de letras*) described in an act of the Cortes.[37] These new judges were to be located in municipalities and district seats (*cabezas de partidos*) with an annual salary of 1,500 pesos. As mayor, Valle challenged the intentions of the deputation, and his opposition focused attention on the inadequacies of the capital and the provinces that drove him from morning till night in his quest for means to guard public order and personal safety and to provide sufficient water, passable roads, and primary education.

On February 16 Mayor Valle reported to the town council that he had received notice from the Jefe Político and the deputation of the decision to establish a new tribunal.[38] Earlier, when the decision was still pending, the municipal council had expressed concern and had asked to be heard. But the deputation, "with disdain," not only failed to answer but also did not acknowledge receipt of the dispatch. Now Valle exhorted the town council to sustain the opposition, explaining that the Constitution invested the monarch with the power to appoint the new judges and stipulated that the tribunals should be located at district seats. And Guatemala, he pointed out, was not yet districted in the manner described by the basic law. Thus the decision of the deputation and the Jefe Político not only violated the Constitution but, by so doing, also "encroached on the authority of the mayors."[39]

But conceding legality to the deputation, Valle still argued against the founding of the court, maintaining that the "public treasury" of the capital could not stand an additional yearly drain of 3,000 pesos for the salaries of two new judges. And the town council had "incontrovertible proof" that the deputation did not have the slightest notion whether the funds existed for paying the

37. AGG, B1.10, 2269, 77. Jueces de letras. The Cortes originally provided for them by an act of October 9, 1812. See AGG, B1.5, 00272, 7. Real decreto de 9 de octubre de 1812, sobre establecimiento de Jueces de Letras.

38. AGG, A1.2.2, 15747, 2194. Libro de cabildos de Guatemala, año 1821.

39. *Ibid.* Valle's argument was published over the signatures of the members of the town council in *El Amigo de la Patria*, February 27, 1821. The record of the town council and *El Amigo* contain basically the same argument, but the record makes clear that it was Valle's argument. A third version of the argument can be found in a letter from the town council to the deputation (AGG, B1.13, 554, 18). The account here draws from all three.

salaries. Only a short time ago, the town council had requested permission from the deputation to spend 600 pesos for new "washing places" (*lavaderos*) at the "only fountain in the district of Havana." The reply received asked the municipal council if there was any surplus in the treasury. The town council, Valle explained, had not yet drawn up the report showing the state of municipal finances. Thus the deputation could not possibly know if funds were available for the new judges. According to Valle's calculations, the treasury, far from having a surplus, groaned under obligations amounting to about 101,000 pesos, and the municipal income from taxes had been declining since 1814.[40]

Mayor Valle preferred to invest the tax receipts in improvements for the capital. Failing to get the necessary permission from the deputation, the town council initiated a public subscription to raise the 600 pesos necessary for new laundry and bathing facilities in the district of Havana. With co-operation from the Church and money from Valle's pocket, the town council was still short of its goal. At this juncture the council sent another dispatch requesting license to take "100 or 200 pesos" from the treasury. "And the Most Excellent Diputación Provincial has not answered." In compliance with an order from the Cortes, the town council sent notes to the Conventos de la Merced and Recolección ordering them to open primary schools. Their replies showed that one needed 100 to 114 pesos and the other 50 before the schools could be opened. The council asked the deputation for permission to provide the money, but "until now," the municipal council attested, the deputation had not answered. In view of the desperate need for schools, Valle went into his own pocket for 50 pesos.[41]

Since the town council had experienced such difficulty in obtaining permission for improvements, Valle, writing for the council, implied that the members of the deputation were blind to the simple yet essential needs of the citizens. He invited them "to look at the wretched districts" of the capital. "None of them

40. AGG, A1.2.2, 15747, 2194; B1.13, 554, 18; *El Amigo de la Patria*, Feb. 27, 1821. The treasurer who submitted the grim financial report to the crown after he refused to accept independence wrote: "Unfortunately, for many years, the Guatemalan treasury was in the grave predicament where expenses greatly exceeded income." See "Informe," *Anales*, XII (Sept., 1935), 4. Also see Solórzano Fernández, *Historia de la evolución económica de Guatemala*, pp. 211-212.
41. AGG, B1.13, 554, 18.

has schools; none of them has a sufficient water supply; none of them has houses of correction; none of them has police; none of them has decent places for recreation and diversion."[42] In the capital, "poverty, misery, nakedness, hunger, and thirst" were the constant companions of those on whom the Constitution so recently had bestowed the title of citizen. But contrasted with the villages, where public funds scarcely existed, the capital was a bustling metropolis. Instead of relieving these "wretched people," who lacked "nearly everything," was it just, Valle asked, that 3,000 pesos annually should go for salaries of judges?[43]

The members of the deputation and the Jefe Político disregarded the opposition from the town council when they appointed temporary judges. After the appointments were announced, snickering and knowing glances must have been exchanged as Valle walked along the streets. The Most Excellent Diputación Provincial and the Jefe Político had appointed Valle as one of the judges, and his name headed the list of forty-eight.[44]

The selection of Valle as one of the judges appeared to be the last shot fired in another exchange between him and the family. Mariano Aycinena, a member of the town council, favored the new tribunal, and he had asked the Jefe Político to name the judges.[45] When Valle and the town council came out strongly against the tribunal, Aycinena refused to support their position and published his own views in *El Editor*, asserting that the town council was a "nearly dead body" that "new individuals" were trying to revive and that the meddling of these individuals in affairs of government would lead only to instability.[46] The Constitution had made the town councils subordinate to the provincial deputation,[47] and that a Pavón, a Beltranena, and Alejandro Díaz Cabeza de Vaca were members of the deputation[48] made

42. *Ibid.* For an equally bleak picture, see the report made in 1810 by Antonio Larrazábal (*Anales*, XXVII [March, 1953-Dec., 1954], 87-93).

43. AGG, B1.13, 554, 18.

44. AGG, B1.14, 660, 20. July 7, 1821.

45. *El Amigo de la Patria*, Feb. 27, 1821; *El Editor Constitucional*, Aug. 20, 1821.

46. March 5, 1821.

47. Tít. VI, Capít. I, Art. 321. Also see Art. 323, which states: "The town councils will discharge all these duties under the supervision of the provincial deputation, to which they will submit an exact account each year of public funds they have collected." For additional information, see Héctor Humberto Samayoa Guevara, *Implantación del régimen de intendencias en el Reino de Guatemala* (Guatemala City, 1960), pp. 121-125.

48. See AGG, B1.10, 2269, 77; *El Editor Constitucional*, March 5, 1821.

more understandable the disdain with which, according to Valle, the town council was treated. And if Valle were motivated, even in the smallest way, to use his office and talent in an attempt to square old accounts with the family, he skilfully concealed that motive by identifying his own with public interest. His financial contributions and tireless efforts to expand education, increase the water supply, and to stimulate agriculture and industry could have been construed by the deputation, perhaps with justification, as an attempt on his part to belittle the importance and functions of the deputation by attracting attention to the town council and to himself. The rivalry between the two bodies doubtless explains the failure of the deputation to answer or acknowledge requests from the town council. And if the literate public concluded that the rivalry was rooted in self-interest, a note in *El Editor* was partly responsible. The anonymous writer, with about equal portions of dismay, disgust, and understanding, wrote: "Jueces de Letras. Words with a curse on them in Guatemala. There is nothing that suffers a more fickle and unworthy fortune than these Jueces de Letras. Applauded and opposed successively by the different authorities, today they exist, tomorrow they don't, and at last will they not be *in saecula saeculorum*. Amen." Among the obstacles confronting the establishment of a new system of government, the writer continued, were "egoism, rivalry, and self-interest." But he attributed the argument over the tribunal to the "natural inconstancy of man."[49]

[4]

In May, 1821, Valle resigned from the town council to accept the position of judge advocate of the army;[50] the hand of Bustamante touched him for the last time. Only eighteen months

49. Aug. 20, 1821.
50. AGG, A1.40, 1768 (legajo), fol. 249. Pases de títulos, 1818-1824. El Lic. José del Valle se nombró Auditor de Guerra de Capitanía General de Guatemala; A1.2.5, 29956, 3099. El ayuntamiento indica al Lic. José Cecilio del Valle, que lamentará su separación de dicho cuerpo al haber optado por el cargo de Auditor de Guerra; A1.39-58, 24946, 2819. Juramento de Auditor de Guerra por José del Valle (May 14, 1821); A1.2.2, 15747, 2194. Libro de cabildos de Guatemala, año 1821. Dn. José del Valle expuso: que S. M. se ha servido agraciarle con el empleo de Auditor de Guerra (May 14, 1821); Crisanto Sacasa to Valle, Granada, April 7, 1821; Pedro Chamorro to Valle, Granada, April 7, 1821, Valle Papers.

earlier, the "pure Spaniard" had recommended Valle for the position.[51] But that short span of time had been an important one for Valle. By September, 1820, when he chose to stand for election, he had accepted the Constitution, and from that point until May, 1821, he supported it to the letter, as his record in the town council and his essays in *El Amigo* show. In response to the basic law and acts of the Cortes, he tried to improve the standard of living in the capital and the provinces, calling for adequate prisons, equitable punishment for crime, additional educational facilities, tax-free indigo and grain, and land free from the grip of the Church. And in the course of five months as mayor, he became involved in a controversy with the deputation that laid bare a society bordering on bankruptcy and indicated that his rivalry with the family continued. But the rivalry, in 1821, prevented the complete co-operation of two governing bodies, boding more grief for Guatemala than all the dreary descriptions of hardship and poverty.

51. Bustamante to José de Alós, Secretario Interino de Estado y del Despacho Universal, Madrid, Nov. 13, 1819, Valle Papers.

Independence, September 15, 1821

[1]

When Valle became mayor in January, 1821, independence appears to have been little more than a desire in the minds of few men who apparently were without any notion of how to translate the desire into reality. Guatemalans of course were aware of the changes that Bolívar, San Martín, and O'Higgins were making in South America and followed closely the devious course of events in Mexico. Valle and his friends, in fact, had been trading information almost since the move began. Colonel Arechavala, for example, wrote in 1817, reporting that news from Mexico told of the defeat of the "traitor Mina" and the capture of the "apostate Mier,"[1] and two years later Mariano Murillo thanked Valle for the papers that spoke of Spanish preparations for an expedition against Buenos Aires.[2] Guatemala also was on the mailing list of the anonymous letter writers who, from Spain and America, contributed in their small way to independence. Less than two weeks after Valle assumed the office of mayor, the town council received another anonymous letter inviting that council to take a stand in favor of independence, warning that justice could not be expected from the Spanish government. The town council labeled these thoughts subversive,[3] but a letter from José Sacasa,[4] substitute deputy for Guatemala, complaining about

1. To Valle, León, Aug. 19, 1817, Valle Papers.
2. *Ibid.*, Sept. 19, 1819.
3. AGG, A1.2.2, 15747, 2194. Libro de cabildos de Guatemala, año 1821 (Jan. 12). This document is reproduced in *Boletín*, IV (1938), 111. The letter was posted in Cádiz.
4. *Ibid.*, pp. 111-112.

the unequal representation in the Cortes, focused attention on a grievance that exercised the writers for *El Editor*.[5] And from a dialogue in the same paper, readers could conclude that independence was the answer to the grievance.[6] But by May, 1821, when Valle retired from the town council, a distinctly different tone rang through the pages of that paper, suggesting that Pedro Molina and others of the staff were bidding fair to break the bond with Spain.

Two unrelated events had occurred between January and May that explained the change in *El Editor* and virtually assured that Guatemala soon would join the ranks of the revolutionaries. The first in time and significance was the radical turn-about of Mexican politics. Following the defeat of Hidalgo and Morelos and the failure of the Mina expedition (1817-1818), the drive for independence languished until 1820, when Ferdinand restored the Constitution. The electoral laws made less certain the control of authority in Mexico by the aristocrats, and the elected Cortes threatened with laws the power and influence of the Church. Thus the upper clergy combined with the aristocrats to promote independence, which they had been fighting against for the last ten years, in order to preserve their colonial heritage. In need of a military leader, they selected Agustín de Iturbide, who had fought the old insurgents until he was retired, suspected of peculation, and in 1820, when the call came, he accepted, happy with the prospects of repairing his fortune. Once in the field, he closed ranks with the old insurgents, and together they marched toward Mexico City and independence under the banner of the Plan of Iguala or, as it also was called, the Three Guarantees: Catholicism, independence, and a Mexican constitutional monarchy.

The importance of these events for the coming of independence in Guatemala was one point on which all contemporaries

5. Jan. 1, 1821.
6. Jan. 22, 1821. The dialogue was between Hernán Cortés and the Conde de la Cadena, a Spanish Officer engaged in fighting the insurgents, and it drew a reply that was investigated by the Board of Censors (Junta de Censura). See *Un americano contradice el sistema de independencia de la América a que inclina el diálogo de Cortés y el Conde de la Cadena, publicado en el periódico Constitucional de Guatemala, con objeto de satisfacer a los españoles europeos que no es pensamiento de lo general de los pueblos americanos sino de quatro necios ingratos preciados de políticos, quando no son más que verdaderos insurgentes*, Feb. 23, 1821 (AGG, A1.1, 57305, 6931).

who left a record agreed, but Manuel Montúfar y Coronado expressed it best. Guatemala, he wrote, lived peacefully in 1821, preoccupied only with the provisions of the Constitution. Freedom of press and the party rivalry during the elections, however, had created opinion favorable to independence. Then, when word arrived of the Plan of Iguala, the patriots began holding meetings, but they soon recognized that they lacked the means of achieving their goal.[7] Thus they waited impatiently (judging from the pages of *El Editor*) for the news of the success or failure of the Plan of Iguala. Guatemalan independence hinged on Iturbide.

The second event that helped to guarantee that Guatemala would become independent occurred quietly and undramatically in Guatemala City. On March 9, 1821, Jefe Político Urrutia, aging and ailing, accepted the advice of Pedro Molina and another physician and turned over the command for a "month or two"[8] to Gabino Gainza, who recently had arrived in Guatemala after an undistinguished tour of duty in Chile.[9] The significance of the transfer of authority, according to all accounts, was that Gainza lacked the qualities of a leader, vacillating between his uncertain loyalty to the crown and his personal desire to exploit independence, should a break occur with Spain.[10] By May, 1821, then, the stage was set for the drama of September 15 and, while attention focused on Mexico, the staff of *El Editor* prepared a receptive audience in Guatemala.

[2]

On May 28, 1821, *El Editor* reported, with more defiance than alarm, that its editor, owing to his forthright way of speaking, had made enemies and that other contributors had been "hated and censured" until they were reluctant to express their views.

7. Montúfar, *Memorias de Jalapa*, p. 45.
8. AGG, A1.23, 1543, 449. Providencia promulgada por el Presidente, Gobernador, Capitán General Carlos de Urrutia.
9. Duke University Library. Convenio celebrado entre los generales de los ejércitos titulados nacional y del Gobierno de Chile (May 3, 1814). Brigadier Gainza signed for the government and Bernardo O'Higgins for the "national" army.
10. Salazar, *Historia de veintiún años*, pp. 216-217; Marure, *Bosquejo histórico*, I, 21; "Informe," *Anales*, XII (Sept., 1935), 11.

El Editor, however, would not be cowed or intimidated, and in the next issue, in a story recalling the style of flamboyant Simón Bergaño, even the most casual reader could discern a more vigorous policy toward Spain. An anonymous writer described a recent journey to the moon, where "a handsome lad with wings, who told me that he was the Spirit of Liberty, conducted me to a town called Airebi where a fierce tyrant ruled, whose name, if I do not forget, was Odnanref le Otargni." In Airebi, the writer witnessed an immense crowd of all "classes, sexes, and dispositions" excitedly running about the streets and plazas. "I could not distinguish clearly the things they were shouting," he related, but, moving closer, he heard these words: "What new monster is this? What plague, so cruel and mysterious, is this . . . ? We possess fertile soil, and we lack profits. We are active and industrious, and we live in poverty. We pay enormous taxes, and they tell us they are not enough. . . What is the enemy that devours us?"[11] Odnanref le Otargni, who was the enemy, the monster, and the plague, was none other than Fernando el Ingrato spelled backwards, and the place, Airebi (Iberia) was Guatemala City or any other city in Spain's dominions.

Among those who read "Journey to the Moon" was Antonio Robles, fiscal for the Board of Censors. After reading the story twice, he accused *El Editor,* on June 8, of libeling Ferdinand VII. Robles lodged the charge before the tribunal of the town council, but before the charge could be processed, a recommendation from the Board of Censors was necessary.[12] The Board, after receiving the accusation, proceeded to examine the disputed story to determine if indeed Ferdinand had been libeled, and in order to avoid a charge of partiality, it published a purported account of the investigation in *El Editor,*[13] but not all the proceedings were published, and the unpublished minutes reveal more clearly the logic of the Board.

The members noted first that *El Editor* had published a story entitled "Journey to the Moon," in which an anonymous writer had described "with liveliness and imagination" the "revolution of a people against an oppressive government." But in the names

11. June 4, 1821.
12. *El Editor Constitucional,* Aug. 6 and Aug. 20, 1821.
13. *Ibid.,* Aug. 20, 1821.

assigned to the place and the tyrant, Robles "saw in anagram
the names of Spain and of Ferdinand the Ingrate" and thus
accused the periodical of libeling "the Sovereign." The Board
immediately found a "great absurdity in the accusation." Robles
had referred to the king with the word *Sovereign*. The word
Sovereign, the Board condescended to explain, was the "august
and exclusive title of the nation" and was applied correctly only
to the people. In these terms, the story, "far from being injurious to the Sovereign," was "exceedingly praiseworthy," because
it brought to light the "imprescriptible right of the nation in
the act [revolution] most characteristic of its sovereignty." Besides, the Board chortled, the story spoke of a fierce tyrant and
Ferdinand was a constitutional monarch. And certainly Robles
realized that an anagram, from the letters of which one might
form various names, was not sufficient evidence to support a
charge of libel. The fact, however, that Robles made the charge
on the basis of such flimsy evidence (the Board was now in dead
earnest) was a threat to the freedom of the press and to the
present "great political system." But in a country where "servilism" had reigned with such sway and where only recently the
government of "D. José de Bustamante strangled the press even
while the Constitution was observed throughout the monarchy,"
the Board was not surprised to find that some *ignorantes adictos*
of that "reign of darkness" remained in Guatemala. These
adictos, the Board asserted, looked upon the "political dogma of
the sovereignty of the people and the faculty of writing" with
great aversion, never missing an opportunity of "obscuring the
first and gazing upon the second of these bastions of liberty."
These "accomplished demagogues" (the Board was now in a bitter mood) were responsible for corrupting and deceiving the
"uneducated and unmannered" people during the popular
elections.[14]

14. AGG, A1.1, 57305, 6931. Junta de Censura (July 27, 1821). Gregorio
Urruela y Ángulo, who was very close to Bustamante and apparently to Valle,
published a pamphlet attacking Liberato Cauto (Molina) and the Board of Censors,
reflecting on their birth and station in life. And Cauto's answer seems to insure
that this was Molina's pseudonym. In a footnote Cauto wrote: "Plebeyuelo sin
nacimiento me llama un forastero, mercader afortunado en mi patria, rico como
un judío y por tanto autorizado para calificarse ante quienes no lo conocen y para
calificar a un criollo a quien él no conoce; pero ésta es antigua usanza entre tales
sujetos. Milagro que no me llame descendiente de África ¿No es lástima que todos

The bitter invective, the mention of the elections, the attack on Bustamante (who fast was becoming the "bloody shirt" of Guatemalan politics), and the decision against Robles came as no surprise to the inhabitants of the capital who knew that the Board included Pedro Molina, José Francisco Barrundia, and José Francisco Córdova.[15]

On August 23, 1821, the Board, convinced of the sanctity of popular sovereignty, the right of revolution, and freedom of the press, asserted again that it could recognize the difference between freedom and license. On that day it received from the town council of Sonsonate a denunciation made by the parish priest, José Antonio Peña, of the reprint of a pamphlet entitled *Constitución secreta de las cortes,* published first in Spain, then in Mérida in 1814 with government license, and now in 1821. That the authors of the pamphlet "were devils descended from human lineage," the Board had on the authority of what "was said in Cádiz." And the purpose of the "absurd, impious, extravagant" essay, it was plain to see, was to start a revolution to destroy the Constitution that the Cortes had given to Spain and "to establish anarchical license," sowing seeds of disaffection for the authorities of the present system. In conclusion, the Board banned the pamphlet, saying: "In this vague and poorly formed plan is seen an author of very limited views but with malignant intentions who has confused truth with error, freedom with license, piety with sacrilege, and the sacred rights of man with subversive principles of disorder." By unanimous vote, the Board declared the pamphlet (which had none of the force of "Journey to the Moon") to be "highly slanderous" of the Cortes and "subversive of the fundamental laws of the monarchy."[16]

---

vengamos de un padre común? Yo me avergüenzo de que este buen hombre pretenda ser mi hermano.

> ¿De onde naciste Angulo?
> (¡Oh maldito consonante!)
> ¿Eres hijo del tonante,
> Ó como todos del cu . . . ?

See *El Editor Constitucional,* Feb. 5, 1821.

15. *El Editor Constitucional,* Jan. 15, 1821. The members originally selected were José María Álvarez, Juan José Batres, Pedro Molina, José Francisco Barrundia, and Juan Venancio López. Álvarez died and was replaced by Pedro Ruiz de Bustamante. José Francisco Córdova was elected secretary. See AGG, A1.1, 57305, 6931. Junta de Censura (Feb. 15, 1821). López was a Baco, and he quarreled with the decision (*El Editor Constitucional,* Aug. 20, 1821).

16. AGG, A1.1, 57305, 6931. Junta de Censura.

While the Board made these decisions, some of its members questioned, in *El Editor,* the justice of Spain's war with Americans and pointed out the threat of the Holy Alliance to Spanish liberalism.[17]   Then, on September 3, immediately below an essay on freedom, appeared a report that Mexico City, Durango, and Vera Cruz were the only areas not submitted to General Agustín de Iturbide, whose successful march already had drawn official recognition in Guatemala City.

[3]

On August 31 Dr. Mariano Larrave, who had succeeded Valle as mayor, reported to the town council that the latest news from Mexico had inspired some fight and was responsible for the growing number of lampoons and rumors which were "directed as much against Spanish Americans as against Europeans."   The "low class" (*pueblo bajo*),[18] the mestizos, mulattoes, and zambos[19] were mainly to blame.   These people, who committed "every crime," were becoming "more bloody and fearful each day," and they were the ones who struck fear in the hearts of all aristocrats and prompted Larrave to urge the members of the town council to guard against further abuses and disorders.[20]

Four days later Jefe Político Gainza manifested another response to the news from Mexico when he addressed the municipal council, saying that he had learned that "some people of the capital" had been canvassing the districts "collecting signatures for the purpose of declaring independence."   He then requested the *ayuntamiento* to consider means for finding out who the leaders were.[21]

At this juncture, Mariano Aycinena received recognition and declared that it was "known for sure" that several provinces of

17. Aug. 13, 1821.

18. AGG. A1.2.2, 15748, 2194.   Libro de cabildos de Guatemala, año 1821.

19. Valle Papers.   In an undated note, most likely in connection with his task of explaining the electoral instructions in 1812, Valle wrote that there was "no exact census" of the capital.   Further, the available census made no distinction with respect to classes—"whites, Indians, mestizos, mulattoes, and zambos."   He went on to say that the number of illegitimates was so great that it nearly equalled that of those born in wedlock.   The men of color and the illegitimates, in the main, made up the "low class" that Larrave feared.

20. AGG, A1.2.2, 15748, 2194.   Libro de cabildos de Guatemala, año 1821.

21. *Ibid.*

Mexico, including nearby Oaxaca, had declared independence, and he was equally sure that general opinion in Guatemala City and its provinces favored the same course. "Out of necessity," he contended, Guatemala "should follow the way of Mexico." The men who were soliciting signatures, Aycinena continued, were trying only to show Gainza that opinion in Guatemala called for independence and to persuade him to take the lead, avoiding in that way any "popular commotion." And, as if to assure Gainza, Aycinena said that it was his understanding that the men who were canvassing did not anticipate, with the coming of independence, any change in the constituted authorities. But he emphasized that some people in the capital were committed to independence, and he did not believe that they would change their minds.[22]

Gainza replied that the very fact that signatures had to be solicited was sufficient proof that no such "general opinion for independence" existed, and the "radicals" (*acaloradores*) who sought the signatures, far from being any service to the government, served only to distract the "youth in the university and *colegio*."[23]

Gainza, according to all accounts, was playing a precarious game. Apparently everyone knew, including Gainza, that Pedro Molina and Mariano Aycinena were the unofficial solicitors for independence. It is contended further, unhappily without much evidence, that they enjoyed the tacit approval of Gainza, who, they promised, would become the first magistrate of the new republic.[24] Aycinena, it is certain, suggested as much in the town council. However, though Gainza doubtless listened to the promises with whetted anticipation, he also remembered his obligations as a Spanish army officer and the possibility of having to account to an irate king for insubordination or worse.[25] Thus he maintained a loyal front for the eyes of Spanish authority by scolding publicly the men whose promises he listened to in private.

22. *Ibid.*
23. *Ibid.*
24. Marure, *Bosquejo histórico*, I, 22; Montúfar, *Memorias de Jalapa*, p. 46; Ramón A. Salazar, *Mariano Aycinena* (Biblioteca de Cultura Popular, XXII; Guatemala City, 1948), p. 47.
25. On September 13 Gainza ordered all military leaders to declare their loyalty to the crown. See Marure, *Bosquejo histórico*, I, 23.

Archbishop Casaus, however, left no doubt about his position. On September 8, a week before independence, he condemned "with greatest vehemence" the "injustice of insurrection" and the "vileness of Iturbide," vowing that he would "shed the last drop of blood" before he would turn against the crown.[26]

While Casaus ranted and Gainza dallied, the patriots, fearing that the crest of emotion built up by events in Mexico might not be sufficient to carry Guatemala to independence, sent Cayetano Bedoya, Molina's brother-in law, to Oaxaca to prevail upon General Nicolás Bravo to support a proclamation of independence in Guatemala. Bedoya never completed his mission. When he arrived in Ciudad Real, in the province of Chiapas (now a part of Mexico), he learned that Ciudad Real already had declared its freedom and had subscribed to the Plan of Iguala.[27]

News of the bold stand taken by Ciudad Real reached Guatemala on September 13, and on the following morning the town council examined two dispatches dated September 5. The first came from Ciudad Real and the second from Tuxtla, also in Chiapas. Both reported that they had declared "independence from Spain" and urged Guatemala City to do the same.[28] In view of the great importance of the news, the town council called an extraordinary session for late that afternoon. Gainza opened the afternoon session, saying that he too had received the dispatch from Chiapas and had resolved to call a general meeting for the following morning of representatives of all corporations and authorities of the capital to consider how to proceed in light of the startling news.[29]

Years later Pedro Molina wrote that the people "were pre-

26. "Informe," *Anales*, XII (Sept., 1935), 11.

27. Marure, *Bosquejo histórico*, I, 22. An indication of the agitation behind the declaration of independence in Chiapas was manifest in the charge against militia captain Joaquín Gutiérrez de Arce of the village of San Bartolomé. On July 11, 1821, about fifty soldiers of the militia, with a violin, marimba, and a guitar, scandalized the village almost until dawn, by shouting throughout the village: "Long live our Captain Joaquín Gutiérrez" and "Down with any other authority of this village." See AGG, A1.1, 57215, 6931. Contra Dn. Joaquín Gutiérrez de Arce y cómplices por perturbadores del sosiego y tranquilidad pública de este pueblo de San Bartolomé (July 12, 1821).

28. AGG, A1.2.2, 15748, 2194. Libro de cabildos de Guatemala, año 1821.

29. *Ibid.* At 5:30 P.M., the rector of the University of San Carlos received a request from Gainza to send two representatives to the meeting. See AGG, A1.34, 12340, 182. Libro de claustros de la Universidad de San Carlos, 1808-1831 (Sept. 14).

pared to ask for independence," but at the same time, "they were timid."[30] Molina probably was in the best position to know, for he and Mariano Aycinena, on the night of September 14, tramped the districts of the capital recruiting support for independence and perhaps intimidating the Serviles,[31] a name that had become synonymous for the Bacos.

The crowd at the palace on the following morning seemed to attest to the effectiveness of Molina and Aycinena's efforts. Before the arrival of the fifty or so representatives to the general meeting, the patio, the antechamber, the corridors, and the vestibule were all filled with people favoring independence.[32] After the representatives had gathered, Gainza opened the session by reading the dispatch from Ciudad Real. Immediately thereafter, according to one contemporary, Valle, who attended as judge advocate, was recognized. In an "eloquent discourse," we are assured, he pointed out the "necessity and justice" of independence but concluded by advising the representatives not to declare until after all the provinces had expressed their opinion. If Valle's plan won any adherents in the partisan crowd, they doubtless were lost when Archbishop Casaus toed the strategic line staked out by Valle. Canon José María Castilla, on the staff of *El Editor*, however, took an absolute stand in favor of independence. Dr. Antonio García Redondo followed Castilla's lead along with Miguel Larreinaga, Mariano Aycinena, Mariano Larrave, and most of the remaining representatives. The enthusiastic crowd greeted each affirmative declaration with peals of approval, each to the contrary with raucous jeers, and soon was mingling on the floor among the delegates, contributing to the complete confusion. Apparently a vote was taken; certainly a majority spoke in the

---

30. Molina, "Memorias," *Centro-Americano*, XIII (April-Sept., 1921), 279.
31. Marure, *Bosquejo histórico*, I, 23; Salazar, *Mariano Aycinena*, p. 47.
32. Marure, *Bosquejo histórico*, I, 23; Montúfar, *Memorias de Jalapa*, p. 47; Molina, "Memorias," *Centro-Americano*, XIII (April-Sept., 1921), 279; Zamora, *El grito de independencia*, pp. 121-126; Miguel García Granados, *Memorias del General Miguel García Granados* (4 vols., Biblioteca de Cultura Popular, XXXVII, XXXVIII, XXXIX, XL; Guatemala City, 1952), I, 20-21. (Hereafter García Granados, *Memorias*.) Concerning the activity in and around the palace on September 15, Granados wrote that he did not see the "immense crowd" that Marure described. On the contrary "the people did not take any part in that movement." The only explanation for this curious statement is that in 1821, García Granados was still an adolescent, and his father, as the son pointed out and as the documents show, was against independence. See AGG, A1.2.2, 15748, 2194. Libro de cabildos de Guatemala, año 1821 (Dec. 1).

affirmative; and as soon as Gainza realized the tenor of the meeting, he proclaimed independence.[33]

After the crowd abandoned the palace to celebrate the occasion, two important matters demanded immediate attention. A provisional government had to be formed and the enthusiasm of the proclamation of independence had to be translated into a written statement. Valle apparently was responsible for writing what has come to be called the declaration of independence, and the document shows clearly that his opinion, which had been defeated amid the confusion of the morning, finally carried the day. Gainza, according to statement number eight of the document, was to be head of the provisional government (Junta Provisional Consultiva), which was to include the members of the provincial deputation and the following to represent their provinces: Miguel Larreinaga, León; José del Valle, Comayagua; the Marquis de Aycinena, Quetzaltenango; José Valdés, Sololá and Chimaltenango; Ángel María Candina, Sonsonate; and Antonio Robles, Ciudad Real. Statements one and two of the declaration made independence temporary, pending a decision by a congress that was to meet on March 1, 1822, in Guatemala City, and number three and four stipulated that one deputy for every 15,000 people (Negroes were to be counted as citizens) would be elected to the congress by the electors who, in March, 1821, had elected deputies to the Cortes.[34]

Closer examination of Valle's declaration, or at least the declaration that he read and corrected, reveals that the only difference in the government of Guatemala, on the morning after September 15, 1821, was that it owed no obligation to Ferdinand VII and Spain. Otherwise everything was the same. The provincial aristocrats were still in control, and they apparently were there more by design than accident. Until Iturbide's success in Mexico, they clung tenaciously to the crown. Afterwards, when Spanish power was broken in nearly all America, only one way lay open to

33. Marure, *Bosquejo histórico,* I, 23-24; Molina, "Memorias," *Centro-Americano,* XIII (April-Sept., 1921), 278-279; Montúfar, *Memorias de Jalapa,* p. 47; "Informe," *Anales,* XII, 12-14.

34. The original document is bound in: Libro de contestaciones de la jura de independencia. When the author examined the document it did not have an archival classification. Valle did not actually write the document. Neither did he sign it. The emendations, however, are his. The document is reproduced in *Boletín,* IV (1939), 127-129, with the comments on the emendations by Professor and Archivist J. Joaquín Pardo, who discovered the Act of Independence in 1934.

them if they were to maintain their position of power and influence: they had to place themselves in the vanguard of the drive
for independence so that they could manipulate it to their own
ends. Mexican independence was a tale told again in Guatemala,
and no single act illustrates it better than when the illegitimate
Molina and the aristocratic Aycinena plodded through the rain
and mud on the night of September 14 to guarantee that a crowd
would gather at the palace on the following morning. While one
might marvel at what Molina and Mariano Aycinena found to
talk about, Molina, Barrundia, and Córdova's complete exclusion
from the provisional government assures us that the conversation
had little to do with what was to happen after independence.
Twenty or so years later a sad but wiser Molina confessed that not
all the Cacos had been in favor of independence.[35]

That the aristocrats compromised independence on the day of
its birth does not mean that they failed to understand the concepts
of democracy, popular sovereignty, and the right of revolution.
On the contrary, they understood them so well that they looked
upon their application in Guatemala as ridiculous, if not suicidal.
They knew their country as well as Valle did, and they knew that
outside the capital and the major cities of the provinces they were
foreigners in their own land, unable to communicate, generally,
unless they happened to know the twenty-five tongues of the
Quiché-language family. As foreigners they stood in fear not only
of the Indians but of all the "uneducated and unmannered"
people that the Board of Censors referred to. Dr. Mariano
Larrave, politically allied with Valle, expressed that fear in the
town council when he spoke of the "low class." *El Editor,* the
Caco paper, shrank from the thought of the nine hundred who
had entered the hospital in 1820. Mariano Aycinena hinted at
the same fear when he spoke of trying to avoid a "popular commotion." Valle recognized it in 1814, in his letter to Castriciones,
in 1817, as crown attorney, and in 1820 and 1821, in *El Amigo.*
And everyone who had a hand in writing the Act of Independence
acknowledged their fear in statement number one, which, with
unabashed candor, explained that Gainza had declared independence "to prevent the consequences that would be fearful in the
event that the people should proclaim it." Their fears, however,

35. Molina, "Memorias," *Centro-Americano,* XIII (April-Sept., 1921), 278-279.

did not spring solely from hospital statistics and the records of the criminal court. They had before them the example of the Indian rebellion in 1820 in Totonicapán, where Atanasio Tzul and Lucas Aguilar, both Indians, assumed authority as "Rey or Fiscal Rey" and "Presidente," respectively.[36] And word of the castration of the "overseas" Spaniards in Almachapán, immediately after independence, only emphasized the fear underlying the words in statement one of the so-called Act of Independence.[37]

This fear, the impoverished state of Guatemala, and the high regard for the contents of the Plan of Iguala were most likely the important reasons behind the attempt of the aristocrats to trade independence, even before it was achieved, for a corner under the canopy of a throne—the one Iturbide was fashioning in Mexico. Though the purpose of the aristocrats was not so apparent on September 15, it became quite clear a month or so later. It is sufficient to say here that Mariano Aycinena, the same aristocratic Aycinena who on September 14 went with Molina, was trying to peddle the prize even before it had been won. Iturbide, in a letter to one of his officers, wrote that "in Guatemala you can rely on Mariano Aycinena, who has corresponded with me since before that capital declared independence." Iturbide planned to use Aycinena's "good connections."[38] To a friend in Chiapas, where allegiance to Iturbide was a fact, the Marquis de Aycinena, a member of the provisional government, wrote: "My friend, I work incessantly to achieve the union of these provinces with the Mexican Empire. Pray God that my work is not in vain."[39]

36. J. Daniel Contreras, *Una rebelión indígena en el partido de Totonicapán en 1820. El Indio y la independencia* (Guatemala City, 1951). p. 38.

37. AGG, B4.2, 1176, 50.   Almachapán sobre juramento de independencia (October 29, 1821). The incident occurred on September 16. Also see the remarks of Archbishop Casaus (Thompson, *Narrative of an Official Visit*, pp. 142-143). Some of these same aristocrats reacted vigorously to an "anonymous proclamation" exhorting the citizens of the capital "to form a party opposing the class called noble."   See AGG, B1.13, 562, 19. Actas de la Junta Consultiva Provisional de Guatemala, instalada el 17 de septiembre de 1821 y disuelta el 21 de febrero de 1822 (hereafter Junta Consultiva Provisional), Oct. 8, 1821.

38. *Boletín,* IV (1939), 308-309. Aycinena's friendship with Iturbide is further illustrated by their correspondence after Iturbide was exiled. See Mariano Cuevas, ed., *El Libertador: documentos selectos de D. Agustín de Iturbide* (Mexico, 1947), pp. 393-394. (Hereafter Cuevas, ed., *El Libertador.*)   After Aycinena was exiled from Guatemala, he published a pamphlet, in 1834, in New York, in which he stated: "In 1821, I say it with frankness, I did not believe the republican regime adaptable to my country. My opinion for a moderate monarchy was founded on the superiority of this form of government." (Quoted in Salazar, *Mariano Aycinena,* p. 51.)

39. *Boletín,* IV (1939), 286.

[4]

Valle's position during the months immediately preceding independence and on September 15 was made beguilingly simple by his writings in *El Amigo*. In nearly every issue and in connection with diverse topics, he embraced the Constitution of 1812 and the laws of the Cortes without any reservation. His constant theme was that knowledge gained from the study of the natural and social sciences was the basis of good government,[40] which he defined, time and again, as the government that provided the greatest good for the greatest number of people.[41] At the same time he criticized openly and harshly the warp and woof of colonial life, condemning the Ley de Partida and the laws of Castile and of the Indies.[42] Justice, he maintained, was not always available in colonial courts, and when it came, whatever the brand, it came at a high price.[43] *Oidores,* he implied, behaved almost as if they were members of an exclusive fraternal organization when they processed accusations against one of their own.[44] And too many times, judges at every level looked first to see who was charged before they considered the accusation and evidence.[45] He pointed the finger of scorn at the system that allowed a person to become a *corregidor,* for example, whose chief qualification was the ability "to make the sign of the cross with his thumb and index finger," declaring before God to fulfil the obligations of office "well and faithfully."[46] Finally and repeatedly, he blamed the colonial period for all the poverty, ignorance, and misery[47] that he saw every time he walked from his large and well-appointed home to the palace. Frequently he anchored his arguments in footnotes and textual citations that told of careful research, not only in the codes of Spain and the Indies, which he knew almost by heart, but also in the works of Buffon,[48] De Pauw,

40. Nov. 18, 1820.   41. Aug. 7, 1821.
42. Dec. 9, 1820; Jan. 25, 1822. Valle, in 1812, indicated that he was unhappy with the laws of the Indies. See Valladares, ed., *Valle,* p. 7; *El Amigo de la Patria,* Oct. 26, 1820.
43. Jan. 25, 1822.   44. *Ibid.*
45. Dec. 23, 1820.   46. Nov. 24, 1820.
47. For example see the issues for May 29, 1821, and September 7, 1821.
48. Valle generally used the works of Count George Louis Leclerc Buffon and the Abbé de Pauw to show how little was known about America (*El Amigo de la Patria,* May 5, 1821). In the issue for April 1, 1822, Valle, commenting on the historians of America, wrote that De Pauw was delirious.

Humboldt, Say,[49] and Montesquieu, among others. And his library shelves until this moment are filled with the volumes of Voltaire, Rousseau, Racine, and a thousand other volumes, papers, and journals that would have compared favorably with the library of any man of the Enlightenment, including even that of Simón Bergaño. In view of what he wrote and what he read, it would be easy, almost irresistibly easy, to conclude that Valle shared the same spirit that drove Pedro Molina to stir the weak of heart and the timid of soul on that rainy eve of independence.

Valle, however, shared the fear of the inarticulate *pueblo bajo*, and he was sufficiently steeped in history to recognize and fear the pattern of revolution. The now classic example of the French was his contemporary, and he must have shuddered with every aristocrat when news arrived of Hidalgo's attack on Guanajuato and the massacre at the *alhóndiga*. But at the same time Valle realized: "The world is on the move and will not turn back. Let's spread knowledge so that its march will be peaceful. We then will enjoy the good that independence promises without suffering the evil that has afflicted other countries."[50] This thought which he expressed in February, 1822, after a second revolution had tied Guatemala to Mexico, seems very close to summing up his views in September, 1821, when he tried to control the direction that independence would take. Molina won the spectacular morning round, but Valle's position prevailed. The final decision concerning independence was left to the congress that was to meet on March 1, 1822, and the representatives to the congress were to be chosen by the same electors who had elected Valle to the provincial deputation and Mateo Ibarra to the Cortes. Thus it appears that the Serviles commanded a majority of the group that planned the declaration on the night of September 14, or at some other time before the act was written. And in this group, Valle doubtless counted Gainza. That Valle should point out the wisdom of waiting for the provinces was probably pre-arranged.[51] In any other terms, the acceptance of Valle's plan, after it had failed on

49. J. B. Say (1767-1832) was a French economist of the same style as the British Manchester school.

50. *El Amigo de la Patria*, Feb. 22, 1822.

51. A better case could be made if it were sure that Valle spoke immediately following Gainza, but the sources do not agree. For example, Marure (*Bosquejo histórico*, I, 23) wrote that Valle did, but Montúfar (*Memorias de Jalapa*, p. 47) claimed that José María Castilla spoke after Gainza.

the floor, would have to be considered coincidence, which is much less plausible than these assumptions. If this relationship between Valle and Gainza did exist on September 15, it is easier to understand why Valle, during the next three months, wrote nearly every important dispatch that appeared over Gainza's signature. But that Valle, on September 15, was not in complete control, is shown by the selection of Larreinaga and the Marquis de Aycinena for the provisional government.

[5]

Thus Valle accepted independence, but the perplexing question is when he made the decision. His life before 1820 assures us that the revolution in Spain, the restoration of the Constitution, and the success of the insurgents in Mexico and South America forced him to re-evaluate the course of his past life and to define what he wanted from the future in terms of the changes that had taken place. The transition began with his decision to remain in Guatemala, continued with his criticism of the colonial period, and culminated with his acceptance of independence and the definition, on November 30, 1821, of his new position. On that date he published his views in the first issue of *El Amigo* to appear since September 15. After much soul searching, Valle tied his future unequivocally and irretrievably to the future of America. Forsaking the title of well-deserving subject, he became citizen Valle. And the argument supporting his decision floods with light the chasm separating the old position and the new and emphasizes the celerity with which he passed from one side to the other.

He proclaimed in italics that Americans possessed the natural rights of man—rights that Spain first trampled when she sent Cortés, Alvarado, and Pizarro to the Indies. Nature had bestowed on Americans and Europeans alike the imprescriptible rights that made man free, equal, and master of his land. In ignorance of the existence of each other, Americans and Europeans had lived happily, but then the conquistadores, booted and spurred, arrived from Spain, and their appearance marked the beginning of the "sufferings" in America and of "wealth" for Europe. Reason denied to Spain a "legitimate title" to conquer America, but what reason denied, Spain took with a strong arm and a blade of steel. That religion licensed Spain to subdue Americans and bring them into the fold was a sophistry. Did the Romans, the Carthaginians, and the barbarians from the north possess the right to conquer Spaniards for the same reason? The "divine Author" commissioned no one to conquer the world.

But in violation of natural rights, the Spaniards came, bringing with them the saddle and side arms of authority that had chafed and subordinated Americans, from Cape Horn to Texas, for three hundred years. By design and calculation, the Spaniards, with an infinite number of laws, isolated America and Americans. Spanish opinion, Spanish education, and Spanish censorship blighted American learning and caused it to lag a century behind that of Europe. Spanish economic policy was the origin of American poverty, and the Spanish caste system was the source of distrust among Americans. The color of a man's skin was not the badge of slavery or superiority. The Spaniards, it was true, were whiter than the Indians, but the Germans were whiter than the Spaniards. Yet those same Spaniards, putting law on law, separated the Indians from all others, forbade the *ladinos* to tread the flagstones of the universities, barred them from careers of honor, and restricted relations between Spaniards and creoles. And to insure that these laws were enforced to the letter, Spain sent to the Indies, as viceroys, men of the military, born and schooled in the Peninsula—pure Spaniards. Thus, since the sixteenth century, Spain had governed, despite all the warnings from the scholars.

Montesquieu had pointed out that the Indies hung by a thread. Buffon had marveled at the ignorance that perpetuated the grip of European nations on their colonies. Adam Smith explained that in the first years Europeans had trampled the Indies with impunity but that the balance, one day, was sure to shift. Condorcet predicted independence, and Raynal (the tears now gone?) saw Americans breaking the shackles forged in Spain, and, beginning from nothing, aspiring to and finally achieving their niche in world history.

"God has heard your voice, wise man and seer." North America revolted against the English and thereby taught a lesson to every American from Mexico to Buenos Aires. Then the

French, defending their freedom in 1789, spread "light to their sons and to the whole world." Gloriously the Spaniards followed the pattern when they revolted in 1808 and later promulgated the Constitution. At length and long last, the light spread to the Spanish colonies: " 'I too am a man,' said the modest and sensible American. 'I also have received from nature those rights that Europe has defended.' " Man, wherever he lived, was blessed with those rights. "In Madrid it was colder in the winter and hotter in the summer than in Guatemala," land of eternal spring. And the "man in Madrid has no more rights than the Guatemalan." Indeed, the same Constitution of 1812, which the Spaniards praised and cursed and praised again, was the document that guaranteed to Americans their independence and inherent rights. Americans should always respect Spain for the precious heritage she left. Spanish blood coursed the veins of countless Americans; the melodic sounds of Castilian were heard from Vera Cruz to Santiago; and the acceptance of Catholicism was nearly unanimous. Filial affection, however, should not take precedence over the obligations imposed by patriotism. Americans were bound to defend their rights. But let the bloody Robespierres stay in France. The character of the American is "sweetness" and sensibility, so plainly apparent in his face and in the soft accents of his speech. But the sweetness should not be mistaken for weakness; Americans would not be persecuted, now that they had received the rights so long denied them.

And with their new freedom, they no longer would poke along aimlessly in the backwash of civilization. Their genius and the natural resources of their land pointed toward a shining future— a future that would lavish on America and her sons the wealth from the richest mineral resources, from a flourishing agriculture, from ports bustling with trade, and from the burst of an industrial revolution. Throughout the length and breadth of the grand design that was America the sounds of the tongues of Germans, Swiss, and English would be heard before they blended with and gave way to Castilian, as these foreigners married Indians and *ladinos*. And the Indian would no longer be a degraded being, his face creased and drawn by three centuries of humiliation, hat in hand, eyes fixed on the ground, a bare toe fidgeting in the dirt. "He will be what a man is: a noble being who, with eyes uplifted, will realize his worth." Both Indians and *ladinos* would abandon the "pleasures of crime," knowing full well that the mere denial would not bring them the rewards of virtue. In the future, "they will make the sacrifices that honor demands," and the grim statistics of the hospital would tell a different, more pleasant story. Finally if America proceeded slowly, not ranging from one extreme to another, she would find her place in the sun, and Guatemala, located in the "best geographical position," would be the focal point of the world.

Valle's transition from "that Ethiopia" with the "doleful" horizon to Guatemala, the focal point of the world, demanded a certain agility. But he made the crossing, and in so doing he selected one of the two alternatives that, between 1775 and 1825, lay open to all Americans of European origin south of the Aroostook River: to remain loyal to the crown and return to the mother country; or to accept independence and remain in America. And who would venture to credit an unqualified answer in favor of independence to each of those men who have passed into history as fathers of American independence, north or south? "Jorge Washington," whose picture Valle carried all the way from Mexico to Guatemala,[52] traveled to New York in 1789 worrying whether his actions as first president would mar the reputation he already enjoyed. Simón Bolívar, beside whose picture Valle wanted to hang that of Washington,[53] declared in a dark mood that all Latin America was not worth the British fleet. And some fathers of Guatemalan independence were instrumental in annexing their country to Mexico.[54]

52. José del Valle, "Manifiesto a la nación guatemalana," Valle and Valle Matheu, eds., *Obras*, I, 76-77.

53. On February 16, 1824, Valle presented the picture to the congress in Guatemala, and the picture was hung. But it had to be taken down. Before Valle had arrived home, the congress had hung portraits of Bartolomé de las Casas and Simón Bolívar. These were full-length portraits, and the one of Washington was only three-quarter length, and it ruined the "symmetry." See AGG, B6.16, 2976, 117. Actas de la Asamblea Nacional Constituyente, February 17, 1824; B6.16, 2899, 107. Comisiones especiales de la Asamblea, April 8, 1824.

54. The possibility exists that Valle and Gainza, together or separately, might have desired, on September 15, to annex the new country to Mexico. If this should prove true, the portrayal of Gainza will undergo a greater change than that suggested by Gordon Kenyon ("Gabino Gainza and Central America's Independence from Spain," *The Americas*, XIII [January, 1957], 241-254). But no future evaluation will portray Gainza as the Guatemalan "Moses" leading his charges from the chains of slavery. See AGG. Libro de contestaciones de la jura de independencia (ayuntamiento de San Sebastián, no date). For additional information about Gainza, see Enrique del Cid Fernández, *Don Gabino de Gainza y otros estudios* (Guatemala City, 1959), pp. 15-74.

A Model of Self Restraint

The Provisional Government and the Annexation of Guatemala to Mexico

[1]

As the last document of colonial Guatemala and the first of Central America was filed in the archive, Valle, appropriately if not symbolically, rendered the *coup de grâce* to the old order and heralded his meticulous efforts in behalf of the new when he successfully proposed that the *audiencia* cease using the royal seal of Spain.[1] The "world was on the move," and Valle, who had served one master "well and faithfully," moved with the tide of the nineteenth century without looking back, ready to serve another with the same talent. Few men in 1821 could lay claim to a record equally distinguished, and no one in the provisional government could match his capacity or approach his pace. His ability to organize, his scrupulous attention to detail, and his facility for synthesizing with economy[2] made him the key administrator in the provisional government.

On September 17, 1821, the government, meeting for the first time, charged Valle with formulating parliamentary procedure. The deputies agreed that the daily sessions should extend from nine in the morning until noon and that the sessions on Monday, Thursday, and Saturday should be public.[3] Each session was to

---

1. AGG, B1.13, 562, 19. Junta Consultiva Provisional, Sept. 29, 1821.
2. This ability is not always so apparent in his published writings, where he frequently was verbose and used phrases for lyrical and symmetrical effect rather than for meaning. His legal opinions were written with scrupulous economy, as were certain dispatches written for the provisional government. In other dispatches his verbosity was intended to cloud issues and avoid direct statements.
3. AGG, B1.13, 562, 19. Junta Consultiva Provisional.

begin with the reading of the minutes from the previous day, and
the deputies were to seat themselves as they pleased (a sure sign
that the colonial period had ended). Jefe Político Gainza, however, was to enjoy a chair of "preference," and since the laws of
Spain would prevail until the congress met in March, 1822, a copy
of the codes, the rules for procedure, and the record of the sessions, were to be placed on the table before him.[4] Further to
facilitate the business of government, Valle proposed committees
for education, defense and security, statistics, agriculture, industry, commerce, and finance.[5] The chairman of each committee
had to be a member of the provisional government but the members could be chosen from the community. Valle, who became
chairman of the committee on finance,[6] immediately presented a
recommendation that provincial deputations and town councils
send reports, describing political and financial problems and suggestions for "consolidating the new government." He was especially interested in seeing appraisals of agriculture, industry, and
commerce,[7] for he knew full well that the new nation not only
had inherited all the financial woes of the colony but also had
acquired new ones.

A dispatch from the town council of the village of San Marcos,
explaining that the mayor had abolished the government monopoly on *aguardiente,* drew a response from Valle that stressed
the new obstacles to a balanced budget.[8] The treasury no longer
could count on the abolished *alcabala,* and the tribute had been
reduced.[9] With the loss of these revenues, Valle calculated that
expenditures for the coming year would exceed income. *Aguardiente,* in the past, had provided one of the best sources, and he

4. AGG, B3.4, 00936, 46. Junta Consultiva Provisional. Valle also proposed
(Oct. 3, 1821) that the government should publish the minutes of the sessions.
Apparently some of them were published, for printer Ignacio Beteta (Feb. 12, 1822)
informed the government that owing to lack of funds he had to discontinue publishing the *Gaceta* (AGG, B1.13, 562, 19).

5. AGG, B1.13, 562, 19. Junta Consultiva Provisional. The committees were
proposed on September 17 and confirmed two days later.

6. AGG, B1.13, 562, 19. Junta Consultiva Provisional, Sept. 29, 1821.

7. *Ibid.,* Oct. 2, 1821. This recommendation was published over the signature
of Gainza. See Gilberto Valenzuela, *La imprenta en Guatemala* (Guatemala City,
1933), p. 7.

8. AGG, B3.6, 1090, 48. El ayuntamiento del pueblo de San Marcos sobre los
motivos que tuvo el alcalde para suspender el estanco de aguardiente (Oct. 6, 1821).
Valle wrote the reply on October 27, but only about one-half of the letter was in
his handwriting.

9. *Ibid.* The *alcabala* was a sales tax, and the tribute was collected from the
Indians.

was counting heavily on the tax it would yield. "The deplorable state of the treasury" simply would not permit anyone to abolish the monopoly. The revenue from the monopoly on gunpowder was important, but the cost to the state of supporting the enterprise exceeded one-half of its total income. Valle's accounting told nearly the same story for the tobacco monopoly. The excise from *aguardiente* for the period of 1814-1819, however, had soared to 212,460 pesos, and his figures did not include the 29,000 pesos for the month of December, 1819. After discounting the expense (13,822 pesos), the net profit had been 198,577 pesos, and a simple calculation told him that the expenses had absorbed only a fraction more than 6 per cent of the gross. "To remove the monopoly would be to abolish the most productive tax," Valle admonished. "If this were an immoral tax" derived from a monopoly that corrupted society, the committee on finance would be first to move against it. Such, however, was not the case. Certainly *aguardiente* would be cheaper and more abundant if it were free from government control, but the increase in drunkenness would offset the advantage. With the monopoly, prices were higher, *aguardiente* was not so abundant, and its abuse was less frequent.[10] "The Reverend P. Fr. José Antonio Goicoechea, who honored these provinces with his knowledge and morality, examined this same question in 1811 . . . in a letter (that should be published) to one of the committee members." According to Goicoechea, abolition of the monopoly would be in the best interests of society only if the "zealous reformers" could guard against a greater abundance of *aguardiente* more easily available. But Goicoechea had known and Valle agreed that to abolish the monopoly would be similar to decapitating the "Hydra of Lerna." Where one source of *aguardiente* now existed "seven" would spring up.[11] These facts

10. Drunkenness apparently was a real rather than an imaginary problem. A member of the *ayuntamiento* complained on November 20, 1821, saying: ". . . there are two taverns where large crowds gather nightly to get drunk, and they cause most serious disturbances in the neighborhood." See AGG, A1.2.2, 15748, 2194. Libro de cabildos de Guatemala, año 1821. On January 20, 1822, in an order nearly twice the length of the declaration of independence, Gainza defined the rules for taverns and promised punishment for the offenders. Among the seventeen separate prohibitions were included those against locating taverns in alleys, against customers remaining in the tavern to "form reunions" on the pretext of listening to music, and against the owners selling alcoholic beverages to those who "ya están tomados, como se dice vulgarmente." See AGG, A1.22, 1510, 46.

11. AGG, B3.6, 1090, 48. El ayuntamiento del pueblo de San Marcos sobre los motivos que tuvo el alcalde para suspender el estanco de aguardiente. Valle quoted (correctly) a paragraph from Goicoechea's letter.

before him, Valle scolded the town council of San Marcos, reproving its members for not educating the youth and for failing to find work for the poor.[12]

Out of necessity, then, Valle was alert to every means that promised to bolster the depleted treasury. He suggested that the deputies, who had been elected to the Cortes, return the 3,000 pesos received for traveling expenses;[13] he opposed the motion to pay salaries, two months in advance of September 15, to crown employees who were returning to Spain;[14] and on November 22, 1821, he proposed to export seven thousand *tercios* (a *tercio* weighed one hundred pounds) of tobacco.[15] But in fairness, he refused to support a petition that demanded a 35 per cent tax on gold and silver, 20 per cent on pearls and precious stones, and 15 per cent on everything else belonging to persons who, refusing to accept independence, were leaving Guatemala.[16]

While Valle, with the help of the committee on finance, vainly sought the means to make the nation solvent, Pedro Molina, José Francisco Barrundia, and José Francisco Córdova initiated a political quarrel that had its roots in the Act of Independence.

[2]

Molina, Barrundia, and Córdova, self-styled representatives of the "people," were determined to have a hand in the provisional

12. The *ayuntamiento* of Quetzaltenango also informed the provisional government that the Indians had forced the selection of a new *alcalde* and the abolition of the monopoly on *aguardiente* (AGG, B1.13, 562, 19. Junta Consultiva Provisional, Nov. 17, 1821).

13. AGG, B3.5, 00936, 46. Junta Consultiva Provisional, Oct. 3, 1821.

14. AGG, B1.13, 562, 19. Junta Consultiva Provisional, Sept. 26, 1821. Among those leaving was Captain General Urrutia.

15. AGG, B3.5, 00937, 46. Junta Consultiva Provisional. On December 18, 1821, Valle called attention to the fact that the *ayuntamiento* of Quetzaltenango had taken from the jurisdiction of the General Director of Tobaccos tobacco valued at 16,000 pesos (AGG, B1.13, 562, 19).

16. AGG, B3.6, 100, 217. Sobre que se cobre un tanto por ciento de los caudales que en oro y plata extraen los europeos que regresan a la península (Oct. 16, 1821). Valle's opposition was based on the following reasoning: "Man is free, and from this freedom comes another that the English call *loco-motivo* and it means that a citizen can move to the country or nation that he prefers. When a government is basically changed, this right becomes clearer than in any other circumstance. Once the bond is cut with the old form, the men who lived under the old government remain free to be members of the new society or to move and become members of another." This well might have been the thread of reason running through his own transition. He continued, saying that the government had a right to tax the goods taken from the country, but he suggested the very

government, despite the fact that they had been excluded from membership. During the second session, Barrundia presented a plan for parliamentary procedure, which was passed to Valle, protesting at the same time that the ports of Omoa and Trujillo were in danger (and they were) and that they were not adequately protected (and they were not).[17] Then, after the government appointed commanders to the ports, all three patriots criticized the appointments.[18] On October 13, 1821, they successfully petitioned permission to establish a patriotic society (*tertulia patriótica*)[19] that, along with *El Genio de la Libertad,* the new name of Molina's paper, served as a launching pad for their opposition. And their primary target, during the first days, was the reform of Article 3 of the Act of Independence.

The disputed article specified that the electors who had voted for Valle and Mateo Ibarra, in March, 1821, should elect the deputies to the congress, which was to make the final decision concerning independence. During the sixth session of the government, Molina presented a petition "written by several citizens of the city" to reform the electoral law. After brief discussion, the deputies divided five to four in favor of reform.[20] Molina scored early, and since Barrundia had been elected secretary to the government on September 24 (a position he refused),[21] the alignment of the Cacos seemed to be holding.

Cheered by their victory, Molina, Barrundia, and Córdova, with their recruits, continued to attend the public sessions, heck-

modest amount of 1 per cent on gold and silver (over 1,000 pesos); 4 per cent on precious stones (over 400 pesos); and the customary tax, if any, on all other items. See AGG, B1.13, 562, 19. Junta Consultiva Provisional, Oct. 17,1821.

17. AGG, B3.5, 00934, 46. Junta Consultiva Provisional, Sept. 18, 1821.

18. AGG, B1.13, 562, 19. Junta Consultiva Provisional, Oct. 21, 1821. Gainza appointed Simón Gutiérrez as commander of the port of Omoa and Francisco Cáscaras of the port of Trujillo. Molina, who happened to be in the antechamber of the assembly room, gained permission to speak, saying that he and "the people" opposed the appointments because the commanders had ideas opposed to independence.

19. AGG, B3.5, 00936, 46. Junta Consultiva Provisional. Larreinaga presented the petition. The University of San Carlos extended the use of one of its buildings to the Patriotic Society, warning that the members of the Society would be responsible for anything broken or damaged. See AGG, A1.3-4, 12340, 182. Libro de claustros de la Universidad de San Carlos, 1808-1831 (Oct. 24, 1821).

20. AGG, B3.5, 00934, 46. Junta Consultiva Provisional, Sept. 25, 1821. Valle, Valdés, Robles, and José Matías Delgado opposed. It is not clear why Delgado joined Valle in the opposition, but one explanation might be that Delgado had been elected to the provincial deputation, which became part of the provisional government, by electors in the province of San Salvador. Thus it behooved him to keep those electors.

21. AGG, B1.13, 562, 19. Junta Consultiva Provisional.

ling, applauding, and challenging the deputies. On September 27, while the government listened patiently to a dispatch from Suchitepéquez, Córdova, a slightly built man with a reputation as wit and raconteur, interrupted proceedings by demanding from the gallery the expulsion from Guatemala of all those who had not sworn to accept independence, and he began reading a list of their names. Deliberations on the floor ground to a halt, and Gainza cleared the hall.[22] On the following day, the deputies debated a motion to suspend public sessions, agreeing finally to admit "1, 2, or 3" persons and warning that permission was necessary before anyone could address the government.[23] Following the disorder and the restriction on public sessions, the deputies argued over the nature of the reform of Article 3,[24] but events outside the capital diminished the importance of the debate and finally destroyed the alignment of the Cacos.

[3]

Before authorities in Guatemala City declared independence, the province of Chiapas, following the lead of Ciudad Real, had pronounced in favor of allegiance to Iturbide and union with Mexico, providing the pattern of dissension that reduced Guatemala to confusion and civil conflict. When the city of León (Nicaragua) learned of the act of independence, Governor Miguel González Saravia, with the aid of Joaquín Arechavala, declared independence from Spain and the capital, favoring annexation to Mexico. In Comayagua (Honduras), José Tinoco repeated the action of González, and in San Salvador, Governor Pedro Barrière

22. AGG, B3.5, 00934, 46. Junta Consultiva Provisional. Manuel Montúfar (*Memorias de Jalapa*, p. 49) wrote that Valle allowed himself to be drawn into arguments with the crowd. Montúfar, however, was a member of the "family" and a dedicated enemy of Valle.
23. AGG, B1.13, 562, 19. Junta Consultiva Provisional, Sept. 28, 1821. Larreinaga, Delgado, and Rivera opined against any innovations. The *ayuntamiento* of the capital, headed by Dr. Mariano Larrave, a friend of Valle, supported Valle's position against public sessions. See AGG, A1.2.2, 15748, 2194. Libro de cabildos de Guatemala, año 1821 (Sept. 28 and Oct. 9). For criticism of the restriction on the sessions, see *El Genio de la Libertad*, Oct. 4, 1821. Finally on November 14 the government decided that the sessions would be secret whenever the "governing power" was exercised and public during the exercise of "legislative" authority. Valle was charged with conveying the decision to the public. See AGG, B1.13, 562, 19.
24. For a discussion of the reform of Article 3, see the minutes of the session for October 4, 1821 (AGG, B3.5, 00936, 46).

apparently had the same pattern in mind when he imprisoned Manuel José Arce and several other so-called "liberals."[25] Three provinces thus were committed to Iturbide, San Salvador was teetering in that direction, and Costa Rica declared herself independent but "neutral."

These declarations and pronouncements in favor of Mexico exposed the unenviable position of the provisional government. Owning no authority to declare either for absolute indepedence or annexation, it staggered under the burden of delivering the former colony to the congress, unity unimpaired. To cope with the disorder that resulted from González and Tinoco's efforts to force other towns and cities to declare for Mexico, the government moved the date of the congress to February 1, 1822, and sent special representatives to each of the troubled areas.[26] But the deputies, for the first two months, studiously avoided any commitment to the issues that caused the disorder. Their commendable objectivity dictated a policy of evasion and delay that they hoped would allow them to retire and bequeath that delicate decision to the congress. When the military commander in Oaxaca, for example, invited the deputies to declare in favor of Iturbide, Valle, accepting the task to avoid a direct answer, replied: "Last September 15 [1821], 108,589 days after June 2, 1524, when Pedro Alvarado arrived in Guatemala with 300 Spaniards, the happy independence of this capital was proclaimed." After scattering more baskets of fragrance, Valle noted that a congress was to determine the future of Guatemala. The deputies approved.[27]

Evasion disguised by grandiose phrase, however, had little appeal in the provinces, where the crisis deepened as González and Tinoco persisted in their attempt to force others to their design. In a futile gesture, however, Valle, commissioned by the government, drafted a manifesto published over the signature of Gainza that pointed out the dangers that the provinces were inviting.[28]

25. For Arce's criticism of Barrière, see Arce's letter to Pedro Molina, Oct. 11, 1821 (AGG, Molina Papers).

26. AGG, B1.13, 562, 19. Junta Consultiva Provisional, Nov. 10, 1821. Valle was responsible for informing the *ayuntamientos* of the purpose of the representatives, and the government ordered 600 copies of his manifesto.

27. AGG, B1.13, 562, 19. Junta Consultiva Provisional, Oct. 6, 1821. Quite understandably this document had been mistaken for the declaration of independence. See Chester Lloyd Jones, *Guatemala Past and Present* (Minneapolis, 1940), p. 35.

28. AGG, B5.4, 01372, 59. José del Valle remite al Jefe Gainza las contestaciones

The "lack of harmony" immediately after independence, Valle wrote, was little more than a difference of opinion, but during the subsequent weeks, the difference had changed to threatening rivalries that, if continued, would surely lead to "civil war." Unity with the provisional government was essential. Man was weak, and owing to his weakness, he had united with other men to form villages. But isolated villages could not long endure, and they had bound themselves together to form districts. Districts, however, were vulnerable and exposed to danger and thus had joined to form provinces. And provinces for the same reason had merged to form states. Here lay the shiny key cast in the eighteenth century that could unlock the axioms of society that were as applicable in nineteenth-century Guatemala as they had been in the wee hours of history. And Valle, changing pace, tried to present the application in what he considered a workable formula. Guatemala had three alternatives: (1) Each province could become an independent state; (2) all could unite with Mexico; (3) each could remain loyal to the provisional government. Students of government, however, had specified a minimum population, income, and power necessary for the success of an independent state. None of the provinces considered separately could lay claim to the prerequisites. The alternatives narrowed to two: Mexico or the provisional government. In order to decide to be a province of one or the other, Valle, on a strident note, declared it was necessary "to form an exact parallel of the advantages and disadvantages" that each choice offered, comparing distances to the capital of Mexico and Guatemala, the ease or difficulty of transportation, and the representation that the provinces would enjoy in the congresses of each nation. These were the practical considerations that should guide those called on to make the decision, which ultimately had to come from the "will of the people." And they could express their will in the congress scheduled for that purpose.[29]

The influence of Valle's manifesto, measured against the events in the provinces, was negligible. Huehuetenango and Quetzaltenango declared for Mexico, along with Santa Bárbara and Sacate-

---

que deben darse a las autoridades de León y Granada, que no están de acuerdo en la independencia, no date [Nov., 1821].

29. AGG, B1.13, 562, 19. Junta Consultiva Provisional, Nov. 10, 1821.

péquez (about ten miles from the capital). In Sonsonate, a corporal wounded a member of the town council,[30] and in the capital, we are assured by Mayor Larrave, few people ventured beyond their doors without a weapon.[31] In short, Guatemala, from Ciudad Real to Cartago, rapidly divided over the issue of absolute independence or union with Mexico, and as the sporadic fighting and disaffection slowly isolated the capital, a dispatch from Iturbide put an even greater burden on the deputies, who cared only to be placeholders for the congress.

[4]

On November 27, 1821, a courier, José de Oñate, carrying dispatches from Iturbide, arrived in Guatemala City.[32] Since September, 1821, when Mexico had declared independence, General Iturbide had earned new titles: the Liberator, General of Land and Sea, and President of the Most Serene Regency. Addressing himself to Gainza, Iturbide veiled a threat of force with a promise of power and prosperity. With pleasantries and congratulatory remarks begging more space, he noted that Guatemala awaited the decision of a "sovereign congress" that should be elected on the basis of one deputy for every 15,000 inhabitants. Now was not "the time to point out the inconveniences" of an electoral law that was difficult under ideal conditions. "My objective is only to manifest to you that the present interest of Mexico and Guatemala is so identical or indivisible that they cannot constitute themselves in separate or independent nations without risking the security of each. . . ." Together under the Plan of Iguala, however, each would be secure in the joys of liberty, free from all threat from within or without. Now, if by chance the deputies were not convinced by his good judgment, he invited them to express their views, promising not to use force even in the interest of their "happiness and well being." And with the purpose of protecting their happiness and well being, "a large and well-disciplined division" already had set out for the

30. *Ibid.*, Nov. 19, 1821.
31. AGG, A1.2.2, 15748, 2194. Libro de cabildos de Guatemala, año 1821 (Nov. 13).
32. AGG, B1.13, 562, 19. Junta Consultiva Provisional.

frontier, marching under the banner of "Religion, Independence, and Union. . . . May God protect you many years."[33]

The threat was not lost on the deputies, but instead of startling them into assuming authority they did not own, it simply hastened them on to the only decision that they considered legally correct. After spending "nearly the whole morning" (November 28) discussing the dispatch, they agreed to inform General of Land and Sea Iturbide that they were without the faculty for resolving the issue but that they were sending copies of his letter to each town council, asking that in *cabildo abierto*[34] they determine the will of the people and inside a month inform the provisional government of the results. The deputies, then, would relay the decision of the people to Iturbide. Valle, who was appointed to draft the manifesto to the town councils, retired from the assembly to begin writing, while the session continued. Hastily he dashed off the message, and upon his return, the deputies read and approved his rough draft,[35] which conveyed the urgency of the moment. Valle stressed that the attached letter from Iturbide demanded attention to questions of singular importance. While the General touched on the "pleasure and joy" of an independent nation whose government nestled in its "bosom," he impressed on the provisional government the undoubted superiority of the "population, power, and wealth" of Mexico and contrasted these advantages with the dissension of Comayagua, León, Chiapas, and Quetzaltenango. On the basis of these expressions and the heavy-handed threat of armed intervention, Valle emphasized, the town councils would have to render a decision.[36]

Four days later (December 3), Valle, changing the cadence of his prose, explained to Iturbide the position of the provisional government.[37] "The people of the nineteenth century are not

---

33. AGG, B5.2, 1264, 57. Apparently two dispatches arrived on that day from Iturbide. Oñate carried one, and another came in the afternoon. See Molina, Barrundia, Córdova to Iturbide, Nov. 3, 1821, Hernández Dávalos Collection, HD, 14-3, 1450, University of Texas Library.

34. The *cabildo abierto* showed the town council in its form that has been compared with the democratic town meetings of English colonial towns. However, these "open sessions" were held infrequently and only those could attend who had been invited.

35. AGG, B1.13, 562, 19. Junta Consultiva Provisional, Nov. 29, 1821.

36. *Ibid.*

37. *Ibid.* On December 3 Valle presented a rough draft of his reply, which was

what they were in the twelfth"; with the advance of civilization, they had become aware that they have rights; and the power of opinion had to be taken into account. Wincing even at the thought of an arbitrary act, the deputies shunned a decision in favor of absolute independence, fearing that the people would turn against those who "had deprived them of the union with a rich and powerful empire." Equally perilous was an avowal for union with Mexico, for the people, always changeable, perhaps would rise against those who had fastened their future to another state, without inquiring about their will. Midway between the extremes ran "a line drawn by prudence," and the provisional government was proceeding along that line.[38] Thus even in the face of Iturbide's threat, the deputies clung to the only position that they believed they could defend. Opinion outside the government, however, fled the line of prudence in favor of the extremes.

[5]

In contrast to the correct expressions of the provisional government, the town council of the capital championed annexation. On November 4, 1821, in response to an invitation from the governor of Oaxaca to join Mexico, Mayor Mariano Larrave asserted that Iturbide's declaration of independence had included "Guatemala and all its provinces" and further that the imperial army was not going "to view with indifference our separation," especially since the principal provinces already had tied their future to the Plan of Iguala. Guatemala, Larrave reasoned, lacked the "arms, money, and military disposition" necessary to oppose Iturbide; consequently it behooved the former colony to pronounce voluntarily for Mexico, achieving in that way more advantages.[39] On November 23, after Larrave had argued against the need of calling the congress, Alderman Quiñones complained that someone had removed the portraits of Pedro de Alvarado and Ferdinand VII and demanded their re-

---

to be sent on the following day. However, according to the *Boletín* (IV [1939], 372-376) the dispatch was not sent until December 29, 1821.
38. *Ibid.*
39. AGG, A1.2.2, 15748, 2194. Libro de cabildos de Guatemala, año 1821.

turn.[40]   Then on November 27 José de Oñate, the courier from Mexico, arrived in the capital, and after presenting his credentials to the provisional government, went to the town council, attracting a curious, news-hungry crowd.   Upon entering the municipal council, he presented a package that the secretary opened, disclosing a letter from Iturbide, inviting Guatemala to "associate herself with his glory."   The invitation, a copy of the Plan of Iguala, and news of the spine-tingling events in Mexico could not have found more receptive hands.[41]

At the opposite extreme, patriots Molina, Barrundia, Córdova, and their friends held tenaciously to the principle of absolute independence, and by means of *El Genio de la Libertad* and the Patriotic Society, they presented their views and opposed vigorously those of the town council.   In October, 1821, when cities and villages began filling the air with hue and cry for Mexico, *El Genio* queried: "Who guarantees that the Mexican congress will be convened?"   (A congress had been called to write a constitution.)   Monarchs were fickle and disposed toward absolutism, especially when they had an army equally fond of "despotism."   And who could force a monarch, "who has an armed force," to fulfil his promise?[42]   While this thoughtful article raised pertinent questions, Córdova, before the Patriotic Society, sneered at the enemies of independence for using the Plan of Iguala as a pretext for promoting their own interests.[43]   The angry Barrundia, who must have realized that the cause was lost, shouted in his frustration: "Ignorant men, do you not have eyes to see the advantages of a country, which until now has been frustrated by tyranny?   Cowards, without the heart to have and defend a fatherland."[44]

As Barrundia suggested, the patriots were beating into the teeth of a gale, hopelessly lost, utterly confused, and surrounded by their enemies.   That they should have written to Iturbide,

40. *Ibid.*
41. *Ibid.*
42. Oct. 15, 1821.   José Matías Delgado, who had become provisional governor of the province of San Salvador, was asking the same questions in a letter to Pedro Molina (AGG, Molina Papers, Dec. 27, 1821).
43. *El Genio de la Libertad,* Nov. 19, 1821.
44. AGG, B5.2, 1264, 57.   Discurso pronunciado por José Francisco Barrundia, Nov. 7, 1821.

plaintively, sincerely, and with the naïveté of innocent youth in an adult world, begging for help against those beating the drums for annexation illumines their plight as does no other single act. Happily they had greeted the news of Mexican independence, but word of Iturbide's desire to annex Guatemala "filled us with confusion" and sapped "our hopes" of ever "seeing our country free." Then by singling out those who favored union with Mexico as "proselytes of odious servilism," the ugly stepchild of Bustamante's "despotic government," they hoped to turn Iturbide away from those whose support he sought.[45]

That the patriots were in a hopeless minority became equally clear during the days immediately following the arrival of Oñate. On the night of November 29 a "well-known orchestra" serenaded Oñate, and "more than three thousand" lusty sons of the capital gathered at his quarters shouting: "Long live the Mexican Empire. Long live Guatemala. Long live the invincible Iturbide. Long live our Liberator. . . . Long live Captain José Oñate. . . . We don't want democracy. We don't want a republic."[46] Leading the parade, according to Molina, Barrundia, and Córdova, were Gainza, Archbishop Casaus, "a man of variable and accommodating character," José del Valle, "the head of the serviles," and the two *alcaldes* of the *ayuntamiento,* Mariano Larrave and Antonio Robles, "drunkards by profession." After praising Iturbide and flattering Oñate, the crowd moved on to the homes of the patriots, shouting, "in their drunkenness," the names that they thought "most reviling," calling them "republicans, serviles, heretics, and freemasons."[47] To retaliate, the patriots apparently were reduced to scribbling on the exterior of houses: "Democracy or blood. Down with Iturbide and long live the republic. Oñate has come to Guatemala . . . to make us miserable. . . . Death to Oñate and all his family." Shaken

45. Molina, Barrundia, Córdova to Iturbide, Nov. 3, 1821, Hernández Dávalos Collection, HD, 14-3, 1450, University of Texas Library.

46. *Boletín,* IV (1939), 323-325; Rafael Heliodoro Valle, ed., *La anexión de Centro América a México* (5 vols., Achivo Histórico Diplomático Mexicano, Series I, nos. 11, 24, 40; Series II, nos. 2, 3; Mexico, 1924-1946), I, 103-106. (Hereafter R. H. Valle, ed., *La anexión.*)

47. Molina, Barrundia, Córdova to Iturbide, Nov. 3, 1821, Hernández Dávalos Collection, HD, 14-3, 1450, University of Texas Library; Bumgartner, ed., "Documentos de la independencia de Guatemala," *Antropología e Historia de Guatemala,* XIII (July, 1961), 50-54.

by these "bloody insults" and an alleged attempt on his life, Oñate armed himself and requested a body-guard.[48]

On the following night (November 30), a number of patriots attended a meeting of the Patriotic Society and heard an address on whether any governing body in Guatemala possessed sufficient authority to annex Guatemala to Mexico.[49] The meeting adjourned about 10:00 P.M., and Molina, his brother-in-law, Mariano Bedoya, and twelve others were walking along "enjoying the moon" (*disfrutando la luna*), shouting "*vivas* and praise for this country, for its freedom, and also for a republican government." As they passed along the street where the Lucrecia tavern was located, they started on their separate ways. But just at that moment, they encountered a patrol of soldiers commanded by corporal Francisco Isla and accompanied by Mariano Larrave, who, as mayor had ordered the patrol. Isla challenged the patriots, who replied: "Guatemala free." Isla, not satisfied, ordered the commander of the patriot patrol to advance and be recognized. They answered that they were not a patrol and had no commander. Isla, after repeating the order and receiving the same reply, fired on the patriots, killing Bedoya and Manuel Meida (or Mayda or Mella). Molina, denied custody of Bedoya's body, claimed that Larrave was "drunk as usual" and charged him and Isla with murder.[50]

Larrave of course told a different story. According to his version, the patriots, after the meeting of the Patriotic Society, began insulting the mayor and the members of the town council, in addition to subjecting José de Oñate to the "worst insults." Some time after the patriots had offended Oñate, they encountered the patrol, and Larrave accused them of carrying weapons. When Isla challenged, the patriots replied with pistol shots, and, given such provocation, he had no choice except to return the fire that killed two men. Larrave concluded by requesting prohibition

48. *Boletín*, IV (1939), 323-325; R. H. Valle, ed., *La anexión*, I, 103-106. For a description of similar events in San Salvador, see J. Joaquín Chávez to Pedro Molina, Dec. 28, 1821, AGG, Molina Papers.

49. AGG, B5.2, 1246, 57. Discurso pronunciado por Lic. José Domingo en la Tertulia Patriótica de Guatemala, November 30, 1821.

50. AGG, B5.2, 1263, 57. Cuaderno que contiene la correspondencia de la Junta Consultiva Provisional. Molina claimed that Larrave quartered a concubine in the "Lucrecia." See Molina, Barrundia, Córdova to Iturbide, Nov. 3, 1821, Hernández Dávalos Collection, HD, 14-3, 1450, University of Texas Library. Physicians Molina and Larrave were also rivals in their profession. See Lanning, *Enlightenment*, p. 301. In addition, Molina claimed that Isla had been prosecuted as a thief. See Molina, "Memorias," *Centro-Americano*, XIII (April-Sept., 1921), 280-281.

of all meetings at night and especially those of the Patriotic Society.[51]

Molina had registered his complaint before the provisional government and thus involved Valle in two ways. As a member of the government, Valle would contribute to any decision coming from that body, and he would sit in judgment, as judge advocate, in the court of first instance, if Isla were brought to trial. Molina of course knew this, and he protested against Valle's participation either in the capacity of deputy or as judge, basing his protest of the "declared enmity that Sr. Valle professes for me" and Valle's "close friendship with Dr. Larrave, and on a thousand other circumstances that are equally well known." The government informed Molina that it had no authority to suspend the rights of any of the deputies, but Valle asked permission to withdraw from any connection with the case. And over a unanimous vote of the deputies, he persisted in his decision. In a move doubtless calculated to cause Valle to remove himself from hearing the case, should it come up, Eusebio Castillo, a lawyer who assisted the judge advocate, withdrew because Molina was the godfather of one of his children.[52]

Two days after Bedoya and Meida were killed, Gainza, with the agreement of the government, issued a decree to restore order in the capital. Henceforth all music in the streets at night without a license was forbidden. All persons caught forming groups or gangs to clamor for any "system of government, any authorities, or officials, or private citizens," or for shouting "death to any class or person of contrary opinion" would be prosecuted. After 8:00 P.M. no more than three men could appear on the streets together, unless they were accompanied by some "decent lady or ladies of their families." Carrying weapons was prohibited (as it always had been), and the Patriotic Society was suspended.[53]

51. AGG, A1.2.2, 15748, 2194. Libro de cabildos de Guatemala, año 1821 (Dec. 1). An unsigned note supporting Larrave's statement can be found in AGG, B5.3, 1248, 58. Cuaderno que contiene los dictámenes e informes del ayuntamiento de la Ciudad de Guatemala (December 24, 1821). Larrave resigned his position as *alcalde* (*Boletín*, IV [1939], 327).

52. AGG, B5.2, 1263, 57. Pedro Molina se queja contra el cabo Francisco Isla por haber hecho fuego y muerte a su hermano político [Molina's], Dn. Mariano Bedoya, la noche del 30 de noviembre (Dec. 3, 1821); B1.13, 562, 19. Junta Consultiva Provisional, Dec. 4, 1821. Barrundia and Córdova also submitted requests asking Valle to withdraw.

53. AGG, B5.3, 1288, 58. Cuaderno que contiene los dictámenes e informes del ayuntamiento de la Ciudad de Guatemala.

Iturbide, observing the chaos and violence bred by the bitter rivalry, rubbed his hands in satisfaction with the "pleasing progress of independence of that Kingdom of Guatemala."[54] And as the fruit of his efforts jarred loose, poised to fall, he ordered Colonel Antonio Flon, the Conde de la Cadena, to Ciudad Real to catch it and bear it back unbruised.[55] Word of Iturbide's order, together with his earlier reference to "well disciplined" troops, was sufficient to perpetuate in Guatemala the gangrenous rumor that five thousand troops were on their way.

[6]

The threat from Iturbide, the deaths of November 30, and the abrasive strife in the provinces began to wear on the deputies, who were awaiting the replies from the town councils. On December 10 Gainza, who earlier had denigrated Iturbide, manifested a fissure in the front of objectivity that the government had shown throughout October and November. Believing that five thousand troops were coming, or afraid not to, he gave credence to the rumor, reporting on the authority of general opinion in the capital that they already had entered the "territory of Guatemala." To avoid the "injurious consequences" promised by armed intervention, he proposed that the government send two deputies to the Mexican congress, emphasizing that it would be cheaper to pay their salaries than to support the sacrifices that the "coming of troops" would demand.[56] More than money was involved in Gainza's suggestion, which was tantamount to conceding annexation. For the moment, then, the deputies would wait for the news from the town councils.

Throughout the remaining days of 1821, the rivalry, at its crest on November 30, slowly gave way to impatience for the

54. *Boletín*, IV (1939), 329; R. H. Valle, ed., *La anexión*, I, 108-109.
55. *Boletín*, IV (1939), 328.
56. AGG, B1.13, 562, 19. Junta Consultiva Provisional, Dec. 10, 1821. On January 2, 1822, Gainza stated that it was always thought that Guatemala "should follow the path of Mexico," claiming that he had heard such expressions before he had arrived. "I always was persuaded of it. So was everyone else until the moment of declaring independence on September 15, and the Junta [Consultiva Provisional] knows what happened then. The events in Mexico produced it. Without them Guatemala would have remained silent." See AGG, B1.13, 562, 19. Junta Consultiva Provisional.

inevitable. Molina, bitter and heartsick, signaled the end of the patriots' opposition when he asked for permission to leave the capital.[57] And by December 18 the Marquis de Aycinena could report to a friend that the provisional government had received the instructions for electing deputies to the Mexican congress, though they had not been circulated. But owing to the effectiveness of Iturbide's dispatch, "all the provinces" were "declaring for union with the empire, and before the end of the month, this capital will also join."[58] A week later, relative Mariano Aycinena, addressing the town council, lauded independence from Spain (*posesión dulce*) but lamented the complete anarchy in which the nation found itself. The remedy, however, was at hand in the person of Iturbide, who rapidly became the panacea for all the national aches. With the "most profound knowledge of politics" and the "skill and perception rarely conceded to mortals," he had shown clearly why Guatemala could not exist as a separate state. "The height of my desire," Aycinena confessed, "is union and conformity with our brothers of Mexico."[59] On December 29, the town council of the capital cast its vote for those "desires," fulfilling the Marquis de Aycinena's prediction.[60]

The provisional government, stolid in its position until the end, met on January 2, 1822, knowing that it had promised Iturbide that an answer would leave Guatemala on the following day. The final decision, however, was not as simple as the deputies had hoped. Instead of counting the votes, determining a majority, and conveying the result to Iturbide, they had to take into account that a number of the town councils still had not answered. Valle, the soul of objectivity in the government, wanted to see as many replies as possible before he voted. He informed his colleagues that he had just received word from Tegucigalpa that its vote was forthcoming, and he begged to delay the decision, volunteering to inform Iturbide of the circumstances by the day's mail. Larreinaga, who wanted to resolve the question immediately, argued that the will of the people was well known. Only "very few town

57. AGG, B3.5, 00938, 46 (Dec. 3, 1821). Molina wanted to take his family to Verapaz.

58. *Boletín*, IV (1939), 349.

59. AGG, B5-3, 1248, 58. Cuaderno que contiene los dictámenes e informes del ayuntamiento de la Ciudad de Guatemala (Dec. 24, 1821).

60. AGG, A1.2.2, 15748, 2194. Libro de cabildos de Guatemala, año 1821.

councils" had failed to answer, and their delay, he said with irritation, should not be permitted to prejudice Guatemala's interest
in the Mexican congress, scheduled to convene in February, 1822.
Besides, the provisional government had given its word—was
honor bound—to dispatch the decision on the following day.
After much agonizing and with the support of Gainza, the deputies agreed to grapple with the question after lunch.[61]

That afternoon, during the second session of January 2, Valle
disclosed another complication. From his study of the votes, he
discovered that the town councils, instead of voting either for
or against, had expressed four different views: (1) only a constituent congress could decide on annexation; (2) unconditional
annexation; (3) the provisional government should decide; (4)
annexation with specific conditions. The first category had been
the position of the provisional government until Iturbide's dispatch arrived. The third had been disavowed, but the second
and fourth were the object of fruitless argument. The Marquis
de Aycinena, in a sentimental mood, thought the name "Guatemala" should appear in that of the Empire. Valle, thinking
about elections to the Mexican congress, wanted to specify certain
electoral procedure. But Larreinaga refused to presume to put
conditions on Iturbide, and, failing agreement on the question
of whether they could attach conditions, they decided to inform
Iturbide that a majority of town councils had voted for union
and to send the decision concerning conditions as soon as it was
made. The dispatch went out on the following day,[62] and annexation was published on January 5, 1822. Nothing remained
for the provisional government except a few loose ends.

But Valle thought the loose ends were important, and he
elaborated on the condition that he wanted to impose. He suggested that the election of deputies to the Mexican congress should
proceed according to the regulations of the Spanish Constitution
of 1812, but in agreement with the Mexican deputy-population
ratio. Larreinaga replied that he thought Valle's proposal was
in the best interest of Guatemala but explained that the elections

61. AGG, B1.13, 562, 19. Junta Consultiva Provisional. For some of the reasons
that delayed the replies from Honduras, which Valle mentioned, see Guillermo
Mayes, *Honduras en la independencia de Centro América y anexión a México*
(Tegucigalpa, 1956), pp. 55-63.
    62. *Ibid.*

would have to conform to the procedure prescribed in Mexico. Dissatisfied with the Mexican regulation that gave town councils the authority to elect deputies, Valle stubbornly persisted, asserting that "the right of the people was very sacred" and that Mexico "trampled" that right with an "unjust law." Thus when the issue came to a vote, he begged to support his verbal opposition in writing "in order that posterity should do him justice."[63]

Gainza, who apparently had no other interest save that of terminating the weary business, raised the question on January 5, and proposed to declare the government in permanent session until the deputies reached a decision. They agreed, and Valle added the qualification that they should have the privilege of submitting in writing all the reasons underlying the vote that each would cast. Preliminaries aside, they concentrated on the motion: Did the provisional government have authority to specify conditions for the annexation of Guatemala to Mexico, in view of the fact that the majority of town councils had voted for union without reservation? Immediately Valle said that in order to resolve the question it was necessary first to review the vote of each town council. But over the protest of Valle, the deputies agreed that they were well informed of the votes, which according to Gainza showed: 104 for unconditional annexation; 11 for union but with conditions; 32 left the decision to the provisional government; 21 wanted the congress to decide; and 2 were opposed to annexation. The rest had not replied.[64] Valle's objection disposed of, the deputies agreed that the provisional government could include only those conditions expressed and that they should apply only to the town councils that had specified them.[65] Doggedly Valle clung to his position even after the motion had

63. *Ibid.*, Jan. 3, 1822.
64. *Ibid.*, Jan. 5, 1822. A few days later, Valle asked secretary Mariano Gálvez for the answers from the *ayuntamientos,* and upon receiving them, he "began to make a prolonged study of them (until 12:30 P. M.), in the presence of the government." Then on the following day (Jan. 8, 1822) he informed the deputies that "the rest" of the *ayuntamientos* that had not replied numbered "seventy-one." This number, more tangible than "the rest," prompted Larreinaga to declare that Valle had counted some *ayuntamientos* "that were not in Guatemala or at least not known to be." See AGG, B1.13, 562, 19. Junta Consultiva Provisional, Jan. 7 and 8, 1822.
65. AGG, B1.13, 562, 19. Junta Consultiva Provisional, Jan. 5, 1822. On December 29, 1821, the Colegio de Abogados proposed that annexation to Mexico should take the form of a federation, permitting Guatemala her own legislature, independent local government, and her own tribunal, which would be supreme and subject to no control from Mexico. See AGG, B5.2, 01264, 57.

carried, saying that the authority of a Guatemalan congress was necessary to impose conditions, but if, as was the case, the congress could not be convoked, the authority devolved upon the provisional government. "Some sovereign power had to exist in order to decide." Patiently Gainza told Valle that he should have presented that point before the question had been resolved. Valle, his persistence equal to Gainza's patience, replied that it had occurred to him after the vote but that he would express the point in writing.[66]

On January 7, five days after the decision to annex Guatemala and two days after the vote on conditions for annexation, Valle with an eye on the future as well as posterity, submitted his written opinion. By this time, however, he had expanded his idea, by coincidence or calculation, in such a manner that it could be construed as his views on annexation, as well as on the faculty of the government for imposing conditions. The "Guatemalan nation," he wrote, had three rights: The people could unite, or choose representatives to unite, for the purpose of dealing with matters pertaining to the legislative power; they could discuss these matters; and they could make decisions. Under no circumstances could the people denounce their rights, for to do so would be to denounce their own existence. Neither could town councils exercise these rights. Sovereign authority was necessary for the binding obligations on which the union should hinge, and the fact that a majority of town councils voted for unconditional annexation was not significant; they were not the sovereign power. The congress that was to have met would have embodied sovereignty, and since circumstances prevented the meeting of the congress, sovereign authority belonged to the provisional government. But the other deputies had overruled his views, which he now submitted.[67]

The provisional government continued into February, 1822, but the crisis had come and gone. An overwhelming majority of town councils had voted to annex Guatemala to Mexico, less than four months after *El Genio de la Libertad,* in an exuberant and swaggering mood, had shouted: "Long live the sovereign

66. *Ibid.,* afternoon session.
67. *Ibid.,* Jan. 7, 1822. Valle's argument has been published in *Boletín,* IV (1939), 396-397.

people of Guatemala. Long live their freedom and Independence. Long live . . ."

[7]

If these four months taught nothing else, they taught by example that the hierarchy of authority in the colonial period, so carefully arranged and calculated to put the reigns of power in the hands of a king, became anathema when the government in the capital no longer was the king's person in the colony. Governors Barrière and Tinoco, after the cloak of purple had been cast aside, enjoyed as much authority as Gainza and the provisional government. And the governors were no less successful in imposing their will on town councils which, more from tradition than respect, clung to the authority in the capital than was Gainza and the government in commanding the loyalty of those that refuted and turned away from the capital. This unfortunate distribution of power plus the resentment that the provinces held for the capital added up to a turn of events that could have been predicted. And to blame the issue of union with Mexico for the strife and chaos is to ignore what happened between 1826-1829. Dionisio de Herrera, intelligent, moderate in his views, and tied closely to Tegucigalpa, where governor González was opposed, expressed what caused many provincials, including Valle, to gnash their teeth:

. . . my character, my principles, and my conscience are opposed to the system of Guatemala. I cannot compromise myself by becoming an instrument of intrigue for the sons of the capital. They surround, they inform, they direct the government—they do everything, as you [Valle] know. This is the cause of the incidents in San Salvador and the discord in Chiapas, Comayagua, León, Tegucigalpa, etc., etc. I would bet ten to one that if the government moved to any other place all again would be stable.[68]

As the confusion mentioned by Herrera enveloped Guatemala, breaking down trade and communications and generally making a normal life impossible, many who had been indifferent or opposed to union with Mexico came to view annexation in the same

68. To Valle, Tegucigalpa, Aug. 9, 1822, Valle Papers. Herrera was explaining why he had just refused, for the second time, the executive authority of his province.

manner that Justo de Herrera, Dionisio's brother, did when he wrote:

What confuses me is that we are independent, and there are Europeans [Spaniards] in our country who control the government, the arms, and the ports. . . . But although it is not the most accommodating government, it will serve as a means for the re-establishment of domestic tranquillity and protect us from the threat from abroad, which demands all the attention of America.[69]

And a large group agreed with brother Próspero de Herrera's friend who, bubbling with enthusiasm, spoke of the "heroes" of the century: "an Iturbide, a Bolívar, and a San Martín."[70] These views, combined with those that saw Guatemala as a part of Mexico even before independence, in addition to the open threat from Iturbide, provided the essentials for annexation.

[*8*]

For Valle, the months following independence were among the most rewarding of his entire career. Throughout the sessions of the provisional government, he provided the key administrative ability, drawing up parliamentary procedure, organizing committees, guarding public funds, and drafting dispatches in the prose demanded by the circumstances. And his presence acted as a check on less patient deputies, when they had to face up to the issue of union with Mexico. Valle, more than any other member of the government, understood the precariousness of the issue for each person who had a hand in making the decision. In the dispatch to Iturbide, Valle recognized the perils when he wrote that the government was following the "line drawn by prudence between the extremes." He knew and shrewdly stated that there would be repercussions, regardless of the decision. That a man, a deputy such as he, could ruin his career by either opposing or supporting annexation was elemental politics to Valle. Thus from the first moment when the government came to grips with the issue until it was resolved, Deputy Valle scrupulously, almost agonizingly, followed the line of prudence. With greatest care, as though he were the personal custodian of all the human rights

69. To Próspero de Herrera, Choluteca, July 22, 1822, Valle Papers.
70. Yanuario García to Próspero de Herrera, Viejo, May 16, 1822, Valle Papers.

imagined in the eighteenth century, he guarded those of the people of Guatemala. So zealous was he in their behalf that he even altered his view concerning the right of the provisional government to exercise sovereign authority. Sovereign power had to be some place. Patiently, meticulously, he sorted out and counted the replies from the municipal councils, begged to wait for the tardy answers, and tried in vain to attach conditions concerning electoral procedure. And never once did he mention the issue in his newspaper. From his actions in the sessions, then, and from what he did not write in *El Amigo* emerges the portrait of a man completely dedicated to the principle of objectivity, so much so that in contrast to the Marquis de Aycinena, whose sympathy we know, Valle appeared to prefer absolute independence. It is also possible to construe his opinions in connection with the authority of the government to specify conditions in such a way that he is seen as a champion of independence. But this opinion and others written so that "posterity" would do him "justice" were drafted and submitted after all the important decisions had been made. Yet his figure in the government was so convincing that the citizens of San Salvador, who opposed annexation with arms, invited Valle to assume executive authority of their province.[71]

There is reason to believe, however, that Valle's personal preference was union with Mexico and that he had held that view since the spring of 1821, when the news of the Plan of Iguala arrived. It is quite likely also that he was thinking in terms of the Mexican Empire when he read and corrected the act of independence. In a sworn statement José Velasco, General Director of the Tobacco and Gunpowder Monopoly, declared that he had known and worked with Valle, dealing with him frequently and with familiarity. In the general meeting convoked to decide on independence, "I heard him vote in favor of it, expressing with eloquence reasons as wise as they were profound." Later, "I heard him several times, in the presence of others, talk in favor of our annexation to the Great Empire, even before they decided to determine the will of the people." At the same time, Valle assured that "if matters reached a point where

71. AGG, B1.13, 562, 19. Junta Consultiva Provisional, Feb. 5, 1822.

order was destroyed, he would put his whole family on the road to the capital of Mexico."[72] In a second statement Nicolás Cobo, chief accountant of the tobacco monopoly, who lived next door to Valle, certified that he had known Valle for many years and had visited and talked with him frequently, as a neighbor would. On one occasion, in May of 1821, Cobo and Valle were chatting, and, among other things, they touched on the Plan of Iguala, which had just arrived in Guatemala. "We talked slowly about it, always agreeing that it was the most useful and wisest plan that could have been drafted." Cobo recalled Valle's saying that, if the Plan were put into effect, Mexico in time would become "the happiest, wealthiest, and most powerful land in the world." And Cobo felt compelled to add that Valle had made this statement when "it was a serious crime to talk about the Plan." Later, but "even before the union of this province with the Empire, he told me that his ideas were to liquidate his interests and take his family to Mexico."[73] In a third statement another accountant swore that Valle had said that the Mexican government was "the most appropriate for his ideas."[74]

Each of these friends made his statement in December, 1822, in extraordinary circumstances. Valle was in prison in Mexico as a result of a conspiracy in which he had become involved. Thus there is reason to suspect the reliability of these witnesses. But there were extraordinary circumstances surrounding his imprisonment (treated below) that indicate that all Valle needed from his friends was the unvarnished truth. Few errors and exaggerations occur in the statements concerning events established as fact. Each praised and commended Valle, but they praised and commended the same qualities that Captains General González and Bustamante and Oidor Polo had lauded. But none of the witnesses approached the enthusiasm that had moved González and Bustamante when they discussed Valle. Further the declarations of Valle's friends fit exactly into the transition that he had to make. Quite understandably it was an easier step from a Spanish

72. Dec. 16, 1822, Valle Papers.
73. *Ibid.*
74. José María Santa Cruz, Dec. 18, 1822, Valle Papers. In a fourth sworn statement (Dec. 17, 1822, Valle Papers), José Vicente del Águila, General Treasurer of the tobacco monopoly, told essentially the same story, though his account makes clear that he did not know Valle as well as the others.

crown to an American crown than from royal authority to republican government, in which persons of little or no background and education could participate. In these terms, annexation for Valle was the fruit of the compromise of September 15. He and the overwhelming majority of men whose financial interests, family background, and formal education were similar to his had taken the position that seemed to promise stability, security, and their continuing influence. It it true that scholar and aristocrat Simeón Cañas, a member of the deputation so detestable to Bustamante, opposed union with Mexico. But Cañas favored a monarchy in Guatemala.[75] These aristocrats knew from experience that a king could keep order as well as oppress, and they understood republican government and knew that the great majority in Guatemala did not.

That Valle could agree with members of the family on the question of annexation did not compromise or end their rivalry. The enmity between him and the family did not feed on differences growing out of conflicting views on types of government but rather on the competition to control whatever government happened to be in Guatemala. The defeat of Article 3 of the Act of Independence demonstrated that the rivalry for control continued and that Valle had lost the majority that had originally put the statement in the declaration. Then after the issue of annexation destroyed the alignment of the family with the patriots[76] and absorbed all attention, there was little over which Valle and the family could disagree. All favored union with Mexico, and the members of the family in the provisional government were content, whether from apathy or inability, to allow Valle to assume the journeywork of administration. Antonio Batres Jáuregui caught the high moment of their agreement when, with the insight that makes his work indispensable, he wrote that Larreinaga, Valle, two Aycinenas, the Beltranenas, and other conservatives worked with many liberals, "all in good faith," to bring about annexation.[77]

75. AGG, A1.3-4, 12340, 182. Libro de claustros de la Universidad de San Carlos, 1808-1831 (Dec. 13, 1821).

76. Pedro Molina ("Memorias," *Centro-Americano*, XIII [April-Sept., 1921], 279-280) confirms that the issue over the union with Mexico destroyed the combination of the patriots with the family.

77. *La América Central ante la historia*, III, 85.

In addition to the reasons that motivated other members of the aristocracy to work for union with Mexico, Valle had personal views that moved him in that direction. One inescapable impression that emerges from a study of his life, before and after 1821, is that he felt that Guatemala was too provincial and thus unappreciative of his talents and that he was missing fame, or at least proper recognition, by reason of geography. He suggested this time and again in his attempt to go to Spain, and it was probably a frank statement to this effect that prompted Oidor González to reply in agreement that Valle would be worth "100 per cent more" in Spain. The same attitude toward living in a remote, if not inferior, corner of the world was expressed repeatedly before 1820 in remarks about the people and the colony that could not be misinterpreted. After 1820 the same attitude runs through his essays on Guatemala that appeared in *El Amigo.* In print he lavished fulsome praise in preface to what needed to be done before Guatemala could hope to achieve what he thought the nations of Western Europe, the darlings of his eye, already had accomplished. Thus his criticism continued, but he put it in palatable phrases. However, his remark about the weather in Madrid, where it was hotter in the summer and colder in the winter than in Guatemala, recalls a fable. Finally his adulation of and identification with the scholars of the Old World, expressed in *El Amigo* and in his unsolicited correspondence with the great and near great, suggested the same feeling of an inadequate audience at home and a longing to test his talent on what he considered a more sophisticated society. In this respect, Valle was similar to Dr. José Felipe Flores, of the University of San Carlos,[78] and judging from Flores' comments, other faculty members shared his feeling. And Valle, in the manner of Flores, thought life in Spain would provide the proper intellectual climate, and when he despaired of achieving that fervent desire, Mexico became his second choice. Thus his expressed intention to move to Mexico and his sympathy for annexation were in harmony with his previous views.

The advantages that Valle stood to gain by practicing objectivity, while privately nourishing the hope for union, was that regardless of the success or failure of union with Mexico his career would not suffer. And as events unfolded, he saw how he could

78. Lanning, *Enlightenment,* p. 274.

use his preference for Mexico to distinct advantage and later how he could turn his calculated objectivity to an advantage equally great, using in the future the documents that he had written for posterity. That Molina saw him parading on November 29 and denounced him as a Servile did not compromise the advantages. Molina's letter was a recommendation of Valle in the eyes of Iturbide. When Guatemala separated from Mexico, time, events in Mexico, and new crises already had blurred the past. Besides, Molina, according to Oñate's count, had seen 2,999 others taking part in the celebration of Iturbide's invitation. Thus placed in the sequence of events after 1821, Valle's actions immediately following the Act of Independence demonstrated that he was a highly skilled politician, a talent that he was to use exceedingly well in Mexico and again when he returned to Guatemala.

To the Capital of Anáhuac

[*1*]

After the dark, uncertain days following independence, a jubilant Valle looked forward to the prosperity and security that was the pledge of the great empire. The revolutions in the English colonies, France, Spain, and Spanish America had turned out for the best; and despite all the heart-rending frustrations and doubts during the last days of the colony, he did live for the moment in the best of all possible worlds. Guatemala was a part of Mexico; Mexico was promised to a constitutional monarch; and Valle could claim citizenship in a nation that sprawled from San Francisco south to Panama. And after the long and dimly lit corridor of the colonial period, the broad, bright span leading into the future lay before him like a dream. "We live in the nineteenth century," he pinched himself editorially, "and the nineteenth century is a liberal century . . . a friend of man."[1] Sober second thoughts, however, told him that much needed to be done before Mexico or Guatemala could compete with European countries, which never lost their appeal for him. But he was firmly committed to America, and since he never demanded less than first place for his own efforts, he felt licensed to demand the same from America. By working together toward the pinnacle, each could contribute to the stature of the other, and finally he and America would stand on the level with Europe. On this basis, Valle struck a bargain with America.

Relaxed and secure in the knowledge that Guatemala had made the right decision, Valle mused on the terms of his bargain. America's terms were clearly stated. Extending from temperate

1. *El Amigo de la Patria*, March 29, 1822.

to torrid to temperate zone, her lush tropics, her mighty rivers, and her towering mountains spoke in the seductive whisper of a jungle breeze, in the churlish voice of the swollen Amazon, and in the strident tone of an Andean blizzard, telling of a home for generations yet unborn and of untold and unimagined wealth. All was there for the taking. These were America's terms. What could he bring to the partnership? Alone in the quiet of his study, surrounded by his books, comfortable in a chair made only for work, pen in hand, and paper on the small table, he allowed his thoughts to spill freely and softly, building steadily and sonorously in majestic Castilian into the torrent that became his song of America—his pledge and his terms.

Thy wishes are mine, those of my friends, and of my compatriots. I swear to uphold them as long as I live. . . . Beloved country accept this oath. . . . America from this moment will be my exclusive occupation—America by day when I write, by night when I think. The study most worthy of an American is America.[2]

His life pledged, he set forth a program leading to the pinnacle that was America's destiny. Valle called for a congress of Americans, from Mexico to Chile, to meet in the province of Costa Rica or León. Each country should send deputies with a summary of its political, economic, and military strength in order to total the sum of America's vigor. The most important objective of the congress should be the formation of an American federation in which every state could come together in "solemn pact" to guarantee each against foreign invasion and domestic strife. Each state should specify the number of troops and the amount of money that it could contribute in the event that a sister state were distressed. To preclude the stamp of oppressor, the troops sent to an American state torn by internal strife should be confined to allowing the legislature of the troubled state to settle its problems peacefully and to enforcing the settlement once it had been made. Equally important, the American deputies should conclude reciprocal trade agreements and draft a plan that would enable each state to achieve the wealth promised by America's resources.

Moved by his grand design for an American federation, Valle exclaimed that his congress would present a "spectacle" never witnessed in the "Old World" nor "dreamed in the New." All

2. *Ibid.*, March 1. 1822.

the benefits that would result from the federation transcended
his powers of imagination, but he knew that such an arrangement,
supported by "14 or 15 million people," would be superior to
any aggressor and give the "weak states the power of the strong."
America, then, bound by the "great bond of the congress," would
form "literally one great family," and the congress thus would be
the initial step in the creation of an *"American system,"* or the
principles that should guide the "political conduct" that one day
would ensconce America next to Europe, whose "system" had put
her astride the globe.[3]

Valle published his plan on March 1, 1822, establishing himself
as one of the early champions for uniting the Spanish American
colonies. Throughout the remainder of the nineteenth century
and into the twentieth, the idea of a united Latin America has
persisted, if only in the fancy of few men. As time has sapped
the idea of practical application, people have imbued it with the
aura of an ideal and have sought out and praised the men of vision
who first spoke the word of the missed opportunity. Generally,
Francisco de Miranda, the precursor of Spanish American independence, is credited with prior claim. Simón Bolívar mentioned
it in his famous Jamaica letter, and owing to the fact that he called
the first American congress, in 1826, he has received the plaudits
for having surpassed all others. A statement, however, by Bernardo Monteagudo, Bolívar's plenipotentiary to Guatemala and
Mexico, suggests that Bolívar might have an unpaid obligation
to Valle. Monteagudo arrived in Guatemala in late 1823, read
Valle's paper, and a short time later wrote: "I am greatly interested
in reprinting in [city illegible] your paper concerning the great
American Federation, and the Liberator [Bolívar] agrees. With
reason, he believes that you are one of the strong defenders of
freedom that the New World has in the south."[4]

3. *Ibid.*
4. Monteagudo to Valle (date and place torn away), Valle Papers. The letter
had to be written some time before the first days of February, 1825, when Monteagudo was murdered. See Bolívar to Francisco de Paula Santander, Lima, Feb. 9, 1825,
Selected Writings of Bolívar, compiled by Vicente Lecuna, edited by Harold A.
Bierck, Jr., and translated by Lewis Bertrand (2 vols.; New York, 1951), I, 467.
(Hereafter Bierck, ed., *Selected Writings of Bolívar.*) For further information
concerning Monteagudo's visit to Guatemala, see AGG, B10.2-1, 3272, 157. Correspondencia de Ministro de Relaciones (Jan. 21, 1824); Andrés Townsend Ezcurra,
"Monteagudo en Guatemala," *Ateneo,* I, no. 1 (Sept., 1953); M. Soto Hall, "Dos
grandes apóstoles del panamericanismo: Bernardo Monteagudo y José Cecilio del
Valle," *Anales,* III (1926-1927), 15-25; Bierck, ed., *Selected Writings of Bolívar,* II,

In addition to Miranda, Bolívar, and Valle, other men talked about the same idea, as did the members of the town councils of Buenos Aires and Caracas. Thus posterity has ascribed more to the wisdom of few men than the teens and twenties of the nineteenth century will ever admit. Since Spain had held her American colonies together for three centuries under a single authority, a profound flash of insight was unnecessary to imagine an American federation. Certainly if two town councils in two small Central American villages could conceive that their future would be more secure in the hands of Colombia or Mexico,[5] the next step could not have been difficult. Bolívar's Gran Colombia was a move in that direction, as was Valle's quiet preference for union of Guatemala and Mexico. Valle, however, never made any great claims for his paper, despite the absence of an earlier more comprehensive plan. But Valle would be the last to refuse the title of "Apostle of America,"[6] should interested parties acclaim it. No one, however, will dispute the fact that a man of Bolívar's stature was necessary if the congress were to become a reality.

[2]

Less than a week after Valle published his plea for an American federation, the province of Tegucigalpa elected him to the Mexican Congress.[7] With the same contagious optimism expressed in his song of America, he set about making preparations

---

383-384; Vicente Lecuna, *Crónica razonada de las guerras de Bolívar* (3 vols.; New York, 1959), III, 302, 394; Juan de Dios Mayorga to Valle, Mexico City, March 27, 1824, Valle Papers. Dios Mayorga wrote: "According to what I hear from his compatriots, I think Monteagudo's departure from Guatemala is a good thing."

5. San Miguel and Santa Anna. See AGG, B4.2, 01167, 50; B4.2, 01168, 50.

6. Eliseo Pérez Cadalso, *Valle, apóstol de América* (Tegucigalpa, 1954). Also see Rubén Leyton Rodríguez, *Valle, padre del panamericanismo* (Tegucigalpa, 1954).

7. Valle to Gainza, April 20, 1822. AGG, B5.8, 1894, 69. Valle also was elected by the *ayuntamiento* of Chiquimula. See AGG, B5.8, 1874, 69. He swore loyalty to the Empire on March 11 (AGG, B5.10, 2208, 74). Later Valle wrote that Tegucigalpa had elected him on March 10, rather than on March 7, as the record shows (Valle and Valle Matheu, eds., *Obras,* I, 67). Valle, who resigned from the provisional government on February 16, 1822, finally succeeded in altering the procedure for electing deputies to the Mexican Congress. The provisional government decided to use the provisions of the Constitution of 1812, except that they would elect deputies on the basis of one for every 27,000 inhabitants. With a population of one and one-half millions as calculated by "Humbol," they planned to send forty deputies to Mexico. See AGG, B1.13, 562, 19. Junta Consultiva Provisional, Jan. 14, 1822.

for his only journey beyond the boundaries of Guatemala. One act, however, illustrates most clearly the change in his thinking brought about by annexation. Instead of liquidating his interests and moving to Mexico, he bought the hacienda "La Concepción,"[8] a solid investment in the security and stability of the Empire.

While he negotiated the sale, he also busied himself with important details. Cousin Dionisio promised to take charge of part of Valle's financial interests,[9] and Cousin Justo doubtless supervised the haciendas near Choluteca, as he had done in the past.[10] Letters of introduction to influential Mexicans were provided by friend Archbishop Casaus.[11]

For Casaus, everything also had turned out for the best. He accepted independence with the same reservations of the aristocracy, knowing that Guatemala could not long remain a colony flanked by independent states. As independence drew near, he suffered some discourtesy.[12] But when annexation became a fact, it was almost as though nothing had changed. He received the Gran Cruz de Guadalupe from "His Majesty Iturbide" with the same boyish pride that an equivalent honor from Ferdinand VII would have evoked.[13] Thus Casaus' remarks in behalf of his faithful friend were as enthusiastic as they had been eight years earlier.

After two months of preparation, Valle was ready for his overland journey to Mexico City. On May 7, 1822, with more sadness than excitement, he embraced the beloved Josefa and two daughters and young son, bidding them goodbye with forced and painful small talk about manners, health, and letter writing that conceals

8. AGG, A1.20, 9964, 1484. Libro de escribano José Antonio de Solís, April 30, 1822.

9. Dionisio de Herrera to María Josefa Valero, Tegucigalpa, July 9, 1822, Valle Papers. Dionisio explained that he had sold ten *tercios* of cacao for 180 pesos and that Valle had asked him to buy silver with the returns from cacao.

10. Justo de Herrera to Valle, Choluteca, July 31, 1818, Valle Papers.

11. Ramón Casaus to Francisco Manuel Sánchez de Tagle, May 4, 1822, Valle Papers. Casaus wrote: "Estimado Compadre y Ahijado: José del Valle, judge advocate of the army, is on his way to congress as a deputy. In the year '12, I had the pleasure of performing his wedding services. I think as highly of him as I do of you. For this reason and because of his talent and personal charm, I am sending him to you so that you might do whatever you can for him, perhaps accompanying him, if it suits you, to meet the General [Iturbide] and the other gentlemen of the Regency, the well-known deputies, and other close friends."

12. AGG, A2.1, 746, 30. Oficio del arzobispo acerca de que prevenga al capitán Rafael Ariza que se respete a la autoridad eclesiástica (Sept. 11, 1821).

13. Casaus to Valle, Sept. 2, 1822, Valle Papers. Casaus noted that he had just received a letter from Valle's brother-in-law, Manuel Valero, congratulating him for having received the honor.

the childlike emotions that, at such moments, surge in the breast of the hardiest traveler. Valle was forty-five when he began the trip that would take him over exceedingly difficult terrain. Older men had endured longer, more difficult journeys, but with few exceptions, such as conquistador Jiménez de Quesada and Valle's friend G. A. Thompson, their previous lives had prepared them for the expeditions they undertook. With calloused hands and wit keen for nature's tricks and the brigand's trap, they had been a match and more for their obstacles. Valle, on the contrary, was not of this breed. He had spent the greater part of his years in the offices of the colonial government and among the books in his study. Writing, not riding, was his forte, and although his pen could be more deadly than a rapier, it is doubtful that he could squeeze a trigger with any accuracy. But in the tradition of the classic traveler, he kept a journal.

Valle spent his first night on the road in Mixco, three leagues from the capital. "It is populated by 2500 Indians and 500 *ladinos;* there is no primary school." While the village claimed no government liquor store (*estanquillo de aguardiente*), six taverns offered *chica*. The prison for women was vacant, but four men were confined, including an "Indian who had killed his wife." On the slope facing the capital, the Indians were without communal lands (*ejidos*), and thus they were obliged to rent their corn patches (*milpas*) from the "few property owners." The rent paid generally consisted of "2 pesos and 2 hens" for the privilege of sowing the seed and "one *fanega* of corn" for every dozen that they harvested.[14] The Indians were grossly ignorant, and their ignorance, Valle protested to his journal, offered "the most decisive proof of the little care and protection that they received from the capital, despite the fact that they live so close." On the opposite side of Mixco, facing away from the capital, a few *ejidos* remained, but they were not sufficiently large to support the population, and thus the Indians on that side were also tenants.

On the following morning, at 7:00 A.M., he left Mixco in the direction of Santa María and Chimaltenango, a steady climb. He wanted very much to measure the altitude at various points but had no instruments. Cherry and apple trees, however, spoke of

14. A *fanega* is equal to about one and one-half bushels.

the increasing height, which began to make him dizzy.[15]   Soon he arrived at the small village of Santiago, immediately before Santa María, where he saw a procession of Indians carrying the images of several Saints and chanting prayers for rain.   "Oh, the thoughts that shot through my mind upon seeing this!"   These "poor, miserable" people were also without a primary school and received no aid or protection from the capital.   Leaving Santiago, he crossed a bridge in bad repair and later contrasted its ruin with the care that it had merited "during the time of its construction." At length he arrived at Santa María, "small, ignorant, and wretched."   He concluded that society outside Guatemala City, instead of progressing, was in full retreat, blaming greed, peculation, and the self-centered capital.[16]

By the first days of June, he had reached Oaxaca,[17] where he mailed gifts to his wife and children.   *"Nuestro amadísimo y muy deseado* José: With inexpressible joy, we received your letter and news of your health,"* Josefa wrote.   The dolls, "two *señoritas,* two infants, an Indian man, and an old lady," were the things that the children enjoyed most.   "Lola and the little one are crazy about them."[18]   Josefa received letters from Puebla and from Mexico City as soon as Valle arrived (July 28, 1822).   When the letter came from the capital of the Empire, she was in church. On her way home, a servant girl, sent by the courier, told Josefa that a letter had arrived.   She ran all the way home.   "We have thanked God" for your safe arrival.[19]

15. It is hard to believe that Valle actually suffered from the height at this point.   Santa María is at about 6,000 feet, or a little more than 1,000 feet above the capital.   Valle was very enthusiastic about his trip and his journal and simply noted what he had read.   He wrote: "Es cierta la observación de los que la han hecho.   A cierta altura el hombre parece beber alegría y contento inspirando el aire plácido de una atmósfera elevada, teniendo la vista por un horizonte más dilatado, y sintiendo el poder de la naturaleza."

16. Diario de mi viage de Guatemala a México en 1822, Valle Papers; Louis E. Bumgartner, ed., "José del Valle's Unfinished 'Diario de Mi Viaje de Guatemala a México en 1822,'" *The Americas,* XVIII (Oct., 1961), 187-190.

17. Casaus to Valle, Aug. 1, 1822, Valle Papers.   Casaus wrote that he had received Valle's letter that had been posted on June 7 in Oaxaca, where Valle had visited some of Casaus' friends.

18. Aug. 3, 1822, Valle Papers.   She wrote that she had received the package from Oaxaca but did not mention the date of Valle's letter.

19. Sept. 3, 1822, Valle Papers.   She noted that she had received the box sent to Casaus for her.   Among other things, it contained a souvenir of the coronation. Casaus (to Valle, Sept. 2, 1822, Valle Papers) wrote that he had delivered the box to Josefa.

[3]

While Valle traveled toward Mexico City, political life in that capital veered sharply to the right. The Constituent Congress, convoked in February, 1822, counted 162 deputies who had aligned themselves in three groups: one insisted on a Bourbon prince for Mexico; a second encouraged Iturbide's ambitions; and the third, the republicans, were playing for time by co-operating with those in favor of a Bourbon, hoping in that way to eliminate the more imminent danger of Iturbide.[20]

Possessing a "Napoleonic complex,"[21] the support of the clergy, much of the aristocracy, and the military, Iturbide staged a popular demonstration for Agustín I. On May 18, 1822, at the urging of Sergeant Pío Marcha, three infantry and several cavalry regiments rushed into the streets, firing their guns and shouting the praise of General Iturbide. They pushed and jostled their way to his quarters, where he appeared, feigned ignorance of their purpose, and listened to the not unpleasant cry of "Viva Agustín I." From his balcony above, he politely refused before he realized that "new sacrifices" were needed from him, and with all humility, he bowed to popular demand.[22]

The next day the Congress convened in special session to consider the petition from cavalry and infantry officers to confirm the elevation of Iturbide to the throne. Without a quorum and in closed session, the deputies began to deliberate. Outside, however, the crowd that had gathered clamored to be admitted to the galleries, making it impossible for the deputies to proceed. To still the crowd, a commission of four prevailed upon the Council of Regency to restore order, but the Council promised nothing. Upon learning this, the Congress invited Iturbide to the session with the vain hope that he would restore order and thus allow the deputies to continue. Iturbide accepted, and when he arrived

---

20. Hubert Howe Bancroft, *History of Mexico* (6 vols.; New York, 1888), IV, 744; Priestley, *The Mexican Nation*, pp. 251-252; Jaime Delgado, *España y México en el siglo XIX* (3 vols.; Madrid, 1950), I, 81; Torres Lanzas, ed., *Independencia de América*, V, 384.

21. Lesley Byrd Simpson, *Many Mexicos* (Berkeley, 1952), p. 199.

22. *Documentos para la historia de la guerra de la independencia, 1810-1822* (Mexico, 1933), XXIII, 215; Simpson, *Many Mexicos*, p. 200; Priestley, *The Mexican Nation*, pp. 252-253.

and entered the chamber, the noisy crowd squeezed in behind him. In these circumstances, the Congress voted to approve his elevation.[23]   Moved by the popular acclaim, Iturbide, choked with emotion, gasped: "My heart throbs."[24]

[4]

The coronation, a makeshift imitation of the courts of Europe, brought temporary relief from the quarrel between Iturbide and the Congress, and during this period of relative quiet, Deputy Valle, on July 28, 1822, entered the capital.[25]   His credentials were approved on July 31;[26] three days later he attended his first session;[27] and on August 5 the president of the Congress assigned him to the committee for drafting the outline of the constitution.[28] Valle, out of habit, put himself on a rigid schedule; he attended sessions in the morning, met with his committee in the library of the cathedral in the afternoon, and at night indulged his taste for reading and writing.   According to his account, he first entered a significant debate on the floor of Congress on August 7.   The record of the proceedings, however, did not record his participation in such a discussion until August 14.[29]

On that date a deputy introduced a motion to remove from all churches the edicts of the "extinguished" Holy Tribunal. Especially obnoxious was the one condemning the theory of popular sovereignty.   No one spoke against the motion, but qualifications were suggested that touched on the hallowed freedoms. Valle, following the discussions closely, inserted himself and pitched the subject on a higher plane, which even the weary secretary noticed and recorded.   Valle saw "no difference between

23. Juan A. Mateos, ed., *Historia parlamentaria de los congresos mexicanos de 1821 a 1857* (25 vols.; Mexico, 1877-1912), I, 481-493.   (Hereafter Mateos, ed., *Historia parlamentaria de los congresos mexicanos.*)
24. *Documentos para la historia de la guerra de independencia, 1810-1822*, XXIII, 223.
25. Valle and Valle Matheu, eds., *Obras*, I, 68.
26. R. H. Valle, *La anexión*, II, 271.
27. Mateos, ed., *Historia parlamentaria de los congresos mexicanos*, I, 729-730. Valle spoke during the first session in connection with the question of whether deputies should be obliged to attend sessions.
28. Mateos, ed., *Historia parlamentaria de los congresos mexicanos*, I, 734.
29. *Ibid.*, pp. 774-775.   For a description of Valle's schedule and his statement on the debate of August 7, see Valle and Valle Matheu, eds., *Obras*, I, 68-69.

thinking and speaking and writing." Since man was free to think, he also should enjoy the freedom of "expressing and publishing his ideas," as long as they did not harm society. Intolerance was much more harmful than full freedom, a point demonstrated by the upheavals and bloody revolutions that were owing to excessive rigor of despotic governments. "Truth," he maintained, "prevails against the deceptions that try to obscure it." Thus freedom to speak and write exposed and destroyed the "false maxims of politics."[30]

The undeclared and uneasy truce between Iturbide and the Congress ended on August 16, when a number of deputies challenged his proposal to appoint the judges of the supreme court. Valle, who had spoken only a few times, had achieved sufficient recognition to feel comfortably confident, to become himself. After two speeches against the Emperor's proposal, Valle gained the floor. With the oratorical ability that he had been polishing since youth, he took charge of the discussion as though he were among Aycinenas and Beltranenas, saying that the question did not beg long discussions but would fall easily before reason. The Spanish Constitution of 1812, for example, invested the executive with the power to appoint judges to the supreme court. The supreme court had the power to try members of the executive department. This arrangement laid bare "one of the defects of the Spanish Constitution," explained Valle, cleaning his scalpel. To permit the executive to appoint the judges encouraged a malignant relationship, and the same reason disqualified members of the judiciary from appointing supreme court judges. The deputies, however, were neither directly nor indirectly responsible to the supreme court, and they, Valle opined, provided the remedy.[31]

This address put Valle's name in the list of voters with Canon Servando Teresa de Mier, republican deputy from the province of Monterrey, outspoken enemy of monarchy, and stinging critic of Iturbide. In addition, Mier had been an active participant in the revolution. After the failure of the Mina expedition in 1817, Mier was imprisoned in Havana for his efforts but managed to escape to the United States. Learning of the rejuvenated move for independence, he returned home, was elected to the Congress,

30. Mateos, ed., *Historia parlamentaria de los congresos mexicanos*, I, 774-775.
31. *Ibid.*, pp. 785-787.

and took the oath on July 15, 1822.[32]   One wonders whether, as Mier spoke supporting Valle's opinion, Valle's thoughts retraced the tortuous course to Colonel Arechavala's remark: the "apostate Mier."

Mier, the antithesis of Valle in many respects, used the debate on the appointment of judges as an opportunity to attack the Emperor.   What Deputy Valle explained with "such eloquence" was true, Mier observed.   The fact, however, that Iturbide had made the proposal demonstrated that it was impossible for the Congress to proceed "without colliding with bayonets."   The source of the evil lay in the Plan of Iguala, which imposed "ridiculous" and "absurd" restrictions on the Congress.   With sovereign power standing mute in "shackles and hand cuffs," Mier was finding it difficult to distinguish "independence from the yoke of the Spaniards."   Who could ever "suffer the insolence" of judges appointed by an emperor with power usurped from the Congress?[33]

Following this discussion, the deputies comported themselves very well, offering His Most Serene Highness no insults, making no accusations.   On August 19 they aired problems relating to salaries.[34]   During the next several days a long debate on the distribution of public lands ensued in conjunction with the idea of attracting foreigners to Mexico.   Valle, who had elaborated on the same theme in Guatemala, inserted that "to attract educated, industrious emigrants" was "to attract talent and wealth."   Others not graced by these virtues would contribute only to "immorality."   Population, he conceded, was one of the first necessities of America, but morality was the bedrock of all wise legislation. Thus he counseled the deputies to agree on some plan for rewarding only the worthy.[35]   On August 24 the Congress held its monthly elections, and the deputies honored Valle with the vice

32. Alamán, *Historia de Méjico,* V, 643-645; Lorenzo de Zavala, *Ensayo histórico de las revoluciones desde 1808 hasta 1830* (2 vols.; Paris, 1831), I, 181-182.   (Hereafter Zavala, *Ensayo histórico.*)   For an excellent presentation of Mier's views on the Constitution, see Nettie Lee Benson, "Servando Teresa de Mier, Federalist," *HAHR,* XXVIII (1948), 514-525.

33. Mateos, ed., *Historia parlamentaria de los congresos mexicanos,* I, pp. 796-798.

34. *Ibid.,* pp. 806.

35. *Ibid.,* pp. 847-848 (Aug. 23, 1822).   In connection with public lands, Valle a few months later was able to accommodate "Esteban F. Austin," who was in Mexico concerning the colony in Las Texas.   See Austin to Valle, March 10, 1823, *Austin Papers,* edited by Eugene C. Barker (American Historical Association, *Annual Report,* 1919; 2 vols., Washington, 1920), I, 584-586.

presidency.[36] On the same day he raised his voice against peculation, and the session of August 26 was devoted largely to a lively discussion of parliamentary procedure.[37] On the following morning Valle and fourteen other deputies awakened in prison.[38]

The immediate cause of the arrest and incarceration of the deputies was not their actions on the floor of the Congress but their alleged clandestine activities outside. Iturbide, living in nearby Tacubaya, had been receiving reports that suggested a conspiracy. According to his information, a number of deputies planned to remove him, substitute a republic for the constitutional monarchy, and convene the Congress outside the capital.[39] Fearing for public safety, he decided to move against the subversives and ordered the arrest of all "deputies included in the denouncement."[40] A plan doubtless was in the making, but according to one contemporary, it was far fetched and could not have endangered the "security of the government." The persons involved numbered no more than eight or ten. Iturbide, the same witness charged, used the "ridiculous" plan as a pretext to still the opposition in Congress and to gain complete control of the government.[41] Whether this was the Emperor's motive is uncertain but the result is clear.

When the arrests were made on the night of August 26, Valle apparently was included by accident. None of the information communicated to Iturbide by his agents contained any reference to Valle.[42] The list of those to be arrested, which Iturbide sent to the military in Mexico City, did not include Valle's name,[43] and the testimony taken from the accused by the crown attorney bears no witness against Valle.[44] A member of the Congress, discussing

36. Mateos, ed., *Historia parlamentaria de los congresos mexicanos*, I, 855.
37. *Ibid.*, pp. 859-860.
38. Alamán, *Historia de Méjico*, V, 649-650; William Spense Robertson, *Iturbide of Mexico* (Durham, North Carolina, 1952), p. 205; Priestley, *The Mexican Nation*, pp. 253-254.
39. *Documentos para la historia de la guerra de independencia, 1810-1822*, XXIII, 248-249.
40. Agustín de Iturbide, *Breve diseño crítico de la emancipación y libertad de la nación mexicana y de las causas que influyeron en sus más ruidosos sucesos, acaecidos desde el grito de Iguala hasta la espantosa muerte del Libertador en la villa de Padilla* (Mexico, 1827), p. 45; Cuevas, ed., *El Libertador*, pp. 412-414.
41. Zavala, *Ensayo histórico*, I, 182.
42. *Documentos para la historia de la guerra de independencia, 1810-1822*, XXIII, 263-278.
43. *Ibid.*, XXIII, 309-311.
44. *Ibid.*, XXIII, 281-384.

the arrest of the deputies, wrote that Valle, "one of the most learned Americans," was imprisoned, although not one scrap of evidence existed that could classify him as a conspirator.[45] A deputy involved in the so-called conspiracy and arrested on August 26 asserted that Valle was blameless.[46] Valle himself wrote that no charges were brought against him and that after "many days" he learned that he was to be questioned "not as a prisoner but as a witness."[47] Valle apparently had been at the wrong place at the wrong time.

According to the scanty evidence, Valle, on the evening of August 26, went to visit José Fagoaga, another deputy from Guatemala, but one marked for arrest.[48] Mier, whose name was on the list,[49] several of his companions, and a citizen of the United States, were also at Fagoaga's house. Some time during the evening, a lieutenant with a detail of troops arrived and arrested everyone except the United States citizen. The soldiers, unaware of the crimes of the deputies, knew only that the arrest was on the authority of Iturbide.[50] Perhaps if Valle had remained at home with his books, he would not have been imprisoned.

Valle's reaction to his arrest portrayed him as a lonely scholar longing for his family. After he was lodged first in the monastery La Merced and later in that of Santo Domingo, he besought the Emperor for release.[51] But as the weeks passed without word of his crime or his final fate, he began to despair and grieve for his family. He knew that in far away Guatemala the news of his misfortune, "exaggerated by the same distance or made worse by maliciousness," would tear at the breast of the beloved Josefa. With this image before him, his "soul suffered sorrow" never before experienced,[52] and he often broke into tears—so often that

45. Zavala, *Ensayo histórico*, I, 187.
46. Carlos María Bustamante, *Diario histórico de México* (Zacatecas, 1896), p. 235. (Hereafter Bustamante, *Diario histórico*.)
47. Valle and Valle Matheu, eds., *Obras*, I, 72.
48. *Documentos para la historia de la guerra de independencia, 1810-1822*, XXIII, 310.
49. *Ibid.*, p. 309.
50. Robertson, *Iturbide of Mexico*, p. 205.
51. *Documentos para la historia de la guerra de independencia, 1810-1822*, XXIII, 317, 339; Noticia de los señores que se hallan presos en los conventos de Santo Domingo, San Francisco, and San Hipólito, con expresión de los que están juntos, de los comunicados, interior y exteriormente, y de los absolutamente privados de comunicación (Dec. 8, 1822), Hernández Dávalos Collection, HD, 15-7, 2016, University of Texas Library.
52. Valle and Valle Matheu, eds., *Obras*, I, 71-72. Iturbide published a mani-

one deputy described him as "pusillanimous" and the callous Mier called him "cry baby."[53]

The Dominicans were kinder to the sensitive Valle, and likely spared him additional hours of black despair by giving him free use of the library. With the scholar's curiosity, he began searching for manuscripts and old journals of the government in order to learn more about Mexico. He found several maps, one by the famous Humboldt and another by Aaron Arrowsmith (1750-1823), an English geographer. He compared the maps for important differences, and badgered his "companions of detention" for descriptions of the provinces of Mexico. He copied many of the manuscripts and began an article on the sciences. Thus he passed the days of his confinement, grieving for his family, protesting the injustice, and doing research and writing.[54]

While the deputies languished in their prisons, Congress reacted vigorously in their behalf. On August 27, 1822, President José Cirilo Gómez de Anaya railed against the arbitrary arrest, pointing out the inviolability of the deputies. Iturbide, Gómez de Anaya charged, not only had violated the rights of the deputies but had flaunted his authority in the face of freedom.[55] Lorenzo de Zavala, a republican leader who later fought for a free Texas, published a pamphlet on individual rights, denouncing Iturbide as a despot.[56] In the face of the opposition, Iturbide remained adamant, assuming the role of the defender of the people. He had sworn to rule under a constitution, and "I shall keep my word," respecting the Congress as long as the deputies did not make it a "tool of anarchy." When this happened, he promised to be the first to call a new congress.[57] In these circumstances the deputies and Iturbide recognized that relations with each other had become impossible.

To destroy the opposition, the Emperor called together a

festo explaining why he had imprisoned the deputies. See Valenzuela, *La imprenta en Guatemala*, pp. 28-29. The news reached Guatemala by October 24, 1822. See José Antonio Marqués and Francisco Suárez to Valle, Tegucigalpa, Oct. 24, 1822, Valle Papers. In expressing their sympathy for his plight, these correspondents suggested that he had been imprisoned by accident.

53. Carlos María Bustamante, *Historia del Emperador D. Agustín de Iturbide hasta su muerte, y sus consequencias, y establecimiento de la república popular federal* (Mexico, 1846), p. 97. (Hereafter Bustamante, *Historia del Emperador*.)

54. Valle and Valle Matheu, eds., *Obras*, I, 72-73.

55. Mateos, ed., *Historia parlamentaria de los congresos mexicanos*, I, 861.

56. Zavala, *Ensayo histórico*, I, 184.

57. Mateos, ed., *Historia parlamentaria de los congresos mexicanos*, I, 884.

number of his followers and announced his intentions to reform the Congress, which finally had led the nation to the brink of anarchy. The deputies did not miss the meaning of "reform," as spoken by Iturbide, and they began making concessions, extending him the privilege of appointing supreme court judges. Iturbide, who no longer wanted a concession or a congress, demanded the right of veto, even of the constitutional provisions that the deputies at that moment were drafting. The demand was unacceptable to the deputies, as Iturbide doubtless had calculated, and on October 31, 1822, he met their refusal with an order to dissolve the Congress, substituting a committee of his own to frame the constitution.[58]

As one student of Mexican history pointed out, Iturbide made the serious error of disregarding legality when he dissolved the Congress.[59] Afterwards he had to depend on force and arbitrariness, and his position as an absolute monarch, his "ruinous fiscal makeshifts, his idiotic pretensions, and his clericalism" welded opposing factions.[60] In December, 1822, Antonio López de Santa Anna, the next master of Mexico, pronounced against Iturbide and later issued the Plan of Casa Mata, which demanded the overthrow of the monarchy and the inauguration of a republic. Disgruntled army officers, frustrated liberals, and naïve republicans saw in Santa Anna the answer to Mexico's political problems and began flocking to his standard.

As the efforts of the opposition gained momentum, Iturbide, isolated in the capital with relatively few troops, resorted to manifestos and bravado to deliver the Empire from the hands of the enemy. On February 11 he issued a proclamation reminding the troops, who were joining the rebels, that he had commanded them in the glorious march to independence, and on the following day he raced his horse through the streets followed by a crowd of paid demonstrators shouting his name. At the same time he began taking precautionary measures, imprisoning those of questionable loyalty and cutting off communications between the capital and the revolting forces.[61] In the midst of the crisis, José del Valle made a curious entrance.

58. Zavala, *Ensayo histórico*, I, 191-195; Bancroft, *History of Mexico*, IV, 784-785.
59. Priestley, *The Mexican Nation*, p. 254.
60. Simpson, *Many Mexicos*, pp. 200-201.
61. Alamán, *Historia de Méjico*, V, 720-721.

[5]

On February 12, 1823, some of the deputies confined in the monastery of San Francisco were transferred to prisons formerly used by the Inquisition, but Valle and his companions remained in Santo Domingo.[62] And while Valle was grieving and copying manuscripts, a letter arrived on February 22, written by Iturbide's personal secretary and addressed to Valle. It is unlikely that he ever received a greater surprise. The Emperor, informed of Valle's "wisdom" and "patriotism," invited him to accept the position of Secretary of Foreign and Domestic Affairs, ordering him to Tacubaya (three miles distant) for an audience on the following day.[63] Valle, desiring his release but not eager to be saddled with the woes of an empire built on sand, vainly supplicated his Most Serene Highness to be excused from a position "so delicate," in "such difficult circumstances" and vainly repeated his supplication two days later.[64] Thus snatched from the privacy of a friend's home, and incarcerated for six months, Valle, apparently as confused as the reader, exchanged his identification as a prisoner for the portfolio of Secretary of Foreign and Domestic Affairs of the Mexican Empire.

Why Iturbide chose Valle is not clear, and the letter from Vicente Filísola, the Mexican commander who replaced Gainza in Guatemala, only adds to the confusion. Filísola, on September 18, 1822, wrote to Iturbide's Secretary of War, explaining that a number of Guatemalans were making every effort to unhinge the union with Mexico. In Guatemala City, Filísola continued, Molina, Barrundia, and Córdova were the chief agitators. In Mexico City they were supported by Valle and Juan de Dios Mayorga, also a deputy from Guatemala. Filísola suggested that Valle, Molina, Barrundia, and Córdova might be won over, or at least rendered harmless, if they were flattered with positions of responsibility.[65] The only explanation for this curious letter is

62. *Ibid.*, p. 721.

63. Archivo General de Relaciones Exteriores (hereafter AGRE), H/131, 385, 979; Francisco de Paula Álvarez to Valle, Feb. 22, 1823, Valle Papers; *Gaceta del Gobierno Imperial de México*, Feb. 25, 26, 27.

64. AGRE, H/131, 385, 979, March 25, 1823. In this letter to Iturbide, Valle noted that he had written on February 23 and February 25, attempting to refuse the appointment.

65. Valle and Valle Matheu, eds., *Obras*, I, lx-lxi.

that Filísola, a complete stranger in Guatemala, could not have learned in a few months the intricacies of local politics and personal preferences, save the obvious. He of course correctly identified Molina and his followers, but the sympathies of these men were daubed in bright red, white, and blue throughout the capital and the provinces. The fact, however, that he thought that Molina, Barrundia, and Córdova could be turned from their objective illustrates plainly that Filísola had only a superficial knowledge of these men. That he failed to comprehend the position of the prudent Valle has been made equally plain.

Iturbide probably saw in Valle the capacity that would enable him to fulfil the obligations of the appointment. The deputies had recognized his ability when they elected him vice president. Mier, despite his lack of sympathy for Valle's sensitivity, was not contemptuous of his learning.[66] The sharp-tongued Carlos María Bustamante, a republican leader, thought that Valle was a country bumpkin and poked fun at his dress (which doubtless was flawlessly correct by English standards), but he was not reluctant to state that Valle was one of the "wisest men in Mexico."[67] In addition to ability, Iturbide, whose position became more tenuous each day, saw that Valle's appointment would not offend any of the factions. He had not been in congress long enough to learn the names of the deputies, much less to identify himself with any group. The final quality that the Emperor would have sought was loyalty to his cause, and the sworn statements made by Valle's friends in December, 1822, would have arrived in Mexico City about the time that Iturbide was casting about for a Secretary. Thus Valle, from Iturbide's point of view, well might have been the man best qualified for the post. The Emperor, however, did not remain in Mexico long enough to realize the advantages of the appointment.

By March 4, 1823, Iturbide realized that his only chance to continue as Emperor lay in making concessions, and in a manifesto bearing that date he summoned the deputies to reassemble,

66. On one occasion Mier corrected a statement that a newspaper had credited to Valle. On April 17, 1823 (Mateos, ed., *Historia parlamentaria de los congresos mexicanos*, II, 272), Valle discussed the merits of Mexico sending a minister to the Vatican. The paper, *Águila Mexicana*, reported that Valle had said that the Pope ought to be considered as a possible monarch of "los estados constituidos." See Servando Mier to the editors of the *Águila Mexicana*, no date, Valle Papers.

67. Bustamante, *Diario histórico*, p. 235.

ordering the Secretary of the Treasury to make funds available for travel expenses. To Iturbide's summons, Secretary Valle added: "All people should unite behind a government that has no other wish than their own. The Mexican nation should be one ruled by wise and liberal principles—a regime distinct from that which formerly existed."[68] Valle was more sanguine than critic Carlos María Bustamante, who wrote that "Valle's line of reasoning" won him many admirers, but "alas, the remedy came too late; the gangrene already was devouring the political body, and the fall of the Empire was inevitable."[69] On March 7 the recalled Congress convened, and Iturbide, in attendance, described that date, with more hope than evidence will allow, as the "happy day of reconciliation." Congress could now resume its "august functions as though it had never been interrupted."[70]

Valle also tried to soothe the discordant factions, publishing plans for increasing prosperity, emphasizing the scholar's contribution to society, and delineating a plan of study for public schools. But to men with strong opinions for or against Iturbide, Secretary Valle's publications appeared strange and a little ridiculous during the critical days of March. Santa Anna was demanding the overthrow of the government; Iturbide was trying to keep his throne; and articulate Mexicans were identifying themselves with one or the other. The insouciant nature of Valle's essays drove Lucas Alamán, a man similar to Valle in many respects, to remark that each "incident" gave Valle another excuse to publish one of his "dogmatic dispatches." But the last straw for Alamán was that Valle chose to publish his plan of study at the moment of "general disorder, when it was unknown whether there was a Congress."[71] What Alamán, in the heat of battle, failed to see, or saw too plainly, was that Secretary Valle, steering clear of extremes, was following the line drawn by prudence, which in other circumstances was familiar to Alamán but never so obvious to the public.

Secretary Valle, however, did react vigorously to a charge that

68. Quoted in Robertson, *Iturbide of Mexico*, p. 243. Also see R. H. Valle, *La anexión*, IV, 162.
69. Bustamante, *Historia del Emperador*, pp. 96-97.
70. Mateos, ed., *Historia parlamentaria de los congresos mexicanos*, II, 118.
71. *Historia de Méjico*, V, 736; Niceto de Zamocois, *Historia de Méjico desde sus tiempos más remotos hasta nuestros días* (18 vols., Mexico, 1879-1888), XI, 487.

implied lethargy or incompetency. The Congress, weighted against the Emperor, asked to see the documents dealing with the negotiations between him and the rebel forces moving on the capital. Before Valle could comply, the deputies intimated that he was taking an undue amount of time. On March 11, 1823, he personally delivered to the Congress and deposited with the secretary seven bundles of papers. Then, turning to the deputies, he protested with candor and acuity. "I have been serving in the ministry for fourteen days, and I defy the most distinguished talent to learn in such short time all that there is to know in the ministry in my charge. I have not rested; I have the satisfaction of having worked day and night."[72] Unjust criticism, he thought, was hardly fair compensation.

Valle and the deputies, however, were working in exceedingly trying circumstances, and their patience was bound to be short. They were not sure whether Iturbide planned to fight or abdicate peacefully; they were sure, however, that the insurgents, who had combined command in a military council of the leading officers, had advanced toward the capital to Puebla. If Iturbide decided on a show of strength, chances were great that deputies and Valle would be under the guns of both sides. However, as Iturbide watched desertion strip him of his troops and add strength to an already strong opponent, he decided, on March 19, to abdicate unconditionally. His personal secretary passed a note to this effect to Secretary Valle,[73] who, with the deputies, doubtless breathed a sigh of relief, despite the fact that they had to work out the tedious details of Iturbide's exile.

The suspicion of the insurgents and the wounded pride of the so-recently-anointed Iturbide guaranteed that arrangements for his departure would be difficult. He wished to await the terms outside the capital, vesting executive authority in parties named by the Congress. Unable to render a decision for want of a quorum, the Congress invited the military council of the insurgents to meet with Iturbide and work out the terms. The council refused, but ordered that Iturbide should reside in one of four specified places until a decision was reached. On the same day, March 25, a committee of deputies and Secretary Valle

72. Mateos, ed., *Historia parlamentaria de los congresos mexicanos*, II, 127-128.
73. Alamán, *Historia de Méjico*, V, 741; Zavala, *Ensayo histórico*, I, 228-230.

visited Iturbide at Tacubaya and explained the plight of the
Congress and that the insurgent generals had refused to treat with
him.   Displeased by the slight, Iturbide again sought an inter-
view with his former officers and again was refused.   The generals
suspected that Iturbide was trying to gain time in order to prepare their defeat and that Valle was working toward the same end.

When Valle and the committee of deputies returned to the
Congress with their reports from the generals, Valle again was
charged with duplicity.   The Congress had been informed that
Iturbide was planning to "retire to Guatemala, because he had
careful plans for that place, and that the motive behind his appointment of Valle as Secretary was that he [Valle] might serve
him [Iturbide] in his plans, owing to the reputation that he
[Valle] enjoys in those provinces."[74]   Valle, called upon to explain
his conduct, dismissed the whole matter quite casually by saying
that he had ignored the rumor, which any "just and thoughtful"
person would not have repeated.   He then reviewed all the negotiations in an attempt to show that he had done nothing to delay
the final disposition of Iturbide.[75]   And owing in part to Valle's
efforts, the details of the abdication were concluded.[76]   Iturbide,
in May, 1823, embarked at Vera Cruz for Italy.

Valle must have grown weary of playing office boy for the
garrulous Congress, the ridiculous Emperor, and the aspiring
rebels.   On March 25, when the Congress charged him with intrigue in behalf of the deposed emperor, Valle sent a letter of
resignation to Tacubaya, plying Iturbide with the strongest
reasons:

I have tried to fulfil my duties; I have been straightforward; my
intentions have been above reproach; and I have had no other goal
than that of the general welfare.   I have worked day and night, and
since I am always interested in the good of the nation, I would continue, but my health is beginning to break.   And by today's mail, I
have received a letter from my family, telling me of the urgent necessity to return in order to protect my interests.   The position of the
Empire is critical, and it will grow worse each day, delaying my journey [home].[77]

74. Mateos, ed., *Historia parlamentaria de los congresos mexicanos*, II, 154-157.
75. *Ibid.*, II, 157-158.
76. A rough draft of the details of Iturbide's departure can be found in Valle
Papers.   It is unsigned and not in Valle's handwriting.   Also see Valle to Captain
General of Mexico, March 24, Hernández Dávalos Collection, HD, 16-2, 3246, University of Texas Library.
77. AGRE, H/131, 385, 979.

He appealed to Iturbide to accept his resignation, but in the margin of the letter appears the note: "His Imperial Majesty did not consent to this request."[78]

On April 1, after executive authority had been lodged in a triumvirate, Valle, much to his satisfaction, relinquished the post of Secretary of Foreign and Domestic Affairs,[79] and by April 17 he had resumed his position in Congress. The six months in prison and the hectic weeks as Secretary, however, had taught him that he had to chart a new course. Mexico no longer was the answer to Guatemala's problem, nor to his own. Mexico in fact suffered from all the aches and pains that Valle had diagnosed for Guatemala. Mexican politics were shot through with rivalries that were to hamstring progress until the great leveler, Porfirio Díaz, could take charge. Her economy was out of joint, and the Indians were no better educated than they were in Guatemala. Valle, alert and curious, could not have missed the plight of Mexico, but the capstone of his disillusion must have come when he helped negotiate the exit of His Most Serene Highness. Valle had a first-hand view of the engineer of the great empire and had been a victim of his careless administration. These thoughts, and the break with Mexico in Guatemala, stripped away the romantic image of Mexico City during the staid, mature days of the colony and made respected monarchy a contemptible mockery. Valle's world was again on the move, and he moved with it, when, for the first time, he assailed annexation and demanded absolute independence for Guatemala.

[6]

The subject of Guatemala was first introduced in the Congress on April 1, 1823. Fourteen deputies presented a proposal requesting Filísola's retirement from Guatemala and admonishing Guatemalans to cease their opposition to annexation. In view of the opposition, however, Carlos María Bustamante, diarist and

78. *Ibid.*
79. *Ibid.*, García Illueca to Valle, April 1, 1823. News concerning the formation of the triumvirate was published on March 31, 1823. See *Colección de órdenes y decretos de la soberana junta provisional gubernativa, y soberanos congresos generales de la nación mexicana* (2 vols.; Mexico, 1829), II, 90-91.

prison companion of Valle, successfully proposed that a committee should be formed to study the relations with the disaffected
provinces. Freedom for Guatemala was not mentioned.[80]

On April 22, after the Congress had approved the minutes of
the previous day, the new Secretary of Foreign and Domestic
Affairs presented to the deputies a paper concerned with the
"separation of several provinces of Guatemala from Mexico" and
then read a dispatch that had accompanied the paper. Valle was
immediately recognized, and when he presented his views on
annexation, he clearly manifested the change that he had under-
gone. Guatemala, he began, had been subordinated to the Spanish monarchy in the same manner as Mexico, possessing the same
inalienable rights. Guatemala, like Mexico, had proclaimed her
independence, and if Mexico had the right to pull herself up
from the humble position of a province to the sublime level of
a sovereign state, Guatemala also had the same right. On September 15, 1821, Guatemala City declared independence, but the
authorities, realizing that the capital could not speak for the
provinces, invited provincial authorities to send deputies to a
congress for the purpose of making a final decision. After September 15 Guatemala "was enjoying the pleasure of being a sovereign state when incidents began to occur that caused the spilling
of the blood of her sons." At this critical juncture Iturbide, believing annexation of Guatemala to Mexico was in the interest
of each nation, invited Captain General Gainza to declare in
favor of union. Gainza and the governors of the provinces supported Iturbide's invitation, but the provisional government, with
Gainza, asked the municipalities to decide the issue. But the
town councils could not exercise sovereign authority. Despite
all, the act of union became official on January 5, 1822.

In vain, I, as a member of the provisional government, informed the
deputies that the municipalities were not the legitimate authority
for resolving the question; in vain, I manifested that even if they
were, they [the deputies] were lacking the replies of many; in vain, I
drew up a list of those that had not responded. The government,
however, swayed by the captain general, agreed to the act of union,
and Guatemala, elevated in 1821 to a sovereign state, saw itself in
1822 reduced to a province of Mexico.

80. Mateos, ed., *Historia parlamentaria de los congresos mexicanos*, II, 185.

In conclusion, Valle declared union with Mexico null and void, asserting that it never had any "legality." The "nation of Guatemala united *en masse* or by means of its representatives" was the only legitimate authority that could make a legal decision.[81]

While the Congress, with many urgent matters before it, sent the Guatemalan question to committee, Vicente Filísola, the Mexican commander, took matters out of the hands of the Congress when he permitted Guatemalans to issue a call for the constitutional congress that was to have met, on February 1, 1822, for the purpose of deciding on the question of independence. Valle, who continued to press the Mexican Congress for a decision,[82] announced, on July 2, that he had received word from Guatemala that the province of Tegucigalpa, which he represented in Mexico, had elected him to the constituent congress of Guatemala.[83] On September 3 he submitted his resignation, freeing himself to return to his family.[84]

[7]

Between September 3 and November 13, when he departed,[85] Valle, homesick as he was, took time to gather material that would be useful to him and to Guatemala. Besides the many manuscripts containing information on agriculture, mining, education, and government, he also brought the debates of the Congress, and copies of ten different newspapers. He ransacked Mexico City for scientific instruments, but he was able to find only a barometer and a Fahrenheit thermometer. With these he planned to measure the altitude at different points along the way, charting the findings of each instrument in order that he might compare the

81. *Ibid.*, pp. 290-291.

82. For example, see *El Sol* (Mexico City), July 3, 1823. Mexico recognized Guatemala's independence on August 20, 1824. See Mateos, ed., *Historia parlamentaria de los congresos mexicanos*, II, 889; AGG, B10.4, 3632, 171. Correspondencia diplomática. Juan de Dios Mayorga wrote that he had received the news on August 21. Dios Mayorga had been appointed as Guatemala's minister to Mexico (Marcial Zebadúa to Pedro Molina, Oct. 13, 1824, AGG, Molina Papers).

83. *El Sol*, July 4, 1823; Mateos, ed., *Historia parlamentaria de los congresos mexicanos*, II, 429.

84. Mateos, ed., *Historia parlamentaria de los congresos mexicanos*, II, 500.

85. Valle wrote to his family on November 12, saying that he was leaving the following day. His family replied (Dec. 18, 1823, Valle Papers), expressing happiness that he was preparing to depart.

results. He also planned to log the distances between villages and observe the opinion of the people—those "who had one"—concerning the independence of Guatemala. An unfortunate accident prevented him from fulfilling all his plans. Before he journeyed far, he broke the barometer that he had "carried with such care." Nevertheless, he kept a journal and brought a collection of seeds and plants from various places. In addition to all these, he found room for a picture of "Jorge Washington," which he presented to the constituent congress of Guatemala.[86]

On January 26, 1824, Valle arrived in Mixco, where he had spent the first night of his journey to Mexico.[87] From Mixco, where he could catch a full view of Guatemala City, he experienced a feeling similar to that of two close friends meeting after long separation. As he made his way into the capital, people recognized the traveler and accompanied him into the city. At that moment "I repeated the vow that I had made of living for my country."[88] After eighteen months he was home, never to leave again.

[8]

The Mexican hayride in Guatemala's history was significant for Valle. When annexation failed, he and the rest of the aristocracy for the first time felt the full impact of the decision of September 15, 1821, which many had made with good faith and the idea of simply shifting ultimate responsibility for basic decisions from a crown in faraway Spain to a crown in not-so-far-away Mexico, assuming then that business and local politics would continue as though nothing had changed. Many aristocrats, doubtless all, in the manner of Valle, caught the contagious spirit of the nineteenth century and paused briefly for idealistic reflection, sure that the constitutional monarchy, in tune with the times, promised the safe, prosperous course for Guatemala. And in any terms save nationalism, it might have done so, given a responsible monarch. But Valle and the 104 town councils had no way of

86. Valle and Valle Matheu, eds., *Obras*, I, 76-77.
87. AGG, B6.26, 2975, 117. Actas de la Asamblea Nacional Constituyente, Jan. 31, 1824.
88. Valle and Valle Matheu, eds., *Obras*, I, 76-77.

knowing that Iturbide was to be the unprincipled clown who would star in the second act of the "comedy" of Guatemala's independence.[89] Still lathered from his efforts in behalf of freedom, Iturbide appeared to nearly everyone in the same light that played on the bronze of San Martín and Bolívar. Then came the sickening moment of truth, when time and another adventurer laid bare the clay of Iturbide. Thus the compromise of September 15 failed and for the first time local leaders had to accept ultimate responsibility for solving local problems with local resources.

Valle's career in Mexico virtually guaranteed that he would be one of the leaders. Incarceration in behalf of freedom, though accidental, was a singular commendation. In addition, he could point to his arguments in Mexico against annexation in the same manner that, in Mexico, he had singled out his belated arguments in Guatemala. His previous preference for the Empire doubtless secured his release from prison and vaulted him into a position that he doubtless did not want. His actions as Secretary of Foreign and Domestic Affairs, however, contributed to the image that depicted him as an advocate of absolute independence, a fact that was not lost on his keen ability to measure an explosive political question and turn it to his advantage without destroying the image that he labored so meticulously to maintain.

The Mexican interlude also contributed to the vast store of knowledge that he had been gathering since his student days at San Carlos. And when in Mexico he stooped to admire the circumference of two onions and then went to the trouble of tracing them on a note card, he demonstrated that the gift of Goicoechea was in good hands.[90]

89. Dionisio de Herrera to Valle, Tegucigalpa, Aug. 9, 1822, Valle Papers. Herrera wrote: "Por mucho que se haya hecho en el asunto de independencia, a lo más, concederé que estamos en la segunda jornada de la comedia."

90. Magnitud de dos cebollas, Aug. 20, 1823, Valle Papers. Years before, Goicoechea, upon crossing the mountains into the valley of Agalta, had to cross one river fifty-eight times. "I counted them to break the monotony and to find out if, according to different opinion, one had to cross 60 or 70 times." See Goicoechea to (?), Gualaco, Feb. 1, 1806, Valle Papers.

T E N

An Apprehensive Executive

[1]

Soon after Valle returned to Guatemala City, the same sentiment that had moved him to repeat his vow filled him with fear as he became fully aware of what was expected from him. He had kept abreast of events at home and thus knew the "delicate position" of the nation.[1] His family had written of the arrival in the capital of Vicente Filísola (June, 1822), commenting on his eating habits, where he lived, and where he quartered his troops, not failing to mention that a member of the "family" had received him.[2] Caustically, Dionisio had spoken of the continuing influence of the "sons of the capital" who, in his eyes, were becoming more odious than those of Spain. He also reported to Valle on the unrest in each of the provinces and blamed the capital for the difficulty with San Salvador, where annexation was opposed with arms.[3] Archbishop Casaus had touched on the same factious conduct, remarking that each day of its duration made compromise more difficult.[4] Mateo Ibarra, Valle's political ally during the days of the Bacos, had written with adolescent enthusiasm that news of Santa Anna's pronouncement ("Eternal glory to Santa Anna") had prompted Filísola to call the congress (March 29, 1823), which was to have met on February 1, 1822. "Here our Filaysola [sic] will be another Wasinton [sic]." And Ibarra assured, as though to persuade Valle to return, that all rivalry had disappeared and that Valle would not be so "secure and esteemed" as Secretary of Foreign and Domestic Affairs in

1. Valle and Valle Matheu, eds., *Obras,* I, 36.
2. June 18, 1822, Valle Papers. A member of the Barrutia family received Filísola on June 12.
3. Aug. 9, 1822, Valle Papers.
4. Aug. 1, 1822, Valle Papers.

Mexico as he would as a "citizen, a deputy, or a scholar" in Guatemala.[5]   The roseate picture that Ibarra etched, if it ever existed outside his imagination, vanished in the heat of competition for the seats in the constituent congress.   On the authority of a letter from José Gabriel O'Horan, Valle learned that his "rivals or emulators" were "venting their fury" on him and like "monsters of envy" were working to bring about his ruin.[6]

From newspapers in Mexico City he could have found out that the congress or National Constituent Assembly, which had convened on June 24, 1823, had declared absolute independence seven days later, denominating the former colony the United Provinces of Central America.[7]   Without knowing who had won the seats, he easily could have guessed their sympathy when he learned that they had elected Canon José Matías Delgado as president of the Assembly[8] and Manuel José Arce, Pedro Molina, and Juan Vicente Villacorta to the Supreme Executive Authority (Supremo Poder Ejecutivo).   Arce, however, was in the United States, and the deputies elected Antonio de Rivera Cabezas, friend of Molina, as Arce's substitute.[9]

Valle also knew that Delgado and Molina had lost much of their initial prestige by September, 1823.   Molina, a good physician and constant patriot, apparently was too emotionally involved to succeed as a member of the executive triumvirate.   According to two contemporaries, he and the others of the Supreme Executive Authority used their positions to even old scores, dispossessing of their offices all those who had received their appointments from

5. April 1, 1823, Valle Papers.   The decree convoking the congress was issued on March 29, 1823.   See *Boletín*, IV (1939), 575-576.   Filísola was kindly disposed toward the idea of calling a congress only after he realized that the day of the Empire was past.   To the *ayuntamiento* of the capital (Jan. 7, 1823), he expressed one of his first reactions to events in Mexico when he wrote that he had received "word of the scandalous events effected in Vera Cruz by the traitor Brigadier General Don Antonio López de Santa Anna."   See AGG, B6.1-4, 02406, 86.   Cuaderno que contiene papeles de la separación de México.

6. Valle Papers (no date).   He spoke of the elections and addressed the letter to Secretary José del Valle; thus the letter was probably written in March or April, 1823.

7. *El Sol*, Aug. 8, 1823.   A preparatory committee, appointed on April 4, 1823, made the arrangements necessary for convening the congress.   See AGG, B6.1-1, 2379, 83.   Cuaderno que contiene los oficios del Jefe Vicente Filísola, nombrando comisionados para que preparen los trabajos del futuro congreso.

8. Delgado received thirty-seven votes.   Pedro Molina received two for the presidency and eight for the vice presidency.   See AGG, B6.1-7, 2439, 89.   Acta de instalación de la Asamblea (June 24, 1823).

9. AGG, B6.26, 2960, 113.   Actas de la Asamblea Nacional Constituyente, July 9, 1823.   Valle received one vote for the third position in the triumvirate.

Spain or Mexico.[10]   Then on September 14 Rafael Ariza de Torres, taking advantage of the fact that Filísola and his troops had departed,[11] staged the first barracks uprising of the new nation, bringing confusion to the capital and imperiling the Assembly.[12] The Serviles (Conservatives), with or without justification, effectively exploited the difficulty when they charged Molina and the Fiebres (Liberals) with ineptitude.[13]   And Molina, Villacorta, and Rivera doubtless added weight to the charge when they resigned from the triumvirate.[14]   On October 4 this change in political sympathy in the Assembly manifested itself in the election to the SPE of Manuel José Arce and José del Valle, both unblemished owing to their absence, and Tomás O'Horan, who had distinguished himself during the uprising of September 14.[15]

10. Marure, *Bosquejo histórico*, I, 68; Montúfar, *Memorias de Jalapa*, pp. 62-63.   Among those dispossessed was Miguel Larreinaga, who went to Mexico, where he published a pamphlet pointing out the injustice.   As he prepared to leave Mexico, Juan de Dios Mayorga, deputy to the Mexican Congress, wrote to Valle: ". . . thank God that Larreinaga and Quiñones are leaving on the 15th.   We will have two less enemies spreading offensive pamphlets about Guatemala" (no date, Valle Papers).   The letter had to be written some time in the fall of 1823, when Larreinaga published his pamphlet.

11. On August 5, 1823, "all the troops of the Mexican division" were on the road to "the territory of their nation" (AGG, B6.26, 2961, 113.   Actas de la Asamblea Nacional Constituyente).   The inhabitants of the capital, wishing to be rid of the Mexicans, contributed thousands of pesos to pay the expenses of the homeward march.   See AGG, B6.1-8, 2445, 90.   Documentos acerca del donativo dado por vecinos de la Ciudad de Guatemala para sufragar los gastos del viage del ejército mexicano.   The author stopped counting after 6,000 pesos.

12. AGG, B6-26, 02692, 113.   Actas de la Asamblea Nacional Constituyente, Sept. 14, 1823.   The best account of the uprising is presented in Andrés Townsend Ezcurra, *Fundación de la república* (Guatemala City, 1958), I, 211-223.   This is the first volume of a projected multivolume work.

13. Cleto Ordóñez, writing to Molina from León (Oct. 7, 1823, AGG, Molina Papers), stated that the Conservatives had spread the word of the uprising to "all the villages of the province," making it seem "a thousand times worse."   Ordóñez worked "night and day" trying to balance the story.   Actually it seems impossible to assign responsibility for the working of a mind such as that of Ariza de Torres, but everyone involved had to share the blame for the attitude of the troops that allowed them to go along with him.   The troops had not been paid and there had been grumbling.   The Assembly and the SPE were aware of the discontent but failed to do anything.   The Secretary of War, only three days before the uprising, informed the Assembly of the ". . . consequencias tristes que están ya produciendo la falta de pago a las tropas de esta guarnición."   See AGG, B6.28, 03003, 121.   Correspondencia recibida por la Asamblea Nacional Constituyente (Sept. 11, 1823).   Apparently this was a chronic condition after independence, for Valle received a letter from a soldier stationed at the prison in Petén, complaining that he had been there four months and had not received "un medio real."   See Lusio Miranda to Valle, March (no day), 1822, Valle Papers.

14. Molina and Rivera apparently submitted their resignations on September 6, 1823, but they were not accepted until after the uprising.   See Townsend Ezcurra, *Fundación de la república*, I, 224.

15. AGG, B6.26, 2963, 114.   Actas de la Asamblea Nacional Constituyente, Oct. 4, 1823.   Pablo Alvarado, deputy from Costa Rica, stated that there were 46 Conservatives and 12 Liberals.   See *Revista de los Archivos Nacionales de Costa Rica,* I (November and December, 1936), 44-46.

Despite the fact that Conservatives commanded a majority in the Assembly, they worked with the Liberals to decree that the form of government for Central America should be republican and federal. The old resentment between the capital and the provinces, however, still continued and became the greatest threat to a peaceful transition. A few weeks before Valle assumed his position in the SPE, his brother-in-law wrote:

The Assembly is going along fine, but the rivalry of the parties will not allow the progress to continue. The bone of contention is the location of the court or the center of government. Some deputies prefer San Salvador to Guatemala City and others the opposite. These are the same parties that divide the people, and the ones who favor San Salvador are called Fiebres. . . . Father Delgado is their oracle. The present executive authority [Valle, O'Horan, and Arce] does not suit them, and they are working secretly to restore the previous executives [Molina, Villacorta, and Arce]. Molina and Rivera belong to this group, and all follow Father Delgado, who was the director and strategist [*disponedor*] of the previous triumvirate. Now the fact that he cannot influence the present executives rankles in his breast.[16]

The location of the capital, which was to be more bitterly contested in the years ahead, was one of the issues in the struggle for power, and though Valle understood Manuel Valero's letter, its simplicity is deceiving. Central America was not divided over the question of locating the capital in either San Salvador or Guatemala City. The rivalry between these two cities when Valle arrived simply happened to be the most glaring example of the suspicion and resentment with which the capital was regarded in the former provinces of the colony and in the nascent states of Central America.[17] Many who feared the consequences of the resentment doubtless shared the opinion that Dionisio de Herrera expressed to Valle soon after he arrived in the capital. "Your friends, the friends of the country, continually have expressed

16. To Valle, Dec. 18, 1823, Valle Papers.
17. Canon José María Castilla, one of the former editors of the defunct *El Editor* and deputy for Cobán, stated succinctly what many influential and articulate men outside the capital believed. On the floor of the Assembly, he said: ". . . that whether it was justified or not, the spirit of rivalry that can be observed in the provinces with respect to their traditional capital made him believe that this rivalry should not be forgotten when they dealt with the residence of the supreme authorities, and our first objective should be to remove the cause that inspires that spirit. Thus Guatemala should no longer be the capital." See AGG, B6.26, 2964, 114. Actas de la Asamblea Nacional Constituyente, Nov. 17, 1823. Matagalpa wanted the capital moved to Granada, and another village wanted it in Tegucigalpa. (AGG, B6.26, 2964, 114, Nov. 7 and 10, 1823.)

their belief in you. Anxiously, all were waiting for you, firmly convinced that your arrival would put an end to the division and rivalry that separates us and that your presence will allow us to constitute ourselves without the difficulty and the obstacles that we have experienced until this moment."[18]

Apprised of the sequence of events during his absence and with full knowledge of the trouble with San Salvador, the confusion in Nicaragua, and the instability of Honduras, an apprehensive Valle wrote a letter of resignation. Further reflection, however, made his duty plain.[19] He tore up the letter and informed the Assembly that he was ready "to make any personal sacrifice in behalf of public interest."[20] The deputies, in receipt of his letter, designated February 5 as the day he should take office.[21]

For Valle February 5, 1824, was not only the scheduled date for his oath of office but also marked his formal homecoming. The committee that called to escort him to the assembly room lent the stamp of solemnity that breeding and tradition allowed him to bear with unconscious ease. After the procession to the rostrum and the solemn oath, he stood before the deputies as a member of the Supreme Executive Authority, an acknowledged leader, roundly hated, rarely loved, always respected, and—at home at last. With confidence tempered by experience, he addressed the Assembly, giving depth and meaning to the strand of history that Central America at that moment was unraveling.

"Guatemala" (he never became accustomed to the name "Central America") had arrived at that delicate moment between the old way and the new. The history of France and of the nations of America told the story of the violence and frustration of their transition and taught him that Guatemala had to anticipate a similar passage. The grim days ahead had caused him to con-

18. Tegucigalpa, Jan. 27, 1824, Valle Papers. Juan Lindo, deputy from Honduras, also wrote in the same manner: "If the ignorance of the people, the local rivalries, and the lack of public funds did not provide obstacles for the Superior Government, I would have nothing to desire. But I am hopeful that your character and knowledge will be the answer to our difficulties." See Lindo to Valle, Feb. 28, 1824, Valle Papers. One of Pedro Molina's correspondents wrote (Feb. 3, 1824) from San Salvador denouncing the rivalry of the factions, saying he thought they would disappear when Valle and Arce arrived (AGG, Molina Papers).

19. Valle and Valle Matheu, eds., *Obras*, I, 36.

20. AGG, B6.26, 2976, 117. Actas de la Asamblea Nacional Constituyente, Jan. 31, 1824.

21. *Ibid.*, Feb. 2, 1824. Two days later the Assembly appointed the committee to escort Valle to the hall and rostrum.

sider resigning, but "after co-operating in achieving absolute independence for Guatemala, it would be opprobrious to abandon her call and those of her sons to consolidate that which had been the object of their desires and mine." These thoughts and those that reminded him that he was a Guatemalan by birth and education made the nation "sacred," and he decided to accept the position. He knew, however, that during the "dangerous transition from one government to another" he would not be able to change "the face of this land," but he pledged to work for the general welfare, concentrating his attention on the stability of government, education, and on the means of securing prosperity. "I shall steal from the geniuses of other nations the thoughts that contributed to their prosperity."

In conclusion and with the prerogative licensed by experience and wisdom, he advised and warned: "A legislator should not confuse himself with a college professor; an immense difference separates one from the other." Professors closeted in their studies deal in abstractions, but a legislator has to consider the realities that he lives with, passing laws appropriate to the level of education of his constituents, to the diverse classes of his society, and to the interests, education, and wealth of each class. The task above all is not to pass "sublime laws" suitable for only an "abstract or an ideal system." The professors would presume to do this. The "experience of the centuries" teaches that the only legislation practical for Guatemala is that dictated by existing conditions in Guatemala. This is the prudent approach to the problems of a nation making the delicate passage to freedom. The "great seal" that should stamp the government is that of "prudence." Guatemala does not have the experience of "independent and free nations." Thus it is "necessary to be guided by prudence, which never takes a step without considering the consequences."[22]

A few weeks after Valle assumed his position in the SPE, Manuel José Arce returned from the United States,[23] and the

22. Valle and Valle Matheu, eds., *Obras*, I, 36-39. For letters praising the speech, see Bishop Nicolás García Jerez to Valle, León, March 9, 1824; Cleto Ordóñez to Valle, Granada, Feb. 18, 1824, Valle Papers. Also see J. Haefkens, *Centraal Amerika, uit een Geschiedkundig, Aardrijkskungdig en Statistiek Oogpunt Beschouwd* (Dordrecht, 1832), p. 85.

23. For information concerning Arce's activities in the United States, see William R. Manning, ed., *Diplomatic Correspondence Concerning the Independence of the*

Assembly scheduled March 15, 1824 for his appearance and oath of office. The triumvirate thus was complete, though Tomás O'Horan was on leave. On March 29 Arce, who apparently had not been home since returning, applied to the Assembly for a month's leave so that he might visit his family in San Salvador.[24] O'Horan returned early in April, but Arce, who suffered an attack of rheumatism that left him unable to attend Mass,[25] was not able to return until May 24.[26]

[2]

During Arce's absence and after his return, Executive Valle tried desperately to accomplish the positive program that he had outlined for the deputies on February 5. He regarded the low level of education as the highest barrier before economic progress and good government. At the same time, he knew that the treasury could not support even the most modest plan for public instruction. But as mayor of the capital he had coped with similar circumstances, and with the same apparent optimism he tried to accomplish his objectives without public funds. He suggested that state and local authorities urge educated men to give classes in the sciences, economics, and politics, allowing them to use any method that they might prefer. Although they were not to receive any pay, they were free to apply to local authorities for a classroom and for whatever financial aid they could get "without prejudice to the treasury."[27] A few days later he asked the rector of the University of San Carlos, the heads of the *colegios,* and the prel-

Latin American Nations (3 vols.; New York, 1925), II, 871-880. (Hereafter Manning, ed., *Diplomatic Correspondence.*)

24. AGG, B6.26, 2978, 117. Actas de la Asamblea Nacional Constituyente, March 8 and 15, 1824; AGG, B6.26, 2980, 118, March 29 and 31, April 6 and 10, 1824; AGG, B10.7, 4038, 184. Correspondencia del ministro de estado, March 15, 1824; Manuel José Arce, *Memorias del General Manuel José Arce, primer presidente de Centro América* (San Salvador, 1947), p. 16. (Hereafter Arce, *Memorias.*)

25. José Matías Delgado to Valle, San Salvador, April 6, 1824, Valle Papers.

26. AGG, B6.26, 2980, 118. Actas de la Asamblea Nacional Constituyente, May 24, 1824.

27. AGG, B10.7, 4038, 184. Correspondencia del ministro de estado. This plan, which was drawn up on March 31, was printed in the *Gaceta de Gobierno,* April 10, 1824. According to one report, the only primary school in Antigua was: ". . . una bóveda, sin la claridad, ventilación, y demás calidades necesarias para la salubridad y buena educación física de los niños que residen algunas horas en ella." See AGG, B10.7, 4040, 185. Correspondencia del ministro de estado, May 21, 1824.

ates of the monasteries to report to the committee on education of the Assembly the classes that were being offered, the methods of teaching, the number of students, and the salaries of the teachers. These data, together with the translation that he had ordered of the project for public instruction that Condorcet and others had presented to the French Assembly, would aid the committee in its task of drawing up the general plan of studies "most adaptable to our circumstances."[28]   Valle, of course, was aware that illiteracy had to be overcome before any formal education could begin, and as a start in this direction he urged the town council of the capital to solicit from the citizens sufficient funds for reprinting Dr. Matías de Córdova's "method of teaching reading and writing."[29]   And with the purpose of raising the level of culture, he appointed a committee to study the possibility of founding an academy of music.[30]

Education as a means to prosperity demanded more specialized instruction. After the "work of Arthur Young," Valle marveled that nations still failed to realize the importance of teaching agriculture, and he tried to restore to Guatemala the interest and enthusiasm for the subject that he had known as a student and as a young lawyer. With the penchant for projects that recalls the activities of the first Economic Society, he extolled the advantages that a professor of botany could bring to Central America. Through his eyes the plants of "our soil" would take on new meaning, and he could teach, what Valle had learned traveling between Mexico and the capital, that on that soil plants not described in the works of Linnaeus abounded. From a purely practical point of view, the research of a botanist well might lead to new products for export and thus to a significant step toward prosperity. To recapture the interest and vigor that had hummed in the capital, he offered to contribute his salary toward the crea-

28. *Gaceta de Gobierno,* April 10, 1824.

29. AGG, B10.7, 4041, 185. Correspondencia del ministro de estado, June 23, 1824. A member of the committee on education suggested the following method for teaching Castilian to the Indians: "Since children begin to form impressions and learn the language that they must speak, it is clear that they must learn that of their mothers. I request, then, that in all the Indian villages where Castilian is not spoken schools should be established for women who, upon learning to speak and read, will pass their knowledge to their children. Thus the barbaric languages that present obstacles to learning will disappear." See AGG, B6.13, 02875, 104. Comisión de instrucción, Feb. 4, 1824.

30. AGG, B10.7, 4041, 185. Correspondencia del ministro de estado, June 23, 1824.

tion of a new botanical garden and succeeded in securing a person to teach classes in botany and agriculture—without salary.[31]

Decadent agriculture lay vulnerable before other approaches. He suggested that the farmers in the vicinity of Chiquimula "should try to cultivate the interesting tobacco plant,"[32] and he tried to revive the interest in cacao of those living near Escuintla and Suchitepéquez.[33] To the Assembly, he recommended the publication of a memorial, which he had copied in Mexico, explaining the cultivation of indigo,[34] and he distributed sketches of a machine for sowing wheat.[35] He called attention to the urgent need of good roads from the interior to the ports, and to exploit the uninhabited northern coasts, he proposed to establish "small colonies of Caribs."[36] After Pedro Molina was appointed minister to Colombia, Valle requested him to send samples of grain, tobacco, and textiles and collections of government publications that might be helpful to Central America.[37] And similar instructions to Antonio José Cañas, minister to the United States, moved him to send copies of the "newspapers of this court," of the congressional debates, and among other things some "docu-

31. *Gaceta de Gobierno*, July 19, 1824. Dionisio de Herrera sent a bright young man, Juan Reyes, to Guatemala City to the classes in "botany and agriculture." José Ignacio Palomo sent an Indian from Verapaz to enroll in the same courses. See Herrera to Valle, Tegucigalpa, Nov. 9, 1824, Valle Papers; AGG, B10.7, 4043, 185. Correspondencia del ministro de estado, August 18, 1824. For a brief survey of Valle's interest in the natural sciences, see José Reina Valenzuela, *José Cecilio del Valle y las ciencias naturales* (Tegucigalpa, 1946), pp. 1-27.

32. AGG, B10.7, 4040, 185. Correspondencia del ministro de estado, Aug. 21, 1824. Marcial Zebadúa conveyed the suggestion to the president of the state of Guatemala.

33. *Ibid.*, May 3, 1824.

34. *Ibid.*, May 10, 1824.

35. Ayuntamiento of Guatemala City to Valle, March 1, 1824, Valle Papers. The council thanked him for the sketch that he had sent.

36. AGG, B10.7, 4042, 185. Correspondencia del ministro de estado, June 28, 1824.

37. Valle to Molina, March 12, 1824, AGG, Molina Papers. Despite the fact that independence from Spain and Mexico had been accomplished, Molina had gone from one frustration to another in his political life. In February, 1824, when he was trying to decide whether to accept the post in Colombia, he had reached a point of despair comparable to that which Valle had experienced in 1818-1819. He laid bare his feelings when he wrote to his wife. "Since I arrived here [San Salvador] and even on the way, I find myself overcome by a kind of insensibility that doesn't allow me to enjoy anything. My sufferings are also cold, and I have just realized that the fire that was driving me has gone out. This feeling will influence my decision with respect to the journey to Colombia. If I return to Guatemala, it will be because I am forced. Neither have I decided to stay here. What, then, shall I do with myself? Valle and Villacorta [probably Juan Vicente], in their letters, urge me to accept. My friends here do the same. It's my duty to serve my country." And on this note, he accepted. See Molina to Dolores Bedoya Molina, San Salvador, Feb. 15, 1824, AGG, Molina Papers.

ments in connection with the opening of canals in New York."[38]

With the same zeal, Valle marshaled all the information at his command for a frontal assault on the mining industry, which never had produced at the level of pristine anticipation. In Mexico he had talked with the eminent Andrés del Río of the College of Mines, asking him if he would recommend one of "his most distinguished students" to come to Central America for the purpose of offering classes in mineralogy and for surveying the resources of the nation.[39] On February 13, 1824, Valle explained in a note to the finance committee the advantages of a resident mineralogist and suggested that the committee secure permission from the Assembly to offer one of Del Río's students an annual salary of 1,200 pesos and 600 for traveling expenses. Valle promised to assume responsibility for the correspondence.[40] The deputies approved the request, and Valle wrote to Del Río, who replied on May 15, saying that one of his students, Francisco Echeverría, would accept the offer. Echeverría, however, wrote (June 27, 1824) that he would need an additional 200 pesos for expenses of travel. The Assembly agreed to meet the request, but whether the student arrived is unknown.[41]

A more vexing problem—one that emerges in connection with each of his projects—was how to overcome the strangling poverty. His experience in colonial offices taught him that the nation had little or no financial reserves to begin with, and his five months in the provisional government following independence assured him that the critical shortage of revenue had grown worse. And if he needed evidence to convince himself that even more fiscal difficulty had been heaped on the government during his absence, Manuel Valero provided it when he wrote: "Fernando, a secretary

38. Cañas to Valle, Washington, Feb. 24, 1825, Valle Papers.

39. AGG, B6.7, 2551, 93. Comisión de hacienda. The note was dated Feb. 13, 1824.

40. *Ibid.*

41. AGG, B6.26, 2976, 117. Actas de la Asamblea Nacional Constituyente, Feb. 14, 1824; *Gaceta de Gobierno*, May 26 and Sept. 13, 1824; AGG, B6.7, 2551, 93. Comisión de hacienda. Much of the *expediente* (2551) of the last citation deals with the project, but notes dated August 13 and 15, 1824, included most of the story. Valle also published a manuscript, which he had copied in Mexico, showing the efficacy of quicksilver for the mining industry. See AGG, B10.7, 4039, 184. Correspondencia del ministro de estado, April 24, 1824; Ayuntamiento of Choluteca to Valle, July 30, 1824; Dionisio de Herrera to Valle, Tegucigalpa, Nov. 6, 1824, Valle Papers. The *ayuntamiento* and Dionisio wrote thanking him for a copy of the manuscript.

of the government, with an annual salary of 1,200 pesos, has not received more than 50 pesos after five months and does not hope to get more than half of his salary. There is no money in the treasury, and they are not imposing any taxes. Without funds, it is impossible to keep employees . . . and it is impossible for a government to exist in such a manner."[42] In a note to the committee on finance, Valle demonstrated that Valero did not greatly exaggerate. "In order to meet the urgent expenses of the treasury," he proposed that the committee use any "funds belonging to overseas heirs." The inheritance had been earned in Central America; the government had guarded it faithfully; thus it was equitable that it should now be used. As Jeremy Bentham had written, "proprietors" were the "sons of the law," and it was just that the "sons" should come to the aid of their "father" in his hour of need. Should Bentham fail to impress, Valle invoked nature's law that laid on all men the obligation of helping each other in troubled times. On the authority of nature and Bentham, the finance committee helped itself to an estimated 680 pesos.[43]

Without any real authority, Valle's efforts to allay the crippling penury were limited to proposals and suggestions, some made for the exigencies of the moment, others aimed at the formulation of fiscal policy. Though his makeshifts showed imagination, his views on the fiscal relationship between the central and state and local authorities were his most significant contribution toward curing the financial ills. As an advocate of a strong central fiscal agency, he used the *Gaceta de Gobierno,* which he edited, and his close relationship with the finance committee to provide a contrast to the overwhelming desire for federalism.[44] As Mateo Ibarra wrote: "A form of government other than that of the United States will not receive 5 votes out of 100 in any place in the Kingdom."[45]

[3]

Valle voiced his views concerning the organization of the government's fiscal agency early in March, 1824. Rumors of pirates

42. To Valle, Dec. 18, 1823, Valle Papers.
43. AGG, B6.7, 2569, 94. Comisión de hacienda, March 6, 1824.
44. Valle and Valle Matheu, eds., *Obras,* I, 79.
45. To Valle, April 1, 1823, Valle Papers.

and foreign aggressors forced the deputies to consider fortification and defense of the ports on either coast. The first prerequisite of course was money, and the Assembly passed a request to the finance committee to assign equitable tax quotas to each of the new states—Guatemala, El Salvador, Honduras, Nicaragua, and Costa Rica—for the purpose of security and defense of the ports. In this connection, Valle, who later said that he was president of the committee, replied, taking the position that he was to defend throughout 1824.

To assign quotas to each state, he affirmed, required precise knowledge of boundaries, of the population of each state, and of the resources or wealth of each. The old boundaries still existed, but without census reports and statements of real property, the committee would have "to roam the field of conjecture." Mistakes were certain to be made and surely would lead to disaffection. When people of one state began making comparisons with those of another, the disgruntled would sue, freighting the courts and the Assembly with litigation sufficient to retard progress and to bring discredit to the government.

Thus far a plea for equity, his narrative, with transition blunted by eagerness, moved suddenly to his primary objective. "A system of taxation established at a central point that exercises control over all is a vigorous and energetic system. A system, however, that has diverse centers is bound to be torpid and lethargic." And the national government would be in the awkward position of encouraging a "number of different systems." If the deputies considered fortification of the ports an urgent necessity, "prudence" demanded that they select "the most vigorous and energetic system" for collecting and administering revenue.

Back to the subject long enough to close one argument, he opened another with more grace than before in which he presented a second theme. "The public treasury is like the national currency; both are sacred. And changes produce effects of great consequence." If he had been present when the Assembly had first met, he "would have manifested that the old system of taxation should not be touched until the nation is constituted." Far from reducing or destroying old forms of revenue, the period of transition demanded that they guard and try to increase them. Now it was too late. Old taxes had been destroyed, and new ones had not been imposed.

His second point made, the question of revenue for the defense of the ports still begged an answer. Characteristically, he addressed himself not to the single question but to the broad issue of raising funds sufficient for seeing the Assembly to a successful close. Circumstances demanded that the finance committee calculate the present income, try to form a reasonable estimate of expenses, and then attempt to cover the deficit (the thought of surplus never entered his mind) by telling the people, "with the frankness that ought to characterize a liberal government," that taxes had to be raised but that they would be reduced as soon as the difficulty of the transition had passed. He then recommended an upward adjustment of import duties, of taxes on certain domestic articles, and of the contributions for "each class" decreed by the Assembly on December 1, 1823. Certainly the Indians, who had paid "sixteen or eighteen reales" in tribute to the "government of their conquerors," should not be offended if they had to pay eight in order to "conserve that of their liberators." The important fact, however, was that the deputies, on the basis of the recommendation of the committee, should levy with one decree enough taxes to see them safely through. Of course there would be grumbling. But by "decreeing a contribution today, imposing another tomorrow, assigning quotas the next, and agreeing to loans on the successive," the Assembly, with these "reiterated acts of exactions," would drive the people to believe that the government, instead of working by plan, shuffled aimlessly from crisis to crisis.[46]

Against Valle's judgment, the deputies assigned tax quotas to each state. The states, however, failed to meet their obligations, and as the fiscal confusion assumed the proportions of chaos, Valle, in translucent terms of grammar school learning, revealed the dark shadows of desperation lurking beneath his narrative. "The public treasury is the basic foundation of all government. Without a treasury, the legislature, the judiciary, and the executive cannot exist. And without the existence of these authorities,

46. AGG, B6.7, 2564, 94. Comisión de hacienda, March 6, 1824.

independence becomes a chimera. The nation that has the best treasury will be the one that establishes itself most easily." The best treasury, according to his reasoning, was the one founded on taxes that the people were accustomed to paying. "All traditional taxes are good," wrote Valle, quoting Nicholas Canard (1750-1833), and the study by which he had arrived "at this great theory would profit those who wish innovations for the treasury, ignorant of the fact that what seems new and brilliant has been abandoned many years ago as complicated and dangerous."[47]

One of the reasons for his growing alarm was the threat to the tobacco monopoly. That tobacco provided a substantial income, which Valle had emphasized after independence, was not lost on the deputies. The question had been brewing since April, 1824, and by October, when it appeared to be destined for the coffers of the states, Valle in a last-ditch stand to save the tax for the national government requested and received permission to address the deputies. Assembly rules failed to mention whether a member of the SPE could be present during the debates. After "some observations," the deputies decided that he should retire from the room immediately after his address. Valle, who probably overheard the decision, "immediately entered," flanked by the Secretaries of State and Treasury. "Taking the seat designated for him, he read the opinion of the committee of finance."[48]

With lawyer-like precision, Valle went immediately to his task, beginning with an outline of his argument: (1) tobacco should continue as a monopoly; (2) the revenue from tobacco should belong to the national government; (3) the administration of the monopoly should be centralized as it always had been. He hastened to say, however, that he opposed monopolies, as such believing that they were unfair. But he was not talking about an abstract idea, and the deputies should realize that they were not making decisions for "the world." Their job, like his, was to think of Central America as it existed in 1824. Laws that worked for the North (it was unnecessary to add the word "America") were not necessarily suitable for the central regions. Thus he urged the deputies to consider the disposition of the tobacco monopoly in light of national needs.

47. *Gaceta de Gobierno*, April 9, 1824.
48. AGG, B6.26, 2992, 119. Actas de la Asamblea Nacional Constituyente, Oct. 11, 1824.

In Guatemala where two thirds of the population, more or less, do not use tobacco, in Guatemala where the majority of the inhabitants do not possess land nor the capital to work it, in Guatemala where tobacco is not an export item, in Guatemala where the transition from a subordinate province to an independent nation has increased the expenses, in Guatemala where the most liberal system of government has been adopted, in Guatemala where the tax from tobacco is a traditional tax, created in the year '66, in Guatemala where it would not be easy to establish a tax to fill the void left by the loss of tobacco, in Guatemala where it is not possible to substitute for it projects proposed in other countries, should tobacco continue as a monopoly or should it be declared free? This is the point that must be decided.

While the drone of the question still lingered, Valle pressed in with evidence. Most people in Central America were poor; the poor were not the ones who used tobacco; and since they lacked the land and capital necessary for its cultivation, they had no vested interest in seeing the weed free of restrictions. The great majority would suffer only if the monopoly were lifted, for without the revenue from tobacco, the Assembly would have to compensate for the loss by subjecting everyone to increased taxation. And the poor, who contributed slightly to the income from tobacco, would have to pay their full share of the new tax.

After demonstrating with Bentham-like procedure that the monopoly provided the greatest good for the greatest number, he asserted that if the deputies voted to continue the monopoly they should also declare that it should be centrally administered—"only one owner, only one director, and only one system of administration." If each of the five states established a separate tobacco monopoly and applied the revenue to the state's financial obligation to the national government (this was the motion before the Assembly), the existence of the "Superior Government," lacking a stable income, would be precarious and the road to anarchy prepared. One of the primary worries of a legislature in a monarchical state was to prevent the accumulation of power in the hands of a monarch, but in a federal republic, the first concern of the deputies should be to guard against the "dissolution or separation of the states." To achieve this objective, they first had to realize that the superior government was the bond in the delicate fabric of federalism that held the states together—it was the government of the nation. And if it were to carry out the obligations that the general interest of the nation imposed, it had to have sufficient revenue, and thus the tobacco monopoly should belong to the national government.[49]

As soon as Valle concluded his paper, the president of the Assembly explained to him that the deputies were going to discuss "the interesting subject of tobacco" and that they would take into consideration what he had said, informing him of the decision as soon as one had been reached. During the weeks following the address, the deputies continued to grope for a solution. Finally, on December 15, 1824, they settled for a compromise that satisfied neither the states nor the national government.[50]

The decision could not have come as a surprise, and a letter from Dionisio pointed up the attitude that foredoomed Valle's hopes.

Dear José: . . . with pleasure, I read your discussion concerning the tobacco tax. You prove that it should remain a monopoly and that it should be administered under one general system, which ought to be the one we always have had. I have written in a similar manner, but I differ with you on the proposition that it should be centralized. . . . Public opinion is against centralization, and the administration of the revenue will not be managed well from Guatemala. . . . I realize the necessity of income for the Supreme Government . . . but it will not come from tobacco. It is necessary to find other sources.[51]

As Valle anticipated, the financial instability began to assume more frightful proportions. In December, 1824, as the work of the Assembly neared completion, the committee on finance submitted a report to the deputies that substantiated what everyone must have known but what few seemed to worry about.

We are obliged to point out to you the state to which the treasury has been reduced. . . .   The only income for sustaining the affairs of the federal government, according to the laws of the National Assem-

49. BNG. *Discurso del Gobierno Supremo de Guatemala sobre la renta de tabaco leído en la Asamblea el día 11 de octubre de 1824* (Guatemala City, 1824): Valle and Valle Matheu, eds., *Obras*, II, 251-264.

50. AGG, A1.22, 1510, 142. Decreto de la Asamblea Nacional Constituyente sobre los productos de las rentas de tabaco y pólvora (Dec. 15, 1824). The law made tobacco a federal monopoly. Profit from domestic consumption belonged to the states, but the states had to apply the profit to the tax quotas assigned by the federal government. Profit beyond the quotas belonged unreservedly to the states. That the law failed was apparent in the vigorous complaints. See AGG, B7.8, 03128, 134. Comisión de hacienda (April 10, 1826).

51. To Valle, Tegucigalpa, Nov. 6, 1824, Valle Papers. When Herrera said that he desired "one general system," he meant that he wanted the states to maintain uniformity of price and of quality and quantity available, hoping to prevent clandestine traffic.

bly, comes from import duties, the postal system, and the monopoly on gunpowder. The first has been assigned to the Consulado, obliging it to pay the garrison; the second is nil, and far from producing anything, it is a rare month when it is not necessary to subsidize it; and the small amount of the third is used for paying the salaries of the secretariat of the Assembly.[52]

One of the most significant points—one that Valle scored in his discussion of the tobacco monopoly—that emerges from the weary repetition of financial reports written from the loss side of the ledger was the failure of the states to meet their tax quotas. The negligence, however, was not owing entirely to lean resources but must be charged in large part to the destructive rivalry within each state and to the withering resentment of all the states for the capital. Dionisio de Herrera, who had finally accepted the presidency of Honduras, observed with as much resolution as despair that "they are working to divide this city [Tegucigalpa] from Comayagua, but I don't think they will achieve it. . . . I will not back up one step, regardless of the danger. I have no army and no money, but I shall exhaust all possible means" to prevent the split.[53] In 1824, however, Nicaragua displayed the most glaring example of internal strife, and the dispute between El Salvador and the national government concerning the means of pacifying Nicaragua brought into the open once more the most ominous sign of the resentment and contributed to the break between the members of the SPE, Arce and Valle.

[4]

The cities of León and Granada in Nicaragua were each controlled by a succession of leaders and supported by a number of villages, and intermittently traded blows throughout 1822 and 1823. The provocations on each side were many, but Alejandro Marure, contemporary historian, summed up the causes when he wrote that the "war of Nicaragua" sprang from personal antipathies, family resentments, village rivalries, contrary opinions concerning the form of government, and the political ambitions of

52. AGG, B6.7, 2643, 96. Comisión de hacienda, Dec. 13, 1824.
53. To Valle, Tegucigalpa, Nov. 27, 1824, Valle Papers. In addition to these difficulties, Herrera was having trouble with counterfeiters (Dionisio de Herrera to Valle, Tegucigalpa, June 27, 1824, Valle Papers).

the clergy.[54]   In December, 1823, when Bishop Nicolás García Jerez swore to recognize established authority, Nicaragua appeared ready to write her constitution and to establish the state government.   An uprising in León, however, fanned dissension anew, and the Assembly sent José Justo Milla to Nicaragua to form a provisional government that would recognize the Assembly.   Inside two months Milla succeeded in gaining recognition of the opposing factions for a government constituted in Managua.   Soon after Milla returned to Guatemala City, happy with his success,[55] León became the scene of further disorder, and it was decided to install another provisional government composed of representatives of the different factions.   The government, however, never met and the fighting continued until January, 1825.

Throughout the spring and summer of 1824, the SPE had sought means to end the strife.   Valle wanted to send Colonel Manuel Arzú to Nicaragua with credentials from the triumvirate empowering him to arbitrate the differences long enough to allow the election of constitutional authorities.   Arce, however, desired to send troops from El Salvador, which he apparently intended to command.[56]   The disagreement within the triumvirate, during the first days of August, delayed a decision.   On August 10, Deputies Argüello and Rosales from León and Granada complained that the government had not reported "one word to the Assembly" concerning Nicaragua.   They proposed that the Secretary of State bring the deputies up to date.[57]

Rather than receive a report from Secretary Marcial Zebadúa, Valle reviewed the crisis and pointed out the difficulty that the triumvirate had been experiencing with the state of El Salvador. That government, on July 6, 1824, ordered that all men between

54. *Bosquejo histórico*, I, 81.   Juan de Dios Mayorga (to Valle, Mexico City, Sept. 29, 1824, Valle Papers), writing in connection with Nicaragua, observed: "It seems to me that the causes . . . are family feuds and the rivalries among the villages."   For a similar statement, see Juan Mora to Pedro Molina, November 17, 1824, AGG, Molina Papers.

55. AGG, B6.22, 02937, 110.   Exposiciones de las autoridades y de particulares. Milla addressed a note (March 20, 1824) to the Assembly describing his success.

56. Earlier El Salvador had organized the Legion of Liberty and had appointed Arce commander.   The war committee protested that Arce could not command the Legion while he served in the SPE, pointing out that Valle had to give up his position of *auditor de guerra*.   The government in San Salvador refused to yield, and Arce continued as commander and finally led the expedition to Nicaragua. For details of this conflict, see AGG, B6.9, 2753, 99.   Comisión de guerra, May 11 and 31; June 2; Aug. 2, 1824.

57. AGG, B6.26, 2991, 119.   Actas de la Asamblea Nacional Constituyente.

the ages of fifteen and forty-five should enlist in either the militia or the reserves and that all forces should prepare to leave for Nicaragua. Then on August 7 the state informed the SPE that the troops would depart as soon as the triumvirate granted permission. Should the SPE refuse, the troops, "perhaps," would march "without it." The outline of the constitution (Valle warming to his task) specified the authority of the states; in none of the provisions could he find anything that authorized a state to raise and train troops for the purpose of invading another state. Such power, when it needed to be exercised, belonged to the national government. Plainly, the armed force that should discipline the factions in Nicaragua "must be an impartial force sent by the Supreme Government." Valle did not believe for a minute that the troops of El Salvador could fit that description. "It is said that a party exists in San Salvador that is thinking of elevating that state over all the other states." Then he softened that rumor by repeating another: "It is also said that another exists in the state of Guatemala that is working against independence." These somber stories well might be the "gloomy origin of most regrettable consequences." Solemnly, he pledged to speak to the government in San Salvador in the "language of reason and law." And with just a hint of panache, as though to contrast his language with that coming from El Salvador, he promised to do so "with the decorum that a government should employ in such instances." He thought the Assembly also should explain to the state that the law on the point in question was so clear that the state would have to revoke the order, commanding that the troops "should not leave the territory of that state without an explicit order from the national government."[58]

Two days later (August 13, 1824), the SPE denied the government of El Salvador the right to send troops to Nicaragua, and on the following day, Executive Arce disclosed his position when he resigned from the triumvirate, complaining that it was impossible for him to continue "suffering the temperament of my colleague, José Cecilio del Valle."[59] Further, Arce wrote that upon assuming his office he learned immediately that Valle possessed the "art of

58. BNG. Colección Valenzuela. The author has lost or misplaced the title of the published pamphlet.

59. AGG, B6.25, 2949, 112. Sesión secreta de la Asamblea Nacional Constituyente, August 14, 1824.

exasperating" and refused to hear opinion distinct from his own. When someone suggested that he might be wrong, he lost his temper. The exasperated Arce, refusing to be a "blind subscriber" to Valle's views, resigned over the protest of the deputies to preserve the decorum of the SPE.[60]

Contemporaries who left an account of the conflict between Valle and Arce over the pacification of Nicaragua cast Valle in a mean role. Alejandro Marure wrote that Valle desired to be the first president of Central America and opposed Arce's plan for fear that it would succeed and that the success would increase Arce's chances of gaining the nation's highest office. Thus Valle was responsible for prolonging the anarchy in Nicaragua.[61] Manuel Montúfar, who never recognized Valle's ability without a conveniently juxtaposed "but," blamed Valle for the continuation of the "anarchy," scorning the puny effort that sent one man, Colonel Arzú, to settle the differences and charging that Valle was trying to identify himself with the strongest faction in Nicaragua.[62] Another contemporary, one without license to express an opinion, observed that Valle, possessing "more ability, foresight, and better sense than Arce," recognized the selfish purpose of the expedition and tried to stop it. The implication was that Arce used the conflict to advance his own ambitions.[63] Valle also considered that possibility. He wrote to Miguel González Saravia, former governor of Nicaragua, who replied, commenting on Valle's remark about the "expedition of Arce to Nicaragua, which you resisted so much." González believed that Arce had been seeking "presidential votes."[64]

The order for the elections had gone out in May, 1824, and at the time of the conflict they were in progress. Valle, who had carried Washington's picture hundreds of miles, wanted very

60. Durón, ed., *Obras de José Cecilio del Valle*, pp. xvii-xviii. Durón reproduced a letter written by Arce on August 19, 1824. Arce wrote a similar letter on September 10, 1824, though it was not phrased so forcefully. See AGG, B6.22, 2940, 110. Exposiciones de las autoridades y particulares. Arce was replaced by José Manuel de la Cerda (Marure, *Bosquejo histórico*, I, 101).

61. *Bosquejo histórico*, I, 107.

62. *Memorias de Jalapa*, p. 69.

63. Vicente Filísola, *La cooperación de México en la independencia de Centro América (Documentos inéditos o muy raros para la historia de México*, XXXVI; Mexico, 1911), pp. 23-24. Filísola arrived in Guatemala City after Valle had gone to Mexico, and he did not return until after Filísola had departed. Thus he did not know Valle, except by reputation.

64. Miguel González Saravia to Valle, Mexico City, December 27, 1826, Valle Papers.

much to be the first president of Central America. He probably used all the influence at his command to secure the office. On August 27, 1824, the following was addressed to him: "I am sending you a copy of the act in connection with the naming of you [by one district] for the president of the republic. It is going well, and the sinister views of our rivals remain ridiculous."[65] Later, Dionisio suggested Valle's legitimate ambition:

Don't worry over what they are saying about you in San Salvador. The people have proof of your conduct and feelings. As for what the writers say in their incendiary papers, they succeed only in bringing discredit to themselves. The votes that you have received for the presidency of the republic are the proof of the pudding. Those who have given their votes to you will not change their minds without reason. By today's mail, several letters against Arce have arrived from San Salvador.[66]

In view of these letters and later events, Marure correctly stated that Valle wanted to be president. That he tried to wring advantage in the elections from the chaos in Nicaragua, however, calls for more evidence.

Montúfar's charge that Valle sent one man to arbitrate the difference in Nicaragua is also correct. But that act was not unusual. The provisional government, following independence, used it successfully, and the Assembly, in January, 1823, commissioned José Justo Milla to settle the dispute in Nicaragua. Milla enjoyed temporary success, and it is possible that Colonel Arzú would have succeeded without Arce and his troops. Arzú received his commission in September or October, and on November 16, Valle wrote to Pedro Molina, in Colombia, that Nicaragua was enjoying "peace and tranquillity."[67] In like manner Juan Mora, president of Costa Rica, wrote that Arzú had arrived and already had begun "to calm the fury of the factions." Hostilities had ceased and some of the armed forces were retiring. Mora thought that the state would soon be organized.[68]

But while Valle was writing to Molina, fighting again broke out, and the SPE invited troops from Honduras, Costa Rica, and El Salvador to assist Arzú and to serve under his orders. The government in San Salvador, which previously had been denied

65. Manuel José Lara to Valle, Aug. 27, 1824, Valle Papers.
66. To Valle, Tegucigalpa, Dec. 27, 1824, Valle Papers.
67. AGG, Molina Papers.
68. *Ibid.*, Nov. 17, 1824.

its request to send troops, now insisted on sending them under secret orders, refusing to reveal them to the SPE. In January, 1825, Arce and his troops, apparently with the slightest effort, brought an end to the fighting. Arce thus has reaped the credit for pacifying Nicaragua, and Valle has been castigated for delaying the settlement with his narrow self-interest.

The exchange of correspondence between San Salvador and Guatemala City during the last days of December, 1824, provided Valle's answer to his critics. A member of the war committee first supplicated the state for a copy of the orders, explaining courteously that the expedition to Nicaragua was a combined operation commanded by the national government. The success of the contingents depended on harmony, and thus the SPE desired a copy of the orders so that the executives could take any measures necessary to avoid the "disaster" promised by a divided command. El Salvador refused to disclose the instructions, saying that her "love and sacrifices for liberty" insured that the troops would conduct themselves for the good of the nation.[69]

Valle replied to the refusal and reviewed the relations of the SPE and the state.

The Superior Government, on August 13, refused to allow the troops of San Salvador to march to León because it shrank from the spirit with which it was intended. These troops would have been received in León not as soldiers of the Government but as prejudiced protectors of one of the belligerent parties, sent because the SPE desired that one group should be destroyed so that the other might rule over cadavers. The zeal with which San Salvador solicited the dispatch of her troops to León—even saying that they would send them if the Government refused—was the main reason why it did refuse. It saw the workings of prejudice rather than reason; it saw capriciousness rather than the wisdom that might terminate by regular means the discord of fellow citizens of the same nation. The opposition to the march of the troops is one of the reasons why the president of Salvador lends an innocent appearance to the arbitrary act of the congress that gave secret orders for operations in Nicaragua, forgetting that such an order attacks the Federal Government, good order, and the authority that belongs to the government of the Republic. . . . Troops that go from a state by order of the Federal Government are subordinate only to that Government; they cannot and must not recognize another authority; and the authority that orders the contrary authorizes disorder. . . . Thus without doubt the Congress of San Salvador has overstepped its authority, as has the president of the state in his

69. AGG, B6.9, 2757, 99. Comisión de guerra, Dec. 16, 1824.

dispatch which abounds with insults authorized only by the desire to use them.

Valle concluded by declaring that the conduct of the congress and the president deserved a reprimand from the Assembly, which also should demand the retraction of the secret orders and charge Arce, who commanded the troops, "to obey religiously the orders of the SPE."[70]

Rather than the narrow, selfish approach attributed to him, Valle tried to apply to the crisis of war and intervention in Nicaragua the same principle that consistently guided his actions in connection with fiscal organization. He appears to have understood the delicacy of federalism, perhaps better than those who chose it, and held the view that the states and the national government should have separate, well-defined areas of authority and that each should enjoy the means of exercising that authority. In connection with fiscal policy, he believed that the national government should not be dependent on the states and that the financial self-sufficiency should come from the power to tax directly the citizens of the five states. In this area the Assembly disagreed in practice, if not in principle. To the national government, the deputies allotted the postal system, gunpowder, import duties, and tobacco, knowing as well as Valle that the combined revenue from these sources would be insufficient. The difference—thus dependency—came from the quotas assigned to the states.[71]

In the area of political relations between the national government and the states, Valle steadily defended the view that there also were well-defined areas of authority. And he believed that the pacification of Nicaragua was the function of the national

70. *Ibid.*, Dec. 31, 1824. This dispatch went to San Salvador over the signature of Marcial Zebadúa, and if he had written it, Valle's case would be stronger. But the author is convinced by the tone and content of the document that Valle either wrote it or told Zebadúa what to write. Also see Valle and Valle Matheu, eds., *Obras*, I, 79.

71. The Constitution also spoke of financial dependency for the national government. In describing the authority of the national congress, Article 69 states: "6. Fijar los gastos de la administración general. 7. Decretar y designar rentas generales para cubrirlos; y no siendo bastantes, señalar el cupo correspondiente a cada estado según su población y riqueza." And in describing the power of the state assemblies, Article 178 shows: "2. Determinar el gasto de su administración y decretar los impuestos de todas clases necesarias para llevar éste, y el cupo que les corresponda en los gastos generales." See *Constitución de la República Federal de Centro-América* (Guatemala City, Nov. 22, 1824). If enough people had wanted the federation to succeed, however, these provisions would have been adequate to insure financial stability. But the naked hostility between the states and the national government made it easy for the states to ignore their quotas.

government. The deputies supported him, at least in theory, for they had drawn up the regulation that empowered the SPE to guard public order.[72] But Valle claimed that one of the reasons for the prolonged anarchy in Nicaragua was the failure of the deputies to support him. In reply to a letter from Valle, Juan de Dios Mayorga, Central America's minister to Mexico, wrote: "Since, as you say, the Assembly has denied the Government the means with which to pacify the province of Nicaragua, I have sent to the Government a dispatch couched in very strong terms in order that you might use it if you see fit."[73] Before receiving this letter, Valle wrote to cousin Próspero: "The Government should smother the factions and sustain our just cause, but the Assembly does not wish to give funds to the Government. Without them, it witnesses the sickness unable to supply the remedy."[74] While it is uncertain exactly what Valle had in mind when he wrote the letter, his views render a citation of Marure and Montúfar, in connection with Valle and Nicaragua, profitable only for showing an attitude.

[5]

On November 22, 1824, the Assembly completed its main task when the deputies signed the Constitution. Later that same day a committee of eight presented the document to the members of the SPE for their signatures.[75] The basic law vested the executive authority in a president, provided for a bicameral legislature, and placed a supreme court at the peak of the judiciary. Juan Arévalo, "the director of the best press," estimated that 2,500 copies of the Constitution would cost between 360 and 400 pesos, and the committee on finance had some difficulty raising the money.[76] Published upon completion, the document apparently was not formally promulgated until April 10, 1825. On that day,

72. AGG, B6.17, 2901, 108. Reglamento del poder ejecutivo, July 8, 1823. The authority to settle the crisis in Nicaragua came from the following: "El poder ejecutivo . . . velará sobre la conservación del orden público en el interior, y sobre la seguridad exterior de este nuevo estado, y protegerá la libertad individual de los ciudadanos y sus propiedades."
73. Mexico City, Jan. 13, 1825, Valle Papers.
74. Dec. 29, 1824, Valle Papers.
75. See the note dated Nov. 25, 1824 (AGG, B10.2-1, 3283, 157).
76. AGG, B6.7, 2639, 96. Comisión de hacienda, Nov. 26, 1824.

according to an anonymous report, at 4:00 o'clock in the afternoon, the members of the court, the cathedral chapter, the cloister
of the University, the Consulado, the Colegio de Abogados, and
the Protomedicato gathered "to celebrate the solemn promulgation of the Federal Constitution." After a parade, the crowd
listened while an official read the Constitution in a loud voice.
At the conclusion, the mayor of the capital city "waved the flag
of the republic, saying: 'Long live the federal constitution.'" The
crowd, restless from the formalities, moved to the hall of the town
council where a table adorned with refreshments awaited.[77]

[6]

Soon after the deputies and the SPE gave the Constitution
legality with their signatures, Valle successfully petitioned a leave
of "twenty or thirty days."[78] Although he was satisfied that he
had done all that he possibly could, he had grave doubts about the
future of the nation. At "La Concepción," which came to be his
favorite retreat during the Christmas season, he relaxed with his
family. "We continue on here without any distractions, happy
and contented." But the happiness and contentment were surface emotions evoked by the beauty and peacefulness of his surroundings and by the rare, undisturbed moment with his family.
"I don't have any desire to leave here; I am enjoying the surroundings and all that they suggest." Then he gave way to the
preoccupation that had intruded with phrases and clauses into the
friendly note at Christmastide. He was genuinely thankful that
he and his family no longer had to be "spectators of intrigue and
maliciousness." And he fumbled for an answer, not understanding what had happened to the stable society that he had known.
Suspicious and given to reporting rumors that he previously might
have scorned, he told Próspero: "Days ago, I said there was a plan
afoot against our independence." Pettishly, he magnified the
importance of an adventurer from Peru or Colombia, J. J. Salas,[79]

77. Valle Papers. Bancroft (*History of Central America,* III, 75) wrote that the
date was April 15, 1825.
78. AGG, B6.26, 2998, 119. Actas de la Asamblea Nacional Constituyente, Dec. 17
and 20, 1824.
79. Salas became involved in the fighting in Nicaragua and soon was leading one
of the factions. Herrera, who wrote that Salas came from Peru, did not regard

accusing him of plans extending far beyond that small mind. With reason, he worried about the two factions in Honduras and "those" in El Salvador.[80]   Similar suspicions and fears were shared by his friends Dionisio de Herrera[81] and Juan de Dios Mayorga,[82] who, in the manner of Valle, seemed to be groping to explain what was happening before their eyes.   In 1824, however, they were still too close to grasp the full significance of the process that had begun immediately after independence.

By December, 1824, when Valle wrote from "La Concepción," the center of authority had shifted from Guatemala City and had splintered among the five states.   As one reads the day-to-day proceedings of the provisional government established after independence and those of the Assembly and of the committees of the Assembly, nothing emerges more clearly than that the authority in the capital, regardless of its composition, did not lead but merely responded to the actions of the former provinces.   When independence lopped off the head of authority, the provinces, scrambling to prevent Guatemala City from becoming the new head, reduced authority in the capital to a wisp tossed by every wind blowing from the provinces.   The capital regained a measure of respect under the rule of Iturbide, but with his downfall, the provinces again took the initiative.   Plainly the deputies in the Assembly worked together to form a federation, but their interest in a federal system was to insure the authority of the states.   Telltale traces of this attitude appear in the constitution,[83] but the act

---

him with the same apprehension that Valle expressed.   Herrera wrote: "Salas wrote to me on the twenty-ninth of last month apologizing for his conduct and saying that he had given up the command.   But on the fourth and fifth of this month, he attacked León, and it seems that he continues to command."   See Herrera to Valle, Tegucigalpa, Nov. 27, 1824, Valle Papers.   Marure (*Bosquejo histórico*, I, 103) noted that Salas came from Colombia.

80. Dec. 29, 1824, Valle Papers.

81. Herrera worried more about Bolívar than Salas: "I suspect that Colombian more each day.   At the moment, Bolívar must have 40,000 troops; they are well paid and well dressed and don't know how to do anything except fight.   No longer are there any Spaniards to fight in Colombia, and there are only a few in Peru. What, then, will he do with those 40,000 men?"   See Dionisio de Herrera to Valle, Tegucigalpa, Dec. 17, 1824, Valle Papers.

82. Dios Mayorga, perhaps with more justification, saw a plot to return Central America to Mexico.   He suspected Miguel Larreinaga, a Montúfar, Antonio García Redondo, and a Beteta, suggesting that "Don Jacobo Villa Urrutia," in Mexico, was the center of the circle.   See Dios Mayorga to Valle, Mexico City, June 5 and Sept. 29, 1824, Valle Papers.

83. Whether Central America was a federation or a confederation still divides opinion.   See Harold Bond Field, "The Central-American Federation, a Political Study, 1826-1839" (unpublished Ph.D. dissertation, Chicago, 1942); Franklin Dallas

that illumined most clearly their desires was the motion: "Will there be any general taxes for the expenses of the federal government?"[84] The division showed fifty-one in the affirmative and one in the negative, but the fact that such a motion ever got on the floor expressed the sympathy for the statement made by Ciriaco Villacorta, deputy from El Salvador, who explained his negative vote by declaring that he opposed "the centralization of any tax."[85] Villacorta, the other deputies from El Salvador, and the president of that state, Juan Vicente Villacorta, were all described as "Liberals," largely because they favored a federal system of government. But if federalism denoted a "Liberal," what name should be applied to these same men and others when they returned to their respective states and proceeded to make their capitals into replicas of the old capital? Baldly put, the party labels—Liberal and Conservative—in the Assembly were meaningless. Only by their actions in the states can the political sympathies of the deputies be determined. In the Assembly, the deputies, for the most part, were state centered and used federalism as a convenient tool to accomplish their purpose. The issue of religion provided an exception, and for a fleeting moment Pedro Molina's consistent liberalism was clearly discernible. But the issue was never in doubt: Catholicism, to the exclusion of all other faiths, became the religion of the republic. Thus the continuing competition between the states and the national government gave added impetus to the centrifugal force that was to turn the third act of the "comedy" into a national tragedy.

Valle, stripped of power as an executive, recognized the shift but viewed the competition in the states as the work of a subversive group whose purpose was the destruction of independence. Apparently there were few who entertained the hope of returning Central America to Mexico or Spain, but the conflict, like that between the states and the capital, appeared as a simple struggle for control of state government. Valle, as he wrote to Próspero, would have used the strength of the national government to control the competing factions. And in view of his ideas concerning

---

Parker, *José Cecilio del Valle and the Establishment of the Central American Confederation* (Tegucigalpa, 1954).

84. AGG, B6.26, 2983, 118. Actas de la Asamblea Nacional Constituyente, May 29, 1824.

85. *Ibid.*

fiscal organization and on the conflict with El Salvador, he doubtless would have preferred a strong central government, perhaps
an oligarchy after the fashion of England.   Certainly he would
have made the national government in a federal system strong
and vigorous.   As it was, he looked forward to the future with
doubt and apprehension.

[7]

On February 25, 1825, a summary of the work of the SPE
appeared over the signatures of the three executives. In the main,
it was a summary of Valle's work and doubtless was written by
Valle. The executives, the summary expressed, had known the
dangers confronting a government not yet established. In the
period of transition there were always those who feared the loss
of all that the old government had given them and those who
wished to acquire benefits from the new. These two groups,
pulling in opposite directions, were bound to clash and thus were
the primary origin of civil war. The SPE tried to protect independence with the limited means at its disposal, realizing that a
government that oppressed with one hand and stifled reaction to
oppression with the other was a despotic government. Armed
forces were necessary, but they had to be used with prudence.
And the SPE always preferred to resolve differences with peaceful
means. In connection with education, the executives again noted
that they worked with limited resources. But poverty did not
change the fact that the ignorant were easy prey for those "capable
of sacrificing an entire people" for narrow self-interest. Thus the
SPE had tried to raise the level of education, and the reader's
attention turned to the list of proposals, suggestions, and projects.
The triumvirate also traced the painful financial picture, reminding the readers that the Assembly had destroyed or pared
down the traditional taxes. At the same time, the number of
employees had increased to meet the demand of the new system.
To arrest the growing deficit and with the vain hope of balancing
the budget, the SPE asked for more taxes and control of the tobacco monopoly. In addition, the executive authority negotiated

a loan with a London firm.[86] Finally, in November of 1824, the deputies completed the Constitution; Central America had made the transition, unity unimpaired.

On the same day that the summary was published, Valle, performing his last function as a member of the triumvirate, addressed the first congress of Central America. His theme brought to light his own fears. He cautioned the new deputies that from the moment they were elected to the congress they were expected to subordinate every vestige of self-interest to the welfare of the nation. In language designed to evoke the patriotism of each and to ennoble the spirit, Valle scorned shallow egoists, agents of intrigue, and small-minded men who in their witless ways would try to seduce members of the congress. And finally he raised his voice against particularism, challenging the deputies to adjust their sights to a national view and to make the congress a "temple of Respect, Prudence, and of Judicious Patriots."[87]

The opening of the national congress signaled the end of Valle's official duties. The summary presented the efforts he had made, and his address to the congress expressed the fear that he had experienced in dealing with Nicaragua and the government in San Salvador. Valle's voice was a warning, but it was to go unheeded.

86. Valle and Valle Matheu, eds., *Obras*, I, 47-63. Barclay, Herring and Company, of London, contracted the loan, but by 1826 the company was bankrupt. However, Marcial Zebadúa, who had become Central America's minister in London, worked out a "convention with the respected House of Reid Irving and Company." See G. A. Thompson to Valle, London, Dec. 7, 1826, Valle Papers; Marure, *Bosquejo histórico*, I, 97; Robert A. Naylor, "The British Role in Central America Prior to the Clayton-Bulwer Treaty of 1850," *HAHR*, XL (Aug., 1960), 369.
87. Valle and Valle Matheu, eds., *Obras*, I, 45-47. A businessman who happened to be in the capital at this time commented on Valle's address: "Señor Del Valle . . . pronounced an eloquent speech at the opening of the congress. It is impossible sufficiently to praise that estimable citizen for the good which he had effected for his country." See Francisco Lavagnino, "Guatemala," *New Monthly Magazine*, XIV (1825), 582-583. Lavagnino knew Valle personally. See Lavagnino to Valle, Quetzaltenango, Dec. 30, 1828, Valle Papers.

If I Were Master of America

[1]

The anxieties that threatened from the periphery of Valle's thoughts before they commandeered his full stream of consciousness were a sincere expression of his misgivings for the future of Central America. The letter that he wrote to Próspero on December 29, 1824, spoke in desperate tones of some imminent but undefined danger that persisted in his mind and again found expression in his address to the first national congress. In the days between the letter and the address, additional correspondence disclosed that he was involved in a personal crisis that became national in scope when the presidential election had to be decided by the deputies.

The order and the instructions for electing the executive had gone out on May 5, 1824. To become president, a candidate had to win a majority of the electoral votes assigned to each of the states on the basis of one vote for each 15,000 inhabitants. Since the Assembly had abolished slavery, all figured in the estimate of the population and enjoyed the franchise. The state of Guatemala possessed thirty-six electoral votes; El Salvador, eighteen; Honduras, twelve; Nicaragua, twelve; and Costa Rica, four. Further, the electoral votes of each state were divided among the districts according to population. Reminders that the elections were in progress cropped up throughout the remainder of the year,[1] and the conflict over the pacification of Nicaragua sug-

1. On June 10, 1824, a deputy to the Assembly suggested that the ballots cast by the states in the presidential election should be locked in a strongbox that required four keys to open. After the box was locked the four keys should be given to the SPE who would lock them in another box that required three keys. Each member

gested the hopes of Arce and Valle. Dionisio's letter to Valle pointed up the sharp rivalry, and Valle's correspondence shed additional light on the elections and explained further his deep anxieties.

After retiring to "La Concepción," he depended for political news on cousin Próspero, a deputy in the Assembly. "I want to know the result of the intrigue that you told me about," Valle urged in reply to a letter. "The objective is clear. They want the majority in the Congress to decide the elections so that they can put someone at the head of the government who will facilitate the plan for submitting us to Mexico and Colombia."[2] A "faction" that did not "love absolute independence" was the antecedent of "they," and the same vague pronoun referred to those who did not wish to elect someone to the presidency who had "decided to dedicate himself to the nation." With pride and the anger and confidence that come from being underrated, he wrote in language stripped of embellishment:

I am a man of honor; I love my country; and I have served it with patriotism. I shall know how to answer. I shall reveal their intrigue, their objective, and the tactics they have used. . . . They will not intimidate me with a heavy hand nor will they deceive me. I am not a child.[3]

The intrigue that worried Valle apparently was an attempt on the part of the leaders of some or all of the political factions to force the election of the president into the Congress by spreading the electoral votes among a number of candidates to prevent anyone from gaining the majority required for election. Should the tactic succeed, the deputies then could test the pliability of the candidates and elect the one that displayed the most promise of cooperation. Whether these were the thoughts of the influential members of the political groups is not clear, but the results of the election gave substance to Valle's fears.

Valle's chances of success rested on his acknowledged ability,

---

of the SPE would possess one of the keys. See AGG, B6.26, 2923, 118. Actas de la Asamblea Nacional Constituyente.

2. Jan. 11, 1825, Valle Papers. Valle received a letter dated October 16, 1824, from a friend in Mexico, "Federico," who assured him that Mexico and Colombia were planning to divide Central America. Valle continued to express fear of this alleged plan and asked Pedro Molina, who was in Colombia, to investigate it. See Valle to Molina, Nov. 16, 1824, AGG, Molina Papers.

3. Valle to Próspero de Herrera, Jan. 20, 1825, Valle Papers.

wisdom, and wide range of knowledge. Arce's early activity in behalf of independence[4] and his opposition to union with Mexico gave him outstanding credentials. When the ballots were opened on April 20, 1825,[5] these two candidates emerged as everyone doubtless had anticipated. Valle received forty-one votes; Arce, thirty-four; Alejandro Díaz Cabeza de Vaca, Valle's old enemy, two; Canon José María Castilla, former Caco and opponent of Valle, one; and Santiago Milla, one. The district of Petén, in the state of Guatemala, lost its vote because two elections had been held and two ballots had been submitted. The deputies, ignorant of which was the valid vote, refused to open them.[6] The votes from Cojutepeque, El Salvador and Matagalpa, Nicaragua did not arrive in time for the "scrutiny." Discounting the three invalidated ballots, the total electoral vote was seventy-nine, and Valle had a majority. But the rules governing the election failed to mention whether a majority should be calculated on the basis of the total vote cast or on the basis of the total number of eligible votes. The deputies in the first Congress decided that the candidate must have a majority of the total eligible votes. Thus the three votes from Petén, Cojutepeque, and Matagalpa, which had been invalidated, raised the total to eighty-two, stripped Valle of a majority, and threw the election of the first president of Central America into the Congress.[7]

The table opposite shows how the states cast their votes.

The significant point of the voting record of the states is that it rejects the tidy assumption that Valle was supported by the "Conservatives" and Arce by the "Liberals." The factions in Nicaragua, described as anarchists, radicals, liberals, conservatives,

4. Future evaluations of this period of Arce's career will have to take into account his claim of innocence and flattery of Bustamante. See Arce to Bustamante, San Salvador, Oct. 26, 1814, AGG, A1.1, 57003, 6924.

5. AGG, B5.8, 2037, 72. *Estado que manifiesta el escrutinio de votos populares, practicado por el congreso en la sesión 20 de abril de 1825 para la elección de presidente de la República, expresando las juntas electorales de los partidos, el número de sufragios correspondiente a cada uno de ellos, y los sugetos que los obtuvieron* (Guatemala City, May 26, 1825). (Hereafter *El escrutinio de votos populares.*) Valle wrote that the votes were opened on April 10, 1825. See Valle and Valle Matheu, eds., *Obras*, I, 80.

6. Among Valle's papers is an unsigned and undated note reporting that both votes submitted from Petén were for Valle, "but no one has opened them and they do not want to open them." It appears that the note was written immediately before the deputies voted for the president and vice president.

7. AGG, B5.8, 2037, 72. *El escrutinio de votos populares.*

State	District	Electoral Votes	Candidate
	Guatemala City	2	Valle
	Sacatepéques	4	Arce
	Chimaltenango	4	Valle
	Sololá	2	Valle
	Totonicapán	4	Valle
	Quetzaltenango	6	Arce
Guatemala	Huehuetenango	2	Valle
	Escuintla	2	Valle
	Chiquimula	2	Valle
	San Agustín	2	Valle
	Verapaz	2	Alejandro Díaz Cabeza de Vaca
	Salamá	2	Valle
	Soconuzco	1	Valle
	San Salvador	4	Arce
	Sonsonate	3	Valle
	Gótera	1	Valle
El Salvador	San Vicente	2	Arce
	San Miguel	2	Arce
	Chalatenango	2	Arce
	Santa Anna	2	Arce
	Sacatecoluca	1	Arce
	Comayagua	1	Valle
	Tegucigalpa	1	Valle
	Choluteca	1	Valle
	Nacaome	1	Valle
	Cantarranas	1	José María Castilla
Honduras	Juticalpa	1	Valle
	Gracias	1	Santiago Milla
	Llanos	1	Valle
	Santa Bárbara	1	Valle
	Trujillo	1	Valle
	Yoro	1	Valle
	Segovia	1	Valle
	León	2	Arce
	Granada	2	Arce
	Managua	1	Arce
Nicaragua	Viejo	1	Arce
	Subtiaba	1	Arce
	Masaya	2	Arce
	Nicaragua	2	Arce
Costa Rica	Costa Rica	4	Valle[8]

8. *Ibid.* The distribution of votes did not include those that had been invalidated; thus those districts failed to appear on the list.

imperialists, and royalists, gave Arce all the state's electoral votes. In Honduras, where the factions bore a similar assortment of labels, all but two votes went to Valle. Costa Rica voted unanimously for Valle, and he won four votes from the state of El Salvador, the stronghold of such "liberals" as Arce and José Matías Delgado. In the state of Guatemala, Valle received twenty-three of the thirty-six votes, but Arce counted the six votes from the district of Quetzaltenango, a stronghold of such conservatives as the Aycinenas and Palomos.

When the deputies had to choose between Arce and Valle, a pattern began to form that well might represent the first signs of national parties. The vote in the Congress was as follows.

State	Deputy	District	Vote
Guatemala	Francisco Carrascal	Sacatepéquez	Arce
	José María Castilla	Cantarranas	Valle
	José Francisco Córdova	Salamá	Arce
	Mariano Córdova	Huehuetenango	Arce
	Domingo Diégues	Chimaltenango	Arce
	José María Echeverría	Chimaltenango	Arce
	Francisco Flores	Quetzaltenango	Arce
	Carlos Gálvez	Quetzaltenango	Arce
	Mariano Gálvez	Guatemala City	Arce
	Manuel Lara	Totonicapán	Arce
	Juan Montúfar	Totonicapán	Valle
	José María Ponce	Escuintla	Arce
	Ramón Solís	San Agustín	Valle
	Doroteo Vasconcelos	Sacatepéquez	Arce
El Salvador	Mariano Fuñes	San Vicente	Arce
	Isidro Menéndez	San Salvador	Arce
	José Antonio Peña	Sonsonate	Arce
	Juan Manuel Rodríguez	Sonsonate	Valle
	Carlos Salazar	San Salvador	Arce
	Ciriaco Villacorta	San Salvador	Arce
Honduras	Santiago Milla	Gracias	Arce
Nicaragua	Toribio Argüello	Nicaragua	Arce
	Francisco Benavent	Masaya	Arce
	Filadelfo Benavent	?	Arce
	——— Quiñones	Masaya	Arce
Costa Rica	Policarpo Bonilla	Costa Rica	Arce
	Pablo Álvarado	Costa Rica	Valle[9]

Total: Arce, 22; Valle, 5

9. AGG, B5.8, 2037, 72. *El escrutinio de votos populares.* This list presented

Arce attracted votes from all sides and Valle was in strange company. Pablo Alvarado and José María Castilla were men of liberal persuasion, and Juan Manuel Rodríguez (alias Malilapa) was a former revolutionary! The men that supported Arce were called Conservatives, and those who opposed him at the time of the election and later were called Liberals.

In view of the results, Valle's suspicions in January, 1825, were not groundless. Before the first Congress ever met, the deputies doubtless possessed a reasonably accurate account of each candidate's votes. Since most of the deputies came from the districts outside Guatemala City, they well might have had first-hand information. Others would have learned as Valle learned— friends would have conveyed the results of the elections. With the knowledge that the vote would be close, talk began, as early as January, 1825, about the possibility that neither Arce nor Valle would receive a majority. How far the "intrigue" extended beyond talk is unknown. But once the votes had been counted, it seems certain that the deputies were determined to eliminate Valle. Otherwise they would have declared him president by simply deciding that a majority of the votes cast was sufficient for election. Instead, they chose to reverse what appeared to be a popular decision and to cloud with doubt and suspicion the election of the first president of Central America. And when they reversed the decision, they likely reversed their own, for there is no reason to believe that the elections of 1824-1825 were different from those of 1820. The deputies were among the most influential men in the nation and probably controlled the district elections. Lists of names, accompanied by threats, doubtless were put in the hands of the *pueblo bajo.*

The question, then, that begs an answer is why Valle received support in the regular elections and then lost to Arce in the Congress. The answer lay in the fact that Guatemala was the key state. In the initial elections, Valle won twenty-three of the

the names of the deputies and how they voted but did not include the district which each represented. The district of each deputy, however, was included in the notes of the thoughtful observer G. A. Thompson (*Narrative of an Official Visit,* pp. 509-511), who was in Central America in 1825. Thompson did not list Filadelfo Benavent as a deputy, and his name has been entered with those from Nicaragua purely for the sake of convenience. But a deputy named Filadelfo Benavent, from Nicaragua, sat in the Constituent Assembly. See Townsend Ezcurra, *Fundación de la República,* p. 73.

thirty-six electoral votes, but in Congress, only three of the fourteen deputies present from Guatemala voted for him. Alejandro Marure suggested that Valle received support in the regular elections because he was considered the only man capable of competing successfully with El Salvador's Arce. At that moment the keen rivalry that existed between Guatemala and El Salvador was sharpened by José Matías Delgado's decision, with the approval of the state government, to create a bishopric in El Salvador and to become the new bishop. Delgado's action stripped Archbishop Casaus of some of his authority, and Casaus refused to recognize the bishop or the bishopric and sought support at Rome.[10] Further, as Marure suggested and as these pages show, a wall of antagonism separated Valle from many of the influential families. Thus the votes cast in the state of Guatemala in the regular elections well might have been cast against the ambitions of El Salvador rather than for Valle or against Arce. When the deputies decided that they should elect the president, they apparently talked to each candidate. Certainly those from Guatemala talked to Arce through José Beteta, who told Arce that the deputies from Guatemala wanted to vote for him but were afraid that he would support the pretensions of his uncle, José Matías Delgado.[11] Arce, according to his own account, pointed out that he had supported Delgado but intimated that the question should be settled by the Congress.[12] Apparently the deputies from Guatemala were satisfied that Arce would not interfere in the question of the bishopric and that he would be more flexible than the independent and self-willed Valle. Thus Arce became the first president of Central America.

The Congress also had to elect the vice president. In the regular election José Francisco Barrundia counted twenty-five votes; Arce, twenty-three; Valle, six; and the remainder of the seventy-nine votes went to ten other candidates. Before proceeding to elect either the president or the vice president, the deputies decided that if Arce should win the nation's first office they would elect the vice president from all the candidates who had received votes for that office. Normally, as the instructions specified, they

10. Marure, *Bosquejo histórico*, I, 138-139.
11. *Ibid.*, p. 139; Arce, *Memorias*, p. 20.
12. *Memorias*, p. 20.

would have considered only those with at least ten votes. But if Arce should have become president, Barrundia would have been the only candidate. By virtue of this fact, he conceivably could have become vice president. The deputies, however, chose to include all the candidates, and then, as though to appease, elected Valle to the nation's second office.[13] But Valle, who doubtless had refused a seat in the Congress to favor his greatest ambition,[14] was enraged by his loss of the presidency and refused the vice presidency, which went to Mariano Beltranena.[15]

Angry because the deputies had deliberately chosen Arce, Valle published a protest in which he reviewed his career since 1821 before addressing himself to the issue. He claimed authorship of the declaration of independence and repeated his arguments in connection with annexation, inviting his readers to peruse the "irrefutable document" that he had submitted to show that neither the municipalities, the captain general, nor the provisional government had possessed the authority to annex Central America to Mexico. Vividly he recalled his suffering as a prisoner in Mexico and in detail reviewed his efforts in the SPE. Throughout the pamphlet, however, he neither flaunted his services nor boasted of his ability. He wrote in anger but it was a controlled anger—sufficiently intense to allow a public review of his career but mastered by years of discipline that disallowed meaningless

13. AGG, B5.8, 2037, 72. *El escrutinio de votos populares.*
14. The districts of Santa Bárbara and Yoro in Honduras had elected Valle to the first Congress. See Juan José Díaz to Valle, Dec. 29, 1824, Valle Papers.
15. AGG, B5.8, 2037, 72. *El escrutinio de votos populares.* When Valle refused the office, the election appeared to be going according to plan. Valle's anonymous reporter (Valle Papers), who well might have been a deputy, wrote: "Just now I have talked with the same deputy. He says that as a result of the meeting last night the others will vote for Mariano Beltranena for vice president, in the event that you [Valle] should refuse it, and for O'Horan for chief justice of the court. He said further that if the Liberals do not agree to this, the Conservatives would vote for you [Valle] for president." The deputies also had to elect the chief justice, and the eligible candidates were Tomás O'Horan and Antonio Rivera Cabezas, a Liberal who had served with Molina in the SPE. On the basis of this thin strand of evidence, it appears that the bargain was the following: The Conservatives of the state of Guatemala would vote for Arce for president. Then the Liberals and Conservatives would elect Valle vice president, believing that he would refuse the office. After he had refused, the Liberals would have to co-operate in electing Beltranena, a son of the capital who had received only four votes in the regular election, and O'Horan, whom the Conservatives preferred over Rivera Cabezas. This is exactly the way the elections turned out (AGG, B5.8, 2037, 72. *El escrutinio de votos populares*), but additional evidence is necessary before a positive statement can be made that such a bargain was made. And any explanation will have to take into account that José Francisco Barrundia was elected vice president after Valle refused. Beltranena, then, became vice president only after both Valle and Barrundia had refused.

and reckless charges. With the directness of an angry aristo-crat, as though smiting an enemy with an empty glove, he de-clared: "I am convinced that the election by the Congress of Citizen Arce is null." Others who were "unimpeachable owing to their impartiality" were persuaded of the "same truth." And the entire nation would be equally convinced if they knew what had happened. "But this is not my objective." All he was trying to do was to defend his good name by disclaiming any part in the clandestine procedure. Head high and hands clean, he then vowed that he was retiring from public life.[16]

The fact that the Congress elected both the president and the vice president and that in each case the deputies refuted the man with the most popular votes was sufficient to send pamphleteers scrambling for pen and paper. When the same elections were denounced as a fraud by the man who commanded more respect throughout the nation than any other, the deputies' decision assumed the dimension of a national crisis. A pamphlet signed "A Liberal" attacked the election of Arce on legal grounds, at-tempting to show that the electoral law of May 5, 1824, and subsequent acts of the Assembly proved that Valle should have been elected.[17] And in a letter Deputy Pablo Alvarado (Costa Rica) wrote: "I repeat that I voted against the election of Arce because it was unconstitutional and dangerous, and I protested its nullity before the whole nation and especially before the Congress and the heads of the states."[18] But the Liberals, Arce's opposition, were in a minority and suffered at the hands of the Conservatives, who supported Arce. "I speak in Congress," Alvarado continued, "with the firmness, clarity, and freedom with which I talk in the

16. Valle and Valle Matheu, eds., *Obras,* I, 64-82. Valle published his protest on May 20, 1825.

17. AGG, B88.9, 4147, 189. *Juicio sobre la primera elección constitucional de presidente de la República que ha hecho el congreso* (Guatemala City, May 16, 1825). For other comments on the election and the candidates, see Doroteo Vascon-celos to Pedro Molina, Oct. 15, 1824, AGG, Molina Papers; Henry Dunn, *Guatimala* [sic], *or the Republic of Central America, in 1827-8; Being Sketches and Memo-randums Made during a Twelve-Month's Residence* (London, 1829), pp. 203-204; Thompson, *Narrative of an Official Visit,* p. 186; C. K. Webster, ed., *Britain and the Independence of Latin America, 1812-1830: Select Documents from the Foreign Office* (2 vols.; London, 1938), I, 330; Pedro Joaquín Chamorro, *Historia de la Federación de la América Central, 1823-1840* (Madrid, 1951), pp. 104-105; Franklin Dallas Parker, "José Cecilio del Valle: Scholar and Patriot," *HAHR,* XXXII (Nov., 1952), 531-534.

18. *Revista de los Archivos Nacionales de Costa Rica,* I (Nov. and Dec., 1936), 57-58. Alvarado wrote on July 7, 1825.

street, in the plaza, or in the countryside." Owing to his unrestrained manner, the Conservatives often denied him the floor or conceded it at awkward hours, interrupting him when he was speaking.[19] Outside the Congress, the newspapers entered the argument,[20] and Valle continued his opposition.[21] The issue finally was seized upon and held up to ridicule by *El Sol* in Mexico City.[22] The net result was that a pall of doubt hung over the election, and Arce was discredited in the eyes of some before he ever exercised executive authority.

Juan de Dios Mayorga, still in Mexico, became exceedingly alarmed about the disrepute that the question heaped on Central America. In straightforward terms of friend to friend, he wrote to Valle.

I am infinitely sorry that the question of the nullity of Arce's election is still a hot one. You will have to realize that for the good of the country you must put an end to it and bury it in eternal silence. The question is a serious one within the Republic as well as outside—outside because it discredits us, for it appears that we are in the midst of a real revolution or that our national government is most unjust and reckless. . . . Domestically, it will inspire in the people ideas that are contemptuous of the national government, and the president will be viewed as a usurper of power. . . . You will remember that when you were in the SPE I always wrote to you deploring the unwise conduct of the *Semanario* of San Salvador in discrediting the Supreme Government. . . . I earnestly beg you to listen to reason, and if you love the country and if you are interested in preserving its reputation and good name, do not say anything more about the presidency.[23]

After a long look at Dios Mayorga's cold reasoning, the angry Valle doubtless agreed that further opposition would serve only to injure the nation. The loss of the election, however, was the sorest frustration that he ever had been asked to accept. Save a

19. *Ibid.*, p. 58.
20. On July 6, 1825, Valle's paper, *El Redactor General,* advertised the pamphlet written by "A Liberal" dealing with the elections and the "Diálogo de D. Melitón y D. Epifanio" dealing with the same subject. The *Semanario* attacked Valle and opposed his protest, for Valle accused his old companion in politics Mateo Ibarra of supplying the *Semanario* with information. Ibarra vehemently denied the charge. See Ibarra to Valle, Aug. 14, 1825, Valle Papers.
21. *El Redactor General,* Oct. 22, 1825.
22. *Ibid. El Sol,* among other things, stated that Valle's protest had not been well received, which Valle denied.
23. Oct. 5, 1825, Valle Papers. Apparently another attempt was made to appease him and perhaps to quiet him when he was appointed minister to England. The news of the appointment arrived on July 8, 1825, and without giving the offer serious thought, he wrote his resignation on the same day (AGG, B10.3, 3596, 169).

decision by the deputies, which well might have been made as early as the time of Captain General González, Valle would have been the first president of Central America. Offended publicly and hurt deeply, he retired to his study, but he did not forget and he continued to oppose, despite the compelling plea from his friend. In June, 1825, Valle founded his second newspaper, *El Redactor General,* and directed some of its columns against the election. But his aristocratic demeanor and political acumen, which never allowed him to paw in the gutter, pitched his opposition on a plain above offensiveness. The high ground was Valle's fortress. Lofty and aloof in the world of ideas, he was unassailable. From these heights he could cut an opponent to pieces without drawing blood. This was the same vantage point that he had held in 1820. While *El Editor* had picked up epithets from the street, *El Amigo,* head high and with an occasional downward glance at its opponent, spoke of statistics, agriculture, elementary education, and the value of scholars for society—ideas that could be read in the quiet aftermath of battle without evoking the pained grimace of shame or the wish that a sentence or phrase had been left unwritten. At the same time, Valle's tactic was extremely effective. He was a front runner in every political race that he entered; and try as his enemies surely did, the worst description of him that they were able to pass on to posterity portrayed him as unpardonably proud and affected in manner.

In the first issue of *El Redactor* (June 12, 1825), temper hobbled to a disciplined pace, he continued his opposition in a theme that he elaborated during the subsequent months. In an analogy, he maintained that "men of wisdom or savants" (*sabios*) performed the same task for society that reason performed for each man. "Wise men are the sense of reason of nations. To them belongs the duty of enlightening the general will; to them belongs the duty of guiding the states." A few months later he explored the same theme when he distinguished between the "voice of the people" and "public opinion." The first was nothing more than the clamor raised by the ignorant on the spur of the moment. Public opinion, however, was the expression of the people who had learned and reflected on the issues of the day. "The savants must be the primary organ of public opinion; this is their first and most sacred obligation." History taught that the great nations did not owe their sinew and splendor to powerful monarchs, wealthy princes, or to any particular government but to "simple individuals who have made progress in science and in the art of governing." Every government should encourage the savants to write and to educate the nation. But unfortunately it was a common practice of modern governments to "ridicule philosophers when they are not persecuting them."[24]

Opposition on this level had many advantages over a protest that might have read: The government is in the hands of ignoramuses. I am not president, but since I am so much wiser than those in the government, I should be the one who runs the show. Such crudities as these would have been destined for the receptacle marked *basura*. Phrased in Valle's language, the same thought, once the issue of the election gave way to another, took on new meaning and redounded to the credit of the author instead of marking him as one more irresponsible journalist. That he was able to write nearly all his public protests in the same style was a measure of his aristocratic bearing and discipline.

In December, 1825, after six months of retirement, he took his family to "La Concepción" for the holidays. While there, he doubtless learned that the district of Guatemala City had elected him to the second national Congress, scheduled to meet on March 1, 1826.[25] He wrote a letter of resignation that appeared to express a sincere desire to remain in retirement. He explained that he had been engaged in the nation's business continually since 1821 and that as a result his health had suffered. A deputy had to attend daily sessions of three or four hours, serve on committees, reflect on various subjects, and debate delicate questions. His nerves would not allow sustained concentration. In December, 1825, it was true, he had consented to serve on a committee appointed to draw up the civil code for the state of Guatemala. Much of the work, however, could be done in the privacy of his study where he experienced no interruptions. The work of a deputy simply was too much for him. "I would deceive the nation

24. *El Redactor General*, Oct. 15, 1825.
25. He was also elected to the Congress by the district of Chiquimula in the state of Guatemala and the district of Santa Bárbara in the state of Honduras. See Valle to the Secretary of the Congress, Feb. 27, 1826, Alejandro Marure Papers, 1131, The Edward Ayer Collection, Newberry Library, Chicago; Francisco Morazán to Valle, March 1, 1826, Valle Papers.

if I presented myself to the Congress as a man capable of such great tasks." Thus he supplicated the Congress to accept his resignation.[26] But the credentials committee of the Congress refused and refused again.[27] Several weeks after the second Congress had convened, Valle took his seat.

[2]

In the course of Valle's brief retirement from public life, relations between President Arce and the state of Guatemala assured that the second Congress would live from crisis to crisis. Soon after Arce had taken office, he became involved in a trivial affair that ballooned to elephantine proportions. The constituent assembly had declared June 24 a national holiday for commemorating the first meeting of the Assembly, prescribing a *Te Deum* and an appropriate address at the University. In Guatemala City members of the national government planned to celebrate the anniversary with local authorities. A local official, however, complained about the seating arrangement, vowed that he would not attend the ceremonies, and sought support from the president of the state, Juan Barrundia, a Liberal and a brother of José Francisco, a member of the Senate. Arce postponed the celebration until June 25 and attempted to persuade Juan Barrundia that the local authorities in the capital should attend the functions along with the national government. Barrundia, however, counseled his subordinate to refuse and explained that the state government, located in Antigua, would celebrate the holiday separately. Arce, who apparently wanted to guarantee respect for presidential authority, ordered a detail of troops to force the officials in the capital to comply.[28]

The relations between Guatemala and the national government were strained again when the state government decided to move to Guatemala City, pointing up the need for a federal district. Since the national government occupied the available office

26. Alejandro Marure Papers, 1131, The Edward Ayer Collection, Newberry Library, Chicago.
27. *Ibid.* His second letter of resignation was written on March 5 (Valle Papers).
28. AGG, B7.9, 3145, 135. Comisión de puntos constitucionales, June 27 and June 30, 1825; Arce, *Memorias*, p. 25.

space, the state government confiscated two private dwellings. The owners protested and petitioned the national government to protect their rights. The Congress authorized Arce to take the measures necessary. Juan Barrundia and the state assembly viewed the action of the Congress as an attempt to block the transfer of the state government, and the assembly granted Barrundia permission to raise troops and manufacture gunpowder, making tax receipts available. The implications were plain, and Arce and the Congress became more circumspect and made available to the state government the building that had housed the offices of the tobacco monopoly.[29]

The debility of the federal system revealed by this petulant and threatening rivalry also disclosed itself in the discord within the Congress. According to a Liberal deputy, Pablo Alvarado, the Conservatives (those who supported Arce) ran roughshod over the Liberals. Smarting from harsh treatment but resolute in spirit, he charged that the Conservatives had tried to terrorize him, confound him, enrage him, insult him, and throw him out of the Congress. He could not finish counting in one day the means taken by the two parties to create trouble between the states and the national government.[30]

Alvarado perhaps exaggerated, for the Congress ratified the Constitution and dealt with matters of general interest. Then, on October 1, 1825, the deputies prepared for the second Congress. The Constitution stated that one-half of the deputies from each state should stand election each year. To decide which districts should hold elections, the deputies drew lots. As a result, those who had to seek re-election were mostly Conservatives. And in the elections they lost heavily to the Liberals, insuring that the second Congress would be hostile toward Arce. This was the Congress that Valle was to enter.

[3]

Valle's attempt to resign doubtless was sincere. He had labored without respite since 1821, and as he pleaded his health probably had suffered. The galling frustration that resulted from

29. Marure, *Bosquejo histórico*, I, 145; Arce, *Memorias*, p. 26.
30. *Revista de los Archivos Nacionales de Costa Rica*, I (Nov. and Dec., 1936), 60. Alvarado wrote on October 7, 1825.

the presidential election, however, did not allow him any peace of mind, and he had driven himself to explain his defeat and to become the nation's sense of reason. Weekly, he had reported not only the significant political events of the world but also commented on those of Central America. Weekly and without charge, he sent twenty copies of *El Redactor* to influential men throughout the states.[31] But despite this continuing interest in politics, he shrank from the thought of the tiring work of a deputy. When his resignation was refused a second time, however, he probably looked forward to his first day. His attitude resembled that of a person anticipating a swim in Lake Atitlán. He winces from sure knowledge that the water will be shockingly cold but knows full well that it also will be stimulating and invigorating, once he screws up enough courage to plunge in. The Congress screwed up Valle's courage when it refused his resignation, and he plunged in and seemed to thrive on the invigorating effect.

On March 28, 1826, he answered his first roll call, and in the course of the day's proceedings he asked for and received recognition. His purpose was to put a motion favoring a government-sponsored newspaper that should carry abstracts of the debates, but he also used the opportunity to explain the circumstances that had resulted in his presence and to announce his determination to help build a stable society. The Congress, he knew, faced the task of trying to create a republic from provinces once ruled by a distant government. To give "the cloth all the beauty that exists in the mind" was not the work of a moment. The creative process was difficult—so difficult that "ingrates" and "traitors" would suggest sacrificing the entire nation to foreign ambition. "Let's divide it and make it for America what the unhappy Poland was for Europe" was their dictum. The "beloved sons of the nation," however, would draw strength from the challenge. "Let's double our work. . . . Let's work night and day and not rest until the last stone of the building is in place." This was Valle's answer. Frightened by schemes to divide Central America, real or imaginary, and dedicated to the welfare of the nation, he offered himself as an object of scorn if ever he deviated from the "line that a

31. He announced this in the undated prospectus of *El Redactor*. It appears, however, that many additional copies went out to the states. Francisco Morazán (to Valle, Comayagua, Aug. 24, 1825, Valle Papers) acknowledged receipt of twenty copies of the paper, which the state government had ordered.

deputy must follow."[32]   Ostensibly a motion to print abstracts of the debates, the essence of his address was a plea for unity and co-operation and a cessation of the destructive rivalry.   But if he had waved a wand and ordered the volcanoes Agua and Fuego to exchange places, the effect would have been the same.

The Congress that Valle spoke to was predominantly Liberal—opposed to Arce; and the principal objective of the Liberals apparently was to embarrass the President.[33]   Actually Arce was in an impossible position.   Until he became president, he had been considered a liberal in his political views.   Yet he owed his office to the Conservatives of Guatemala, and this fact alienated a number of Liberals.   Then, during the first months of his administration, he tried to become president in fact as well as name when he chastised with a heavy hand the Liberal government of Guatemala.   The Liberals in the second Congress and many of their followers throughout the nation interpreted Arce's desire to gain respect for the executive office as a strike at the Liberals.   The Conservatives, who supported him, gave the same meaning to his acts.   Thus anything that Arce did was bound to be viewed as a partisan gesture.   Without the ability for the office, the well-meaning Arce blundered from one crisis to another, unable to imagine any means but force for gaining the respect the executive office deserved.   Instead of accomplishing his objective, he stripped himself of all support save that of the "family."

After Arce's message to the second Congress (March 1, 1826), the Liberals began to draw up a bill designed to regulate the

32. Valle and Valle Matheu, eds., *Obras*, I, 116-121.   A Scottish observer of the Congress commented that the deputies appeared as "tradesmen in their Sunday clothes," and he saw one "without stockings and shoes."   See James Wilson, *A Brief Memoir of the Life of James Wilson (late of Edinburgh) with Extracts from His Journal and Correspondence, Written Chiefly during a Residence in Guatemala, the Capital of Central America* (London, 1829), p. 115.   In contrast was G. A. Thompson's experience (*Narrative of an Official Visit*, pp. 138-139). "I could not help remarking the Englishman-like well dressed appearance.   One of them [one of the deputies], a young man with broad cloth pelisse particularly well furred and frogged, seemed much engaged in contemplating my habiliments: they were far from correct.   I had on a blue frock dress coat, with canary silk linings, which I need not add is by no means a morning dress."   Thompson's baggage had been swamped in landing, and he had nothing else to wear.   In addition see J. Haefkens' (*Centraal Amerika*, p. 341) drawing of the citizens of the capital walking along main street.   Wilson probably saw an Indian who had become a *ladino* by trading his native costume for European dress and had not become accustomed to shoes and stockings, if he could afford them.   He could have been a messenger for the deputies.

33. Marure, *Bosquejo histórico*, I, 148-150.

armed forces but contrived to lodge control of the military with the states. In this connection, Liberal deputies solicited the services of Nicholas Raoul, a French soldier of fortune. While in Colombia, Pedro Molina, following the instructions of Executive Valle, invited Raoul to accept a commission from the government of Central America.[34] Raoul accepted, and soon after his arrival, he threw in with the Liberals. Upon learning of Raoul's connection with the military project of the deputies, Arce ordered him to reconnoiter the northern coasts of the nation. At the same time, the President set about strengthening his position with the military. On the pretext of danger from a Spanish invasion from Cuba and for the immediate purpose of settling the renewed strife in Nicaragua, he decided to add four thousand troops to the national army. The Liberals protested that Arce was building up the army in order to gain control of the nation for himself and the Conservatives. On March 30, in contravention of Arce's order, the deputies ordered Raoul to remain in the Capital. Arce then commanded that he should begin his mission within three days. Raoul obeyed.

El Salvador, unstinting in her support of Arce, declared, on April 21, 1826, that nothing could be expected from the Congress as long as it remained in Guatemala City. The first Congress, dominated by Conservatives from Guatemala, stirred the fires of provincialism; the second Congress, under the thumb of "Guatemalan Liberals," was doing the same.[35] On June 2, acting on instructions from their state government, the deputies from El Salvador withdrew from the Congress, followed by those from Costa Rica and most of the Conservatives. The purpose apparently was to prevent opposition to Arce by stripping the Congress of a quorum. Ten days later, after the Liberals had promised not to initiate measures against Arce or the Conservatives, the

34. Valle to Pedro Molina, March 12, 1824, AGG, Molina Papers. Valle explained that some wanted Molina to secure the services of a number of officers and enlisted men. "I was not of this opinion." Thus Molina's instructions called for only "4 captains," two artillerymen and two engineers. "Friend Arce, who just arrived, has told me that Bolívar has 6 thousand criminals in his army and wants to get rid of them. Take care that none of those comes." Raoul accepted Molina's invitation a year later. See Raoul to Molina, March 12, 1825, AGG, Molina Papers. For an extensive treatment of Raoul, see Adam Matthias Szasdi, "The Career of Nicholas Raoul in Central America" (unpublished MA thesis, Tulane University, 1954).

35. Quoted in Arce, *Memorias*, p. 32.

second Congress resumed, though the deputies from El Salvador and Costa Rica did not return. On this ominous note the session closed on June 30, 1826.[36]

Amid this welter of rivalry, Valle's position remains uncertain. Alejandro Marure wrote that Valle joined the Liberals in order to overthrow Arce. The "colossus tumbled," Valle hoped to become president.[37] Manuel Montúfar claimed that Valle, upon entering Congress, was submissive but later gave free reign to his resentment against Arce.[38] Valle, always mindful of history, published and distributed a number of his congressional speeches. On April 7, 1826, he spoke on the need in the Americas of a scientific expedition headed by someone such as Alexander von Humboldt. Ten days later he addressed the Congress on the topic "Our Sovereignty and the Principle of Non-Intervention." On April 21 he pointed out that time was slipping by and that an enormous amount of work begged completion, suggesting how they might proceed with more efficiency. Six days later, the possibility of a canal through Nicaragua attracted his attention and also was the subject of his address on May 2 and May 12. A week later he spoke on the past injustice of military courts. For several days he tried to explain that freedom of speech was not absolute, and on June 29, the day before the Congress adjourned, he protested against a motion that would demand a unanimous decision from a court of law before a deputy could be convicted of a charge.[39]

In view of these topics, Valle apparently followed the "line drawn by prudence" that had guided his actions during the days of the provisional government and while he served as a minister for Iturbide. Cousin Justo de Herrera caught the spirit of Valle's participation: "I have read the three notebooks containing your addresses in the Congress. They bestow on you an honor that your enemies cannot obscure."[40] And a second letter from Justo suggested who the enemies were. "I have reason to believe that all those in the capital and in the states who are called Conserva-

36. Marure, *Bosquejo histórico*, I, 158; Bancroft, *History of Central America*, III, 84-85.
37. *Bosquejo histórico*, I, 149-150.
38. *Memorias de Jalapa*, p. 86.
39. For the text of these addresses, see Valle and Valle Matheu, eds., *Obras*, I, 124-167.
40. Justo de Herrera to Valle, Choluteca, Aug. 5, 1826, Valle Papers.

tives are your enemies and, consequently, ours [the Herreras] and that we also have them among those called Liberals."[41]

Probably if Valle had been forced to choose between the two groups, he would have chosen the Liberals, not for their political philosophy, if indeed they had one, but because they opposed Arce. But Valle at this time did not have to make the choice, which he could have considered only as the lesser of two mean ones. Early in 1826, soon after he returned from "La Concepción," the government of the state of Guatemala, controlled by Liberals, demonstrated that it was quite as ready to resort to force as President Arce was. And Valle was one of the targets. "I demand the fulfilment of the basic law. I ask the Assembly of the state of Guatemala to take into consideration the breach of the law. I beg that it have the goodness to order the retirement of the detail of troops that has custody of my house and that it assume that I have fulfilled the obligation of giving 640 pesos to the last subscription, in addition to all the previous ones."[42] That Valle could have identified himself with the president of the state, Juan Barrundia, and "his satellites"[43] seems implausible.

[4]

The second Congress was to reconvene on October 1, 1826. Events during the summer, however, virtually promised that the rivalry between the states and the national government would not be settled by legislators. Raoul, who had begun his mission, decided to resign his commission and return to the capital. His letters of resignation, however, were attacks on President Arce, who began proceedings to court-martial Raoul. Captain José María Espínola, with orders for Raoul's arrest, apprehended and imprisoned him. Upon learning of Raoul's incarceration, Juan Barrundia reported the news to the state assembly, declaring that Arce had encroached upon state authority by ordering the arrest of Raoul in the territory of Guatemala without previous permission. To guard against future infringement, the state assembly,

41. *Ibid.*, Oct. 25, 1826.
42. Valle Papers. The note, dated February 22, 1826, was not addressed and not signed but was in Valle's handwriting.
43. Pedro Valenzuela to Valle, Antigua, March 10, 1825, Valle Papers.

on August 16, 1826, encouraged Juan Barrundia to meet force with force, and five days later Barrundia ordered Captain Cayetano de la Cerda with 300 men to arrest Captain Espínola and to free Raoul. At the same time the state assembly refused to meet its tax quota. A few days after Arce learned that Espínola had surrendered to state troops, he heard rumors that Barrundia planned to overthrow the national government. After long reflection, Arce decided to move first. On September 5, 1826, he ordered the arrest and imprisonment of Barrundia, and the order was carried out early the following morning. Cirilo Flores, vice president of the state, assumed the presidency.[44]

On the day that the second Congress was to reconvene (October 1, 1826), the number of deputies in attendance was short of a quorum. Arce, in an attempt to eliminate Liberal opposition and to end the influence of the capital, called for an extraordinary congress to meet in Cojutepeque, El Salvador. The states, according to Arce's order, were to send one deputy for each 15,000 inhabitants rather than one for each 30,000 as the Constitution specified. A few days later the state government of Guatemala disintegrated. On October 8, 1826, Cirilo Flores moved the state government to Quetzaltenango. Five days later a mob of Indians assassinated Flores and sent others scurrying for their lives. Arce then assumed executive authority of the state, and on October 31 ordered the election of a new president and vice president of Guatemala. With the opposition in that state destroyed and the promise of a friendly congress in Cojutepeque, Arce doubtless believed that order would be restored. But at this juncture El Salvador, under the new executive guidance of Mariano Prado, refused to recognize Arce's decree convoking a new national congress in El Salvador. Prado began raising troops.

To guarantee further that peace and order would not come cheaply, the long-smoldering rivalry in Honduras between Dionisio de Herrera and his enemies exploded. The constitutent assembly met in the autumn of 1824, and Herrera, on September 16, became president of the state. Skeptical of the deputies' ability, he wrote Valle that men were in the assembly who thought they were capable of writing "ten constitutions," though

44. Marure, *Bosquejo histórico*, I, 161-169; Bancroft, *History of Central America*, II, 85-87.

this was not the opinion expressed by men of good judgment.[45] At any rate, the deputies finished their task, and within four months gave way to the first state assembly. Herrera continued as president, though one faction claimed that he had been elected provisionally and should resign and allow a new election. He failed to do so, and thus a number of cities and villages, apparently under the leadership of Bishop Nicolás Irías, refused to recognize his authority. The rivalry increased, and on November 3, 1826, Herrera's enemies attempted to assassinate him. A week later, he described the event for Valle. "This is going to terrify you. On the third of this month, at 2:00 o'clock in the morning, they fired five shots at me through the windows of my house." He blamed Irías but also held Arce responsible. The "President of the Republic has kept up correspondence with my enemies and with the most immoral men of Honduras." Here, they say, generally, that "these happenings are the result of his plans."[46]

By this time the state of El Salvador apparently had decided that Arce had to be removed. Herrera wrote that "the government of San Salvador has invited me to proceed with it to sustain the Constitution, as they say."[47] In March, 1827, Arce dispatched troops to Honduras and Herrera came to Guatemala City under arrest. During the same month troops from El Salvador began their march on Guatemala City, and Arce, with the aid of the new president of Guatemala, Mariano Aycinena, prepared for the attack and the beginning of the civil war that was to last until 1829.

Valle was a spectator as the crisis developed in the autumn of 1826. He had been prepared to take his seat in the Congress that failed to attract a quorum, but he regarded Arce's decree calling for a new congress as unconstitutional. And as he became more alarmed at the willingness of men on all sides to resort to force, he shouted editorially: "Law. Law. That is what saves nations from the most imminent dangers."[48] He realized, however, that editorials were futile, and when the fighting began, he accepted it philosophically. Domestic strife plagued "all the republics of

45. Tegucigalpa, Nov. 6, 1824, Valle Papers.
46. Comayagua, Nov. 10, 1826, Valle Papers; Louis E. Bumgartner, ed., "The Attempted Assassination of Honduran President Dionisio de Herrera, November 3, 1826," *HAHR*, XLII (Feb., 1962), 60-62.
47. *Ibid.*
48. *El Redactor General*, Oct. 26, 1826.

America," but instability, chaos, and civil wars were inevitable for nations making the transition from one form of government to another. "This is one of the invariable laws that have been discovered in the [history] of political societies." Personally, he continued on in Guatemala City "without changing my way of life." But in the midst of the "torrent of events," his own cool detachment allowed him to see more clearly the wisdom of the "theories of the philosophers."[49]   On this reflective note Valle weathered the worst that a society could offer that had cast off one authority and yet had failed to find another that it could respect.

[5]

The war, however, did provide him with his first span of free time since 1818-1820. But a decade earlier he had been forced out of public life by persons as ambitious as he had been. Frustrated and garrulous, he had spent the greater part of his time in his study nursing his own interests. From 1827 until 1829, when the war ended, it was a wiser Valle who sought refuge in that same study. He still entertained ambition for the talent that he knew was his, but he identified his hopes for the future with those that he held for Central America. He knew, probably better than most of his contemporaries, that the nation possessed the resources necessary for a stable national life. At the same time, he recognized that the gross ignorance of the great majority and the inexperience of the educated in government were the two serious flaws in the national character. To give the "cloth all the beauty that existed in the mind"—to substitute strength for weakness— was the herculean task that he marked for himself. Education was his answer and had been since independence. To educate for a responsible citizenry and skilful leadership, he well knew, was not the work of a moment. What he proposed, then, fancifully and sincerely, was leadership by the gifted few until the uncertain time when his society accepted the obligations of freedom. Lathered and lean from freedom's burdens, each citizen would exercise with prudence the privileges of freedom—a stable

49. Valle to Miguel González Saravia, July 23, 1827. This letter was partially destroyed.

society would have evolved—and the savants, weary and wreathed with the nation's gratitude, could retire to their studies, still the keepers of the nation's sense of reason. Here lay the vital connection between his own hopes and those he fondled for the nation. He saw himself as one of the gifted few capable of providing leadership until the society of Central America matured. And if he appeared during the war years as an intellectual Walter Mitty, it was owing to his belief that few others in Central America were capable of the leadership that he fancied for himself, aided only by the savants of Europe.

"I love Europe and those that are her beautiful adornments [savants],"[50] he wrote with hymnal reverence. "It is my desire that every savant in Europe should dedicate his talent to designing a plan that America should follow in her foreign and domestic affairs. . . . If I were Master of America, this already would be done."[51] Certainly he nodded his agreement upon reading that the origin of Central America's difficulty could be traced to the departure of Captain General Bustamante, when authority fell into weak hands. "Yours were the only capable ones."[52] Valle, however, put it differently. "My will is not omnipotent. If it were, permit me to say that the Republic would present a different appearance." The change, however, would have been owing not only to his own efforts but also to those of the European savants that he would have attracted to Central America.[53] "More than two thousand years ago, Plato said: 'The troubles of mankind will not end as long as the savants do not control the government.' "[54] For Valle, the savants were the "supreme Beings of the human species." Each person had his own niche; and that "is mine."[55]

During the war years, Valle tried to enlist for Central America the talent of European scholars. In 1825, cousin Próspero de Herrera journeyed to London in an attempt to form a company to exploit the Herrera mines with English capital. Valle gave him explicit instructions to send books, journals, newspapers, and addresses of leading scholars. Through Próspero, Valle began

50. Valle to Álvaro Flórez Estrada, March 24, 1830, Valladares, ed., *Valle*, p. 182.
51. *Ibid.*, Oct. 7, 1828, p. 176.
52. Miguel González Saravia to Valle, Mexico City, Dec. 27, 1826, Valle Papers.
53. Valle to Flórez Estrada, March 24, 1830, Valladares, ed., *Valle*, p. 182.
54. Valle and Valle Matheu, eds., *Obras*, I, 187.
55. Valle to Flórez Estrada, March 24, 1830, Valladares, ed., *Valle*, p. 182.

corresponding with Jeremy Bentham, Count Giuseppe de Pecchio (1785-1835), an Italian economist whose marriage allowed him to live luxuriously in exile in Brighton, and Álvaro Flórez Estrada (1769-1853), a well-known Spanish economist also spending his exile in England. Valle, however, was personally responsible for initiating correspondence with Alexander von Humboldt. He sought the services and advice of each of these men and implored Humboldt to make a survey of Central America,[56] which he had missed during his classic expedition. When Flórez Estrada published a volume on political economy, Valle invited him to send copies so that he might sell them in Central America, and reliable Próspero boxed and shipped forty copies.[57] Pecchio sent his survey of the works of the Italian economists,[58] but from Bentham came the greatest reward. In a letter to Herrera (in English), Bentham said, "Have the good fortune to add to my letter to Del Valle what follows. After my death, Bowring shall have instructions to send you any such future works of mine as I shall not myself have sent you."[59] Also from Bentham came copies of his *Westminster Review*,[60] and Próspero sought Bentham's advice concerning the list of books that Valle requested. Upon seeing the list, Bentham inquired "if the books were for enriching the congressional library." Próspero might have answered in the words of G. A. Thompson that they were only for Valle's "inordinate . . . requisitions at the feast of the intellect." Instead, Próspero replied that Valle "could use them for that purpose."[61]

56. Humboldt to Valle, Paris, Nov. 30, 1825, Valladares, ed., *Valle*, pp. 156-157; Valle and Valle Matheu, eds., *Obras*, I, 124.

57. Próspero de Herrera to Valle, London, Sept. 12, 1829, Valle Papers; Flórez Estrada to Valle, London, Aug. 14, 1829, Valladares, ed., *Valle*, p. 180. The title of the book was *Curso de economía política* (London, 1828). Later, Valle publicly praised the book. See *Boletín Oficial*, July 1, 1831.

58. Próspero de Herrera to Valle, London, Sept. 12, 1829, Valle Papers; Valle to Pecchio, March 24, 1830, Valladares, ed., *Valle*, p. 196. The title of the book was *Storia dell' economia pubblica in Italia* (Lugano, 1829).

59. Próspero de Herrera to Valle, London, Oct. 7, 1829, Valle Papers. Valle doubtless could read Próspero's English much better than he could Bentham's. Próspero wrote (to Valle, London, September 15 [no year], Valle Papers): "I have seen copies of letters that he is sending to you, and let me warn you now that reading them will take a lot of work. Despite the fact that I am more accustomed to his handwriting and that of his secretaries, I have to pause on many paragraphs and guess at others. But the contents of those that he is sending to you and the consideration and esteem that he has for you make the small task worthwhile." John Bowring was Bentham's secretary.

60. Próspero de Herrera to Valle, Jan. 20, 1831, Valle Papers.

61. *Ibid.*, Sept. 15 [no year].

Valle also used his correspondents to address himself to a wider audience, sending them copies of his own publications. And momentarily the harsh lines that years of work and frustration had put on his brow softened when he read their comments. Flórez Estrada told Próspero: "Although I do not agree with all his [Valle's] reasoning, I did not think there was anyone in America with such knowledge of economics."[62]   With contentment, he read Alexander von Humboldt's praise: "Your address at the opening of the Congress, which you were kind enough to send me, displays noble sentiments together with a profound knowledge of the true foundation of freedom."[63]   Again from Próspero came more tinsel: "Count Pecchio, who has read all your papers . . . has published an essay on Guatemala in which he included your name with distinctive praise."   To Pecchio, Valle owed his membership in a Paris society dedicated to the improvement of elementary education.   "I am sending you the diploma," wrote Próspero.[64]   Bentham also read all the papers that Valle sent, and according to Próspero, Bentham had a very good opinion of Valle.[65]   But the corners of his mouth must have drooped a bit when he read another letter from his cousin: "I have told him [Bentham] that you want his portrait.   He doesn't have any, but he is going to send you one as soon as he can."[66]

Próspero also tried to publish Valle's works.   "Please send me all your writings that you have published, especially those that have been published since our independence from Spain. . . .   I have only *El Amigo de la Patria*."[67]   He also wrote for more copies

62. *Ibid.*, Oct. 30, 1827.   Próspero thought highly of Flórez Estrada but remarked: "Although he has said that the independence of America is dictated by the laws of nature, he is in the final analysis a Spaniard, and once a Spaniard always a Spaniard."

63. Paris, Nov. 30, 1825, Valladares, ed., *Valle,* p. 156.

64. Aug. 5, 1826, Valle Papers; Valle to Pecchio, March 3, 1828, Valladares, ed., *Valle,* p. 190; Valle and Valle Matheu, eds., *Obras,* I, 178.   The essay that Herrera mentioned probably was the one recently reprinted.   See Giuseppe de Pecchio, "Bosquejo de la República de Centro-América," *Anales,* XXV (1951), 29-39.   Pecchio based his essay on the journal that Francisco Lavagnino kept when he visited Guatemala in 1824-1825.   Pecchio, in the manner of Lavagnino, spoke kindly of Valle.

65. Próspero de Herrera to Valle, London, Jan. 3, 1828, Valle Papers.

66. *Ibid.*, September 15 [no year].   But Valle doubtless was cheered when he read: "I am now sending you the Mountain Barometer, the best . . . that one can find here."   See Próspero de Herrera to Valle, London, May 29, 1828, Valle Papers. By the same letter, Valle learned that copies of the *Times* were on the way.   After a trip to Paris, Próspero sent addresses of other scholars (that of Jean Baptiste Say, for example) and his impressions of Paris (London, April 4, 1827, Valle Papers).

67. Paris, Dec. 4, 1831, Valle Papers.

of *El Redactor General*. "I left the first ones in Paris to be published."[68] In addition, Próspero convinced a friend that he should write an article about Valle for the *Westminster Review*.[69]

While Valle spent most of the war years in a world apart from Central America, unpleasant reminders of the war occasionally intruded. In the manner of the Liberal Government of Barrundia, the Conservatives under Arce, Beltranena, and Mariano Aycinena also resorted to forced loans. In 1828 the Conservatives demanded 2,000 pesos from Valle, and when he claimed that he was unable to raise the money, a detail of soldiers forced him to sacrifice some of his belongings in order to cover "said sum."[70] The same government, however, exempted from service in the army Valle's hired hands, Cecilio Chinchilla and Sebastián Burgos, who worked at "La Concepción."[71]

Early in 1829 Guatemala City, the last stronghold of the Conservatives, fell to the Liberal Army under Francisco Morazán, who imprisoned Arce and Aycinena along with others who had served with them or who had supported them. Juan Barrundia was restored to the presidency of Guatemala, and his brother, José Francisco, the senior senator, was appointed to finish Arce's term as president of the Republic. The national Congress, of which Valle was a member, assembled on June 22, and one of the most

68. London, Jan. 3, 1828, Valle Papers.

69. Próspero de Herrera to Valle, London, April 18, 1831, Valle Papers. The person who was going to write the article had to go to France, but Próspero thought it would appear in 1831. The article, however, did not appear.

70. Oct. 5, 1833, Valle Papers. In 1829 when many regular and secular clergymen were expelled, the government acquired ownership of the mortgages held by the ecclesiastical organizations. Valle received a note from the secretary of the commission named for collecting unpaid mortgages asking for 2,000 pesos that Valle owed for "La Concepción." Valle replied that he had owed 2,000 pesos to the Convento de la Merced but had satisfied it "years ago." He then explained: "In the year of 1828, the government of this state demanded of me a loan of 2,000 pesos, and upon [my] showing that I did not have this amount, it sent a detail of soldiers to my home and forced me to sacrifice some belongings and pay the said sum. The federal congress, in 1829, passed the law of October 3, in which Article 3 says: Those who were neither instigators nor accomplices in the revolution and who can show the amount that the government, legitimate or illegitimate, asked of them have a right to indemnification. Article 8 adds that full compensation will be allowed to those who should be indemnified if they acknowledge their mortgage to the suppressed monasteries." Valle then pointed out that the mortgage on his hacienda had been paid by the forced loan and that: "I had been a victim of the revolution, not an accomplice." For an analysis of Morazán's policy toward the clergy, see Mary Wilhelmine Williams, "The Ecclesiastical Policy of Francisco Morazán and the Other Central American Liberals," *HAHR*, III (May, 1920), 119-143. For a general work on church and state, see Mary P. Holleran, *Church and State in Guatemala* (New York, 1949).

71. Francisco Cáscaras to Valle, Sept. 19, 1828, Valle Papers. Cáscaras was one of Arce's generals.

important matters that the deputies had to take into consideration was the disposition of the prisoners. The Congress declared them traitors and sentenced them to death but on the same day declared a general amnesty, reducing the death penalty to permanent exile. Manuel Montúfar, who spent his exile in Mexico, claimed that Valle was the author of the penalty and excoriated him for his vengeance. Whether Valle wrote the decree that Congress passed is uncertain. Certainly he had no sympathy for Arce and Aycinena.[72] A letter from Próspero de Herrera, in reply to Valle's letter of May 20, 1829, may offer a clue to Valle's feelings. "If the exile of such a considerable number of persons is decreed . . . the families and relatives of all those who suffer this punishment surely will become embittered and the number of enemies outside the country, already large, will increase. I do not approve of this type of general punishment." Banishment, according to Herrera, should have been applied only to those "who started the war."[73]

With the war at an end, Valle was ready to begin putting the pieces back together. "We have suffered incalculable damage," he wrote. "The Republic has retrogressed immeasurably." But Central America possessed the raw materials for wealth and stability. "We have fertile lands [and] mineral wealth in the mountains. . . ." But, he reported pessimistically, "we do not have the men necessary to fill the offices that we must have for the adopted system." Where could he find, he asked rhetorically, "80 or so individuals worthy of being legislators, 10 capable of being sena-

72. An indication of Valle's feelings for the Aycinenas might be inferred from a letter that he received from cousin Próspero (London, March 27, 1830, Valle Papers). "The first of last month, [given name unintelligible] Aycinena left here . . . for New York. Do you know that during the time that his family predominated there he did not visit me. Then came the humiliation of coming to ask for recommendations. . . . Forgetting the many injuries that my family and my dearest relatives received from him, I gave him a letter of recommendation. . . ." Próspero continued that he would have refused if he had known about Aycinena's activities in London. "He left a debt with every person with whom he dealt, and the worst part is that none was contracted in good faith. His last trick was to empower Mr. [name unintelligible] of the House of Barclay to receive his correspondence and the *consignments* made to him, on the basis of which he received a loan of fifty pounds sterling. At the same time, he had given the same authority to Mr. Hill[?], who had paid, according to what he has told me, the mentioned debts, which amounted to a thousand pounds." The fraud was discovered when a letter arrived for Aycinena, and each of the men with Aycinena's power of attorney claimed the letter, thinking that it contained news of a "large shipment of indigo." When the letter was opened, they found not a title to a cargo of indigo but the "sad complaints from his grieved grandmother or aunt about the expulsion of the friars."

73. London, Sept. 12, 1829, Valle Papers.

tors, 20 or so with the aptitude for deputies, 2 for president and vice president of the Republic, 10 presidents and vice presidents of the states," and a multitude of others?[74]

Valle planned to continue his efforts to build the nation on the solid foundation of an educated citizenry, but he was not optimistic about the results of his efforts. In the course of four years, he had seen the Constitution promulgated and the constitutional authorities take office, only to fall victim of the competition for power. He felt the new republic had taken its first step under a cloud of doubt that had resulted from the election of Arce. Valle protested that the election was a fraud and probably contributed to the disaffection, as Dios Mayorga had suggested. As a deputy to the second Congress, he apparently let prudence be his guide. He accepted the war with pensive repose and used those years to satisfy his desire for recognition beyond the boundaries of Central America and to secure knowledge that would benefit the nation. The end of the war caused him to consider again his political career, but the jaunty optimism that in the past had tempered his apprehension gave way to cold realism. "Politically, America is the same as it is physically: the land of earthquakes."[75]

74. Valle to Flórez Estrada, Oct. 27, 1829, Valladares, ed., *Valle*, p. 181. If Valle's will had been "omnipotent," he would have established a school for executives, legislators, and judges. See Valle and Valle Matheu, eds., *Obras*, I, 179. For an expression from the British Consulate in Central America concerning the resources for "wealth and greatness" in Central America, see John O'Reilly to George Canning, Feb. 22, 1826, R. A. Humphreys, ed., *British Consular Reports on the Trade and Politics of Latin America* (London, 1940), p. 299. For a sympathetic appraisal of Central America's natural resources, see John Baily, *Central America; Describing Each of the States of Guatemala, Honduras, Salvador, Nicaragua, and Costa Rica; Their Natural Features, Products, Population, and Remarkable Capacity for Colonization* (London, 1850). If this is the same Bailey that acted as agent for the London firm that contracted the loan for Central America, he had reason to be unsympathetic. During the final days of the civil war, Arce forced him to aid in the fight against Morazán. After defeating Arce, Morazán put Baily in jail. Indignant and confused after "more than ten weeks" in prison, Baily tried to gain freedom by beseeching Valle to use his influence. In the course of the letter, Baily said he had lived five years in Central America, or since 1824 when the loan was negotiated. See Baily to Valle, Prisión de Belén, July 5, 1829, Valle Papers.

75. Valle to Flórez Estrada, July 26, 1833, Valladares, ed., *Valle*, p. 187.

T W E L V E

The Final Years

[1]

A detached, almost indifferent Valle faced the years following the civil war. "I continued vegetating here, alone with nature and my thoughts."[1] He wrote in March, 1830, three months before the results of the presidential election held in late 1829 were announced. Though he was a candidate, he seemed disinterested. His attitude might be explained by the popularity that his opponent, the triumphant General Francisco Morazán, was enjoying. Yet he appeared content for the first time in his career to stay out of public life. In 1831 he refused appointment as Central American minister to France,[2] and two years later he had to refuse the vice presidency three times before his desire was respected. "How can one govern without taxes, without strength, and without authority?"[3] he asked, suggesting the classic gesture of finality. While the elections of 1829 continued, he occupied himself with his haciendas and his correspondence, and when Morazán won, few were surprised and Valle apparently was not disappointed. Guided by new instructions, the states cast 357 electoral votes for 11 candidates. Morazán received 202 votes against Valle's 103. José Francisco Barrundia, who finished Arce's unexpired term, was a poor third with 34 votes.[4]

1. Valle to Pecchio, Valladares, ed., *Valle*, p. 197.
2. *Boletín Oficial*, April 1, 1831. Cousin Próspero became minister to France, perhaps through Valle's help. See Próspero de Herrera to Valle, London, April 20, 1831, Valle Papers.
3. Valle to Flórez Estrada, July 26, 1833, Valladares, ed., *Valle*, p. 187.
4. Estado general de los individuos que han tenido sufragios para presidente y vice presidente de la república y fiscal de la suprema corte de justicia, June 15, 1830, Valle Papers. The citation is to a rough draft written by Valle, "at 12:30 at night," explaining the outcome of the elections. The report was unaddressed and unsigned. Valle received twenty-six votes for vice president and ninety-four for Chief Justice of the Supreme Court. Congress must have decided that election and

Valle, who seemed content not to be president, well might have seen himself in the role of the nation's sense of reason and perhaps as the guiding hand of Morazán's administration. Writing in 1831, cousin Próspero suggested Valle's influence. "The people here [London] who know your writings and your feelings thought that you would be elected president. I have told them that Morazán has good intentions, is a patriot, and is determined to profit from your wisdom in order to succeed in his new career."[5] Certainly Morazán, in his continuous military campaigns, had little use for Valle's advice. But when the General from Honduras was inaugurated on September 16, 1830, his words about public education destroying errors and preparing the way for the triumph of reason had a familiar ring. And his statement about the alliance of the American people had been expressed earlier.[6]

Events following the elections denied the peace that the defeat of Arce and the Conservatives seemed to promise. Arce attempted an invasion from Mexico; an uprising against the national government occurred in Honduras; and José María Cornejo, the new president of El Salvador, became recalcitrant and, on January 7, 1832, declared the federation at an end and El Salvador an independent state. Nicholas Raoul beat back Arce's poorly prepared expedition; Colonel Terrelonge smashed the outbreak in Honduras, and Morazán defeated the forces of El Salvador, replacing Cornejo with Joaquín de San Martín.[7] In 1833 rumor spoke of a new invasion by Arce, and the states, momentarily free of internal strife, had time to remember their resentment of the influence of the state of Guatemala. In an attempt to allay the suspicion, the national government moved the capital to San Salvador, which

also the one for fiscal, for none of the candidates received a majority of the votes cast. Barrundia apparently made a poor showing because he was not interested and favored Morazán. See David Vela, *Barrundia ante el espejo de su tiempo* (2 vols.; Guatemala City, 1956), I, 207. Other accounts of the election explain that Morazán did not receive a majority of the total eligible vote but that Valle favored Morazán's election on the basis of a majority of the total vote cast. See Bancroft, *History of Central America*, III, 111-112; Lorenzo Montúfar, *Reseña histórica de Centro América* (7 vols.; Guatemala City, 1878-1888), I, 267-268. (Hereafter L. Montúfar, *Reseña histórica*.)

5. To Valle, London, March 6, 1831, Valle Papers.
6. Arturo Humberto Montes, *Morazán y la federación centroamericana* (Mexico, 1958), p. 107.
7. Joaquín de San Martín to Valle, San Salvador, July 4, 1833, Valle Papers. San Martín wrote: "I had the misfortune, I can say, of receiving the first office of the state. Today, before the assembly, I was inaugurated."

promptly became the object of the suspicion previously reserved for Guatemala City.

[2]

Valle, before and after the presidential election, was chiefly concerned with business. During the civil war, "La Concepción" had fallen into disrepair—the house (*casa grande*) needed the hands of a carpenter, fences were down, and the cane press was broken.[8] Likely as not his haciendas near Choluteca also had suffered. As soon as the war ended, he began repairing and restocking. In December, 1829, he bought twenty-one mares and in the course of the following year purchased ten mules, seventeen mares, fifteen studs and geldings, and a burro. His meticulous records for the next two years showed similar acquisitions.[9]

Some time during 1832 or 1833, he formed a business arrangement with Joaquín de San Martín, who became president of El Salvador in 1833.[10] Judging from their correspondence, Valle shipped cheese and cattle from his haciendas near Choluteca to San Salvador, where San Martín sold them. Political instability, periodic failure of mail service, and improperly prepared cheese were some of the obstacles to success.[11] But the threat that alarmed Valle and his associates more than anything else was an attempt by the national government to control the sale of meat.[12] The purpose was to create another source of revenue. On October 29, 1832, Valle published a protest against the government's proposal, citing the works of the major economists to support his argument for free trade.[13] Apparently the monopoly was established,[14] but Valle and San Martín continued their business throughout 1833.

8. D. Carios to Valle, "La Concepción," Nov. 4, 1829, Valle Papers.
9. Razón de las yeguas, caballos, y mulas que compré en 1829, 1830, 1831, 1832, 1833, Valle Papers. He kept a separate record for each year, but for the sake of convenience they appear in the citation as one.
10. Demostración de la liquidación hecha sobre cuentas de la casa de Señor José del Valle con la del Señor San Martín, July 1, 1835, Valle Papers.
11. For example, see San Martín to Valle, San Salvador, June 28, Sept. 28, and Oct. 29, 1833; Valle to San Martín, Sept. 9, 1833, Valle Papers.
12. See Atemacia Galarza de Murillo to Valle, León, Sept. 8, 1832; Valle to San Martín, July [day torn away], 1833; Juan Cabrera to Valle, León, Dec. 8, 1832, Valle Papers. Murillo referred to the restriction as "el maldito monopolio."
13. Valle and Valle Matheu, eds., *Obras*, II, 265-285. For another of his essays defending free trade, see *Boletín Oficial*, July 1, 1831.
14. Atemacia Galarza de Murillo to Valle, León, Sept. 8, 1832. Murillo wrote: "Veo con dolor la marcha triste que sigue el abasto de carnes."

Following the war, Valle also continued his efforts in behalf of education. In 1829 he became director of the re-established Economic Society.[15] Four years later, after the University of San Carlos had been reorganized, he accepted the charge to direct the division of humanities.[16] He continued his correspondence with Bentham,[17] and upon receiving news of his death in 1832, Valle was responsible for the congressional decree to mourn the passing of the "light of Westminster."[18] In addition, he wrote an essay on the value of mathematics[19] and was commissioned by Morazán to found a patriotic society dedicated to education.[20]

Late in December, 1833, as was his custom, Valle took his family to "La Concepción." Throughout January, 1834, he enjoyed the best of health, but during the following month, he began to tire easily. Then on February 22, at five o'clock in the afternoon, he suffered an overwhelming feeling of fatigue and a burning sensation in his chest. The family sent for a physician who arrived three days later. By this time Valle felt better and could explain what he had experienced. The physician, called by business of the Senate to El Salvador, regarded the illness lightly

15. Valle to Flórez Estrada, March 24, 1830, Valladares, ed., *Valle*, p. 182; Valle to Bentham, May 21, 1830, John Bowring, ed., *The Works of Jeremy Bentham* (11 vols.; Edinburgh, 1843), XI, 71. (Hereafter Bowring, ed., *Bentham*.)

16. AGG, B80.2, 22661, 1074. El Dr. Molina, presidente de la dirección de estudios, comunica al Secretario General del Supremo Gobierno sobre las tres secciones de la Academia de Estudios; *Boletín Oficial*, June 15, 1831; Antonio Batres Jáuregui, *El Doctor Mariano Gálvez y su época* (Guatemala City, 1925), p. 53; Héctor Humberto Samayoa Guevara, *La enseñanza de la historia en Guatemala* (Guatemala City, 1959), pp. 31, 37; Alejandro Marure, *Efemérides de los hechos notables acaecidos en la República desde el año de 1821 hasta el de 1842* (Guatemala City, 1895), pp. 72-73 (hereafter Marure, *Efemérides*); José M. Gavarrete to Valle, August 30, 1833, Valle Papers. Of the humanities, Valle probably found most pleasure in history, and he intended, one day, to write the history of Central America (see Valle and Valle Matheu, eds., *Obras*, I, 95-102). If Valle had written a history of Central America, he doubtless would have contributed information that we sorely need today. But his interpretation would have been the now familiar but unacceptable one that blames the colonial period for all the ills of the national period.

17. On one occasion, Bentham mildly reproached Valle. In a long letter (May 19, 1829), Valle presented his thoughts concerning what should appear on the coins of a free nation. Bentham, on September 13, 1829, replied: "Coins—what you say on this subject shows the expansiveness of your mind. It would, however, have been still more gratifying to me to have seen it when applying itself to subjects on which its labor might have been employed in the production of effects, in which contribution to public happiness had been more determinate and unquestionable." See Bowring, ed., *Bentham*, XI, 17-19; Rafael Heliodoro Valle, ed., *Cartas de Bentham a Valle* (Mexico, 1942), pp. 42-47.

18. Marure, *Efemérides*, p. 72.

19. Valle and Valle Matheu, eds., *Obras*, I, 215-223.

20. AGG, B85.1, 26290, 1148. Sobre establecimiento de la sociedad patriótica, May 14, 1829.

(*graduó de cosa de poco o de ningún cuidado*) and departed on the following day, leaving medication and approving Valle's transfer to Guatemala City. On March 1 the Valle family, the necessary servants, and the priest who had been at the hacienda moved Valle on a litter into a carriage and began the homeward journey. After traveling only three leagues they arrived at the hacienda "Jute," where they spent the night. Valle seemed to be gaining but early the next morning he suffered another attack that rendered him delirious. When he calmed, the family set out for the hacienda "Corral de Piedra." At ten o'clock, March 2, 1834, when they had covered half the distance, Valle suffered his third and final stroke. Among his last words were those to the priest: "I know that I'm going to die, and I need spiritual help to return my soul to the Creator." Upon receiving the sacrament of extreme unction, "he died with the tranquillity, simplicity, and resignation of a philosophic and virtuous man." A stiff wind stirred the dust on the road.[21]

[3]

At the time of Valle's death sealed envelopes containing the states' electoral votes for president and vice president were waiting to be opened. Morazán's term expired in 1834, and the regular elections had been held during the last months of 1833. According to all accounts, Valle received the necessary majority, defeating Morazán for the presidency.[22] Valle had an inkling of his success and perhaps even knew that he had been elected. On December 3, 1833, a friend from Cartago wrote that Costa Ricans were convinced by sad experience that order and honor would never grace the nation as long as it lacked competent leadership. In this spirit, the eastern district of the state cast all its votes for the third

21. To Justo de Herrera, no date, Valle Papers. The letter was written by a member of the family, probably his wife, who reproached herself because Valle, in his last moments, was not protected against the sun and "los horribles ventarrones que se habían desatado por aquellas llanuras." For a similar description, see Manuela Valero to Próspero de Herrera, Guatemala City, March 15, 1834, Valle Papers.

22. The elections were held during the last months of 1833, but the ballots had not been opened and counted. See L. Montúfar, *Reseña histórica*, I, 95-96; Bancroft, *History of Central America*, III, 121.

time for José del Valle, the only person capable of saving the Republic.[23]

Whether Valle could have saved the federation from flying apart was doubtful. The plain fact was that the states, since the declaration of independence, had absolutely no intention of submitting to central authority, regardless of its name. Nothing save a strong, well disciplined, regularly paid army could have held the states together in the course of the four years following 1834. Morazán, who succeeded himself after the death of Valle, was better suited than Valle for the demands of the time. Valle would have talked about agriculture, mineral resources, and education, while the dry rot of particularism continued its disintegrating process. And "without taxes, without strength, and without authority," he would have been more helpless than General Morazán, who could put himself at the head of an army. By 1838, when Valle's term would have expired, the federation could be pronounced dead, though in fact it never really had existed.

Central America ceased to act as a political unit on September 15, 1821. The first four months of "freedom" were spent denouncing the capital and declaring for or against Mexico. The Mexican interlude brought respite but no real change toward central authority. After annexation failed, the states gave their particularism the force of law when the deputies wrote and promulgated the Constitution. Then the tactless and heavy-handed Arce tried to be president in fact as well as name and civil war was the result. Morazán emerged as the hero of the Liberals, but as soon as he asserted presidential authority, he found himself in the same position that Arce had occupied, except that Morazán spent his last moment before a firing squad. Thus the states went their separate ways, and in freedom, educated and influential men created governments that rivaled the fondest dreams of Ferdinand VII. If Valle had become president in 1825, the course of Central American history might have been changed. But in 1834 time ran out for Valle and was fast running out for the federation.

23. A. Peralta to Valle, Valle Papers.

THIRTEEN

The Measure of the Man

Valle, in the course of his life, never veered sharply or strayed far from the pattern of thought molded by his background and education. Born a creole aristocrat, he remained an aristocrat until his death on that hot and windswept road.

One of the traditional privileges of his class was admission to the universities that aristocratic Spaniards, with their discriminating respect for knowledge, had established with the same enthusiasm that prompted them to found churches. Associated with San Carlos for about ten years, he fell under the influence of such men as Goicoechea, José Felipe Flores, and José Matías de Córdova, immersing himself in the new learning. The information that he gleaned, however, was not nearly so important as the approach to learning that his teachers instilled in him. Owing largely to the efforts of Goicoechea, investigation and experimentation replaced authority. Knowledge in his hands became a versatile tool rather an overbearing master. When Valle entered San Carlos, the break with the decadent Schoolmen was sufficiently recent to allow the rigorous discipline of scholasticism and the method of the Enlightenment to exist side by side. Thus Valle gained the best of the old and the bright spirit of the new.

In the manner of his teachers, Valle sought knowledge not for the sake of knowledge but for a useful purpose. When he posted the temperature for nearly twenty-five years, he did it for the same reason that Goicoechea counted his crossings of a river and for the same reason that impelled Flores to explore the crater of Vesuvius. They wanted to find out if all they had heard and read was true. The same restless spirit that caused these men to fill their spare time with small projects drove them to search for means of improving their society. Valle did not decide suddenly that Central America was not ready for independence. He had known the problems of his society since his student days. Goicoechea, Córdova, the *Gazeta de Guatemala,* and the first Economic Society gave him a social conscience and then tweaked it regularly, long before the patriots "discovered" the same conditions.

Valle, however, did not emerge from San Carlos as a democrat; nor did he ever become one. Before 1821, he turned his talent and discipline to building a law practice and to carving out a career in colonial administration. After 1807 his driving ambition was to secure the office of *oidor* in an *audiencia* in Spain. Captains General González and Bustamante showered him with offices and each recommended him for a toga. When the crown in 1818 replaced Bustamante, ambitious members of the "family" successfully sought the favor of Captain General Urrutia and elbowed Valle out of his traditional position of influence. For the next two years he tried desperately to go to Spain as an *oidor.*

Throughout the years of his colonial career, his unflinching loyalty to the crown distinguished him as a *vasallo benemérito.* He reacted to the Napoleonic invasion of Spain by drawing closer to the crown, and as a loyal subject, he viewed the insurrections in San Salvador, León, and Granada in the same light as Bustamante did. He regarded the Constitution of 1812 as completely out of touch with reality and thought that Antonio Larrazábal was extremely naïve. In 1820 the revolution in Spain likely prompted him to remain in Central America and allowed him to accept the restored Constitution. Then independence forced his hand, and he decided to accept and try to control it, as the declaration of independence showed. With the authority of the crown removed, he favored union with Mexico, an easier, more prudent step than a sudden leap to a republic. Mexico under the Three Guarantees—independence, Catholicism, and constitutional monarchy—seemed safer. If Iturbide had been a responsible, intelligent monarch, Central America well might have continued as a part of Mexico until this moment. Certainly in the beginning the arrangement satisfied most of the whites in Central America. And who ever consulted the *ladinos* and Indians? When the Empire failed, Central America stood on the threshold of the chaos that

Valle had feared as early as 1814—the old system was gone and he believed that his society was not prepared for the new.

He returned from Mexico too late to do anything about the Constitution, but his arguments in favor of the government monopoly on tobacco and the dispute over the pacification of Nicaragua expressed his wish for a strong central government. Indifferent and disgusted in 1833, he expressed his feeling more succinctly. "The authors of the Constitution showed very little foresight." They made each state sovereign of its internal affairs and forced the national government to a position of precarious dependency on the states.[1] An indication of the degree of centralization that would have satisfied him readily can be discerned from his constant theme of the place of the savant in society. Surely if his will had been "omnipotent," the world would have witnessed a spectacle without parallel in modern history. His oligarchy of the gifted few would have educated society, turning over the reigns of government to competent hands when the process was completed. Thus Valle's political views changed slowly and never ranged far from his belief at any given moment of his mature life. Before 1821 he apparently thought little about government, accepting what had existed for three centuries. Independence made him appraise and evaluate, and his conclusion was that government by the gifted few was the answer until the uncertain time when his society could govern itself. Was this concept far removed from the society that he had known before 1808, when San Carlos, the *Gazeta de Guatemala,* and the Economic Society furnished leadership?

But if all this is true, how can his writings in *El Amigo* ever fit into the pattern? The question stands surly and defiant because of Valle's singular skill as a politician, but the answer lay in the ambition whose satisfaction depended on that skill. Between 1818 and 1820 he decided to remain in Central America. After the Constitution of 1812 was restored, he concluded either that constitutional monarchy was to be a permanent fixture for the Spanish Empire or that Central American independence was inevitable. In either case, he knew that in order to succeed politically, he had to convince the articulate members of his society

1. Valle to Flórez Estrada, July 26, 1833, Valladares, ed., *Valle,* p. 187. Also see Durón, ed., *Obras de D. José Cecilio del Valle,* pp. 227-237.

that he had not been so close to the crown as they might have supposed. This could not have been very difficult, for a great number of his class faced the same problem. Yet at the same time he could not be sure that the Constitution would be permanent or that independence would come. Thus the course that he charted for himself was the "line drawn by prudence." When he wrote about politics or criticized Spain, he did so in connection with a decree of the Cortes, which, after all, Ferdinand VII had convoked. He never went beyond the bounds of the constitutional monarchy, and he never mentioned the word "independence" in connection with Central America, never reported news of the revolutions in South America, and above all never reported the news from Mexico. In short, he never ventured beyond the point of no return. But what he wrote in connection with the decrees together with his expressions about science, statistics, agriculture, and education became another "irrefutable document." All that he wrote can be used to show the far reaches of his expansive mind, but to conclude on the basis of his published writings that he was a democrat or that he intended to prepare the nation for independence is to accept exactly what he intended for his contemporaries to believe after 1821 and what he likely hoped historians would believe. This tactic of patient waiting and preparation for any eventuality was the same one that he employed so effectively in the provisional government when the question of annexation awaited an answer. He employed it again as Iturbide's Secretary of Foreign and Domestic Affairs, and he apparently used the same tactic in the second Congress. As soon as a critical issue was resolved, he then could capitalize on what he had written regardless of which way the decision had gone. Thus with pride he pointed out that he had written the declaration of independence, that he had opposed annexation to Mexico, and that he had suffered for freedom at the hands of Iturbide. Frequently and with pride, he mentioned the offices he had held and the services that he had performed since 1821, but he rarely referred to his distinguished career before that date. The fact, however, that the Bacos were called the "Spanish party" shows that he did not succeed completely in obscuring his earlier career. But that he succeeded beyond his fondest hope is attested to not only by the offices that he held but by the place that history generally has assigned to him.

Valle's political acumen stands out more clearly when viewed from other angles. Miguel Larreinaga, Mariano Aycinena, Mariano Beltranena, and Miguel González Saravia, for example, held basically the same view that Valle held before 1821. But Valle was the only one to succeed. A view from another angle is still more revealing. Pedro Molina, José Francisco Barrundia, and José Francisco Córdova were beyond question among the stoutest precursors of independence. Yet not one matched Valle's political success or evoked the respect that he enjoyed after 1821. As Molina reported in his memoirs, Valle was a friend of independence but knew how "to conceal his views."[2] Finally, the qualities that made him successful and respected were the same ones that made him the one man who had any chance of saving the federation.

Valle's economic thought followed close to his political thought. In 1803 he demonstrated that he understood Adam Smith, or at least the less abstruse parts. But, understandably, he did not follow Smith to his conclusion of free trade, which went against royal economic policy. In 1817 he asserted that the crown possessed the only authority to restrict trade.[3] In 1818 he feared that free trade would prepare the way for the independence of Central America. In 1820 he apparently won the support of the weavers owing to his opposition to free trade. In 1824 he supported the government monopoly on tobacco, in which he had no interest; and in 1832 he protested against the proposed monopoly on meat, in which he had a large interest. He protested against the grip on the land by the Church but failed to say anything about the grip of the landed aristocracy. He criticized absentee landlords but continued to be one for the remainder of his life. He kept slaves at least until 1824 and criticized slave

2. "Memorias," *Centro-Americano*, XIII (April-Sept., 1921), 278-279. When Molina wrote, Valle was dead and the federation was dead. In a mellow mood, he could forget his charges in *El Editor*, his declared enmity for Valle, and the events leading to annexation. If Molina, however, referred to the days after independence was achieved, Valle of course was a friend of independence.

3. The reference is to Valle's opinion as temporary fiscal of the *audiencia* (see p. 88). When Valle, in 1832, referred to this opinion, he gambled that his readers would not check on the document. See Valle and Valle Matheu, eds., *Obras*, II, 265.

labor.[4] And the inescapable conclusion is that his economic views were determined by his own interests, which he projected as the best interests of the nation.

After independence destroyed royal economic laws, he thought that savants should draw up economic policy; that entrepreneurs should breathe life into the policy; and that labor should be paid a living wage.[5] The shift of control, then, was from a small group of royal economic advisers to a small group of savants and capitalists. Valle of course was both. His thoughts on economics thus were as modern as any, but the change was slight.

The quality that set Valle apart from most of his contemporaries was his breadth of view. He thought not only of Central America and the Americas but also of the civilization of mankind. His knowledge of history allowed him to range to the farthest reaches of man's past and to place Central America, at any given moment of her history, in the context of world history. His chief aim was to make Central America a stable, cultured, and respected nation and to put the nations of the New World on the same level with the leaders of the Old. He was as ambitious for his nation and for the Americas as he was for himself. The success of one complemented the others. And it is well-nigh impossible to separate his own interests from those that he held for his nation and for America.

4. On April 24, 1824, the Constituent Assembly abolished slavery. According to Batres Jáuregui (*La América Central*, III, 93), Valle was among the first to free his slaves.

5. Valle and Valle Matheu, eds., *Obras*, I, 167-176.

Bibliography of Sources Cited

MANUSCRIPTS

El Archivo General del Gobierno de Guatemala

The manuscripts from the Archivo are arranged according to the letter and number specifying the *sección* assigned to the manuscript by the archivist, Professor J. Joaquín Pardo. Further, the division of the manuscripts according to periods (colonial and national) has been maintained. The dates that appear at the end of an entry apply generally to the part of the *legajo* and *expediente* cited. In some cases, a title for the manuscript did not appear, and in these cases, I have supplied a brief English title. In other cases, no *expediente* number is given owing to the fact that a volume of manuscripts (*pases de títulos,* for example) composes the *legajo,* and the citation thus can be traced easily by date or folio number. Even though a *legajo* may contain hundreds of pages, any given *expediente* can be secured, owing to the careful work of Professor Pardo, in the time it takes one of his assistants to go and get it. However, in some cases an *expediente* may run to several hundred pages (in tracing a deed to property, for example), and in this case the only sure way of finding the citation is to begin reading. Dates offer some clues, but they also confuse. In the span of several pages dates may be mentioned that refer to events more than a century before the time when the manuscript was written. The litigation over the hacienda "San Antonio" is an example of such an *expediente.*

[COLONIAL PERIOD]

A1.1, 4347, 37. Elecciones de los ayuntamientos de León, Tegucigalpa y San Vicente, 1809.

A1.1, 57003, 6924. Contra D. Manuel José Arce por infidencia que le resultó en sublevaciones de 5 de noviembre de 1811 y 24 de enero de 1814.

A1.1, 57215, 6931. Contra Don Joaquín Gutiérrez de Arce, 1821.

A1.1, 57305, 6931. Junta de Censura, 1821.

A1.2.2, 15732, 2187. Libro de cabildos de Guatemala, año 1805.

A1.2.2, 15733, 2187. Libro de cabildos de Guatemala, año 1808.

A1.2.2, 15738, 2190. Libro de cabildos de Guatemala, año 1812.

A1.2.2, 15739, 2190. Libro de cabildos de Guatemala, año 1813.

A1.2.2, 15740, 2191. Libro de cabildos de Guatemala, año 1814.

A1.2.2, 15741, 2191. Libro de cabildos de Guatemala, año 1815.
A1.2.2, 15742, 2192. Libro de cabildos de Guatemala, año 1816.
A1.2.2, 15743, 2192. Libro de cabildos de Guatemala, año 1817.
A1.2.2, 15745, 2194. Libro de cabildos de Guatemala, año 1819.
A1.2.2, 15747, 2194. Libro de cabildos de Guatemala, año 1821.
A1.2.5, 2835 (legajo). Cuaderno de correspondencia del ayuntamiento.
A1.2.5, 29956, 3099. El ayuntamiento indica al Licenciado José Cecilio del Valle, que lamentará su separación de dicho cuerpo al haber optado por el cargo de auditor de guerra, 1821.
A1.3-4, 12340, 1892. Libro de claustros de la Universidad de San Carlos, 1808-1831.
A1.5, 1273, 51. El Real Tribunal de Consulado, sobre fomentar la agricultura, industria, y comercio, April 15, 1817.
A1.5.7, 2411, 18341. Entre Don Pedro José de Górriz y la testamentaría de Don José Biedna sobre treinta y cuatro tercios de tinta, August, 1806.
A1.6, 31117, 4035. Oficio del Capitán General Antonio González, transcribiendo la orden por cual es restablecida la Sociedad Económica, December 12, 1812.
A1.6, 31118, 4035. Autos relativos al restablecimiento de la Sociedad Económica, 1812.
A1.15, 1818, 181. Francisco Estrada con Don Joseph Antonio Díaz del Valle sobre la propiedad de la hacienda nombrada San Antonio, 1780-1782.
A1.15, 1821, 182. Autos de Joseph Díaz del Valle con Don Manuel Batres y Juan Manrique sobre la venta de la hacienda nombrada Santa Cruz, perteniente a los bienes de Juan Félix Briceño, 1781-1787.
A1.15, 7084, 335. José del Valle pide incitativa para que las justicias de Comayagua remitan los autos con Juan Jacinto Herrera sobre la partición de bienes, 1804.
A1.15, 26038, 2867. Señora María Josefa Ramírez, sobre que se le nombre de abogado al Sr. Don Josef Tomás de Zelaya, y otros, 1804.
A1.15, 35435, 4361. Don José C. del Valle solicita el nombramiento de curador *ad litem* y propone al Procurador Ballesteros, February 21, 1799.
A1.15, 36409, 4415. Manuela García demanda daños y perjuicios de Don Julián González, 1805.
A1.15, 37619, 4466. Contra José María Flores por arma corta, 1813.
A1.15, 37774, 4474. Contra María Arriola por homicidio en Gregorio Mendoza, 1817.
A1.15, 37781, 4474. Contra Mariano Garóz, 1817.
A1.15, 37812, 4477. Sobre la formación de estados y modo de dar cuenta en las causas criminales para que se arreglen a lo dispuesto en la real cédula de 1800, March 12, 1817.
A1.15, 37839, 4477. Contra Gaspar Lucho por homicidio en Vicente Pacheco, 1817.
A1.15, 37856, 4479. Contra Rito Orantes por homicidio en José María Fuentes, 1817.

A1.15, 37856, 4479. Contra Manuel Eugenio Lito por homicidio en Miguel Lemús, 1817.

A1.17.1, 13999, 2020. Autos formados sobre la real cédula para que esta real audiencia, con la brevedad y reserva posible, remita una relación individual de los corregimientos y alcaldías mayores de este reyno, 1763.

A1.20, 9964, 1484. Libro de escribano José Antonio de Solís, April 30, 1822.

A1.20, 39013, 4561. José C. del Valle transpasa un poder a José Antonio Solís, para que siga cierta mortual, October 5, 1800.

A1.20, 39045, 4562. Obligación escrita entre José del Valle y José Antonio García Zelaya, sobre la venta de una partida de novillas, 1819.

A1.22, 1510, 46. Providencia promulgada por el Capitán General Gainza, January 20, 1822.

A1.22, 1510, 142. Decreto de la Asamblea Nacional Constituyente sobre los productos de las rentas de tabaco y pólvora, December 15, 1824.

A1.22.22, 5772, 262. Autos acerca de la falta de maíz en Comayagua, 1817.

A1.23, 1543, 449. Providencia promulgada por el Presidente, Gobernador, Capitán General Carlos de Urrutia, March 9, 1821.

A1.23, 2317, 273. Declaración y pronunciamiento de las autoridades civiles, eclesiásticas, y militares sobre que no reconozcan ni reconocieren en tiempo alguno la abdicación de Fernando VII, August 14, 1808.

A1.23, 4609 (legajo). Copias de títulos y reales cédulas de los años de 1731 hasta el de 1737.

A1.29, 25427, 2841. El ayuntamiento de Guatemala protesta por el asiento asignado al auditor de guerra, Licenciado José C. del Valle, 1814.

A1.30-4, 22002, 2639. Peticiones del ayuntamiento en la residencia contra el Capitán General Bustamante, 1818-1819.

A1.38.3.4, 655, 23. Instrucción sobre la plaga de langosta; medios de exterminarla, o de disminuir sus efectos; y de precaver la escasez de comestibles, 1803.

A1.39, 1758 (legajo). Mercedes y nombramientos, 1805-1807.

A1.39-58, 24946, 2819. Juramento de auditor de guerra por José del Valle, May 14, 1821.

A1.40, 1768 (legajo). Pases de títulos, 1818-1824.

A1.40-29, 22383, 2657. Juramento del fiscal interino José del Valle, January 30, 1817.

A1.40-58, 14218, 2045. Juramento de José del Valle, auditor de guerra de ejército, June 10, 1813.

A1.43, 3242, 348. Recurso de José Antonio Díaz del Valle, residente en Tegucigalpa, sobre la mortual de su padre, José del Valle, 1780-1789.

A1.47, 23784, 2756. Colegio de Abogados, 1810-1814.

A1.47, 44962, 5333. Listo de los individuos del Ilustre Colegio de

Abogados de este Reyno de Guatemala, y de los que componen tan noble cuerpo, año 1813.

A1.47, 44942, 5334. El Ilustre Colegio de Abogados sobre nombramientos de los individuos que despachen los asuntos criminales y de pobres con el sueldo de 800 pesos anuales cada uno, 1811.

A1.47-1, 24915, 2818. Autos del examen de abogado de José del Valle, 1803.

A1.47.2, 32250, 4072. El Señor Licenciado Don José del Valle sobre continuar despachando los negocios en que estaba encargado antes de separarse de la carrera de abogado, 1813-1814.

A2.1, 746, 30. Oficio del arzobispo acerca de que prevenga al Capitán Rafael Ariza que se respete la autoridad eclesiástica, September 11, 1821.

A3.1, 380, 18. This document lists the cost of Simón Bergaño y Villegas' care and keep in Cuba, July 28, 1814.

A3.1, 2852, 1790. Minuta del informe sobre que a fines de noviembre de 1814 fué ejecutado el ex-presidente Antonio González por Morelos, May 12, 1815.

A3.10, 1729, 178. Capitán José Díaz del Valle, regidor de la villa de Chuluteca [sic], pide que se le otorgue título al oficio de alférez real, 1736.

A3.10, 3561, 193. Títulos y méritos de Joseph Díaz del Valle, 1769.

[NATIONAL PERIOD]

B1.1, 00002, 1. Minuta del oficio circulado por el ayuntamiento de la Ciudad de Guatemala con motivo de la prisión de la familia española, August 18, 1808.

B1.4, 582, 20. Correspondencia general.

B1.5, 00272, 7. Real decreto de 9 de octubre de 1812.

B1.9, 00426, 12. Oficio del Exmo. Sor. Capitán General sobre que la Real Audiencia se restablezca el estado del año 1808, January 16, 1815.

B1.10, 2269, 77. Jueces de letras, 1821.

B1.13, 478, 16. Actas de la diputación provincial, 1820.

B1.13, 345, 18. Papeles indiferentes de la diputación provincial, February 21, 1821. This is a letter from the town council of Guatemala City protesting against the establishment of jueces de letras.

B1.13, 545, 18. Papeles indiferentes de la diputación provincial, April 6, 1821. This is a letter written by Mayor Valle to the provincial deputation suggesting means of preserving public order.

B1.13, 562, 19. Actas de la Junta Consultiva Provisional, 1821-1822.

B1.13, 8337, 494. Testimonio de los autos tramitados en la Antigua, Guatemala, contra los asistentes a la junta celebrada el 17 de noviembre, en la casa de Don Tomás Arroyave, convocada por Don Mateo Ibarra, para tratar de la elección de miembros del ayuntamiento de dicha ciudad, 1820.

B1.13, 8338, 494. Several citizens complain that their freedom to vote was obstructed in the elections of 1820.

B1.13, 8361, 494. Manuel José Górris a la Junta Provincial, villa de Tuxtla, January 5, 1821.

B2.2, 701, 24. El gobernador de Nicaragua al ayuntamiento de la ciudad de Granada y León, July 7, 1813.

B2.7, 777, 31. Sobre averiguar la conducta de Simón Bergaño y Villegas, 1808.

B2.7, 778, 31. Autos pronunciados por la Real Sala del Crimen denegando la aplicación del indulto a favor de Don Simón Bergaño, 1812.

B2.7, 779, 31. Contra Simón Bergaño y Villegas, oficial escribiente de la secretaría de la capitanía general de Guatemala, por díscolo, 1808.

B3.4, 00934, 00937, 00938 (expedientes), 46. Junta Consultiva Provisional, 1821-1822.

B3.6, 1090, 48. El ayuntamiento del pueblo de San Marcos sobre los motivos que tuvo el alcalde para suspender el estanco de aguardiente, October, 1821.

B3.6, 100, 217. Sobre que se cobre un tanto por ciento de los caudales que en oro y plata extraen los europeos que regresan a la península, October 16, 1821.

B4.2, 1167, 50. Almachapán sobre juramento de independencia, October 29, 1821.

B4.2, 1167, 50. Town council of San Miguel to Gainza (October 12, 1821) suggesting an offensive and defensive alliance with Mexico, Colombia, and Chile.

B4.2, 1168, 50. Town council of Santa Anna to Gainza (October 13, 1821) suggesting an offensive and defensive alliance with Mexico and Colombia.

B5.2, 1263, 57. Cuaderno que contiene la correspondencia de la Junta Consultiva, 1821-1822.

B5.2, 1264, 57. Conditions proposed by the Colegio de Abogados for annexation of Guatemala to Mexico, December 29, 1821.

B5.2, 1264, 57. Discurso pronunciado por José Francisco Barrundia, November 7, 1821.

B5.2, 1264, 57. Discurso pronunciado por Licenciado José Domingo en la Tertulia Patriótica de Guatemala, November 30, 1821.

B5.3, 1248, 58. Cuaderno que contiene los dictámenes e informes del ayuntamiento de la Ciudad de Guatemala, 1821.

B5.4, 01372, 59. José del Valle remite al Jefe Gainza las contestaciones que deben darse a las autoridades de León, no date (1821).

B5.8, 1894, 69. Valle al Jefe Gainza, April 20, 1822.

B5.10, 2208, 74. This is a note explaining that Valle swore loyalty to Mexico on March 11, 1822.

B6.1-1, 2379, 83. Cuaderno que contiene los oficios del Jefe Vicente Filísola, nombrando comisionados para que preparen los trabajos del futuro congreso, April 4, 1823.

B6.1-4, 02406, 86. Acta de instalación de la Asamblea Nacional Constituyente, June 24, 1823.

B6.1-8, 2445, 90. Documentos acera del donativo dado por vecinos de la Ciudad de Guatemala para sufragar los gastos del viage del ejército mexicano, 1823.

B6.7, 93, 94, 96 (legajos). Comisión de hacienda, 1824.

B6.9, 99 (legajo). Comisión de guerra, 1824-1825.
B6.13, 104 (legajo). Comisión de instrucción, 1824.
B6.16, 106 (legajo). Comisiones especiales de la Asamblea Nacional Constituyente, 1824.
B6.17, 2901, 108. Reglamento del poder ejecutivo, July 8, 1823.
B6.22, 02937, 110. Exposiciones de las autoridades y de particulares, 1824.
B6.25, 2949, 112. Sesión secreta de la Asamblea Nacional Constituyente, August 14, 1824.
B6.26, 113, 114, 117, 118, 119 (legajos). Actas de las sesiones de la Asamblea Nacional Constituyente, 1823-1825.
B6.28, 121 (legajo). Correspondencia recibida por la Asamblea Nacional Constituyente, 1823-1825.
B7.8, 03128, 134. Comisión de hacienda, 1826.
B7.9, 3145, 135. Comisión de puntos constitucionales, 1825.
B10.2-1, 157 (legajo). Correspondencia del ministro de relaciones, 1824.
B10.3, 3569, 169. This is a note from Valle refusing an appointment as minister to England, July 8, 1825.
B10.7, 184, 185 (legajos). Correspondencia del ministro de estado, 1824-1825.
B80.2, 22661, 1074. El Dr. Molina, presidente de la dirección de estudios, comunica al Secretario General del Supremo Gobierno sobre las tres secciones de la Academia de Estudios, 1833.
B85.1, 26290, 1148. Sobre establecimiento de la sociedad patriótica, May 14, 1829.

Manuscripts in El Archivo General del Gobierno de Guatemala without an Archival Classification

Libro de contestaciones de la jura de independencia, año 1821.
Molina Papers.

Valle Papers

Unlike the manuscripts housed in the government archive, the Valle Papers, preserved by Valle's descendants in Guatemala City, are not available to the public, and while they are bound, boxed, and carefully stored, they are not arranged in any order. As the footnotes indicate, they are composed chiefly of letters to Valle and of rough drafts of papers that he wrote in connection with his work and varied interests. I first decided to list each manuscript in the bibliography, but such a list would have added more than 250 separate entries. Further, explanations already made in the footnotes would have had to be repeated in the bibliography in order to make many of the entries comprehensible. Thus, sheer bulk and added expense have ruled out my first intention.

Archivo y Biblioteca Nacional de Honduras

Relación de los ejercicios literarios, grados, títulos, y méritos patrióticos de Don José Cecilio del Valle, Auditor Honorario de Guerra del ejército y provincia de Guatemala.

Archivo de la Catedral de Guatemala

Libro de entierros de la Parroquia Sagrario de Guatemala, 1816-1870.
Libro de matrimonios españoles de 1729 a 1821, Parroquia Sagrario.
Volumen sexto de bautismos de españoles, desde 6 de febrero de 1772
hasta el año de 1822, de la Parroquia Sagrario.

Archivo General de Indias

Audiencia de Guatemala, 629. El presidente y capitán general de
Guatemala acusa el recibo de la real orden de 31 de julio del
año próximo pasado, acompañando quatro documentos en comprobación de inconvenientes que se pulsaron para escribir por
ahora las memorias que previene dicha real orden y hasta que
S. M. en su vista se digne resolver lo que sea de su soberano agrado,
1815-1816.

Archivo General de Relaciones Exteriores, Mexico

H/131, 979, 385. Correspondencia del Secretario de Relaciones Exteriores, 1823.

Duke University Library

Convenio celebrado entre los generales de los ejércitos titulados nacional y del Gobierno de Chile, May 3, 1814.

General Cemetery of Guatemala City

Libro de inhumaciones en mausoleos.

Newberry Library, Chicago

The Edward Ayer Collection. Alejandro Marure Papers.

University of Texas Library

Hernández Dávalos Collection.

PRINTED DOCUMENTS, GENERAL

ALAMÁN, LUCAS *Historia de Méjico.* Mexico, 1849-1852. 5 vols.
ARCE, MANUEL JOSÉ. *Memorias del General Manuel José Arce, primer
presidente de Centro América.* San Salvador, 1947.
BAILY, JOHN. *Central America; Describing Each of the States of Guatemala, Honduras, Salvador, Nicaragua, and Costa Rica; Their
Natural Features, Products, Population, and Remarkable Capacity
for Colonization.* London, 1850.
BARKER, EUGENE C., ed. *Austin Papers* (American Historical Association. *Annual Report,* 1919). Washington, 1920.
BERGAÑO Y VILLEGAS, SIMÓN. *Proclama.* Guatemala City, no date.
BERISTAIN DE SOUZA, JOSÉ MARIANO. *Biblioteca hispano americana
septentrional; o, catálogo y noticias de los literatos, que o nacidos,
o educados, o florecientes en la América septentrional española,*

han dado a luz algún escrito, o lo han dexado preparado para la prensa. Mexico, 1816. 3 vols.

BIERCK, HAROLD A., ed. *Selected Writings of Bolívar.* Compiled by Vicente Lecuna. Translated by Lewis Bertrand. New York, 1951. 2 vols.

BOWRING, JOHN, ed. *The Works of Jeremy Bentham.* Edinburgh, 1843. 11 vols.

BUMGARTNER, LOUIS E., ed. "The Attempted Assassination of Honduran President Dionisio de Herrera, November 3, 1826," *Hispanic American Historical Review,* XLII, 1962.

——. "Documentos de la independencia de Guatemala," *Antropología e Historia de Guatemala,* XIII, 1961.

——. "José del Valle's Unfinished 'Diario de mi viaje de Guatemala a México en 1822,'" *The Americas,* XVIII, 1961.

BUSTAMANTE, CARLOS MARÍA. *Diario histórico de México.* Zacatecas, 1896.

——. *Historia del Emperador D. Agustín de Iturbide hasta su muerte, y sus consequencias; y establecimiento de la república popular federal.* Mexico, 1846.

COSTA RICA. *Revista de los Archivos Nacionales de Costa Rica.* 1936.

DÍAZ DEL CASTILLO, BERNAL. *The True History of the Conquest of New Spain.* Edited by Genaro García. Translated by Alfred Percival Maudslay. London, 1908-1916. 5 vols.

DUNN, HENRY. *Guatimala [sic], or the Republic of Central America, in 1827-8; Being Sketches and Memorandums Made During a Twelve-Month's Residence.* London, 1829.

DURÓN, RÓMULO, ed. *Obras de Don José Cecilio del Valle.* Tegucigalpa, 1906.

FILÍSOLA, VICENTE. *La cooperación de México en la independencia de Centro América (Documentos inéditos o muy raros para la historia de México,* XXXVI). Mexico, 1911.

GARCÍA GRANADOS, MIGUEL. *Memorias del General Miguel García Granados* (Biblioteca de Cultura Popular, XXXVII, XXXVIII, XXXIX, XL). Guatemala City, 1952. 4 vols.

GUATEMALA. *Boletín del Archivo General del Gobierno.*

——. *Constitución de la República Federal de Centro-América.* Guatemala City, November 22, 1824.

——. *Escritos de Pedro Molina* (Colección Documentos, X, XI, XII). Guatemala City, 1954. 3 vols.

——. *Instrucciones para la constitución fundamental de la monarquía española y su gobierno de que ha de tratarse en las próximas cortes generales de la nación.* Guatemala City, 1953.

——. *Junta pública de la Real Sociedad Económica de la Patria de Guatemala.* Guatemala City, 1796.

"Guatemala, hace ciento catorce años. Informe (inédito hasta ahora) del ministro tesorero de las reales cajas de Guatemala, acerca del estado deficiente del erario antes y después de 15 de septiembre de 1821," *Anales de la Sociedad de Geografía E Historia de Guatemala,* XII, September, 1935.

HAEFKENS, J. *Centraal Amerika, uit een Geschiedkundig, Aardrijkskundig en Statistiek Oogpunt Beschouwd.* Dordrecht, 1832.

HUMPHREYS, R. A., ed. *British Consular Reports on the Trade and Politics of Latin America.* London, 1940.

ITURBIDE, AGUSTÍN DE. *Breve diseño crítico de la emancipación y libertad de la nación mexicana y de las causas que influyeron en sus más ruidosos sucesos, acaecidos desde el grito de Iguala hasta la espantosa muerte del libertador en la villa de Padilla.* Mexico, 1827.

JUARROS, DOMINGO. *Compendio de la historia de la Ciudad de Guatemala.* Guatemala City, 1937. 2 vols.

LANNING, JOHN TATE, ed. *Dr. Narciso Esparragosa y Gallardo* (Colección Historia, II). Caracas, 1953.

———. *Reales cédulas de la Real y Pontificia Universidad de San Carlos de Guatemala.* Guatemala City, 1954.

LAVAGNINO, FRANCISCO. "Guatemala," *New Monthly Magazine,* XIV, 1825.

LEÓN PINELO, ANTONIO DE. *Tratado de confirmaciones de encomiendas, oficios, i casos, en que se requieren para las Indias Occidentales.* Madrid, 1630. 2 vols.

LÓPEZ DE VELASCO, JUAN. *Geografía y descripción universal de las Indias.* Madrid, 1894.

MANNING, WILLIAM R., ed. *Diplomatic Correspondence Concerning the Independence of the Latin-American Nations.* New York, 1925. 3 vols.

MARURE, ALEJANDRO. *Bosquejo histórico de las revoluciones de Centro América desde 1811 hasta 1834.* Guatemala City, 1877. 2 vols.

———. *Efemérides de los hechos notables acaecidos en la república desde el año de 1821 hasta el de 1842.* Guatemala, City, 1844.

MATEOS, JUAN A., ed. *Historia parlamentaria de los congresos mexicanos de 1821 a 1857.* Mexico, 1877-1912. 25 vols.

MEDINA, JOSÉ TORIBIO. *La imprenta en Guatemala (1660-1821).* Santiago, Chile, 1910.

MEXICO. *Colección de órdenes y decretos de la soberana Junta Provisional Gubernativa, y soberanos congresos generales de la nación mexicana.* Mexico, 1829. 2 vols.

———. *Documentos para la historia de la guerra de independencia* (Publicaciones del Archivo General de la Nación, XXIII). Mexico, 1933.

MOLINA, PEDRO. "Memorias acerca de la revolución de Centro América, desde el año de 1820 hasta el de 1840," *Centro-Americano,* XIII, 1921.

MONTÚFAR Y CORONADO, MANUEL. *Memorias para la historia de la revolución de Centro América.* Guatemala City, 1934.

PECCHIO, GIUSEPPE DE. "Bosquejo de la República de Centro-América," *Anales de la Sociedad de Geografía E Historia de Guatemala,* XXV, 1951.

PINEDA, JUAN DE. "Descripción de la provincia de Guatemala, año 1594," *Relaciones históricas y geográficas de América Central*

(Colección de Libros y Documentos Referentes a la Historia de América, VIII). Madrid, 1908.

"Relación de los ejercicios literarios, grados, títulos, y méritos patrióticos de Don José Cecilio del Valle, Auditor Honorario de Guerra del ejército y provincia de Guatemala." *Revista del Archivo y de la Biblioteca Nacional de la República de Honduras,* I, 1905.

SPAIN. *Constitución Política de la Monarquía Española.* Cádiz, 1812.

——. *Recopilación de las leyes de los reynos de las Indias.* Madrid, 1791. 3 vols.

THOMPSON, G. A. *Narrative of an Official Visit to Guatemala from Mexico.* London, 1829.

TORRES LANZAS, PEDRO, ed. *Independencia de América, fuentes para su estudio. Catálogo de documentos conservados en el Archivo General de Indias de Sevilla.* Madrid, 1912. 6 vols.

VALENZUELA, GILBERTO. *La imprenta en Guatemala.* Guatemala City, 1933.

VALLADARES RODRÍGUEZ, JUAN, ed. *El pensamiento económico de José Cecilio del Valle.* Tegucigalpa, 1958.

VALLE, JOSÉ DEL, AND JORGE DEL VALLE MATHEU, eds. *Obras de José Cecilio del Valle.* Guatemala City, 1929-1930. 2 vols.

VALLE, RAFAEL HELIODORO, ed. *La anexión de Centro América a México* (Archivo Histórico Diplomático Mexicano, Series I, nos. 11, 24, 40; Series II, nos. 2, 3). Mexico, 1924-1946. 5 vols.

——. *Cartas de Bentham a Valle.* Mexico, 1942.

——. *Valle* (El Pensamiento de América, X). Mexico, 1943.

VÁZQUEZ DE ESPINOSA, ANTONIO. *Compendium and Description of the West Indies.* Translated by Charles Upson Clark (Smithsonian Miscellaneous Collection, CII). Washington, 1942.

WEBSTER, C. K., ed. *Britain and the Independence of Latin America, 1812-1830. Select Documents from the Foreign Office.* London, 1938. 2 vols.

WILSON, JAMES. *A Brief Memoir of the Life of James Wilson (Late of Edinburgh) with Extracts from His Journal and Correspondence, Written Chiefly During a Residence in Guatemala, the Capital of Central America.* London, 1829.

ZAVALA, LORENZO DE. *Ensayo histórico de las revoluciones desde 1808 hasta 1830.* Paris, 1831. 2 vols.

PRINTED DOCUMENTS WITH AN ARCHIVAL CLASSIFICATION

A1.1, 56930, 6921. *El Presidente, Gobernador y Capitán General de Guatemala, Teniente General de la Real Armada D. José de Bustamante a todas las autoridades y habitantes del reyno de su mando.* Guatemala City, April 13, 1811.

A1.1, 57305, 6931. *Un americano contradice el sistema de independencia de la América a que inclina el diálogo de Cortés y el Conde de la Cadena, publicado en el periódico Constitucional de Guatemala, con objeto de satisfacer a los españoles europeos que no es*

pensamiento de lo general de los pueblos americanos sino de quatro necios ingratos preciados de politicos, quando no son más que verdaderos insurgentes. Guatemala City, February 23, 1821.
A1.3-12, 12813, 1927. *Propositiones de rebus naturalibus defendenae a D. Josepho Cecilio del Valle.* Guatemala City, 1794.
A1.38.3.4, 22150, 2646. *Instrucción sobre la plaga de langosta; medios de exterminarla, o de disminuir sus efectos; y de precaver la escasez de comestibles.* Guatemala City, 1804.
B5.8, 2037, 72. *Estado que manifiesta el escrutinio de votos populares, practicado por el congreso en la sesión 20 de abril de 1825 para la elección de presidente de la república, expresando las juntas electorales de los partidos, el número de sufragios correspondiente a cada uno de ellos, y los sugetos que los obtuvieron.* Guatemala City, May 26, 1825.
B88.9, 4147, 189. *Juicio sobre la primera elección constitucional de presidente de la república que ha hecho el congreso.* Guatemala City, May 16, 1825.

PRINTED DOCUMENTS IN THE BIBLIOTECA NACIONAL DE GUATEMALA, COLECCIÓN VALENZUELA

Discurso del Gobierno Supremo de Guatemala sobre la renta de tabaco leído en la Asamblea el día 11 de octubre de 1824. Guatemala City, 1824.
Report by the Supreme Executive Authority of Central America concerning San Salvador and the pacification of Nicaragua. Guatemala City, August 11, 1824. (The correct title of this pamphlet has been misplaced or lost.)

PUBLISHED AUTHORITIES

AZNAR LÓPEZ, JOSÉ. *El Doctor Don José de Flores: una vida al servicio de la ciencia.* Guatemala City, 1960.
BANCROFT, HUBERT HOWE. *History of Central America.* New York, 1883-1887. 3 vols.
——. *History of Mexico.* New York, 1888. 6 vols.
BATRES JÁUREGUI, ANTONIO. *La América Central ante la historia.* Guatemala City, 1915-1949. 3 vols.
BENSON, NETTIE LEE. "Servando Teresa de Mier, Federalist," *Hispanic American Historical Review,* XXVIII, 1948.
CHAMORRO, PEDRO JOAQUÍN. *Historia de la federación de la América Central, 1823-1840.* Madrid, 1951.
CHAPMAN, CHARLES E. *A History of Spain.* New York, 1918.
CHINCHILLA AGUILAR, ERNESTO. *La inquisición en Guatemala.* Guatemala City, 1953.
CID FERNÁNDEZ, ENRIQUE DEL. *Don Gabino de Gainza y otros estudios.* Guatemala City, 1959.

CONTRERAS, J. DANIEL. *Una rebelión indígena en el partido de Totonicapán en 1820. El Indio y la independencia.* Guatemala City, 1951.

DELGADO, JAIME. *España y México en el siglo XIX.* Madrid, 1950. 3 vols.

DUHEM, PIERRE. *The Aim and Structure of Physical Theory.* Princeton, 1954.

DURÓN, RÓMULO, ed. "Primer centenario de la muerte de Don Dionisio de Herrera—vida, hechos, y escritos del prócer," *Revista del Archivo y de la Biblioteca Nacional de la República de Honduras,* XXVIII, 1950.

——. "José Cecilio del Valle," *Bulletin of the Pan American Union,* LXIX, 1935.

FERNÁNDEZ GUARDIA, R. "La independencia: una gran sorpresa," *Revista de los Archivos Nacionales de Costa Rica,* IV, 1940.

FLOYD, TROY S. "The Guatemalan Merchants, the Government, and the *Provincianos,* 1750-1800," *Hispanic American Historical Review,* XLI, 1961.

GÁNDARA DURÁN, CARLOS. *Pedro Molina.* Guatemala City, 1936.

GAVIDIA, FRANCISCO. *Historia moderna de El Salvador.* San Salvador, 1918.

GUATEMALA. *Noticia biográfica del Señor D. Manuel Francisco Pavón, Consejero de Estado y Ministro de lo Interior del gobierno de la República de Guatemala.* Guatemala City, 1855.

GUILLÉN, FLAVIO. *Un fraile prócer y una fábula poema (estudio acerca de Fray Matías de Córdova).* Guatemala City, 1932.

HERR, RICHARD. *The Eighteenth-Century Revolution in Spain.* Princeton, 1958.

HOLLERAN, MARY P. *Church and State in Guatemala.* New York, 1949.

JONES, CHESTER LLOYD. *Guatemala Past and Present.* Minneapolis, 1940.

KENYON, GORDON. "Gabino Gainza and Central America's Independence from Spain," *The Americas,* XIII, 1957.

LAMADRID, LÁZARO. *Una figura centroamericana, Dr. Fr. José Liendo y Goicoechea, O.F.M.* San Salvador, 1948.

LANNING, JOHN TATE. *The Eighteenth-Century Enlightenment in the University of San Carlos de Guatemala.* Ithaca, New York, 1956.

——. *The University in the Kingdom of Guatemala.* Ithaca, New York, 1955.

——. "La recepción, en la América española con especial referencia a Guatemala, de la ilustración del siglo XVIII," *Anales de la Sociedad de Geografía E Historia de Guatemala,* XXI, 1946.

LARDÉ Y LARÍN, JORGE. "Orígenes de la villa de Choluteca," *Revista del Archivo y de la Biblioteca Nacional de Honduras,* XXIV, 1946.

LECUNA, VICENTE. *Crónica razonada de las guerras de Bolívar.* New York, 1950. 3 vols.

LEONARD, IRVING A. *Books of the Brave, Being an Account of Books and of Men in the Spanish Conquest and Settlement of the Sixteenth-Century New World.* Cambridge, Massachusetts, 1949.

LEVENE, RICARDO. *Historia de la nación argentina (desde los orígenes hasta la organización definitiva en 1862)*. Buenos Aires, 1936-1941. 10 vols.

LEYTON RODRÍGUEZ, RUBÉN. *Valle, padre del panamericanismo*. Tegucigalpa, 1955.

MACH, ERNST. *The Science of Mechanics, a Critical and Historical Account of Its Development*. London, 1942.

MARTÍNEZ DURÁN, CARLOS. "La Sociedad Económica de Amigos de Guatemala," *Universidad de San Carlos*, XXVI, 1952.

MAYES, GUILLERMO. *Honduras en la independencia de Centro América y anexión a México*. Tegucigalpa, 1956.

MONTES, ARTURO HUMBERTO. *Morazán y la federación centro-americana*. Mexico, 1958.

MONTÚFAR, LORENZO. *Reseña histórica de Centro América*. Guatemala City, 1878-1888. 7 vols.

MORENO, LAUDELINO. "Guatemala y la invasión napoleónica de España," *Anales de la Sociedad de Geografía E Historia de Guatemala*, VII, 1930.

——. "Independencia de la Capitanía General de Guatemala," Asociación Española para el Progreso de la Ciencia de Cádiz. Madrid, 1927.

NAYLOR, ROBERT A. "The British Role in Central America Prior to the Clayton-Bulwer Treaty of 1850," *Hispanic American Historical Review*, XL, 1960.

OTS CAPDEQUÍ, JOSÉ MARÍA. *Instituciones sociales de la América española en el período colonial*. La Plata, Argentina, 1934.

PARDO, J. JOAQUÍN, ed. *Bibliografía del Doctor Pedro Molina* (Colección Documentos, XVI). Guatemala City, 1954.

PARKER, FRANKLIN DALLAS. *José Cecilio del Valle and the Establishment of the Central American Confederation*. Tegucigalpa, 1954.

——. "José Cecilio del Valle: Scholar and Patriot," *Hispanic American Historical Review*, XXXII, 1952.

PARRY, J. H. "The Sale of Public Offices in the Spanish Indies under the Hapsburgs," *Ibero-Americano*, XXXVII, 1953.

PÉREZ CADALSO, ELISEO. *Valle, apóstol de América*. Tegucigalpa, 1954.

PRIESTLEY, HERBERT INGRAM. *The Mexican Nation, a History*. New York, 1924.

REINA VALENZUELA, JOSÉ. *José Cecilio del Valle y las ciencias naturales*. Tegucigalpa, 1946.

ROBERTSON, WILLIAM SPENCE. *Iturbide of Mexico*. Durham, North Carolina, 1952.

RODRÍGUEZ BETETA, VIRGILIO. *Evolución de las ideas*. Paris, 1929.

ROSA, RAMÓN. *José Cecilio del Valle* (*Obras de José Cecilio del Valle*. Edited by José del Valle and Jorge del Valle Matheu.) Guatemala City, 1929-1930. 2 vols.

SALAZAR, RAMÓN A. *Desenvolvimiento intelectual de Guatemala*. Guatemala City, 1897.

——. *Historia de veintiún años; la independencia de Guatemala.* Guatemala City, 1928.

——. *Mariano Aycinena* (Biblioteca de Cultura Popular, XXII). Guatemala City, 1948.

SAMAYOA GUEVARA, HÉCTOR HUMBERTO. *La enseñanza de la historia en Guatemala (desde 1832 hasta 1852).* Guatemala City, 1959.

——. *Implantación del régimen de intendencias en el Reino de Guatemala.* Guatemala City, 1960.

SHAFER, ROBERT JONES. *The Economic Societies in the Spanish World (1763-1821).* Syracuse, New York, 1958.

SIMPSON, LESLEY BYRD. *Many Mexicos.* Berkeley, California, 1952.

SMITH, ROBERT S. "Indigo Production and Trade in Colonial Guatemala," *Hispanic American Historical Review,* XXXIX, 1959.

——. "Origins of the Consulado of Guatemala," *Hispanic American Historical Review,* XXVI, 1946.

——. "The *Wealth of Nations* in Spain and Hispanic America," *The Journal of Political Economy,* LXV, 1957.

SOLÓRZANO FERNÁNDEZ, VALENTÍN. *Historia de la evolución económica de Guatemala.* Mexico, 1947.

SOTO HALL, M. "Dos grandes apóstoles del panamericanismo: Bernardo Monteagudo y José Cecilio del Valle," *Anales de la Sociedad de Geografía E Historia de Guatemala,* III, 1926-1927.

TOBAR CRUZ, PEDRO. *Valle, el hombre, el político, el sabio.* Guatemala City, 1961.

TOWNSEND EZCURRA, ANDRÉS. *Fundación de la república.* Guatemala City, 1958.

——. "Monteagudo en Guatemala," *Ateneo,* I, 1953.

VALLE, RAFAEL HELIODORO, ed. *Oro de Honduras. Antología de Ramón Rosa.* Tegucigalpa, 1948.

VELA, DAVID. *Barrundia ante el espejo de su tiempo.* Guatemala City, 1956. 2 vols.

VILLACORTA, J. ANTONIO. *Historia de la Capitanía General de Guatemala.* Guatemala City, 1942.

WILLIAMS, MARY WILHELMINE. "The Ecclesiastical Policy of Francisco Morazán and the Other Central American Liberals," *Hispanic American Historical Review,* III, 1920.

WOLF, ABRAHAM. *A History of Science, Technology, and Philosophy in the Sixteenth and Seventeenth Centuries.* New York, 1935.

WOODRUFF, L. L., ed. *The Development of the Sciences.* New Haven, Connecticut, 1941.

ZAMOCOIS, NICETO DE. *Historia de Méjico desde sus tiempos más remotos hasta nuestros días.* Mexico, 1879-1888. 18 vols.

ZAMORA CASTELLANOS, PEDRO. *El grito de independencia.* Guatemala City, 1935.

UNPUBLISHED AUTHORITIES

FIELD, HAROLD BOND. "The Central-American Federation, a Political Study, 1826-1839." Unpublished Ph.D. dissertation, University of Chicago, 1942.

LANNING, JOHN TATE. "Grados académicos en el Reino de Guatemala." Unpublished manuscript.
STANGER, FRANCIS MERRIMAN. "The Struggle for Nationality in Central America." Unpublished Ph.D. dissertation, University of California, 1930.
SZASDI, ADAM MATTHIAS. "The Career of Nicholas Raoul in Central America." Unpublished MA thesis, Tulane University, 1954.

NEWSPAPERS

El Amigo de la Patria. Guatemala City, 1820-1822.
Boletín Oficial. Guatemala City, 1831-1832.
El Editor Constitucional. Guatemala City, 1820-1821.
Gaceta de Gobierno. Guatemala City, 1824.
Gaceta del Gobierno Imperial de México. Mexico City, 1823.
Gazeta de Guatemala. Guatemala City, 1804-1809.
El Genio de la Libertad. Guatemala City, 1821.
Periódico de la Sociedad Económica de Guatemala. 1815-1816.
El Redactor General. Guatemala City, 1825-1826.
El Sol. Mexico City, 1823.

Index